MOON

D0017657

MONTEREY & CARMEL

STUART THORNTON

Feb 2016

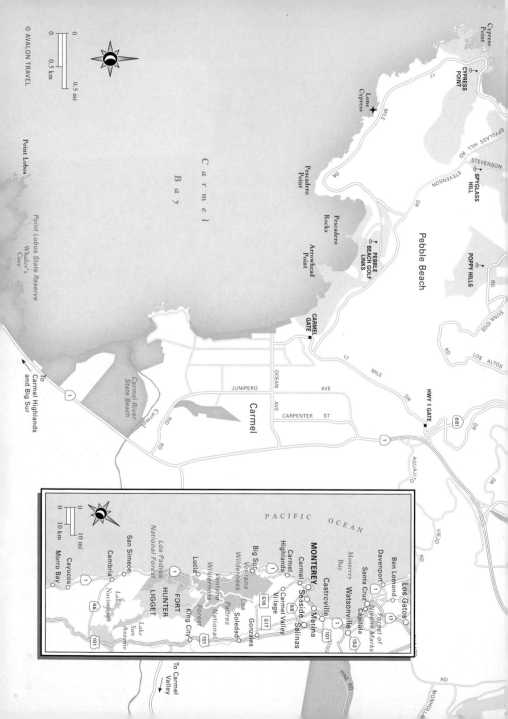

MONTEREY & CARMEL

PACIFIC OCEAN

Seal Rock

Bird Rock

Point Joe

17 MILE DR

MONTEREY
PENINSULA
COUNTRY CLUB

SLOAT RD

SLOAT RD LOPEZ RD

Forest
Lake

SFB Morse
Botanical
Preserve

South Moss
Beach

North Moss
Beach

SPANISH
BAY

FOREST LODGE RD

CONGRESS

SFB MORSE DR

COUNTRY
CLUB GATE

CONGRESS

SFB MORSE
GATE

681

681

Asilomar
State
Beach

SUNSET DR

ASILOMAR

Point Piños

OCEAN AVE

SINEX

PICO

LIGHTHOUSE DR

VIEW

Pacific Grove Marine Gardens Fish Refuge

17 MILE DR

DEL MONTE

AVE

AVE

AVE

BLVD

FOREST AVE

AVE

CENTRAL AVE

Shoreline
Park

Pacific Grove

17-MILE DRIVE PACIFIC
GROVE GATE

Huckleberry
Hill
Preserve

TAYLOR ST

DAVID AVE

PRESCOTT AVE

RIFLE RANGE

SKYLINE DR

MAR VISTA

Quarry
Park

Veterans
Memorial
Park

Via
Paraiso
Park

JEFFERSON ST

FRANKLIN ST

PRESIDIO OF
MONTEREY

Monterey

MUNRAS AVE

PACIFIC ST

LIGHTHOUSE AVE

CANNERY
ROW

MONTEREY BAY
AQUARIUM

Point
Cabrillo

Greenbelt

MONTEREY
PENINSULA
COLLEGE

El
Estero
Park

Monterey
State Beach

DEL MONTE AVE

Monterey
Bay

1

MARK THOMAS DR

SLOAT AVE

2ND ST

POSTGRADUATE

NAVAL

SCHOOL

DEL
MONTE

Contents

DISCOVER
Monterey & Carmel

Monterey Bay is California in microcosm. Here, you can experience the best the Golden State has to offer—without the big-city crowds and complications.

The best days in Monterey are spent in the water. Dive into a kelp forest. Explore the scenic coastline on a kayak or stand-up paddleboard. Scout for migrating whales passing near the shores.

The idyllic village of Carmel possesses seaside charm. From white-sand beaches to luxurious hotels, it promises a refined, high-class vacation bursting with art galleries and tasting rooms. Nearby Pebble Beach offers world-class golfing and stunning scenery.

Not far away, excursions range from quirky beach town Santa Cruz to opulent Hearst Castle. Big Sur is the region's most dramatic stretch of coastline, and the perfect geography for an unforgettable road trip.

Monterey Bay is not just a collision of land and sea, but also a juxtaposition of jarring colors and symbiotic ecosystems. From world-class wines and fine foods to a wonderland of marine life, Monterey encapsulates the California dream.

Clockwise from top left: the bell tower at Carmel Mission; Big Sur coastline; a seagull by Monterey Bay Aquarium; sunset from the Monterey coast; monarch butterflies in the Pacific Grove Monarch Butterfly Sanctuary; Julia Pfieffer Burns State Park.

Planning Your Trip

Where to Go

Monterey

Visit the **Monterey Bay Aquarium** to learn about the area's fascinating marine life, then head out on a **kayak, stand-up paddleboard,** or on a **whale-watching trip** to view sea otters, harbor seals, and migrating whales. Visit adjacent **Pacific Grove** to experience the town's colorful Victorian buildings and scenic coastline including **Lover's Point Park** with its bay views and protected beach.

Carmel

Wander around in the art galleries of **Carmel-by-the-Sea** and then take a stroll on the light sands of **Carmel Beach.** Get a dose of history at the **Carmel Mission** or **Tor House.** If you are a wine lover, be sure to hit the wineries in downtown Carmel-by-the-Sea or head out to **Carmel Valley** to taste some of the region's best varietals.

Salinas

Stroll around **Oldtown** Salinas before a visit to the **National Steinbeck Center,** a museum devoted to famed writer and Salinas native John Steinbeck. Drive south down Salinas Valley to spend some time in **Pinnacles National Park** and gawk at the amazing rock formations.

Santa Cruz

Have some throwback fun on the Giant Dipper roller coaster at the **Santa Cruz Beach Boardwalk** and then experience Santa Cruz's vibrant downtown by walking down **Pacific Avenue.** Drive up into the **Santa Cruz Mountains** for redwoods at **Big Basin Redwoods State Park** or see a colony of elephant seals at **Año Nuevo State Park.**

Big Sur coastline

Big Sur

Some of the most beautiful coastline in the world is along this section of the **Pacific Coast Highway.** Make sure your camera or phone has lots of room for photos of **Pfeiffer Beach** and **McWay Falls.** Slip on your hiking boots for a longer day hike at **Julia Pfeiffer Burns State Park** or **Andrew Molera State Park.**

Cambria, San Simeon, and Morro Bay

Tour grandiose **Hearst Castle** in San Simeon. Take time to visit the area's unique natural features, like Cambria's **Moonstone Beach** or **Montaña de Oro State Park,** outside of Morro Bay.

When to Go

The Monterey region's best feature is its **all-season** appeal. In **summer,** expect significant crowds at popular attractions, wineries, beaches, and campgrounds. In **fall,** the crowds have mostly left, but the weather is still warm. It's also when some of the best surfing waves occur along the coast. **Winter** is the rainy season, though the days between storms are often clear with mild temperatures. The crowds are lightest at this time, except on holiday weekends. During **spring,** the land is green and colored with wildflowers. The winds can really kick up in the afternoon along the coast.

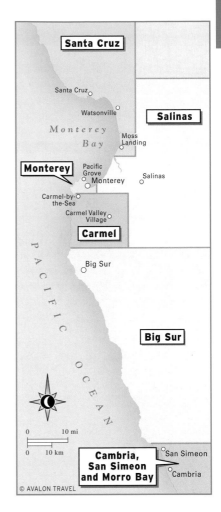

Know Before You Go

It is essential to make advance reservations for lodging in **Big Sur, Monterey, Carmel,** and **Santa Cruz,** especially during summer. It's necessary to reserve a spot on a **Hearst Castle tour** before arriving. Finally, an advance reservation is the only way you'll be able to play on **Pebble Beach's famed golf courses.**

If you're road-tripping through the region, visit the **California Department of Transportation website** (www.dot.ca.gov) before leaving for **current road conditions,** especially for trips to Big Sur and up into the Santa Cruz Mountains.

Summer fog is likely along the coast. Bring **layered clothing.** Also bring **sunscreen;** that coastal fog doesn't stop UV rays.

The Best of Monterey and Carmel

The major attractions of the Monterey Bay region can be explored in a long weekend, but taking up to five days will allow for a more immersive experience. The two best approaches to exploring the area are to choose a home base (like Monterey or Pacific Grove) and plan day trips; or take a road trip through the region, beginning in Santa Cruz, continuing into Monterey, Carmel, and Big Sur, and ending in Cambria or Morro Bay.

Monterey: Maritime Escape

Time in Monterey should be spent exploring the bay itself, whether by visiting the world-renowned Monterey Bay Aquarium or heading out in the water on a kayak, stand-up paddleboard, or whale-watching vessel.

Day 1
After an early arrival in Monterey, take a leisurely walk around the **Monterey Harbor** on the **Monterey Bay Coastal Recreation Trail.**

Be sure to head out on the **Coast Guard Pier** if you want to view some harbor seals and sea lions up close.

Grab a quick lunch of fish tacos at **Turtle Bay Taqueria** or a fine Greek salad at **Epsilon** before heading over to **Cannery Row** to spend the afternoon taking in furry sea otters and swirling jellyfish at the **Monterey Bay Aquarium.** Recall all the cute critters over a happy hour beer at the nearby **Cannery Row Brewing Company**

Monterey Bay

whale-watching in Monterey Bay

or enjoy a cocktail with a bay view at the **C Restaurant & Bar.** Head a few blocks up the hill for an elegant seafood dinner at **The Sardine Factory,** a steak at the **Whaling Station,** or a more casual dinner with tiki drinks at **Hula's Island Grill.**

The **Jabberwock Inn** offers a quiet bed-and-breakfast experience a few blocks up from Cannery Row, while the **Spindrift Inn** is perched right on McAbee Beach with sweeping panoramic bay views. Budget travelers can bed down at the **HI-Monterey Hostel,** conveniently located just a few blocks from the aquarium.

Day 2

It's time to experience Monterey's amazing marine life firsthand. Mornings are the best time to hit the water, before the wind comes up. Rent a **kayak** or **stand-up paddleboard** from **Monterey Bay Kayaks** and paddle out into the bay from nearby **Monterey State Beach.** Or head underwater by **scuba diving** or **snorkeling** off Monterey's **Breakwater Cove,** one of the best beginner dive spots in the state.

Another way to experience the bay is to secure a seat on a **whale-watching** tour leaving from Monterey Harbor. During the winter and spring migration, gray whales swim right off Monterey's coast. Pack a sandwich from **Mundo's Café** or from **Parker-Lusseau Pastries & Café.**

For dinner, opt for seafood at the **Sandbar & Grill** on the Municipal Wharf or creative New American fare at the **Montrio Bistro.** Enjoy a nightcap on the outdoor patio of **The Crown & Anchor** or sip a beer at **Alvarado Street Brewery.**

Day 3

Begin the day with a breakfast near the water at **LouLou's Griddle in the Middle,** a microdiner perched on the Municipal Wharf, or **First Awakenings,** located a block from the aquarium.

Monterey is chock-full of historic buildings. The **Monterey State Historic Park** has historic adobes and old government buildings scattered around downtown that are well worth visiting. The **Custom House** and **Pacific House Museum** located around Custom House Square are good places to start. On weekends, **guided**

Monterey Bay features coastline directly in the impact zone of ocean swells as well as tranquil, protected areas uncommon to most of the California coast. These conditions make the region suitable for lots of different water-based recreation.

SURFING

Santa Cruz is the surf capital of this region. **Steamer Lane** has surfers from around the world drooling with anticipation, while many beginners have caught their first waves at **Cowell's Beach.**

Carmel Beach has a fun break in spring and summer and is home to the Sunshine Freestyle Surfabout, Monterey County's only annual surf contest.

KAYAKING AND STAND-UP PADDLEBOARDING

Monterey is one of the best places on the California coast to kayak or stand-up paddleboard. The relatively protected waters from Monterey's **Municipal Wharf** to the **Monterey Bay Aquarium** make for a great paddle. If the swell or winds kick up, duck into **Monterey Harbor** for protection.

Though known for its golf courses, Pebble Beach also has **Stillwater Cove,** a superb paddling spot. Moss Landing's **Elkhorn Slough** provides a place to see sea otters and seals without being exposed to ocean swells.

One of the highlights of **Morro Bay** is getting out in the bay on a kayak or stand-up paddleboard. Cross the bay to the **Morro Bay Sandspit** for access to a slice of coast most people don't visit.

SCUBA DIVING AND SNORKELING

The best way to see the multitude of sea life, kelp forests, and reefs off the Monterey shoreline is to put on some snorkeling or scuba gear and get underwater. People come from all over California to dive in Monterey. **Breakwater Cove** is a popular, easy-to-access spot where lots of people have done their certification dives. Nearby, Pacific Grove's

stand-up paddleboarding off Monterey's Cannery Row

Lover's Point Park has a protected cove and kelp forest for snorkelers and scuba divers.

Carmel's **Monastery Beach** is for advanced divers and features a steep drop-off into a deep underwater canyon. **Point Lobos State Reserve** has underwater attractions in addition to terrestrial sights. Make reservations in advance to dive the park's **Whaler's Cove** and the deeper **Bluefish Cove.**

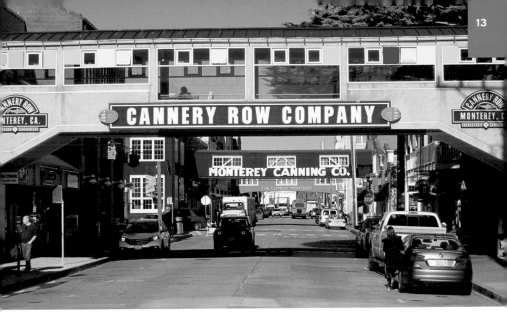

Monterey's popular Cannery Row

tours of the park provide an overview of the area's history.

Fans of old Victorian buildings should head to nearby **Pacific Grove** and take in its quaint downtown along **Lighthouse Avenue.** Be sure to detour down to **Lovers Point Park** for its views of the curving bay.

Stay in Pacific Grove for dinner. **Passionfish** is known for serving sustainable and tasty seafood, while the **Jeninni Kitchen & Wine Bar** showcases Mediterranean-inspired small plates and entrées. Or head to **Il Vecchio** if you're craving Italian food.

Day Trip to Salinas

Break a sweat and then crack open a bottle of wine on a day trip around inland Monterey County. Start by embarking on the hour-long drive to the country's newest national park: **Pinnacles National Park,** a wonderland of rock spires, sheer walls, steep canyons, and caves. The park's west end, the closest entrance from Monterey, provides access to a handful of trails. One recommended hike is the **Juniper Canyon Loop,** which goes up to the impressive High Peaks.

Cool off afterward by crossing the Salinas Valley to reach the **River Road Wine Trail,** a string of wineries in the Santa Lucia Highlands. Post up on the outdoor deck at **Hahn Winery Tasting Room** for views of Pinnacles rising in the distance as you sample pinot noir and chardonnay.

Head to **Salinas** for dinner. Choose between upscale European fare at **Patria** on Main Street or go for hearty Italian food at the family-friendly **Gino's.**

Carmel: Art, Wine, and Beaches

Carmel-by-the-Sea has one of the state's best beaches along with a downtown full of art galleries and tasting rooms. Carmel Valley is home to an up-and-coming wine industry.

Day 1

Start your time in Carmel with an open-faced breakfast sandwich made with organic ingredients at **Carmel Belle.** Then stroll along **Ocean Avenue,** taking time to peer into the art galleries and upscale boutiques. Make your way west as the road starts its descent to **Carmel Beach,** one of the finest beaches in the entire state. Once on the sugar-white sands, take off your shoes and let your dog run on the beach. Save some energy for the walk back up Ocean Avenue.

Having returned to your vehicle, head three miles south on CA-1 to reach **Point Lobos State Reserve,** which is rumored to have inspired Robert Louis Stevenson's *Treasure Island.*

There, the **Cypress Grove Trail** boasts twisted Monterey cypress trees and stunning coastline views.

Return to Carmel-by-the-Sea for a drink and snack on the rooftop bar at **Vesuvio,** or go to **Mundaka** for tapas and wine. Save some room for fine French dining at **Casanova** or a lively Mediterranean meal at **Yafa,** where your server may break out in song.

Spend the night with the sounds of the nearby sea at **La Playa Carmel** or stay in the Far East-inspired **Tradewinds Carmel.** Traveling with a furry friend? Consider the pro-pup **Cypress Inn,** co-owned by actress and animal-rights activist Doris Day.

Day 2

Get a hearty breakfast at the **Little Swiss Café** or drive to the **Lafayette Bakery** in the Barnyard Shopping Center for some wonderful pastries. Then take in the grounds of the San Carlos

scenic Carmel Beach

Catch of the Day

The Monterey Bay region is known for its seafood and abounds with superb seafood restaurants.

MONTEREY

- **The Sandbar & Grill** (page 61) has some of Monterey's best golden-fried calamari. Its location hanging over Monterey Harbor means you may be able to watch sea otters do the backstroke during your meal.

- Get a taste of local Sicilian recipes like squid pasta at **Monterey's Fish House** (page 60).

- Prefer your seafood raw? **Crystal Fish** (page 65) serves up fresh fish in sushi rolls bestowed with tasty sauces and unique supporting ingredients.

PACIFIC GROVE

- One of Monterey Peninsula's most popular seafood restaurants is **Passionfish** (page 75), which is known for its commitment to sustainable seafood and its staff's extensive knowledge of coastal cuisine.

MOSS LANDING

- Tucked between the harbor and the ocean in Moss Landing, **Phil's Fish Market** (page 83) serves up hearty and tasty cioppino and sea scallops.

CARMEL

- Japanese cooking methods meet California cuisine in the seafood entrées at the **Flying Fish Grill** (page 106).

- A hole-in-the-wall sushi restaurant in Carmel, **Akaoni** (page 106) does some of the area's freshest and tastiest rolls and nigiri.

SAN SIMEON, CAMBRIA, AND MORRO BAY

- The **Sea Chest Oyster Bar** (page 241), in

Pacific Grove's Passionfish

a cottage across from Moonstone Beach, wows seafood lovers with everything from calamari strips to cioppino.

- Just off Cayucos Beach, **Rudell's Smokehouse** (page 247) serves seafood tacos with big flavors, including smoked salmon and smoked albacore, along with an unexpected topping: chopped apples.

- Right on Morro Bay's Embarcadero, **Tognazzini's Dockside Restaurant** (page 259) is the place for fresh barbecued oysters in garlic butter.

Borromeo de Carmelo Mission, better known as the **Carmel Mission.**

Following a self-guided walk around the mission, take a tour of the nearby **Tor House,** a fascinating castle-like structure on Carmel Point constructed by nature poet Robinson Jeffers. Tours are only offered on Fridays and Saturdays.

It's late afternoon, and you deserve some wine. Carmel-by-the-Sea has a handful of **tasting rooms** downtown, including the popular **Scheid Vineyards Tasting Room.**

For dinner, enjoy the hip atmosphere at the New American restaurant **Affina** or get some of the freshest sushi around at the hole-in-the-wall **Akaoni.**

Day 3

For your third day in this area, head inland to **Carmel Valley.** Save your appetite for a hearty down-home breakfast at the **Wagon Wheel** or a more creative egg dish at **Jeffrey's Grill & Catering.**

Work off those calories with a hike at **Garland Ranch Regional Park,** an expansive parcel of land with steep hikes, ridges, and fine views of the valley. One option is the **Mesa Trail.**

Carmel Valley is a burgeoning but unassuming wine region, so be sure to head to the **Carmel Valley Village** for some **wine tasting.** Seven tasting rooms are located in a small strip mall and several more are a short walk away. Had your fill of reds and whites? Head to **Baja Cantina** for a cold margarita on its sunny deck instead.

Enjoy dinner at **Will's Fargo,** a classic Old West steakhouse helmed by a classically trained French chef.

Santa Cruz: Coast and Mountains

Visit Santa Cruz to experience an eclectic California surf town, explore redwood-cloaked mountains, and take in the lightly developed north coast.

Day 1

Getting to **Santa Cruz** is an easy 50-minute drive (44 miles) up CA-1 from the Monterey Peninsula. The eclectic beach city is an ideal place to try and catch a wave, whether you are a novice or an accomplished wave rider. **Cowell's Beach** is great for learning, while both **Pleasure Point** and **Steamer Lane** have larger waves. Afterward, visit the one-room **Santa Cruz Surfing Museum,** just above Steamer Lane.

Walk along **West Cliff Drive** and stop into **The Picnic Basket** for a sandwich or salad. Wander across the street to the **Santa Cruz Beach Boardwalk** to ride the wooden Big Dipper roller coaster.

Head to downtown Santa Cruz's lively **Pacific Avenue** and check out local shops like the wonderful **Bookshop Santa Cruz.** Dinner options include the sleek Afghan restaurant **Laili,** island cuisine at the **Pono Hawaiian Grill,** or rustic Californian fare at **Assembly.**

To hear some live music, make for the **Kuumbwa Jazz Center,** an intimate venue that hosts jazz and acoustic performances, or **The Catalyst,** the place for indie, rap, and reggae bands.

Now it's sleepy time. The **Seaway Inn** has basic motel rooms in a location that can't be beat, while the adjacent **West Cliff Inn** offers an upscale bed-and-breakfast experience in a gleaming white mansion. Across the street, the **Santa Cruz Dream Inn** reflects the playfulness of the nearby boardwalk and has a view of Cowell's Beach.

Day 2

To see the big trees, drive eight miles to the Santa Cruz Mountains town of **Felton.** Experience the impressive coast redwoods by taking a ride on the **Roaring Camp Railroads.** Hop on the **Redwood Forest Steam Train** that chugs up a small mountain or take the **Santa Cruz Beach**

surfing at Santa Cruz's Steamer Lane

Train down through the redwood-cloaked San Lorenzo River Canyon to the Santa Cruz Beach Boardwalk.

Stay in Felton for lunch. The **Cowboy Bar & Grill** does creative comfort food, while **The Cremer House** serves sandwiches and salads in the town's oldest building.

Felton is just 15 miles from **Big Basin Redwoods State Park,** which boasts the largest continuous ancient coast redwood forest south of San Francisco. Be sure to do the easy **Redwood Loop Trail.**

Return to Santa Cruz for dinner. Enjoy tacos and margaritas at **El Palomar** or creative sushi at **Akira.**

Day 3

The coastline just north of Santa Cruz is worth your time if you have an extra day. On the way out of town, stop in for a Brazilian breakfast at **Café Brasil.** Continue north on CA-1 where buildings cede to farmland, marine terraces, and secluded beaches. Two miles north of the city boundary is **Wilder Ranch State Park,** a great place to get a feel for this landscape. The **Old Cove Landing Trail** walks along the coast's edge.

Six miles farther up CA-1, **Davenport** is a small community perched on coastal bluffs. If it's migration season, keep your eyes peeled here for whales traveling offshore. One of the region's best beaches is **Davenport Landing Beach.**

Continue north about eight miles on CA-1 to reach **Año Nuevo State Park,** where up to 10,000 elephant seals can be found on the beach. Make sure to get a reservation for the guided tour before heading up to the park.

Return south on CA-1 to Davenport. Get a burger or sandwich at the **Whale City Bakery Bar & Grill** and then walk over to the nearby **Bonny Doon Vineyard Tasting Room** for a glass of wine.

Big Sur to Cambria Road Trip

Big Sur is the 90-mile stretch of stunning coastline that spans Carmel to San Simeon, the coastal town best known for being the home of Hearst Castle. The drive along CA-1 can be done in less than three hours, but you'll want to set aside more time, as you'll be driving past some of the state's best parks, beaches, and trails.

Day 1

Steer your vehicle down the **Big Sur Coast Highway** (CA-1) for a stunningly scenic drive. Make sure to stop 15 miles south of Carmel to photograph the **Bixby Bridge,** an architectural marvel spanning a deep canyon with the Pacific Ocean in the background.

For breakfast, opt for one of two worthy restaurants: the **Ripplewood Café,** which does home-style breakfasts, and the **Big Sur River Inn Restaurant,** where you can dine on an outdoor deck near the Big Sur River.

Big Sur has superb hiking options. To take

in the coastal bluffs and beaches, head out on the **Eight-Mile Loop** at **Andrew Molera State Park.** Want redwoods and coastal views? At **Julia Pfeiffer Burns State Park,** the **Ewoldsen Trail** is the ticket. Afterward, make sure to walk across the highway and take in **McWay Falls,** an 80-foot waterfall that plummets into the Pacific.

Catch sunset at **Pfeiffer Beach** and snap a selfie with the offshore rocks as a backdrop. Head south again to **Nepenthe Restaurant** for a late dinner of the Ambrosia burger and a terrific view.

Check if the **Henry Miller Library,** just a quarter mile south of Nepenthe, has an evening event, like its summer short-film series or a music performance. Otherwise, head to the **Fernwood Tavern** to mingle with locals and tourists from around the world.

Fall asleep in a tent within the **Pfeiffer Big Sur State Park Campground** or in an artfully decorated room at **Glen Oaks Big Sur.** For a

the world-famous Big Sur coast

the boardwalk above Cambria's Moonstone Beach

splurge, have a once-in-a-lifetime overnight experience at the luxury **Post Ranch Inn.**

Day 2

Fuel up for a drive at Big Sur's **Deetjen's** restaurant, known for its cozy atmosphere and eggs Benedicts. For something quicker, swing into the **Big Sur Bakery** for a pastry and coffee.

Big Sur's south coast has two worthy stops for travelers headed towards San Simeon and Cambria. **Sand Dollar Beach** is 60 miles south of Carmel and one of Big Sur's best beaches. **Salmon Creek Falls** is an impressive roadside waterfall located eight miles south of Gorda.

Drive past **San Simeon** to **Cambria,** where you'll stroll on scenic **Moonstone Beach.** When hunger hits, head back to Cambria for dinner. The **Main Street Grill** is a casual eatery with a tasty tri-tip sandwich, while **Robin's** has an eclectic international menu.

Get a full night's sleep at **Sand Pebbles Inn** across from Moonstone Beach or the **Bridge Street Inn HI-Cambria,** a small hostel in a former parsonage.

Day 3

Drive to opulent **Hearst Castle.** Tours of this ranch, built for newspaper magnate William Randolph Hearst, offer insight into the lifestyle of the rich and infamous. Be sure to make a tour reservation in advance!

Just down from the castle is **Sebastian's Store,** an informal eatery where for lunch you can dine on burgers and sandwiches made of Hearst Ranch beef.

Drive a half hour south to the scenic Central Coast town of **Morro Bay** and stare up at **Morro Rock,** a 576-foot volcanic plug looming over the active harbor area. Then walk along the **Embarcadero** to check out **The Shell Shop** and stop in for a craft beer at the **Libertine Pub.**

Dine on seafood for dinner with fish tacos at **Taco Temple** or barbecued oysters at **Tognazzini's Dockside Restaurant.** Spend the evening at the **Masterpiece Hotel** or enjoy the **Beach Bungalow Inn & Suites,** just two blocks up from the bustling Embarcadero.

Best Beaches

The Monterey Bay region has an impressive range of beaches, from sweeping expanses of sand to pocket beaches crammed between towering headlands. Many of these beaches provide access to the area's myriad ocean-based recreation opportunities, from sea kayaking and surfing to scuba diving and snorkeling.

Monterey

SAN CARLOS BEACH PARK
Best for Scuba Diving, Picnicking
This sliver of sand is located right in Monterey, south of Monterey Harbor. It's a superb place to picnic and take in the curving bay or don scuba equipment and head offshore to one of the area's most popular dive spots (page 46).

MONTEREY STATE BEACH
Best for Long Strolls, Kayaking, Stand-Up Paddleboarding
This large strand of beach begins just north of the Monterey Harbor and stretches to the neighboring city of Seaside. Head out for a long walk or paddle out from the wharf in a kayak or SUP (page 46).

MOSS LANDING STATE BEACH
Best for Fishing, Birding
A long stretch of beach with frequently powerful waves offshore, this state beach draws both anglers and birders for its substantial wildlife (page 82).

Pacific Grove

LOVERS POINT PARK
Best for Families, Snorkeling, Wading
The small, protected beach here allows a spot for kids to dip their feet into the cool Pacific, while the waters offshore feature a kelp forest that provides snorkelers and beginning divers with an introduction to the region's underwater features (page 67).

Lover's Point Park, Pacific Grove

Andrew Molera State Park Beach

ASILOMAR STATE BEACH
Best for Strolling
Take a walk south toward Pebble Beach on this scenic, mile-long beach. Return on the wooden boardwalk above the sand (page 68).

Carmel
CARMEL BEACH
Best for Scenery, Sunsets, Dog Lovers
With its pale sand and contrasting blue-green ocean water, Carmel Beach is a jewel of Monterey Bay. It's also one of the state's friendliest beaches for dogs (page 92).

Santa Cruz
COWELL'S BEACH
Best for Surfing
Santa Cruz's Cowell's Beach has slow, rolling waves perfect for beginners. Even though it gets crowded, the surfers here are usually friendly (page 156).

SANTA CRUZ BEACH BOARDWALK
Best for Families, Mild Thrill Seekers
Just feet away from Cowell's, the Santa Cruz Beach Boardwalk makes families happy with its rides, games, and entertainment. The Boardwalk's Giant Dipper roller coaster has been thrilling folks since 1924 (page 146).

SEACLIFF STATE BEACH
Best for Shipwreck Lovers, Fishing
How many beaches in California have their own hulking shipwreck right offshore? The pier offers the best views of the concrete vessel and is also a preferred spot for local anglers (page 167).

DAVENPORT LANDING BEACH
Best for Beachcombing, Kitesurfing
The northern coast of Santa Cruz County has a handful of scenic, rugged beaches. Davenport Landing Beach is one of the best and easiest to access. The beach has two rocky headlands on either end (page 172).

AÑO NUEVO STATE PARK
Best for Wildlife, Scenery
At Año Nuevo, gigantic elephant seals turn the beach into a battleground. You can also catch a glimpse of an eerie, abandoned light station right offshore (page 174).

Pfeiffer Beach

Big Sur

ANDREW MOLERA STATE PARK BEACH
Best for Scenery, Views
The beach here is accessed via an easy one-mile walk, worth doing to see the Big Sur River spilling into the sea and a beach decorated with driftwood huts. Take the Headlands Trail to get a view of the beach from above (page 187).

PFEIFFER BEACH
Best for Photo Ops, Sunsets
Make sure that your camera has fully charged batteries for a trip to Big Sur's windswept Pfeiffer Beach, with picture-perfect rock formations offshore (page 188).

SAND DOLLAR BEACH
Best for Picnics
Protected by cliffs on windy days, crescent-shaped Sand Dollar Beach is a great spot for a picnic (page 192).

San Simeon, Cambria, and Morro Bay

MOONSTONE BEACH
Best for Beachcombing
Hunt for the eponymous moonstones on this Cambria beach. Its impressive driftwood structures are also worthy discoveries (page 230).

CAYUCOS STATE BEACH
Best for Sunbathing, Lounging
The primary attraction of the seaside community of Cayucos is this protected beach and its pier, perfect for a day of lazing in the sun (page 243).

SPOONER'S COVE
Best for Scenery, Picnics
Soak up the natural beauty of Spooner's Cove, in Montaña de Oro State Park. A scenic arch decorates the bluffs on the south end of the cove (page 249).

MORRO ROCK BEACH
Best for Photo Ops, Surfing
Take a photo in front of 576-foot-high Morro Rock. The beach to its south is popular with surfers of all skill levels (page 253).

Wine Time

Monterey

After a day of sightseeing, stay in the seaside city and sample its tasting rooms. The **Pierce Ranch Vineyards Tasting Room** is housed in a cozy cottage and occasionally hosts live music. **A Taste of Monterey** pours wine from over 95 local wineries in a stunning Cannery Row location with views of the bay (page 39).

Carmel

Tasting rooms are popping up all over downtown **Carmel-by-the-Sea.** One of the best is the **Scheid Vineyards Carmel-by-the-Sea Tasting Room,** a social spot where you can sample wines, including the popular claret. **Trio Carmel** offers olive oil tasting in addition to wine tasting. Check out the displays of contemporary art on the walls (page 93).

Make a day of exploring the many wineries of **Carmel Valley. Chesebro Wines** has affordable, high-quality wines, while **Cima Collina** has a great patio where you can sip their acclaimed pinots (page 112).

Salinas

The **River Road Wine Trail** has a string of wineries known for their valley views, fine chardonnays, and exemplary pinot noirs. **Hahn Winery Tasting Room** has a superb outdoor deck for wine sampling, while **Paraiso Vineyards Boutique & Tasting Room** is known for its Rieslings (page 127).

Santa Cruz

On the Santa Cruz coast is the town of Davenport. Here, the **Bonny Doon Vineyard Tasting Room** is the place to taste the products of winemaking iconoclast Randall Grahm, especially his flagship Le Cigare Volant (page 173).

San Simeon, Cambria, and Morro Bay

The Central Coast has a few worthy tasting rooms. The San Simeon-based **Hearst Ranch Winery** pours wines within a historic general store down the hill from Hearst Castle (page 232).

Morro Bay's **Stax Wine Bar & Bistro** is a fine place to taste local varietals while gazing out at imposing Morro Rock (page 251).

the fabulous outdoor deck at the Hahn Winery Tasting Room

The Monterey and Carmel region contains outstanding hiking trails for all levels of hikers. Options include everything from an easy leg-stretching hike to a strenuous multiday backpacking adventure.

EASY HIKES

• The Skyline Trail (0.8 miles round-trip) in Jack's Peak County Park offers a view of Monterey from the peninsula's highest point (page 51).

• Point Lobos State Natural Reserve has plenty of easy hikes that pay impressive dividends with stunning scenery, abundant wildlife, and unique natural features. The Cypress Grove Trail (0.8 miles round-trip) is one of the best with its twisty cypress trees and vantage points of the sea (page 91).

• Most visitors to Big Sur want to view McWay Falls, the 80-foot waterfall that drops precipitously into the ocean. It can be seen from an observation deck by doing the Overlook Trail to McWay Falls Trail (0.66 miles round-trip) in Julia Pfeiffer Burns State Park (page 190).

• Andrew Molera State Park occupies a big parcel of Big Sur's spectacular coastline. At the end of the Trail Camp Beach Trail (two miles round-trip) hikers are rewarded with a wild beach where the Big Sur River spills into the sea (page 195).

• Also in Julia Pfeiffer Burns State Park is the Partington Cove Trail (0.8 miles round-trip), which ventures out from the highway, over a bridge, and through a tunnel to a rocky cove (page 198).

INTERMEDIATE HIKES

• For a view of the Carmel coast from above, take Palo Corona Regional Park's Inspiration Point Hike (1.3 miles round-trip) to a bench where the shoreline spreads out below.

Be sure to first secure a permit to hike in the park (page 92).

• Pinnacles National Park has rock formations that seem to be nature's take on castles and towers. The Juniper Canyon Loop (4.3 miles round-trip) travels up to some fine examples, especially on the steep and narrow portion of the trail (page 133).

• Take the Ridge Trail and Panorama Trail Loop (eight miles round-trip) in Andrew Molera State Park for views of the Big Sur coast (page 195).

• In Julia Pfeiffer Burns State Park, the Ewoldsen Trail (4.5 miles round-trip) combines redwoods and coastal views, two of Big Sur's best assets, for one of the region's best day hikes (page 197).

• Towering above the south coast of Big Sur, Cone Peak in the Ventana Wilderness is a giant, rocky mountaintop with fantastic 360-degree views. The Cone Peak Trail (five miles round-trip) is a doable day hike to the summit of Big Sur's second-highest peak (page 199).

BACKPACKING HIKES

• A backpacking trip that goes mostly downhill? That's the Skyline to Sea Trail (30 miles one-way) in the Santa Cruz Mountains. The hike begins in Castle Rock State Park before heading into Big Basin Redwoods State Park, where it continues past towering trees and scenic waterfalls on the way to Waddell Beach (page 178).

• For an overview of Big Sur's rugged backcountry, consider a multiday backpacking excursion in the Ventana Wilderness on the Pine Ridge Trail from China Camp to Big Sur Station (24 miles one-way). This hike travels along the Big Sur River with a stop at popular Sykes Hot Springs (page 201).

Monterey

Look for ★ to find recommended sights, activities, dining, and lodging.

Highlights

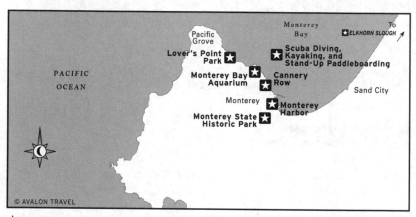

© AVALON TRAVEL

★ **Cannery Row:** Made famous by John Steinbeck's novels, this was once a working neighborhood lined with fish canneries. Today it's been reinvented as a tourist destination overlooking a scenic strip of Monterey Bay (page 30).

★ **Monterey Bay Aquarium:** This mammoth aquarium astonishes with a vast array of sea life and exhibits on the local ecosystem (page 33).

★ **Monterey State Historic Park:** This state historic park preserves the old adobes dotting Monterey's downtown and allows people to imagine what life was like here in the 1800s (page 34).

★ **Monterey Harbor:** The best way to see one of the most scenic harbors on the Central Coast is by strolling along the Monterey Bay Coastal Recreation Trail (page 37).

★ **Scuba Diving, Kayaking, and Stand-Up Paddleboarding:** Experience Monterey Bay's calm water and unique wildlife by getting into the water (pages 46 and 47).

★ **Lover's Point Park:** This Pacific Grove park is located on a scenic peninsula that juts out into the bay, offering a protected beach and great views (page 67).

★ **Elkhorn Slough:** Get some of the best views of the bay's marine mammals at this estuary in Moss Landing (page 81).

Monterey has roots as a fishing town. Native Americans were the first to ply the bay's waters, and fishing became an economic driver with the arrival of European settlers in the 19th century.

Author John Steinbeck immortalized this unglamorous industry in his 1945 novel *Cannery Row*. The city's blue-collar past is still evident in its architecture, even if the cannery workers have been replaced by tourists.

This coastal city has one of California's oldest and richest histories. Spanish explorer Sebastian Vizcaino noted that the bay and harbor would make for a great port way back in 1602. In 1770, the Spanish constructed the Presidio of Monterey to protect the port. After that, Monterey became the capital of the Spanish territory of Alta California; later, it would be the capital of California under Mexican and U.S. military rule. When California composed the documents to apply for U.S. statehood in 1849, it did so in Monterey.

Today, Monterey is the "big city" on the well-populated southern tip of the wide-mouthed bay. There are two main sections of Monterey: the old downtown area and "New

Monterey," which includes Cannery Row and the Monterey Aquarium. The old downtown is situated around Alvarado Street and includes the historic adobes that make up Monterey State Historic Park. New Monterey bustles with tourists during the summer. The canneries are long gone, and today the Row is packed with businesses, including the must-see Monterey Bay Aquarium, seafood restaurants, shops, galleries, and tasting rooms. The aquarium is constantly packed with visitors, especially on summer weekends. One way to get from one section of town to the other is to walk the Monterey Bay Coastal Recreation Trail, a paved path that runs right along a stretch of coastline.

PLANNING YOUR TIME

Monterey and its immediate surroundings can be explored over 2-3 days. The communities of the Monterey Peninsula have distinct characters, so you can stay in the town that best

---

Previous: Monterey State Historic Park's Pacific House; Asilomar Beach; **Above:** Cannery Row.

Monterey Peninsula

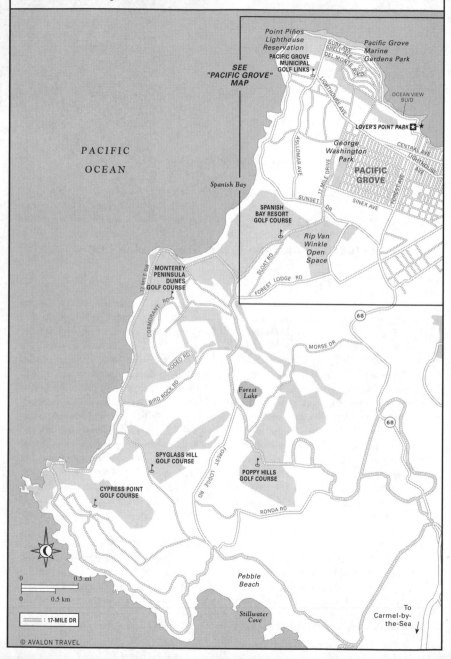

PACIFIC OCEAN

Point Piños Lighthouse Reservation

PACIFIC GROVE MUNICIPAL GOLF LINKS

SEE "PACIFIC GROVE" MAP

SURF AVE
SHELL AVE
DEL MONTE BLVD

Pacific Grove Marine Gardens Park

OCEAN VIEW BLVD

LIGHTHOUSE AVE

LOVER'S POINT PARK

CENTRAL AVE

LIGHTHOUSE AVE

George Washington Park

PACIFIC GROVE

ASILOMAR AVE

17-MILE DRIVE

FOREST AVE

Spanish Bay

SUNSET DR

SINEX AVE

SPANISH BAY RESORT GOLF COURSE

Rip Van Winkle Open Space

SLOAT RD

FOREST LODGE RD

MONTEREY PENINSULA DUNES GOLF COURSE

CORMORANT RD

17-MILE DR

RODEO RD

BIRD ROCK RD

68

MORSE DR

Forest Lake

68

SPYGLASS HILL GOLF COURSE

FOREST LODGE RD

POPPY HILLS GOLF COURSE

CYPRESS POINT GOLF COURSE

RONDA RD

0   0.5 mi

0   0.5 km

: 17-MILE DR

Pebble Beach

Stillwater Cove

To Carmel-by-the-Sea

© AVALON TRAVEL

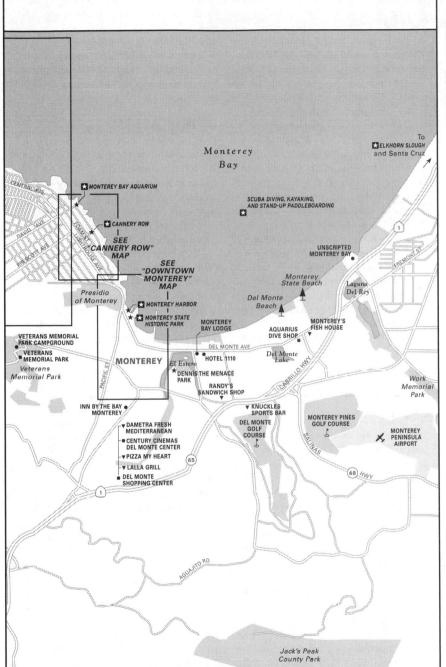

Monterey
Bay

To
★ ELKHORN SLOUGH
and Santa Cruz

★ MONTEREY BAY AQUARIUM

SCUBA DIVING, KAYAKING,
AND STAND-UP PADDLEBOARDING
★

★ CANNERY ROW

*SEE
"CANNERY ROW"
MAP*

UNSCRIPTED
MONTEREY BAY

*SEE
"DOWNTOWN
MONTEREY"
MAP*

Monterey
State Beach

Laguna
Del Rey

Del Monte Beach

*Presidio
of Monterey*

★ MONTEREY HARBOR

★ MONTEREY STATE
HISTORIC PARK

MONTEREY
BAY LODGE

AQUARIUS
DIVE SHOP

MONTEREY'S
FISH HOUSE

VETERANS MEMORIAL
PARK CAMPGROUND

VETERANS
MEMORIAL PARK

*Veterans
Memorial Park*

MONTEREY

DEL MONTE AVE.

HOTEL 1110

Del Monte
Lake

*Work
Memorial
Park*

El Estero

DENNIS THE MENACE
PARK

RANDY'S
SANDWICH SHOP

INN BY THE BAY
MONTEREY

DAMETRA FRESH
MEDITERRANEAN

CENTURY CINEMAS
DEL MONTE CENTER

PIZZA MY HEART

LALLA GRILL

DEL MONTE
SHOPPING CENTER

KNUCKLES
SPORTS BAR

DEL MONTE
GOLF
COURSE

MONTEREY PINES
GOLF COURSE

MONTEREY
PENINSULA
AIRPORT

65

1

68 HWY

AGUAJITO RD

*Jack's Peak
County Park*

CENTRAL AVE.
DAVID AVE.
PRESCOTT AVE.
FOAM ST.
LIGHTHOUSE AVE.
PACIFIC ST.
SALINAS
CARRILLO HWY.
FREMONT ST.

suits your needs. To be near the aquarium, opt for lodging in Cannery Row. If you're a history buff, stay next to some of the state's oldest buildings in downtown Monterey. If you love old Victorians and bed-and-breakfasts, stay in Pacific Grove. To experience a Central Coast harbor community, overnight in Moss Landing. No matter where you stay, you'll be able to easily explore the nearby towns.

The Monterey Bay Aquarium is the area's most popular attraction. While it is expensive—adult admission is $40—the aquarium's artfulness makes it worth a visit. Cannery Row, the area surrounding the aquarium, has a few sights, most notably Ed Ricketts' Laboratory, but otherwise it's a lot of gift shops and restaurants.

History buffs should not miss Monterey State Historic Park, a collection of historic government buildings and residences in downtown Monterey. Water enthusiasts should get out in the calm waters off Monterey, whether it is to kayak, stand-up paddleboard, or scuba dive.

Pacific Grove is worth a visit for its unique Victorian residences and fine stretch of coastline, including Lovers Point Park. Seaside has some of the best inexpensive eateries in the area, while Marina has Fort Ord Dunes State Park, one of the California coast's newest state parks. Head up to Moss Landing to explore Elkhorn Slough, a tidal marsh that's home to abundant wildlife.

ORIENTATION

Alvarado Street is the main street of **downtown Monterey,** while Lighthouse Avenue is lined with a lot of New Monterey's businesses and restaurants. **Cannery Row** is a touristy street by the bay, three blocks from Lighthouse Avenue.

Pacific Grove is southwest of Monterey. Its main street is **Lighthouse Avenue,** which connects the two towns. Upon entering Pacific Grove, Lighthouse Avenue becomes Central Avenue, while Lighthouse Avenue moves two blocks up from the bay.

Highway 1 connects Monterey with the northern Monterey County cities of **Seaside, Marina,** and **Moss Landing.**

Sights

★ CANNERY ROW

Cannery Row (www.canneryrow.com) did once look and feel as John Steinbeck described it in his famed novel of the same name. In the 1930s and 1940s, fishing boats offloaded their catches straight into the huge warehouse-like cannery buildings. Low-wage workers processed the fish and put it into cans, ready to ship across the country and around the world. But overfishing took its toll, and by the late 1950s Cannery Row was deserted; some buildings even fell into the ocean.

A slow renaissance began in the 1960s, driven by new interest in preserving the historic integrity of the area, as well as a few savvy entrepreneurs who understood the value of beachfront property. Today, what was once a workingman's wharf is now an enclave of boutique hotels, big seafood restaurants, and souvenir stores selling T-shirts adorned with sea otters. Cannery Row is anchored at one end by the aquarium and runs for several blocks that include a beach; it then leads to the Monterey Harbor area.

The Monterey Bay Aquarium is the best attraction around, but the new **Monterey Mirror Maze and Highway 1 Golf** (751 Cannery Row, 831/649-6293, http://montereymirrormaze.com, hours vary, mirror maze adults $12, children 4-6 $8, mini golf adults $12, children 4-6 $8) offers touristy family fun. Navigate the mirror maze with its disorienting lights and music or putt 9 to 18 holes of mini-golf on a glow-in-the-dark course with attractions inspired by California's Highway 1.

Central Monterey

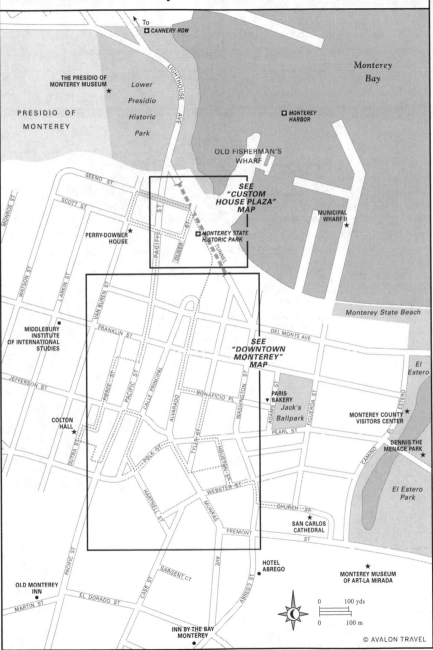

To
CANNERY ROW

Monterey
Bay

THE PRESIDIO OF
MONTEREY MUSEUM ★

Lower
Presidio
Historic
Park

PRESIDIO OF
MONTEREY

MONTEREY
HARBOR

OLD FISHERMAN'S
WHARF

SEENO ST

SCOTT ST

MONROE ST

WATSON ST

LARKIN ST

PACIFIC ST

OLIVER ST

SEE
"CUSTOM
HOUSE PLAZA"
MAP

MUNICIPAL
WHARF II ★

PERRY-DOWNER
HOUSE ★

MONTEREY STATE
HISTORIC PARK

TUNNEL

Monterey State Beach

VAN BUREN ST

FRANKLIN ST

MIDDLEBURY
INSTITUTE
OF INTERNATIONAL
STUDIES

DEL MONTE AVE

SEE
"DOWNTOWN
MONTEREY"
MAP

El
Estero

JEFFERSON ST

PIERCE ST

PACIFIC ST

CALLE PRINCIPAL

BONAFICIO PL

ALVARADO

WASHINGTON ST

ADAMS ST

PARIS
BAKERY ▼

Jack's
Ballpark

FIGUEROA ST

EL ESTERO

MONTEREY COUNTY
VISITORS CENTER ★

COLTON
HALL ★

DUTRA ST

POLK ST

TYLER ST

HOUSTON ST

PEARL ST

DENNIS THE
MENACE PARK ★

CAMINO EL ESTERO

WEBSTER ST

El Estero
Park

HARTNELL ST

MUNRAS

CHURCH ST

FREMONT

SAN CARLOS
CATHEDRAL
ST

PACIFIC ST

CASE ST

SARGENT CT

AVE

ABREGO ST

HOTEL
ABREGO ●

★ MONTEREY MUSEUM
OF ART-LA MIRADA

OLD MONTEREY
INN ●

EL DORADO ST

MARTIN ST

0   100 yds

0   100 m

INN BY THE BAY
MONTEREY ●

© AVALON TRAVEL

Cannery Row

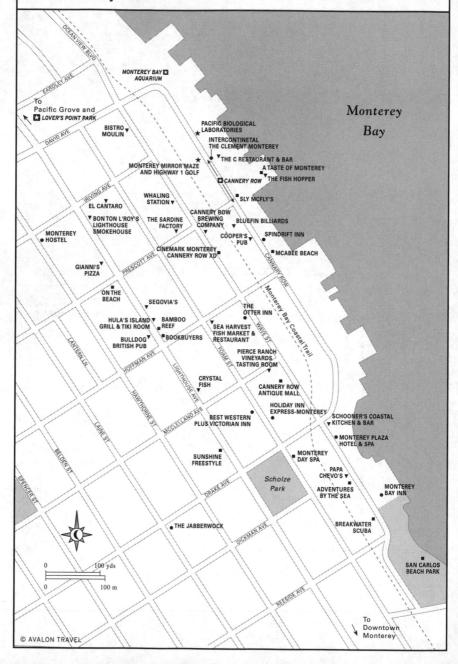

OCEAN VIEW BLVD

EARDLEY AVE

To
Pacific Grove and
LOVER'S POINT PARK

DAVID AVE

MONTEREY BAY
AQUARIUM

*Monterey
Bay*

PACIFIC BIOLOGICAL
LABORATORIES

BISTRO
MOULIN

INTERCONTINETAL
THE CLEMENT MONTEREY

THE C RESTAURANT & BAR

MONTEREY MIRROR MAZE
AND HIGHWAY 1 GOLF

A TASTE OF MONTEREY

THE FISH HOPPER

CANNERY ROW

IRVING AVE

WHALING
STATION

SLY MCFLY'S

EL CANTARO

BON TON L'ROY'S
LIGHTHOUSE
SMOKEHOUSE

THE SARDINE
FACTORY

CANNERY ROW
BREWING
COMPANY

BLUEFIN BILLIARDS

MONTEREY
HOSTEL

COOPER'S
PUB

SPINDRIFT INN

CINEMARK MONTEREY
CANNERY ROW XD

MCABEE BEACH

PRESCOTT AVE

GIANNI'S
PIZZA

ON THE
BEACH

SEGOVIA'S

THE
OTTER INN

CANNERY ROW

HULA'S ISLAND
GRILL & TIKI ROOM

BAMBOO
REEF

SEA HARVEST
FISH MARKET &
RESTAURANT

Monterey Bay Coastal Trail

WAVE ST

BULLDOG
BRITISH PUB

BOOKBUYERS

LANTERN LN

HOFFMAN AVE

LIGHTHOUSE AVE

TOM ST

PIERCE RANCH
VINEYARDS
TASTING ROOM

CRYSTAL
FISH

CANNERY ROW
ANTIQUE MALL

HAWTHORNE ST

HOLIDAY INN
EXPRESS-MONTEREY

MCCLELLAND AVE

BEST WESTERN
PLUS VICTORIAN INN

SCHOONER'S COASTAL
KITCHEN & BAR

MONTEREY PLAZA
HOTEL & SPA

LANE ST

SUNSHINE
FREESTYLE

MONTEREY
DAY SPA

PAPA
CHEVO'S

BELDEN ST

*Scholze
Park*

ADVENTURES
BY THE SEA

MONTEREY
BAY INN

SPENCER ST

DRAKE AVE

THE JABBERWOCK

BREAKWATER
SCUBA

DICKMAN AVE

REESIDE AVE

0   100 yds

0   100 m

SAN CARLOS
BEACH PARK

To
Downtown
Monterey

© AVALON TRAVEL

The Steinbeck Effect

John Ernst Steinbeck was born in Salinas, then a tiny, isolated agricultural community, in 1902. He somehow managed to escape life as a farmer, a sardine fisherman, or a fish canner and ended up living the glamorous life of a writer for his too-short 66 years.

Steinbeck's experiences in the Salinas Valley farming community and in the fishing town of Monterey informed many of his novels. The best known of these is *Cannery Row*, but *Tortilla Flat* is also set in working-class Monterey (though no one knows exactly where the fictional Tortilla Flat neighborhood was supposed to be). The Pulitzer Prize-winning novel *The Grapes of Wrath* takes more of its inspiration from the Salinas Valley. Steinbeck used the valley as a model for farming in the Dust Bowl during the Great Depression.

Steinbeck was fascinated by the plight of the worker; his novels and stories depict ordinary folks going through tough and terrible times. Steinbeck lived and worked through the Great Depression, and thus it's not surprising that many of his stories don't feature Hollywood happy endings. Steinbeck was a realist in almost all of his novels, portraying the good, the bad, and the ugly of human life and society. His work gained almost immediate respect: In addition to his Pulitzer Prize, Steinbeck also won the Nobel Prize for Literature in 1962. Almost every American high school student from the 1950s onward has read at least one of Steinbeck's novels or short stories, and his body of work forms part of the enduring American literary canon.

As the birthplace of California's most illustrious literary son, Salinas became famous for inspiring his work. You'll find a variety of Steinbeck-related maps online (www.mtycounty.com) that offer self-guided tours of the regions made famous by his various novels. Steinbeck's name is taken in vain all over now-commercial Cannery Row, where even the cheesy wax museum tries to draw customers in by claiming kinship with the legendary author. More serious Steinbeck fans prefer the **National Steinbeck Center** (page 125) and **The Steinbeck House** (page 126), both in the still-agricultural town of Salinas. And if the museums aren't enough, plan to be in Monterey County in early August for the annual **Steinbeck Festival** (page 128), a big shindig put on by the Steinbeck Center in order to celebrate the great man's life and works in fine style.

Thankfully, a few remnants of Cannery Row's past remain in the shadows of the area's touristy shops. The most important is a battered little shack located between the Monterey Bay Aquarium and the shiny new InterContinental luxury hotel. The **Pacific Biological Laboratories** (800 Cannery Row, 831/646-5648, www.monterey.org, only open for infrequently scheduled public tours and group visits by reservation) was the workplace and home of famed marine biologist Ed Ricketts, a good friend of Steinbeck's who appeared as "Doc" in Steinbeck's classic novel *Cannery Row*. Following Ricketts' death in 1948, the building hosted a men's club where ideas were batted around over drinks and card games. One of the ideas to make it out of the lab was Jimmy Lyon's concept of putting on an annual music festival in Monterey, an event that would eventually become the long-running Monterey Jazz Festival. The club still meets to this day. Now owned by the city, the lab is open for tours at certain times of the year including days to commemorate Ricketts' birthday (May 8) and for group tours by reservation. The shack's interior has not changed much since Ricketts' time. It's essentially decorated with books and bottles.

★ MONTEREY BAY AQUARIUM

The first aquarium of its kind in the country, the **Monterey Bay Aquarium** (886 Cannery Row, 831/648-4800, www.montereybayaquarium.org, daily 9:30am-6pm, adults $40, students and seniors $35, children $25) is still unique in many ways. From the very beginning, the aquarium's mission has been conservation, and they're not shy about it. Many of the animals in the aquarium's tanks were rescued, and those that survive may eventually be returned to the wild. All the exhibits you'll see in this mammoth complex contain only local sea life.

The aquarium displays a dazzling array of species. When you come to visit, a good first step is to look up the feeding schedules for the tanks you're most interested in. The critters always put on a show at feeding time, and it's smart to arrive several minutes in advance to get a good spot near the glass. Current feeding times are also listed on the aquarium's website.

The living, breathing **Kelp Forest** is just like the kelp beds outside in the bay. Between the swaying strands of kelp, leopard sharks glide over the aquarium floor, anchovies coalesce in silver clouds, and warty sea cucumbers and starfish adorn rocks.

The deepwater tank in the **Open Sea** exhibit area always draws a crowd. Inside its depths, hammerhead sharks sweep the bottom like vacuum cleaners, while giant bluefin tuna cruise by. The aquarium has even had one of the ocean's most notorious predators in this tank: the great white shark. The aquarium has great whites infrequently, but if one is on display, it's definitely worth looking at this sleek and amazing fish up close.

The **Wild About Otters** exhibit gives visitors a personal view of rescued otters. The adorable, furry marine mammals come right up to the glass to interact with curious children and enchanted adults. These fellows might be the true stars of the aquarium. Another of the aquarium's most popular exhibits is the **Jellies Experience,** which illuminates delicate crystal jellies and the comet-like lion's mane jellyfish.

The aquarium is a wildly popular weekend destination. Especially in the summer, the crowds can be forbidding. Weekdays can be less crushing (though you'll run into school groups during much of the year), and the off-season is almost always a better time to visit. Almost all exhibits at the aquarium are wheelchair accessible.

★ MONTEREY STATE HISTORIC PARK

Monterey State Historic Park (831/649-7118, www.parks.ca.gov, gardens May-Sept. daily 9am-5pm, Oct.-Apr. daily 10am-4pm, free) pays homage to the long and colorful history of the city of Monterey. This busy port town acted as the capital of California when it was under Spanish rule, and then later when it became part of the United States. Today, this

The Monterey Bay Aquarium is perched on the water.

park provides a peek into Monterey as it was in the middle of the 19th century when it was a busy place filled with dockworkers, fishermen, bureaucrats, and soldiers. And yet it blends into the modern town of Monterey as well, and modern stores, galleries, and restaurants sit next to adobe structures dating from the 1800s.

It's tough to see everything in just one visit to Old Monterey. If you only get to one spot on your first trip, make it the **Custom House** (20 Custom House Plaza, Fri.-Mon. and holidays 10am-4pm, adults $3, children under 12 free). Built in 1827, it's California State Historic Landmark No. 1 and the oldest government building still standing in the state. You can spend some time wandering the adobe building, checking out the artifacts on display, or even just looking out the upstairs window towards the sea. Also on the plaza is the **Pacific House Museum** (Fri.-Mon. and holidays 10am-4pm, adults $3, children under 12 free). The first floor shows a range of Monterey's history from the Native Californians to the American Period, while the second floor has a plethora of Native American artifacts.

The other buildings that compose the park were built mostly with adobe and/or brick between 1834 and 1847. These include: the **Casa del Oro** (210 Oliver St., 831/649-3364, Thurs.-Sun. 11am-3pm); the **Cooper-Molera Adobe** (525 Polk St.); the **First Brick House** (Fri.-Mon. and holidays 10am-4pm, free); the **Larkin House** (464 Calle Principal, tours Fri. and Sun. 12:30pm, Sat. noon, $5); the **Old Whaling Station** (not open to public); the **Sherman Quarters** (not open to public); and the **Stevenson House** (530 Houston St., Sat.. 1pm-4pm, free), once a temporary residence of Robert Louis Stevenson.

Famous artists, writers, and military men have stayed in some of these spots, most of which have long histories playing several different roles. Look down as you walk to see if you're stepping on antique whalebone sidewalks. And be sure to take a few minutes to admire the many beautiful gardens surrounding the adobes, which are lovingly maintained by local groups.

A great way to get an introduction to the park is to take a **guided tour** (meet at the Pacific House, Fri.-Mon. and holidays 10:30am, 12:30pm, and 2pm, $5). Approximately an hour long, the short walk begins at the Pacific House and includes the Custom House, the First Brick House, the Old Whaling Station with its whalebone sidewalk out front, and California's First Theatre.

Colton Hall, the site of the signing of California's first constitution

Downtown Monterey

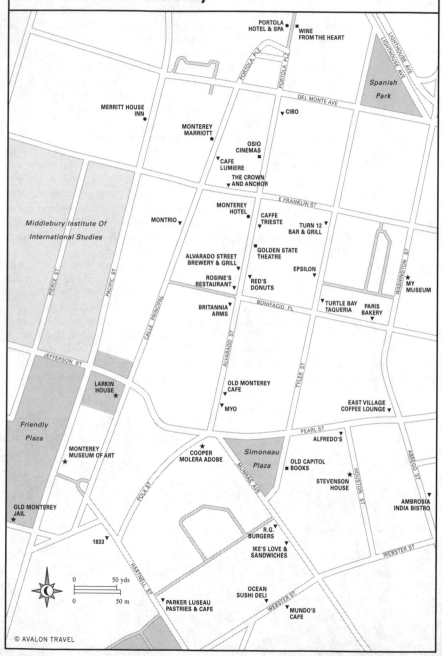

PORTOLA
HOTEL & SPA
WINE
FROM THE HEART

PORTOLA PLZ

PORTOLA PLZ

LIGHTHOUSE AVE

LIGHTHOUSE AVE

Spanish
Park

DEL MONTE AVE

MERRITT HOUSE
INN

CIBO

MONTEREY
MARRIOTT

OSIO
CINEMAS

CAFE
LUMIERE

THE CROWN
AND ANCHOR

E FRANKLIN ST

Middlebury Institute Of
International Studies

MONTRIO

MONTEREY
HOTEL

CAFFE
TRIESTE

TURN 12
BAR & GRILL

WASHINGTON ST

MY
MUSEUM

PIERCE ST

PACIFIC ST

GOLDEN STATE
THEATRE

ALVARADO STREET
BREWERY & GRILL

EPSILON

ROSINE'S
RESTAURANT

RED'S
DONUTS

CALLE PRINCIPAL

BONIFACIO PL

TURTLE BAY
TAQUERIA

PARIS
BAKERY

BRITANNIA
ARMS

ALVARADO ST

JEFFERSON ST

LARKIN
HOUSE

OLD MONTEREY
CAFE

TYLER ST

MYO

EAST VILLAGE
COFFEE LOUNGE

Friendly
Plaza

PEARL ST

ALFREDO'S

MONTEREY
MUSEUM OF ART

COOPER
MOLERA ADOBE

Simoneau
Plaza

OLD CAPITOL
BOOKS

ABREGO ST

MUNRAS AVE

STEVENSON
HOUSE

HOUSTON ST

POLK ST

OLD MONTEREY
JAIL

AMBROSIA
INDIA BISTRO

1833

R.G.
BURGERS

IKE'S LOVE &
SANDWICHES

WEBSTER ST

HARTNELL ST

0   50 yds

0   50 m

PARKER LUSEAU
PASTRIES & CAFE

OCEAN
SUSHI DELI

WEBSTER ST

WEBSTER ST

MUNDO'S
CAFE

© AVALON TRAVEL

37

MONTEREY
SIGHTS

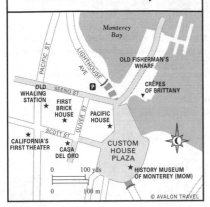

Custom House Square

Visitors can also learn about the historic buildings by taking a cell phone tour, where a two-minute rundown on each building is accessible by dialing 831/998-9458 and entering the code listed outside the structure.

COLTON HALL

The grand white-stone building of **Colton Hall** (Pacific St. between Jefferson St. and Madison St., 831/646-5640, www.monterey. org, summer daily 10am-4pm, winter Mon. and Wed.-Sat. 10am-4pm, Tues. and Sun. noon-3pm, donations appreciated) is where the state of California was born, when 48 delegates met for a month and a half in the fall of 1849 to draft California's first constitution. Among the subjects that were debated were the state's eastern boundary and whether California would allow its citizens to own slaves.

Upstairs is a museum, housed in the long, wood-floored room where the constitution was drafted. The constitution itself is now in Sacramento, but there are other documents from the convention under glass, including a piece of paper where the delegates practiced their signatures. A large portion of the building still houses the working offices of Monterey's city hall.

The rear of Colton Hall is the location of the **Old Monterey Jail** (831/646-5640, www.

monterey.org, daily 10am-4pm, free), which makes an appearance in John Steinbeck's 1935 novel *Tortilla Flat*. Wander into the granite jailhouse that hosted Monterey's malcontents from 1854 to 1956 and peer into its cells.

One final aspect of Colton Hall worth mentioning is the **Moon Tree,** which can be found in front of the building in Friendly Plaza. This towering coast redwood has the unique distinction of growing from a seed that traveled to the moon in 1971 before it was planted here in 1976.

★ MONTEREY HARBOR

The **Monterey Harbor** (Del Monte Ave., www.monterey.org) has always been an important part of Monterey, from its fishing past to its tourism-focused present. Sailboats creak and clank in the Municipal Marina, while fishing boats head out in search of squid and other seafood. A superb way to survey the scene is to walk the one-mile section of the **Monterey Bay Coastal Recreation Trail** (831/646-3866, www.monterey.org) along the harbor's edge.

Three piers jut out into the water and provide nice views of the harbor. The most popular is **Fisherman's Wharf** (1 Old Fisherman's Wharf, www.montereywharf.com, daily, hours vary), which resembles a smaller version of San Francisco's popular tourist attraction of the same name. Where tons of sardines were once shipped out of Monterey Harbor, you'll now find a collection of seafood restaurants, touristy gift shops, and whale-watching boats. (Most of the wharf's seafood restaurants offer free shots of their competing clam chowders to those walking by. It might be enough to stave off your hunger until the next meal.) To dive deeper into Monterey's fishing history, consider taking a **walking tour** (831/521-3394, www.montereywaterfrontcanneryrowtours.com, first Sat. of the month, 10am, adults $20, children 10-15 $15) of the wharf with local historian Tim Thomas. Tours start at the base of Old Fisherman's Wharf, by Harbor House Gifts.

The **Coast Guard Pier** is a 1,700-foot-long

Abalone Underfoot

Visitors walking out onto Municipal Wharf II might be surprised to learn that there is a hidden farming operation right under their feet. The **Monterey Abalone Company** (160 Municipal Wharf II, 831/646-0350, http://montereyabalone.com, Mon.-Fri. 8am-5pm, Sat. 10am-3pm) grows abalones in cages that dangle down from the wharf's underside. Due to the destruction of the mollusk's wild populations, farmed abalone are the only ones available for retail sale. You can stop by the storefront to purchase your own abalone. The kind folks at the Monterey Abalone Company can also provide you with some recipe ideas.

breakwater on the north end of the harbor. It is one of Monterey's best wildlife-viewing areas, and it's a guarantee that you'll be able to see some sea lions and harbor seals if you walk out on the structure.

Municipal Wharf II is located on the eastern edge of the harbor. It still has working fishing operations along with a few wholesale fish companies, a couple restaurants, an abalone farm underneath its deck, and fine views of the harbor and nearby Del Monte Beach.

SAN CARLOS CATHEDRAL

The **San Carlos Cathedral** (500 Church St., 831/373-2628, www.sancarloscathedral.com) is integral to Monterey and early California's history. It has the distinction of being the oldest building in Monterey, the oldest continuously operating church on the West Coast, and California's first cathedral. The first chapel on the site was a wood hut constructed in 1771, a year before Carmel Mission was built. The current Spanish Colonial-style building dates back to 1794.

It is best to visit to the cathedral, which is also known as the Royal Presidio Chapel, when the **Heritage Center** (Sun. 1pm-3pm, 2nd and 4th Mon. 10am-noon and 1:15pm-3:15pm, Wed. 10am-noon, Fri. 10am-3pm, Sat. 10am-2pm) is open. The two-room museum displays artifacts that were discovered during the cathedral's restoration in 2007 and 2008 along with exhibits on different eras of the church and the presidio. In addition, the docents in the museum will give visitors guided

tours of the grounds when the Heritage Center is open.

The T-shaped chapel has a handful of interesting features. The niche at the top of the cathedral's façade holds a statue of Our Lady of Guadalupe that is the oldest non-indigenous sculpture in California. Inside the long, narrow building are a few exposed sections that showcase old friezes and panels. Another fascinating aspect is a crypt for a local Monterey family that is buried under a slab right in front of the altar.

MONTEREY MUSEUM OF ART

Monterey has two venues for taking in art. The Pacific Street location of the **Monterey Museum of Art** (559 Pacific St., 831/372-5477, www.montereyart.org, Thurs.-Mon. 11am-5pm, adults $10, students, military personnel, and children free) is a three-story building across the street from historic Colton Hall. Its eight galleries showcase works from paintings to photographic art with a focus on works created by California artists.

Less than a mile away, the Monterey Museum of Art's **La Mirada location** (720 Via Mirada, 831/372-3689, Thurs. 11am-8pm, Fri.-Mon. 11am-5pm, adults $10, students, military personnel, and children free) is the place to go to see rotating special exhibitions. Past shows have included exhibits of Ansel Adams and Chuck Close's art.

La Mirada is the more interesting space, having been a private estate where Richard Burton and Elizabeth Taylor stayed while filming their 1965 film *The Sandpiper* in nearby Big Sur. When taking in art within the building's drawing room, it feels like you are visiting the home of a wealthy art enthusiast; you'll pass by an old fireplace and a piano amid the hanging works. The room even hides a secret: a hidden Prohibition-era bar that is accessed by a door located at the far end of the room. After visiting the interior galleries, take a few minutes to stroll around La Mirada's outside rose garden and admire its nice view of Lake Estero. When you pay to get into one location of the museum, you receive a pass (with no expiration date) to visit the other location without further charge.

MY MUSEUM

The goal of **MY Museum** (425 Washington St., 831/649-6444, www.mymuseum.org, Tues.-Sat. 10am-5pm, Sun. noon-5pm, adults and children $8, children under two free) is to entertain the youngest members of your family. Touting itself as a "playground for the mind," this downtown kids' museum aims to show wee ones what makes Monterey special. It does this with exhibits including a beach area where children can make sand castles from sand blocks and a mini putting green where budding golfers can work on their technique. The museum also maintains a regular schedule of children's classes, concerts, and craft-making sessions.

PRESIDIO OF MONTEREY

Monterey has long been a military town. Back in 1792, Spain constructed a fortification called El Castillo on a hillside, with cannons pointed down to protect the harbor. When the United States claimed California, it built its own military installation called Fort Mervine on the hill just above the El Castillo site. Today the area, known as the **Presidio of Monterey,** is home to the Defense Language Institute, a school that teaches members of the American military foreign languages.

While the Upper Presidio, where the Defense Language Institute is located, is closed to civilians, the Lower Presidio is open to the public as the **Lower Presidio Historic**

Park (Artillery St. and Private Bolio) and the **Presidio of Monterey Museum** (Corporal Ewing Rd., Bldg. 113, 831/646-3456, www.monterey.org, Mon. 10am-1pm, Thurs.-Sat. 10am-4pm, Sun. 1pm-4pm, donations appreciated). The one-room museum is located in an old military administrative and storage building. It interprets the history of Monterey through a military lens, with exhibits and artifacts, including cannonballs from El Castillo, field uniforms, and more.

Downhill from the museum is a stone statue of Father Junipero Serra stepping out of a small boat and looking toward Monterey Harbor. On the hillside above the museum there is a large monument to U.S. commodore John Drake Sloat that is topped with a concrete eagle. Every night at 10pm, the strains of "Taps" drift into town from the Defense Language Institute, where the song is played at the close of the day.

DENNIS THE MENACE PARK

The brainchild of Hank Ketcham, the creator of the *Dennis the Menace* comic strip, **Dennis the Menace Park** (777 Pearl St., 831/646-3860, 10am-dusk daily) opened in 1956. Ketcham was heavily involved in the design process; he moved to the area after World War II, and lived here until his death in 2001. There's a nine-foot climbing wall, suspension bridge, curvy slides, brightly colored jungle gyms, a (fenced in, non-working) locomotive, and a whole lot more, as well as a bronze sculpture of the little menace near the entrance.

WINE TASTING

Right up from Cannery Row is the **Pierce Ranch Vineyards Tasting Room** (499 Wave St., 831/372-8900, www.piercevineyards.com, Mon.-Thurs. noon-7pm, Fri.-Sat. noon-8pm, Sun. noon-6pm, tasting $5), which looks like a small family home. Inside, they pour glasses of cabernet sauvignon, petite sirah, and zinfandel made from grapes grown on their southern Monterey County vineyard.

They host frequent events, from wine-tasting parties to performances by national touring bands.

A Taste of Monterey (700 Cannery Row, Ste. KK, 831/646-5446, www.atasteofmonterey.com, Sun.-Wed. 11am-7pm, Thurs.-Sat. 11am-8pm, tasting $10-20) provides an unbeatable view of the bay while you sample wines from 95 Monterey County wineries. The tasting room, in a renovated sardine cannery building, also has a bistro that makes small plates, flatbreads, and sandwiches to pair with the fine wines.

Wine from the Heart (241 Alvarado St., 831/641-9463, www.sovinowinebar.com, Sun.-Thurs. 1pm-9pm, Fri.-Sat. 1pm-10pm, tasting $10) has a good location at the end of Alvarado Street. Sample wines from all over California and maybe take a bottle home.

SIGHTSEEING TOURS

Over 215 movies have been filmed in Monterey County, from Clint Eastwood's directorial debut *Play Misty for Me* to the goofy Tom Hanks comedy *Turner & Hooch*. **Monterey Movie Tours** (800/343-6437 or 831/372-6278, www.montereymovietours.com, $55) provides a three-hour bus tour that visits film locations on the Monterey Peninsula. The tour bus pulls up to Monterey sights like the historic Colton Hall, where you'll see a clip from 1959's *A Summer Place* on the video screen mounted in the bus. Then, at the Monterey Bay Aquarium, you'll watch footage from *Star Trek 4: The Journey Home,* where scenes from the movie were filmed. The scenic tour also heads into Pebble Beach and stops at the Lone Cypress and The Lodge at Pebble Beach. Owner and operator Doug Lumsden uses the tour to impart impressive knowledge about the peninsula's history and notable attractions, including anecdotes about legendary Carmel resident Clint Eastwood. Some tourists zip around and see the sights in bright yellow, convertible scooter cars that resemble souped-up golf carts. Rent one yourself at **Sea Car Tours** (230 Alvarado Plaza, 831/884-6807, www.seacartours.com, $60/hour). There is a one-hour tour of Monterey, a two-hour tour that covers Monterey and Pacific Grove, and a three-hour tour where you can do your own thing.

Dennis the Menace Park

Hotel Del Monte

Monterey's reputation as a travel destination began with one massive resort: the Hotel Del Monte. The sprawling 20,000-acre resort was built by railway tycoon Charles Crocker in 1880. In 1919, developer Samuel F. B. Morse—a distant relative of the inventor of the same name—and his company Del Monte Properties acquired the hotel and began to highlight the resort's recreation facilities, including an auto racetrack, polo fields, a horse-racing track, and a Roman plunge pool. Pebble Beach's popular 17-Mile Drive was developed as an attraction for the Hotel Del Monte's guests (though its route has since changed). During its heyday, the resort hosted an impressive range of notable guests, including President Theodore Roosevelt, actor Charlie Chaplin, actress Marlene Dietrich, surreal artist Salvador Dali, aviation pioneer Amelia Earhart, and author Ernest Hemingway.

Today, the grounds are no longer open to the public. The U.S. Navy bought the resort in 1947, and it is currently home to the Naval Postgraduate School. Visitors can glimpse views of the old resort while driving by its grounds on Del Monte Avenue.

Entertainment and Events

BARS AND CLUBS

Descending down into **The Crown & Anchor** (150 W. Franklin St., 831/649-6496, www.crownandanchor.net, daily 11am-1:30am) feels a bit like entering a ship's hold. Along with the maritime theme, The Crown & Anchor serves up 20 international beers on tap. Sip indoors or on the popular outdoor patio. They also have good pub fare, including cottage pies and curries; the curry fries are a local favorite. Lively but not a pickup joint, The Crown & Anchor is a go-to place for locals, tourists, and even celebrities like Jon Hamm, who passed several nights here in 2014 during the filming of *Mad Men* in nearby Big Sur.

Britannia Arms (444 Alvarado St., 831/656-9543, www.britanniaarmsofmonterey.com, daily 11am-2am) is a British pub right on Alvarado Street owned by an actual Brit. The "Brit," as it's known to locals, is usually packed with a younger crowd on Thursday, Friday, and Saturday nights, when there's a DJ spinning or a band performing. There's also karaoke three times a week (Tues.-Wed. and Sun.). At less crowded times, the Brit is a good place to watch sports, and if you are an English Premier League soccer fan,

this pub has you covered. Choose between 24 beers on tap and a full bar.

The location of the **London Bridge Pub** (256 Figueroa St., Wharf II, 831/372-0581, http://lbpmonterey.com, daily 11:30am-11pm) sets it apart from Monterey's other drinking establishments. Situated right beside the Monterey Harbor, adjacent to the Municipal Wharf, the pub takes advantage of the setting with an outdoor heated patio that has views of the boats docked in the harbor.

A good bet for a beer or cocktail is the **Cannery Row Brewing Company** (95 Prescott Ave., 831/643-2722, www.canneryrowbrewingcompany.com, Sun.-Thurs. 11:30am-midnight, Fri.-Sat. 11:30am-2am), just a block up from bustling Cannery Row. They pour 73 beers on tap, ranging from hefeweizens to barley wine. Sip your suds in the large dining room, at the bar, or outside on the back deck by a fire pit. Expect good happy hour deals on food and beer 3pm-6pm. The occasional band or DJ performs in a little alcove facing the bar on some evenings.

The **Bulldog British Pub** (611 Lighthouse Ave., 831/658-0686, daily 11:30am-2am) is one of New Monterey's favorite watering holes. The long, narrow bar entices with friendly bartenders, a handful of TVs for viewing sporting events, and a popular jukebox. If you have a group, opt for the table next to the door that has windows looking out on Lighthouse Avenue.

The best place in Monterey to watch your favorite sports team is **Knuckles Sports Bar** (1 Old Golf Course Rd., 831/372-1234, http://monterey.hyatt.com, Mon.-Tues. 4pm-10pm, Wed.-Fri. 4pm-11pm, Sat. 11am-11pm, Sun. 9am-10pm). Its 24 flat-screen TVs have individual detached speakers that you can bring to your table so you can actually hear the commentators. There are free peanuts and popcorn, along with a better-than-average bar menu if you need something more substantial.

Blue Fin Billiards (685 Cannery Row, 831/717-4280, Sun.-Thurs. noon-midnight, Fri.-Sat. noon-1:30am, pool tables $12/hour) provides a place to tap into your competitive side while sipping a beer or cocktail. Occupying a large upstairs space in Cannery Row, Blue Fin has 11 pool tables, seven big-screen TVs, dartboards, and foosball tables.

A true dive bar, **Segovia's** (650 Lighthouse Ave., 831/646-3154, Mon.-Fri. 2pm-2am, Sat.-Sun. 10am-2am, cash only) doesn't have windows, draft beer, or a cash register that takes credit cards. It does have cheap drinks, a jukebox, a fireplace, a smoking patio, and some interesting matador decor.

A distinct stone building just a couple blocks off Alvarado Street, **Alfredo's** (266 Pearl St., 831/375-0655, Sun.-Thurs. 10am-midnight, Fri.-Sat. 10am-2am, cash only) is a cozy dive bar for the downtown Monterey crowd. This comfortable drinking establishment has dim lighting, a gas fireplace, cheap drinks, and a good jukebox. It's a fine place for a drink if you actually want to hear what your companion is saying.

LIVE MUSIC

Downtown Monterey's historic **Golden State Theatre** (417 Alvarado St., 831/649-1070, www.goldenstatetheatre.com) hosts live music, a speaker series, and dance, comedy, and theater productions. The theater dates

historic Golden State Theatre

back to 1926 and was designed to look like a Moorish castle. Performers in its ornate main room have included music legends like Patti Smith, Willie Nelson, and Darlene Love. The current owners also run the Fox Theatre in Redwood City.

Cibo (301 Alvarado St., 831/649-8151, www.cibo.com, daily 4pm-close) does live music six nights a week on Alvarado Street and draws a mostly middle-aged crowd. It hosts mellow jazz on Sundays, Tuesdays, Wednesdays, and Thursdays before heating up with funk, soul, and more upbeat genres on Friday and Saturday.

Sly McFly's (700 Cannery Row, Ste. A, 831/649-8050, daily 11am-11:30pm) is one of the only places in the area that guarantees live music seven days a week. On weekends, a middle-aged crowd spins and dips on the wooden dance floor in front of the stage. There are also lots of TVs for catching sporting events. Also on Cannery Row, **Cooper's Pub** (653 Cannery Row, 831/373-1353, www.cooperspubmonterey.com, Sun.-Thurs.

Monterey Pop Festival

The 1967 Monterey Pop Festival changed popular music forever. It launched the careers of icons including Jimi Hendrix, Janis Joplin, and Otis Redding, while basically creating the blueprint for the current multi-act music festival. It all began as an idea hatched by a small group of music industry heavyweights including producer Lou Adler and John Phillips of the folk act The Mamas & the Papas.

During their show at the Monterey County Fairgrounds, The Who wowed an American audience by smashing their instruments onstage. This was the same event where Hendrix set his guitar on fire during his performance, and the same place where Otis Redding made inroads into mainstream music due to a well-received set he played with Booker T. & the MGs as a backing band.

The Monterey Pop Festival is immortalized in D. A. Pennebaker's legendary concert film *Monterey Pop.*

11:30am-10pm, Fri.-Sat. 11:30am-1am) has live bands on Friday and Saturday nights. In the summer, bands play out on a large patio that has a stage, heat lamps, and fire pits. The music moves inside to the front dining room during the winter.

For old-school cool, stop into the **Sardine Factory** (701 Wave St., 831/373-3775, www.sardinefactory.com, Sun.-Thurs. 5pm-10:30pm, Fri.-Sat. 5pm-11pm) any night from Tuesday to Saturday between 7:30pm and 10:30pm to see local musician David Conley play piano in the restaurant's lounge. He takes requests, and it's a kick hearing piano bar versions of modern songs.

CINEMA

Head to Cannery Row to see the latest blockbuster on a giant floor-to-ceiling screen at the **Cinemark Monterey Cannery Row XD** (640 Wave St., 831/372-4645, www.cinemark.com). There's also a 13-screen movie theater, the **Century Theatres Del Monte Center** (1700 Del Monte Center, 831/373-8051, www.cinemark.com), that's located in Monterey's shopping mall.

When Monterey's art house movie theater, **Osio Cinemas** (350 Alvarado St.), closed abruptly in 2015, community desire influenced a new group to step in and revive the local institution. The Osio is once again the place to view independent movies, foreign films, and documentaries in Monterey.

FESTIVALS AND EVENTS

The Monterey region hosts numerous festivals and special events each year. Whether your pleasure is fine food or funky music, you'll probably be able to plan a trip around some sort of multiday festival. There are dozens of events and performances scheduled during Monterey's busy year.

Every April, hordes of spandex-clad cyclists take over the Laguna Seca Recreation Area and beyond for the **Sea Otter Classic** (Laguna Seca Recreation Area, 800/218-8411, www.seaotterclassic.com, Apr.), which is touted as the largest cycling festival on the continent. This "celebration of cycling" includes everyone from amateurs to Olympians competing in mountain bike and road bike races.

Monterey is connected to many foreign countries thanks to the presence of the Middlebury Institute of International Studies, the Defense Language Institute, and the Naval Postgraduate School. Having debuted in 2015, the **Language Capital of the World Cultural Festival** (20 Custom House Plaza, 831/649-6544, www.lcowfest.com, early May) celebrates Monterey's many cultural connections with music, dance, and food from around the world over two days.

Since debuting in 2010, the three-day **California Roots Music & Art Festival** (Monterey County Fairgrounds, 2004

Fairground Rd., http://californiarootsfestival.com, late May) has become the world's largest reggae-rock festival. The 2015 installment included Steel Pulse and Slightly Stoopid, along with outside-the-box acts like John Butler Trio, The Roots, and Fishbone.

In keeping with the Central Coast's obsession with food and wine, the annual **Monterey Wine Festival** (Custom House Plaza, 800/422-0251, www.montereywine.com, June) celebrates wine with a generous helping of food on the side. The wine festival is also incongruously home to the West Coast Chowder Competition. This festival offers the perfect opportunity to introduce you to Monterey and Carmel wineries, many of which have not yet hit the "big time" in major wine magazines. It is set outdoors in Monterey's Custom House Plaza.

Gearheads love **Monterey Car Week** (peninsula-wide, www.montereycarweek.com, Aug.) when classic cars clog up the area's motorways. There are also high-dollar car auctions, vintage car races, and the accompanying Concours d' Elegance at Pebble Beach.

The Monterey County Fairgrounds is known nationally for events like the Monterey Jazz Festival, but it's also the place where the **Monterey County Fair** (Monterey County Fairgrounds, 2004 Fairground Rd., 831/717-7167, www.montereycountyfair.com, Aug.) occurs every year. Enjoy deep-fried foods, amusement park rides, 4-H animals, and live concerts.

Monterey's Italian heritage is honored in early September every year during the **Festa Italia** (Custom House Plaza, 831/625-9623, www.festaitaliamonterey.org, Sept.). The three-day fest showcases music, a bocce tournament, and plenty of terrific Italian food.

One of the biggest music festivals in California is the **Monterey Jazz Festival** (Monterey County Fairgrounds, 2004 Fairground Rd., 831/373-3366, www.montereyjazzfestival.org, Sept.). As the site of the longest-running jazz festival on earth, Monterey attracts 500 artists from around the world to play on the fest's eight stages. Held each September at the Monterey County Fairgrounds, this long weekend of amazing music can leave you happy for the whole year. Recent acts to grace the Monterey Jazz Festival's stages include Herbie Hancock, Booker T. Jones, and The Roots.

Come to Monterey to celebrate the coastal lifestyle during the **Monterey Beach Sportsfest** (Del Monte Beach, 831/383-8520, www.montereybeachsf.com, Oct.). Events and competitions include ocean swims, ocean-based water polo matches, and beach volleyball games, all to highlight healthy living.

Monterey is flush with history. To celebrate it, the city hosts the annual **Monterey History Fest** (Monterey, 831/646-5640, www.historicmonterey.org, Oct.) with tours, reenactments, and lectures that bring the past to life.

One way to get into the holiday spirit and explore Monterey's historic buildings is to secure a ticket to **Christmas in the Adobes** (downtown Monterey, www.parks.ca.gov, Dec.). This popular event allows you to experience the city's downtown adobes along with actors in period dress and music performances.

Shopping

CANNERY ROW

Cannery Row is mostly home to shops selling touristy T-shirts, candy, and refrigerator magnets. One of the best shops in Cannery Row is the **Monterey Bay Aquarium's Gift & Bookstore** (886 Cannery Row, 877/665-2665, www.montereybayaquarium.org, late May-early Sept. daily 10am-5pm, early Sept.-late May daily 9:30am-6pm). There are field guides, children's books, Monterey Bay-inspired art, and squishy stuffed sea otters. If you are not buying a pass to the aquarium, you can ask an aquarium manager to escort you into the shop by calling 877/665-2665 on weekdays from 10am to 4pm.

Lighthouse Avenue, a couple of blocks away from Cannery Row, is the place to find locally owned shops. Between Cannery Row and Lighthouse Avenue is the **Cannery Row Antique Mall** (471 Wave St., 831/655-0264, www.canneryrowantiquemall.com, Mon.-Fri. 10am-5:30pm, Sat. 10am-6pm, Sun. 10am-5pm), which is located in a former cannery building. It boasts 100 antique dealers selling all sorts of items, from jewelry to sports memorabilia.

If a visit to Monterey is inspiring you to re-read some of John Steinbeck's classic works (or read them for the first time) stop into **BookBuyers** (600 Lighthouse Ave., 831/375-4208, http://bookbuyers.com, daily 11am-7pm), a used bookshop that almost always has some Steinbeck titles as well as other books about the Monterey Bay area.

DOWNTOWN MONTEREY

Downtown Monterey is dominated by restaurants and bars, but there are a few local shops worth seeking out as well. The **Old Monterey Business Association** (831/655-8070, www.oldmonterey.org) has a directory of downtown businesses on their website.

Old Capitol Books (559 Tyler St., 831/333-0383, http://oldcapitolbooks.com, Wed.-Mon. 10am-6pm, Tues. 10am-7pm) deals in used and out-of-print books with an emphasis on California's history. They also host book signings, open mics, and reading groups.

DEL MONTE SHOPPING CENTER

Del Monte Shopping Center (1410 Del Monte Center, 831/373-2705, www.delmontecenter.com, shop hours vary) is an open-air shopping mall just off the Munras exit of Highway 1. The mall is home to usual suspects like the Apple Store, Forever 21, and The Gap, but there are also some local gems as well, including Green's Camera World and worthwhile dining options Dametra Café and Lalla Grill. It's also the place to go to see the latest blockbusters at **Century Theatres** (1700 Del Monte Ave., 831/373-8051, www.cinemark.com).

Sports and Recreation

Monterey Bay is the premier Northern California locale for a number of water sports, especially scuba diving. It's also one of the best areas on the California coast for kayaking and stand-up paddleboarding due to its protection from the open ocean and its vibrant marine life.

BEACHES

Monterey State Beach

Monterey State Beach (Del Monte Ave., 831/649-2836, www.parks.ca.gov, daily dawn-sunset) is a fee-free beach stretching from the Monterey Municipal Wharf II to Seaside. The relatively flat state beach is good for walks or beach runs, while the protected waters offshore are usually nice places to paddle out into the bay in a kayak or on a stand-up paddleboard. Access points include the Monterey Municipal Wharf II and the end of Canyon del Rey Boulevard in Seaside. You can access a popular locals' section by turning left onto Casa Verde Way off Del Monte Avenue while heading toward Seaside from downtown Monterey. The street then turns into the one-way Surf Way, which dead-ends into Tide Avenue; that street offers parking right along the beach. A section of the state beach is known as Del Monte Beach, which can be a bit confusing.

Between the state beach and El Estero Park is the city's **Monterey Bay Waterfront Park** (831/646-3860, http://monterey.org, daily 6am-10pm), which has volleyball courts, picnic tables, and barbecue pits.

San Carlos Beach Park

One of the most popular places for scuba divers to access the bay, the **San Carlos Beach Park** (Cannery Row at Reeside Ave., 831/646-3860, www.monterey.org, daily 6am-10pm) is west of the Coast Guard Pier and Monterey Harbor. This small spit of beach is backed by a grassy lawn.

McAbee Beach

To get some sand in your shoes while walking around Cannery Row, check out **McAbee Beach** (Cannery Row and Hoffman Ave., 831/646-3860, www.monterey.org, daily 6am-10pm), a little pocket beach tucked between the Spindrift Inn and El Torito Restaurant. This 0.14-acre sliver of sand still has a few ruins from Cannery Row's fishing heyday. The little beach boasts a vibrant history: It was once a launching spot for Portuguese whalers and the site of a small Chinese fishing village. Learn more by reading the interpretive panels above the beach.

★ SCUBA DIVING

Any native Northern Californian knows that there's only one really great place in the region to get certified in scuba diving: Monterey Bay. Even if you go to a dive school up in the Bay Area, they'll take you down to Monterey for your open-water dive. Accordingly, dozens of dive schools cluster in and around the city of Monterey.

One of the best places for novices and more experienced divers is in **Breakwater Cove** (novice to advanced, 10-60 feet) off San Carlos Beach. It's easy to access with lots of parking and a beach entry. Breakwater's accessibility results in busloads of folks from Bakersfield to Berkeley coming to the spot to do their checkout dives. Despite this, it rarely feels crowded in the water. You can spot fish, Dungeness crab, and harbor seals along the rocks of the cove's namesake breakwater. To the west is a reef with a kelp bed. It's shallow enough that even snorkelers can see their fill of sea life.

A more advanced dive off San Carlos Beach is on the **Metridium Field** (advanced, 35-60 feet), which involves a swim out into the bay. Once there, you'll be treated to reefs covered in Metridium anemones that look like white underwater mushrooms. To reach the site, swim 50-60 feet out from the beach pump

Sea Sanctuary

Monterey Bay is in a federally protected marine area known as the **Monterey Bay National Marine Sanctuary** (MBNMS, http://montereybay.noaa.gov). Designated a sanctuary in 1992, the protected waters stretch far past the confines of Monterey Bay to a northern boundary seven miles north of the Golden Gate Bridge and a southern boundary at Cambria in San Luis Obispo County. The sanctuary was created for resource protection, education, public use, and research. The MBNMS is the reason so many marine research facilities including the Long Marine Laboratory, the Monterey Bay Marine Laboratory, and the Moss Landing Marine Laboratories dot the Monterey Bay's shoreline.

MBNMS holds many marine treasures including the Monterey Bay Submarine Canyon, which is right offshore of the fishing village of Moss Landing. The canyon is similar in size to the Grand Canyon and has a rim to floor depth of 5,577 feet. In 2009, MBNMS expanded to include another fascinating underwater geographical feature: the Davidson Seamount. Located 80 miles southwest of Monterey, the undersea mountain rises an impressive 7,480 feet, yet its summit is still 4,101 feet below the ocean's surface.

house. Look for a large pipe and follow it to the end. Then swim north for another 30 feet.

An easy-access dive spot is off Cannery Row's **McAbee Beach** (novice to advanced, 10-50 feet). Swim out from the beach 30-40 feet to reach a kelp forest colored with invertebrates.

Breakwater Scuba (225 Cannery Row, 831/717-4546, http://breakwaterscuba.com, Mon.-Fri. 9am-6pm, Sat.-Sun. 7am-6pm) occupies an enviable spot close to the Breakwater Cove diving spots. They rent equipment, teach classes, and conduct tours of the Breakwater Cove area.

A locals' favorite, **Bamboo Reef** (614 Lighthouse Ave., 831/372-1685, www.bambooreef.com, Mon.-Fri. 9am-6pm, Sat.-Sun. 7am-6pm) offers scuba lessons and rents equipment just a few blocks from popular dive spots, including Breakwater Cove. The aquamarine storefront on Lighthouse Avenue has been helping people get underwater since 1980.

Another of the many dive shop options is the **Aquarius Dive Shop** (2040 Del Monte Ave., 831/375-1933, www.aquariusdivers.com, Mon.-Fri. 9am-6pm, Sat.-Sun. 7am-6pm). Aquarius offers everything you need to go diving in Monterey Bay, including air and nitrox fills, equipment rental, certification courses, and help booking a trip on a local dive boat. Aquarius works with five boats to create great trips for divers of all interests and ability levels. Call 831/657-1020 for local dive conditions.

★ KAYAKING AND STAND-UP PADDLEBOARDING

With all the focus on sustainable tourism in Monterey, coupled with the lovely recreation area formed by Monterey Bay, it's no wonder that sea kayaking is popular here. Monterey's coastline is as scenic a spot as any to learn to kayak or stand-up paddleboard (SUP). Whether you want to try paddling for the first time or you're an expert who hasn't brought your own gear out to California, you'll find a local outfit ready and willing to hook you up.

The coast off Monterey is an ideal place for paddling. It is less exposed than other spots along the California coast. If the swells are big, duck into Monterey Harbor, where you can paddle past moored boats and harbor seal colonies. When the surf is manageable, the paddle from San Carlos Beach to the aquarium and back (1.16 miles round-trip) pretty much guarantees that you will see an otter or a harbor seal in the water near you. The Monterey Bay National Marine Sanctuary regulations require all paddlers to stay 150 feet from all sea otters, sea lions, and harbor seals.

Adventures by the Sea (299 Cannery Row, 831/372-1807, www.adventuresbythesea.com, summer daily 9am-8pm, winter daily 9am-6pm, kayak tours $60-85 pp, kayak rentals $30/day, SUP rentals $50/day) rents kayaks by the day to let you choose your own route around the magnificent Monterey Bay kelp forest. If you're not confident enough to go off on your own, Adventures offers tours from Cannery Row. Your guide can tell you all about the wildlife you're seeing: harbor seals, sea otters, pelicans, seagulls, and maybe even a whale in the winter. The tour lasts about 2.5 hours and the tandem sit-on-top kayaks make it a great experience for school-age children. Adventures by the Sea also runs a tour of Stillwater Cove at Pebble Beach. Reservations are recommended for all tours, but during the summer the Cannery Row tour leaves regularly at 10am and 2pm, so you can stop by and see if there's a spot available. They have several other locations in Monterey (685 Cannery Row and 210 Alvarado St.).

Rent a kayak or SUP from **Monterey Bay Kayaks** (693 Del Monte Ave., 831/373-5357, www.montereybaykayaks.com, Nov.-Feb. daily 8:30am-5pm, March-late May daily 8:30am-6pm, late May-early Sept. daily 8:30am-7pm, kayak tours $55-150, kayak rentals $30-45 pp, SUP rentals $30/two hours) and paddle into the bay from the beach right south of the Municipal Wharf. (There's also a branch in Moss Landing on the Elkhorn Slough.) You can also choose to paddle out with an experienced guide. The tours include kayak fishing, Sunday sunrise excursions, and a Point Lobos paddle. If you really get into it, you can also sign up for closed-deck sea kayaking classes to learn about safety, rescue techniques, tides, currents, and paddling techniques.

SURFING

Monterey is not the best place on the Monterey Peninsula to surf. (That would be Carmel Beach and Pacific Grove's Asilomar Beach.) That said, occasionally the break off Monterey State Beach's Casa Verde stretch has waves. When the swells get big, an easy beginner wave sometimes forms off Monterey's Municipal Wharf.

Sunshine Freestyle (443 Lighthouse Ave., 831/375-5015, http://sunshinefreestyle.com, Mon.-Sat. 10am-6pm, Sun. 11am-5pm, surfboard rental $30/day, wetsuit rental $15/day) is one of two Monterey surf shops. Loved by the area's hard-core surfers, this shop can rent you the necessary equipment to get out into the water. These are also the guys who put on the annual Sunshine Freestyle Surfabout in Carmel, the only surf contest in Monterey County. **On the Beach** (693 Lighthouse Ave., 831/646-9283, http://onthebeachsurfshop.com, Sun.-Thurs. 10am-6pm, Fri.-Sat. 10am-7pm, surfboard rental $30/day, wetsuit rental $15/day) is on the same street a few blocks away and rents boards. It is a large, organized shop with lots of gear.

WHALE-WATCHING, FISHING, AND BOAT TOURS

Whales pass quite near the shores of Monterey year-round. While you can sometimes even see them from the beaches, any number of boats can take you out for a closer look at the great beasts as they travel along their own special routes north and south. The area hosts many humpbacks, blue whales, and gray whales, plus the occasional killer whale, minke whale, fin whale, and pod of dolphins. Bring your own binoculars for a better view, but the experienced boat captains will do all they can to get you as close as possible to the whales and dolphins. Most tours last 2-3 hours and leave from Fisherman's Wharf, which is easy to get to and has ample parking. If you prefer not to rise with the sun, pick a tour that leaves in the afternoon.

Monterey Bay Whale Watch (84 Fisherman's Wharf, 831/375-4658, www.montereybaywhalewatch.com, adults $40-145, children 4-12 $29-39, children 3 and under $15) leaves from an easy-to-find red

Fast Raft Ocean Safaris

fishing license, you can purchase a one-day license at the shop before your trip. While you can try to walk up to their bright teal shop at Fisherman's Wharf, it's best to get tickets for your trip in advance; either call or buy online from Randy's website. For another option in catching your own seafood, consider heading out with **Westwind Charter Sport Fishing & Excursions** (66 Fisherman's Wharf, 831/392-7867, www.westwindcharter. com, $140-150). Depending on what's in season, you can catch salmon, rock cod, halibut, or albacore.

Fast Raft Ocean Safaris (Monterey Harbor, 800/979-3370, www.fastraft.com, $140/pp) offers an intimate way to see the Monterey coastline and the wildlife of Monterey Bay. The "fast raft" is a 33-foot-long inflatable boat with a rigid hull that accommodates just six passengers. The raft does whale-watching trips out of Moss Landing and coastal safaris that depart from Monterey and head south to Pebble Beach's Stillwater Cove and Point Lobos when the weather cooperates. The vessel has a few advantages over the other larger whale-watching ships for those who want to see marine mammals up close and personal. It is low to the water and open, which makes any nearby whale that is surfacing, spouting, or breaching an even more incredible experience to behold. The engine is also quieter, and the captain doesn't use amplified speakers to address the passengers, making it easy to hear the exhalations of surfacing and diving whales. Though the six shock-absorbing straddle seats look like something you'd find on an amusement park roller coaster, they provide a surprisingly comfortable sit even in bumpy ocean conditions. It's worth noting that the fast raft does not have a restroom, and it doesn't allow passengers under 12 years old.

SAILING

A good way to see the bay is by sailboat. **Monterey Bay Sailing** (78 Old Fisherman's Wharf, 831/372-7245, www.montereysailing. com, bay cruises adults $39/hour, children

building on Fisherman's Wharf and runs tours in every season. You must make a reservation in advance, even for regularly scheduled tours. Afternoon tours are available. **Princess Monterey Whale Watching** (96 Fisherman's Wharf, 831/372-2203, www.montereywhalewatching.com, $45 pp) prides itself on its knowledgeable guides/marine biologists and its comfortable, spacious cruising vessels. The *Princess Monterey* offers morning and afternoon tours, and you can buy tickets online or by phone.

If you'd rather catch fish than watch mammals, **Randy's Fishing Trips** (Fisherman's Wharf, 831/372-7400 or 800/251-7440, www. randysfishingtrips.com, $75-80) can take you out for salmon, halibut, albacore, mackerel, rock cod, flatfish, and even squid and Dungeness crab in season. They can also take you out for a whale-watching trip if that's your preference. The half-day trips can be scheduled for the morning or afternoon. You can bring your own food including a small cooler for your drinks. If you don't have a California

$25/hour, boat rentals $200-350/day) does all sorts of cruises, sailboat rentals, and even sailing lessons. **Carrera Sailing** (Municipal Wharf II, A-Tier, 831/375-0648, www.sailmonterelbay.com, cruises $38-50 pp) can also get you out on the water, whether it's a nature excursion, romantic sunset cruise, or sailing lessons.

The Monterey Bay Aquarium takes folks out on their 65-foot eco-friendly sailboat the *Derek M. Bayliss* during the summer. Hop onboard for their **Summer Sailing Adventures** (831/647-6886 or 866/963-9646, www.montereybayaquarium.org/adventures, June-Aug., adults $55-69, children $59), where you can opt to work with an aquarium naturalist on an ocean-monitoring program or simply enjoy an evening wine-and-cheese outing on the water.

PARKS
El Estero Park
El Estero Park (bordered by Del Monte Ave., Camino Aquajito, Fremont Blvd., and Camino El Estero, 831/646-3866, www.monterey.org, daily 6am-10pm) has a variety of facilities, including the very popular **Dennis the Menace Park** (777 Pearl St., 831/646-3860, 10am-dusk daily), a playground park.

Rent a paddleboat (some are designed to look like giant swans) at **El Estero Boating** (corner of Camino El Estero and Del Monte Ave., 831/375-1484, summer daily 10am-6pm, winter daily 10am-5pm, regular paddleboats $23/hr, swan paddleboats $35/half hour) and cruise around the goose-laden waters. Or walk the path around the lake, where you can utilize the park's physical fitness equipment (parallel bars, balance beam) if you need a workout. The park's other features include a nice group barbecue area, a baseball diamond, a youth center, a dog park, and the **Monterey Skate Park** (daily 9am-dusk), which has obstacles like stairs and rails.

Veteran's Memorial Park
Veteran's Memorial Park (Skyline Dr. and Jefferson St., 831/646-3860, www.monterey.org, daily 6am-10pm) is uphill from downtown Monterey and has fine views of the bay. With a large lawn and barbecue facilities, it's a good place for a picnic. There are also hiking trails and a basketball court. It's the access point for **Huckleberry Hill Nature Preserve.**

Jack's Peak County Park
Jack's Peak in **Jack's Peak County Park** (25020 Jacks Peak Park Rd., 831/775-4895, www.co.monterey.ca.us, daily 10am-close, vehicles Mon.-Fri. $4, Sat.-Sun. and holidays $5) is the Monterey Peninsula's highest point at 1,068 feet. The park is located a few miles east of downtown Monterey and has some nice views of the city and its harbor. There are 8.5 miles of trail here, including a self-guided nature trail that shows off some fossils from the Miocene epoch. The park also has picnic areas and bathrooms.

CAR RACING
If you're feeling the need for speed, you can get lots of it at the **Mazda Raceway Laguna Seca** (1021 Monterey-Salinas Hwy., 831/242-8201, www.laguna-seca.com), one of the country's premier road-racing venues. Here you can see historic auto races, superbikes, speed festivals, and an array of Grand Prix events. The major racing season runs May-October. In addition to the big events, Laguna Seca hosts innumerable auto clubs and small sports car and stock car races. Be sure to check the website for parking directions specific to the event you plan to attend—this is a big facility. There is even a campground here known as the **Laguna Seca Recreation Area** (888/588-2267, www.co.monterey.ca.us, RV sites $35, tent sites $30) that is run by the Monterey County Parks Department.

HIKING
If you want to explore Monterey's coastline without getting wet, head out on the **Monterey Bay Coastal Recreation Trail** (831/646-3866, www.monterey.org). The 18-mile paved path stretches from Pacific Grove

in the south all the way to the north Monterey County town of Castroville. The most scenic section is from Monterey Harbor down to Pacific Grove's Lovers Point Park.

Jack's Peak County Park (25020 Jacks Peak Park Rd., 831/775-4895, www.co.monterey.ca.us, daily 10am-close, vehicles Mon.-Fri. $4, Sat.-Sun. and holidays $5) is home to the highest point on the Monterey Peninsula. Its 0.8-mile-long **Skyline Trail** passes through a rare Monterey pine forest and offers glimpses of fossils from the Miocene epoch before reaching the summit, which offers an overview of the whole peninsula.

An interesting little hike in **Veteran's Memorial Park** (Skyline Dr. and Jefferson St., 831/646-3860, www.monterey.org, daily 6am-10pm) leads to a former quarry. The **Quarry Park Trail** (1.3 miles round-trip, easy) can be found northeast of the park's large, grassy lawn. It traverses a hillside before winding down into the former quarry, where it is said rocks were taken to build Monterey Harbor's breakwater. Now the quarry feels like a tranquil box canyon.

Accessible from Veterans Memorial Park, **Huckleberry Hill Nature Preserve** has an intact Monterey pine forest. The **Huckleberry Hill Loop Trail** (1.88 miles round-trip, moderate) gains 300 feet as it makes a loop around the perimeter of the preserve.

BIKING

A terrific way to see Monterey's coastline is to hop on a bike and hit the **Monterey Bay Coastal Recreation Trail** (831/646-3866, www.monterey.org), which allows you to bike past Monterey Harbor and Cannery Row and out to Pacific Grove's Lover's Point Park. **Adventures by the Sea** (299 Cannery Row, 831/372-1807, www.adventuresbythesea.com, summer daily 9am-8pm, winter daily 9am-6pm, bike rentals $20/four hours, $30/all day) rents bikes in various locations (685 Cannery

Row, 210 Alvarado St.) along the Rec Trail. Try your team building skills by renting a two to six-person surrey bike ($20-30/hour).

GYM

If you have been indulging in the Monterey Peninsula's excellent dining scene, work off some of your added pounds at the **Monterey Sports Center** (301 E. Franklin St., 831/646-3730, www.monterey.org, Mon.-Fri. 5:30am-9:30pm, Sat. 7am-6pm, Sun. 8:30am-6pm, adults $9, seniors $6.50, 6-17 years old $5.50, under 5 $3.75). This clean city-run facility has a weight-training center, a cardio fitness room, two indoor pools, a new sauna facility, and a waterslide. They also offer over 100 group exercise options every week, from aqua Zumba to Pilates, for an added fee.

GOLF

The **Monterey Pines Golf Course** (Fairground Rd. and Garden Rd., 831/656-2167, www.montereypeninsulagolf.com, Mon.-Fri. $18-34, Sat.-Sun. $20-37) might boost your confidence after a lousy day playing on Pebble Beach's challenging greens. The course is a beginner-friendly 18 holes next to the Monterey County Fairgrounds.

The Pebble Beach Company manages the **Del Monte Golf Course** (1300 Sylvan Rd., 831/373-2700, www.pebblebeach.com, $110). It opened as a nine-hole course way back in 1897 as a place for guests of the Hotel Del Monte to play. Now expanded to 18 holes, it claims to be the oldest continuously operating course west of the Mississippi.

DISC GOLF

A lot of people travel to the Monterey Peninsula to play golf at Pebble Beach, but there's another, less expensive way to tee off in Monterey. The **Ryan Ranch Disc Golf Course** (10 Park Dr., 831/277-5941, daily dawn-dusk, free) is a challenging 29-hole disc golf course that includes oak-lined fairways and difficult wooded sections.

SPAS

Monterey is as good a place as any on the California coast to spoil yourself. The **Monterey Day Spa** (380 Foam St., Ste. A, 831/373-2273, www.montereydayspa.com, Sat. 10am-7pm, Sun.-Fri. 10am-6pm, massages $85-140) will freshen you up with massages, facials, waxing, nail care, and more. The spa packages range from a "Girlfriend Getaway" to a "Couples Sanctuary." You can also throw a sparty (spa party) at Monterey Day Spa to celebrate a wedding, a birthday, or any other important life event.

"Elysium" is an ancient Greek word for perfect happiness. **Elysium** (157 Sargent Court, 831/375-1976, www.elysiumtotalbliss.com, Mon.-Fri. 9am-7pm, Sat. 10am-6pm, Sun. by appointment, massages $95-130) does massages, body treatments, and cosmetic work (teeth whitening, hair removal) to help you get to your happy place.

Creative Hands (555 Webster St., Ste. D, 831/737-7353, www.creativehands.biz, Mon.-Sat. 10am-7pm, $60-130) is a one-woman operation that does classic Swedish, deep tissue, and express massages.

Accommodations

DOWNTOWN
Under $150

The section of Munras Avenue between the Highway 1 exit and downtown Monterey has a string of hotels and motels including chains like Days Inn and Best Western. One of the most popular inexpensive options on this stretch is the **Inn By the Bay Monterey** (936 Munras Ave., 831/372-5409, http://innbythebaymonterey.com, $89-199). The rooms come with basic amenities including Wi-Fi and flat-screen TVs with cable.

$150-250

A cute, small budget motel, the **Monterey Bay Lodge** (55 Camino Aguajito, 831/372-8057, www.montereybaylodge.com, $110-159) brings a bit of the Côte d'Azur to the equally beautiful coastal town of Monterey. With small rooms decorated in classic yellows and blues, a sparkling pool with a fountain in the shallow end, and an on-site restaurant serving breakfast, lunch, and dinner, the lodge makes a perfect base for budget-minded families traveling in the Monterey region.

A boutique hotel just a few blocks from downtown, the **Hotel Abrego** (755 Abrego St., 831/372-7551, www.hotelabrego.com, $139-220) has 93 rooms, each with a balcony or patio. Most rooms also have fireplaces.

Amenities include complimentary Wi-Fi, free parking, an exercise studio, an outdoor heated pool, and a hot tub.

The **Casa Munras Hotel & Spa** (700 Munras Ave., 831/375-2411, www.hotelcasamunras.com, $149-359) is named after a former residence that was built in the same spot back in 1824. A portion of the original adobe walls can still be viewed within the modern hotel's Marbella Meeting Room. The 170 rooms of the Casa Munras are designed to recall Monterey's old style. The comfortable but somewhat basic rooms provide a great base for exploring downtown Monterey's adobes, including some that are just a few hundred yards away. Amenities include a heated kidney-shaped pool, a fitness center, and a complimentary DVD library that provides guests an eclectic mix of films. The hotel grounds also include the terrific tapas restaurant **Esteban Restaurant** (831/375-0176, Mon.-Thurs. 5pm-9pm, Fri.-Sat. 5pm-10:30pm, Sun. 5pm-9pm, $8-35) and a spa (831/372-1829, daily 9am-7pm).

The 17-room **Hotel 1110** (1110 Del Monte Ave., 831/655-0515, www.hotel1110.com, $160-225) feels like the kind of boutique hotel you'd find in a big city. The common areas range from artful to borderline extravagant, and there's a rooftop deck to take in views of the small city including a glimpse of Monterey's Municipal Wharf jutting out into the bay. Every room is different but they all have electric fireplaces, bamboo flooring, and comfortable beds. Fourteen of the rooms also include jetted soaking tubs. The third-floor offerings even have bidets, a unique feature for a small American hotel. Enjoy a complimentary afternoon beer or wine at the lobby bar or upstairs at the rooftop bar if the weather is nice. In the morning, a multicourse breakfast is served in the ornate downstairs dining room. The hotel is located just a half mile from downtown's Alvarado Street and right across the street from Del Monte Beach. There are a few quirks here including doors that are difficult to open along with the occasional pile of cleaning supplies in the hallway, but there are also some unexpected amenities for such a moderately priced hotel.

The **Portola Hotel & Spa** (2 Portola Plaza, 831/649-4511, www.portolahotel. com, $179-260) has an enviable perch at the end of Alvarado Street and overlooking the Custom House Plaza. Reflecting its proximity to Monterey Harbor, which is just a couple hundred yards away, the hotel's 379 rooms have a nautical decor that includes items such as mirrors that resemble a ship's porthole. This is a sprawling complex with a fitness center, outdoor pool, the on-site **Jack's Restaurant** (831/649-2698, Mon.-Fri. 6am-10:30am, 11:30am-2pm, and 5pm-10pm, Sat.-Sun. 6am-2pm and 5pm-10pm, $24-36), **Peter B's Brewpub** (831/649-2699, Mon.-Thurs. 4pm-11pm, Fri.-Sat. 11am-1am, Sun. 11am-11pm, $9-18), and the **Spa On the Plaza** (831/647-9000, daily 9am-7pm, $80-250).

The **Monterey Hotel** (406 Alvarado St., 831/375-3184 or 800/966-6490, www.montereyhotel.com, $190-490) was once called "the finest European hotel west of Chicago." With its red awnings shading Alvarado Street's sidewalk, it still has a striking presence downtown. All of its 45 rooms have Victorian furnishings and fireplaces for a comfy stay that recalls an earlier time.

The Merritt House is an adobe built in 1830 and where Monterey County's first judge resided. Now it is part of the **Merritt House Inn** (386 Pacific St., 831/646-9686, www.merritthouseinn.com, $140-250), which is conveniently located a block up from downtown Monterey and the harbor area. The old adobe is now split into three suites, each one with

Casa Munras Hotel & Spa

a fireplace and a parlor. The inn also has 22 rooms with fireplaces, fridges, and coffeemakers. Enjoy the expanded continental breakfast in the morning.

Beach lovers can opt for the **Unscripted Monterey Bay** (2600 Sand Dunes Dr., 800/242-8627, www.montereybeachresort. com, $219-350), which is right on Monterey State Beach with waves breaking out front. The rooms include flat screens, fridges, and coffeemakers. The on-site features include a fitness center, heated pool, and hot tub. The best thing about the resort is its proximity to the sand.

Over $250

The **Monterey Marriott** (350 Calle Principal, 831/649-4234, www.marriott.com, $250-400) is in downtown Monterey and is connected to the Monterey Conference Center by a sky bridge. This is a big hotel with 319 rooms and 22 suites. In addition to its location, other pluses include an outdoor heated pool, a fitness center, and the on-site **Characters Sports Bar & Grill** (831/647-4023, Mon.-Thurs. 2pm-11pm, Fri. 2pm-midnight, Sat. 9am-midnight, Sun. 9am-11pm) in case you want to see the game while in town.

CANNERY ROW
Under $150

The ★ **Monterey Hostel** (778 Hawthorne St., 831/649-0375, http://montereyhostel.org, dorm bed $34-37, private room $129, family room with five beds $179) offers inexpensive accommodations within walking distance of the major attractions of Monterey. This hostel has a men's dorm room, women's dorm room, private rooms, a five-person family room, and a coed dorm room with 16 beds—earplugs not included. There's no laundry facility on-site, but there is a laundromat within walking distance. It's also close to some good restaurants, but there's a large, fully stocked kitchen if you want to save money and make meals on site. The hostel has an unexpected perk in the morning: a free pancake breakfast. Linens are included with your bed, and there are comfy, casual common spaces with couches and musical instruments. And then there's that location—you can walk to the aquarium and Cannery Row, stroll the Monterey Bay Coastal Recreation Trail, or make a short drive over to Carmel to see a different set of sights.

The Otter Inn (571 Wave St., 831/375-2299, $130-400) is one of the least expensive lodging options in the Cannery Row area. Just two blocks from the aquarium, this gray hotel

the rooftop deck of Hotel 1110

resembles an old canning building. It has 33 rooms, including a family suite with a king bed in one room and another bedroom with two queen beds.

$150-250

Tucked into a residential street within New Monterey, the ★ **Jabberwock Inn** (598 Laine St., 831/372-4777, www.jabberwock-inn.com, $209-399) is named after a non-sense poem written by Lewis Carroll that is contained in his 1871 novel *Through the Looking Glass*. Despite its name, the amenities and pluses of this comfortable former convent turned eight-room bed-and-breakfast are no-nonsense. The common area includes a covered wraparound sun porch with views of the Monterey Bay and two fireplaces to warm up by during the winter months. The morning breakfasts are tasty and filling, while the innkeepers are warm and knowledgeable. There are also nice little perks including free parking and late-afternoon wine and appetizers along with evening milk and cookies. In addition, the B&B is just a short walk to Cannery Row, the aquarium, and the businesses on Lighthouse Avenue. The lowest-priced room has a private detached bathroom down the hall, while the Borogrove Room has

a long list of worthwhile features that includes a large Jacuzzi tub, gas fireplace, and sitting area with a coastal view. There are no TVs or telephones here, but there are books, including a few by Steinbeck, and, of course, a number by Carroll.

The ★ **Monterey Bay Inn** (242 Cannery Row, 831/373-6242 or 800/424-6242, www.montereybayinn.com, $249-449) has a generic name, but its setting is anything but. Located between San Carlos Beach and the start of Cannery Row, the boutique hotel's oceanfront rooms have private balconies that allow guests to peer right down into the clear waters of Monterey Bay. In-room binoculars are handy for spotting diving cormorants, bobbing harbor seals, and playful otters. The rooftop hot tub offers another vantage point to take in the marine action offshore. Enjoy a continental breakfast delivered to your room in the morning and some tasty cookies in the evening.

A locally operated hotel under an international chain umbrella, the **Best Western Plus Victorian Inn** (487 Foam St., 831/373-8000 or 800/232-4141, www.victorianinn.com, $199-339) is just two blocks up from Cannery Row. Rooms have marble fireplaces, and guests are treated to a deluxe continental

Jabberwock Inn

breakfast in the morning. The inn has two family suites that sleep up to six guests.

Just a block up from Cannery Row, the **Holiday Inn Express Monterey** (443 Wave St., 877/834-3613, www.montereyhie.com, $180-400) has modern rooms with niceties like TVs carrying HBO. Enjoy an afternoon wine-and-cheese reception along with a morning breakfast buffet with hot items.

Over $250

Luxury hotel **InterContinental The Clement Monterey** (750 Cannery Row, 831/375-4500, www.ictheclementmonterey. com, $250-850) has a can't-be-beat location just a splash away from the bay and feet from the Monterey Aquarium. The hotel has 208 rooms and 12 luxury suites that are decorated with tasteful Asian elements including a bonsai tree, a book-sized Zen garden, and some live white orchids. Most of the marble-floored bathrooms have a separate soaking tub and walk-in shower. The oceanside rooms have views of the bay, while the units on the other side of Cannery Row all have fireplaces. There are a lot of amenities and features outside the comfortable rooms, including a fitness room, an outdoor whirlpool, **The Spa** (831/642-2075, daily 9am-7pm,

massages $80-175), **The C Restaurant & Bar** (831/375-4800, daily 6:30am-10pm, $29-58), a sliver of an outdoor pool long enough to swim laps in, and an artsy jelly-fish-inspired staircase connecting the first and second floors.

Want to stay right on Cannery Row in a room overlooking the bay? You'll pay hand-somely at the **Monterey Plaza Hotel & Spa** (400 Cannery Row, 831/646-1700, www.montereyplazahotel.com, $250-650). This on-the-water luxury hotel has it all: restaurant, coffee shop, spa, private beach, room service, and upscale guestroom good-ies. Rooms range from "budget" garden and Cannery Row-facing accommodations to oceanview rooms with private balconies and huge suites that mimic posh private apart-ments. They also offer a complimentary shuttle to locations in Monterey and nearby Pacific Grove.

Hear the barks of seals and the squawks of seagulls at the ★ **Spindrift Inn** (652 Cannery Row, 831/646-8900, www.spin-driftinn.com, $239-719), a boutique hotel towering above the golden sand and clear green waters of scenic McAbee Beach. This 45-room establishment has been called the country's most romantic hotel, and with

Spindrift Inn is right on the bay.

good reason. Most of the hardwood-floored rooms have gas fireplaces that burn real wood, and full or half canopy beds. Stare out of your window after dark as the lights of Monterey and its surrounding cities ring the bay and listen to one of your room's Monterey-related CDs (a Dave Brubeck live at the Monterey Jazz Festival album, John Tesh's *Monterey Nights*, and more). The very friendly staff serves up a wine-and-cheese reception every day from 4:30pm to 6pm and delivers a complimentary continental breakfast to your room in the morning. The only problem with staying at the Spindrift is that you'll never want to leave.

CAMPING

A mile up a hill from downtown Monterey, the 50-acre **Veterans Memorial Park** (Via Del Rey and Veterans Dr., 831/646-3865, www. monterey.org, $27/single vehicle, $32/two vehicles) has 40 first-come, first-served campsites with views of the Monterey Bay below.

There's also a campground at Laguna Seca, known as the **Laguna Seca Recreation Area** (888/588-2267, www.co.monterey. ca.us, RV sites $35, tent sites $30) and run by the Monterey County Parks Department. The year-round RV campsites have water and electricity, while the 70 tent-camping sites are only available from April to October.

Food

The organic and sustainable food movements have caught hold on the Central Coast. The Monterey Bay Seafood Watch program (www. montereybayaquarium.org) is the definitive resource for sustainable seafood, while the Salinas Valley inland hosts a number of organic farms.

DOWNTOWN
New American

Inside an old brick firehouse, ★ **Montrio** (414 Calle Principal, 831/648-8880, www. montrio.com, daily 4:30pm-close, $18-38) is an elegantly casual Monterey eatery. The ever-changing menu includes meat and seafood entrées, but Montrio is also an ideal place for a lighter dinner, due to its nice small bites and appetizer offerings. One such dish is the Butchers Butter, delicious meat from the top of a ribeye cut. There's also a 40-ounce prime ribeye steak ($110) served family style. Montrio mixologist Anthony Vitacca is well known around town for his creative cocktails that employ ingredients as far ranging as sea salt caramel and pickle juice. Dine inside, under ceilings decorated with art that resembles clouds, or out front on their patio.

★ **Restaurant 1833** (500 Hartnell St.,

831/643-1833, www.restaurant1833.com, Sun.-Thurs. 5:30pm-10pm, Fri.-Sat. 5:30pm-1am, $18-50) is housed in one of Monterey's most historic buildings, a seven-room adobe built in 1833, gussied up for a big-city crowd. At a white onyx bar, patrons can try interesting intoxicants, or lounge in the library for small bites by a roaring fire. Executive chef Jason Franey does approachable cuisine with a real love of details, like the tasty Hawaiian bread appetizer that is made in house (sometimes a matter of minutes before arriving at your table). The menu changes frequently but may include freshly made pastas and meat entrées like tender beef short ribs in a pool of polenta. For parties of six or more (and a week's advance notice), they offer the Gallatins Throwback menu: a whole suckling pig, roasted salmon, or baby goat cooked over a wood fire. The restaurant is owned and operated by Coastal Luxury Management, who put on the Pebble Beach Food & Wine Festival every year.

Del Monte Shopping Center's **Lalla Grill** (1400 Del Monte Center, 831/324-4632, www.lallagrill.com, Mon.-Wed. 11am-10pm, Thurs.-Sat. 11am-11pm, Sun. 10:30am-10pm, $9-22) is a great place for a snack or sipper before taking in a movie at the adjacent Century Theatres. Or discuss the film you just saw over an oversized cocktail (in 14- or 22-ounce glasses) and a flatbread, taco, or burger in the ultramodern interior or on the patio.

Four miles out of downtown Monterey on the way to Salinas is the long-running restaurant **Tarpy's Roadhouse** (2999 Monterey-Salinas Hwy., 831/647-1444, http://tarpys.com, daily 11:30am-10pm, $11-31). A complex of patios, gardens, and a unique stone building, Tarpy's does creative American comfort food under the direction of Chef Todd Fisher, host of the TV program *The United States of Bacon*. Expect steak, chops, ribs, and the popular cast iron-seared sea scallops with bacon and grits.

Classic American

The **Turn 12 Bar & Grill** (400 Tyler St., 831/372-8876, www.turn12barandgrill.com, Mon.-Fri. 11:30am-1am, Sat.-Sun. 10am-1am, $10-30) pays tribute to the nearby Laguna Seca Raceway with vintage motorbikes and framed images of racecars and motorcycles. The space is massive and includes a 50-foot-long pewter bar that is ideal for watching sporting events on the flat-screen TVs behind the bar while enjoying food and drinks. The menu includes salads, pizzas, pastas, meats, and seafood.

Rosine's Restaurant (434 Alvarado St., 831/375-1400, www.rosinesmonterey.com, Sun.-Thurs. 8am-9pm, Fri.-Sat. 8am-10pm, $10-30) is a longtime family-run restaurant that is very popular with families. This Alvarado Street institution serves hearty breakfasts, lunches, and dinners. It's known for its homemade lasagna, meatloaf, and slabs of cake that tower over a foot high. In 2014, Rosine's became even more popular when it was featured in an episode of the Food Network's *Diners, Drive-Ins and Dives*.

Above downtown Monterey and close to the Defense Language Institute is **Duffy's Tavern** (282 High St., 831/644-9811, Mon. 11am-10pm, Tues.-Thurs. 4pm-11pm, Fri. noon-2am, Sat. 10am-1am, $10-20). This is a hidden gem for hearty tavern fare. It's

especially known for its burgers, which come in many varieties.

Burgers

Not feeling up for seafood or a gourmet meal? **R.G. Burgers** (570 Munras Ave., No. 30, 831/372-4930, www.rgburgers.com, Sun.-Thurs. 11am-9pm, Fri.-Sat. 11am-10pm, $8-11) stands for really good burgers, and if they aren't always really good, they are definitely quite good. You get to choose your burger style (cheeseburger, Mediterranean, Hawaiian, etc.) along with the type of meat used.

Breakfast

Old Monterey Café (489 Alvarado St., 831/649-1021, daily 7am-2:30pm, $6-10) is a local favorite for hearty eggs Benedict, egg scrambles, and pancake dishes. The interior is cramped, and there is frequently a line out the door on weekends.

LouLou's Griddle in the Middle (Municipal Wharf II, 831/372-0568, www.loulousgriddle.com, Sun.-Mon. 7:30am-3pm, Wed.-Sat. 7:30am-3pm and 5pm-8:30pm, $7-12) is a red-and-yellow microdiner sitting atop Monterey's Municipal Wharf. The tiny interior includes a sit-down counter and a few booths. Suiting its location on Monterey Harbor, LouLou's serves up a few unique seafood breakfast items including a squid-and-eggs dish and a crab cake-and-eggs plate.

Red's Donuts (433 Alvarado St., 831/372-9761, http://redsdonuts.com, Sun.-Mon. 6:30am-12:30pm, Tues.-Sat. 6:30am-1:30pm, $1-6) has been serving up sugary breakfast treats since 1950. Enjoy your glazed, coconut, maple, or chocolate donut at the counter with other locals. There's also a Seaside location (1646 Fremont Blvd., 831/394-3444, Mon.-Fri. 4am-3pm, Sat. 4am-2pm, Sun. 4am-1pm).

Brewpubs

Peter B's Brewpub (2 Portola Plaza, behind Portola Hotel & Spa, 831/649-2699, www.portolahotel.com, Mon.-Thurs. 4pm-11pm, Fri.-Sat. 11am-1am, Sun. 11am-11pm, $8-18) opened in 1978 as the area's first craft

5,000-square-foot space or dine on the nice enclosed patio out front.

Crepes

Other restaurants on Old Fisherman's Wharf ladle clam chowder into bread bowls and serve up seafood, but **Crepes of Brittany** (6 Old Fisherman's Wharf, Ste. C, 831/649-1825, www.crepesofbrittany.com, summer Sun.-Fri. 8am-6:30pm, Sat. 8am-8pm, winter Mon.-Fri. 8am-3pm, Sat. 8am-6:30pm, Sun. 8am-4pm, $4-10) does something different. The tiny restaurant makes giant, flat, and tasty sweet and savory crepes that are served on paper plates. There are two tiny booths inside and a small seating area out front by the edge of the wharf.

Greek

The best place for Greek food in the area is ★ **Epsilon** (422 Tyler St., 831/655-8108, www.epsilonrestaurant.com, Mon. 11am-2pm, Tues.-Fri. 11am-2pm and 5pm-9:30pm, Sat.-Sun. 5pm-9:30pm, $19-28). Inside, attentive black-vested waiters deliver upscale Greek items to tables draped in white tablecloths. The walls showcase a mishmash of Greek art, while the dishes highlight a range of Greek staples including gyros, spanakopita, and shish kebabs. There's a nod to seafood as well, like whole grilled boneless trout and flash-grilled octopus. Their Greek salads, which can be topped with grilled meats, are the best around.

Indian

Crave the colorful flavors of Indian food? The **Ambrosia India Bistro** (565 Abrego St., 831/641-0610, www.ambrosiaib.com, Sun.-Thurs. 11:30am-2:30pm and 5pm-9:30pm, Fri. Sat. 11:30am 2:30pm and 5pm 10pm, $12-30), just a couple blocks off Alvarado Street, creates mouthwatering curry and tandoori dishes. Dine on chicken tikka masala, butter chicken, lamb vindaloo, or seafood curry indoors on linen-covered tables or outside in a courtyard that is warmed by heat lamps. To sample more of the menu, come earlier for the weekday lunch buffet (Mon.-Fri.

Alvarado Street Brewery & Grill

brewery; it's now run by brewmaster Kevin Clark and chef Jason Giles. The beers include five house beers along with four or five seasonal offerings including some experimental brews. The menu includes salads, burgers, pizzas, and entrées along with worthwhile appetizers like the jumbo Bavarian pretzel. There's a pet-friendly patio with four fire pit tables, and 18 flat-screen TVs indoors so that you can catch whatever game is on.

Operating in a large space that used to be a movie theater, the ★ **Alvarado Street Brewery & Grill** (426 Alvarado St., 831/655-2337, www.alvaradostreetbrewery.com, daily 11:30am-10pm, $7-27) is a welcome addition to downtown Monterey. The 10 barrel brewpub focuses on superbly crafted West Coast ales and Belgian-inspired ales. The Minesweeper IPA is the most popular choice, but getting a sample of the spicy Muay Thai IPA made with Thai chilies, coupled with the pilsner as a spice reducer, is an inspired order. They also do flatbreads, a few entrées, and a pork belly poutine. Sit inside the massive

11:30am-2:30pm, $11) or the weekend champagne lunch buffet (Sat.-Sun. and holidays 11:30am-2:30pm, $14), which includes a mimosa or soda.

Mediterranean

An offshoot of Carmel's Dametra Café, **Dametra Fresh Mediterranean** (Del Monte Center, 831/275-5555, daily 11am-9pm, $7-11) in the Del Monte Shopping Center does a fast-casual style of dining. Choose a main ingredient (chicken kebab, lamb kebab, falafel, etc.), then wrap it or put it on a plate, or toss it in a salad.

Mexican

Brightly colored **Turtle Bay Taqueria** (431 Tyler St., 831/333-1500, www.turtlebay.tv, Mon.-Thurs. 11am-8:30pm, Fri.-Sat. 11am-9pm, Sun. 11:30am-8pm, $4-14) blares salsa music while serving up a healthy, seafood-heavy menu. This isn't a typical Mexican food joint: The hearty burrito wraps include items like calamari and locally caught sand dabs (when in season) over beans, rice, cabbage, and salsa. The sopa de lima, a Mexican-style chicken soup, hits the right spot on cold days when Monterey is socked in with fog. They also have a Seaside location (1301 Fremont Blvd., 831/899-1010, Mon.-Sat. 11am-8pm).

Pizza

Located in the Del Monte Shopping Center, **Pizza My Heart** (660 Del Monte Center, 831/656-9400, http://pizzamyheart.com, daily 11am-10pm, $3.50-4.25) is a great place to grab a slice of pizza. Go for a traditional cheese or choose a specialty like the chicken-and-bacon pie made with a white sauce. Dine inside among surfing photos.

Sandwiches

Ike's Love & Sandwiches (570 Munras Ave., Ste. 70, 831/643-0900, http://ilikeikesplace.com, daily 11am-7pm, $9-13) is part of a Bay Area chain of sandwich shops that has penetrated down into Monterey Bay. People are quite excited by the giant, creatively

made sandwiches that include the "Jaymee Sirewich," a delectable fried chicken creation, and the "Joe Montana," which combines halal chicken, bacon, avocado, and jack cheese under a dripping of sesame dressing.

Monterey locals swear by **Randy's Sandwich Shop** (1193-D 10th St., 831/375-9161, http://randyssandwichshop.com, $4.50-6, cash only), a tiny spot that serves large breakfast and lunch sandwiches to go. The Godfather is a popular Italian-style sub, while the Jaws 2 is an impressive pile of meats and cheeses. They also do some specials like a calamari sandwich on Fridays. Take cash because they don't accept debit or credit cards.

Mundo's Café (170 Webster St., 831/656-9244, www.mundoscafemonterey.com, daily 10am-9pm, $6.50-9) impresses with giant sandwiches. The best of the bunch is the Argentinean beef brisket with a chimichurri sauce. They also do burgers including a beef/chorizo hybrid. Their original location is at 2233 Fremont Street (831/656-9244, Mon.-Fri. 10am-9pm), and they also have a Marina location (3156 Del Monte Blvd., Marina, 831/884-6904, Mon.-Fri. 11am-5pm, Sat.-Sun. 11am-4pm).

Seafood

On weekends there is typically a line out the door at ★ **Monterey's Fish House** (2114 Del Monte Ave., 831/373-4647, Mon.-Fri. 11:30am-2:30pm and 5pm-9:30pm, Sat.-Sun. 5pm-9:30pm, $11-30), one of the peninsula's most popular seafood restaurants. Once you get inside, you can expect attentive service and fresh seafood including snapper, albacore tuna, and calamari fished right out of the nearby bay. Nods to Monterey's Italian fishermen include Sicilian calamari and seafood pastas.

Out on Fisherman's Wharf, **Abalonetti** (57 Fisherman's Wharf, 831/373-1851, www.abalonettimonterey.com, daily 11:30am-9pm, $13-43) serves up fresh Monterey Bay calamari in the standard fried variety and the surprisingly good buffalo style, with tentacles and rings drenched in the tangy sauce usually reserved for chicken wings. More substantial and pricier options include cioppino and grilled Monterey abalone. Dine with a fine view of Monterey Harbor.

One seafood dish that is on almost all of the menus around Monterey is fried calamari. ★ **The Sandbar & Grill** (Municipal Wharf II, 831/373-2918, www.sandbarandgrillmonterey.com, Mon.-Sat. 11am-9pm, Sun. 10:30am-9pm, $12-30) has the best fried squid appetizer around: a plate of tender, flat pieces of calamari golden fried in a seasoned batter. They are also known for their fresh sand dabs and Dungeness crab sandwich with bacon. The restaurant hangs off the Municipal Wharf over Monterey Harbor, which means you might be able to catch a sea otter stroking by as you dine.

Sushi

Ocean Sushi Deli (165 Webster St., 831/645-9876, www.oceansushi.com, Mon.-Sat. 11am-9pm, Sun. 11am-8pm, $7-16) has a dizzying menu of 194 items. Chilly? Try the udon, ramen, or miso soup. In the mood for seafood? Opt for some very fair-priced sushi or sashimi. Really hungry? The teriyaki donburi bowls are a hearty mix of your choice of meat cooked in teriyaki sauce and vegetables over a bed of rice. Less expensive than other area sushi restaurants, Ocean Sushi Deli is set up like a café where you place your order at the counter.

Tapas

Esteban Restaurant (Casa Munras Hotel & Spa, 700 Munras Ave., 831/375-0176, www.hotelcasamunras.com, Mon.-Thurs. 5pm-9pm, Fri.-Sat. 5pm-10:30pm, Sun. 5pm-9pm, $8-35) is the place to go for an evening of Spanish-inspired delights and well-crafted cocktails. Sit inside at the stone bar, beside the fireplace, or outside on the patio while grazing the menu's creative vegetable, seafood, meat, and paella dishes. Some standouts include a blue cheese-stuffed date wrapped in bacon and pulled pork empanadas with feta cheese and green tomatillo salsa. Tuesdays are paella nights, where a three-course paella meal is served for $48 a couple. On warm Monterey afternoons, come early for happy hour (daily 5pm-6:30pm) to enjoy the patio and half-priced draft beers, house wines, mojitos, and glasses of house-made sangria.

Bakeries and Coffee Shops

Connected to the Osio Cinemas, Monterey's art-house movie theater, ★ **Café Lumiere**

outdoor seating at Esteban Restaurant

(365 Calle Principal, 831/920-2451, daily 7am-10pm) is where Monterey's old Sicilian anglers hang out in the morning while sipping coffee drinks and munching on pastries. There are a lot of tempting options behind the counter's glass case, but the café also offers made-to-order breakfast, lunch, and Sunday brunch dishes. In addition, the café has weekday lunch specials including a very popular giant bowl of pho (Vietnamese noodle soup) on Thursdays.

Part of a Bay Area chain of Italian-style coffeehouses, **Caffe Trieste** (409 Alvarado St., 831/241-6064, http://caffetriestemonterey.com, daily 7am-10pm) has a wide range of espressos. It also serves breakfast all day, while lunch and dinner items include pastas, pizzas, and paninis. Order at the counter and then take a seat inside or outside overlooking Alvarado Street.

The **East Village Coffee Lounge** (498 Washington St., 831/373-5601, http://eastvillagecoffeelounge.com, Mon.-Tues. and Thurs.-Fri. 6am-8pm, Wed. 6am-10pm, Sat.-Sun. 7am-8pm) occupies a cool stone building with a tower at the intersection of Washington and Pearl Streets. There's coffee, tea, beer, wine, sandwiches, wraps, and salads. Sip your caffeinated drink inside under art or out front in the plaza.

Many Monterey businesses are housed in historic adobes. Among them is **Parker-Lusseau Pastries & Café** (539 Hartnell St., www.parkerlusseau.com, 831/641-9188, Mon.-Fri. 7am-5:30pm, Sat. 7:30am-3:30pm), which occupies a charming adobe that was built in 1847. Inside, the café feels like Paris, where colorful macarons, tarts, baked goods, and quiches are displayed. There are also breakfast croissants and small but tasty lunch sandwiches available.

It's difficult to resist the baked temptations on display behind glass at the **Paris Bakery** (271 Bonifacio Place, 831/646-1620, www.parisbakery.us, Mon.-Sat. 6am-6pm, Sun. 6:30am-4:30pm). These include pastries, cakes, breads, and cookies. They also serve coffee, soup, salads, and sandwiches.

Desserts

Myo (491 Alvarado St., 831/649-3769, http://myofrozenyogurt.com, Sun.-Thurs. 11am-10pm, Fri.-Sat. 11am-11pm) does frozen yogurts that you can load up with sweets and fruits from the topping bar. Just don't go overboard because they charge by the ounce.

Parker-Lusseau Pastries & Café is located in a historic adobe.

Markets

The primary farmers market in the county, the **Monterey Farmers Market** (Alvarado St. between Del Monte and Pearl, 831/655-2607, www.oldmonterey.org, Oct.-Apr. Tues. 4pm-7pm, May-Sept. Tues. 4pm-8pm) fills over 3.5 blocks of downtown Monterey with fresh produce vendors, restaurant stalls, jewelry booths, and live music every Tuesday afternoon.

If you miss the downtown Tuesday farmers market, the local community college hosts the **Monterey Farmer's Market at Monterey Peninsula College** (Monterey Peninsula College, 930 Fremont St., www.monterey-bayfarmers.org, Fri. 10am-2pm) on Fridays.

Located in an old railroad station adjacent to the Monterey Bay Coastal Recreation Trail, **The Wharf Marketplace** (290 Figueroa St., 831/649-1116, www.thewharfmarketplace.com, Wed.-Mon. 7am-7pm, Tues. 7am-2pm) touts itself as being the place to buy the "bounty of the county." This means local produce and fresh seafood. The marketplace café (Wed.-Mon. 7am-3pm, Tues. 7am-2pm) also serves breakfast (breakfast sandwiches, quiches) and lunch (salads, sandwiches, pizzetas).

CANNERY ROW

Barbecue

Exercise your jaws and work up a serious appetite before a trip to **Bon Ton L'Roy's Lighthouse Smokehouse** (794 Lighthouse Ave., 831/375-6958, Mon.-Tues. 8am-10pm, Wed. 11am-midnight, Thurs.-Sun. 8am-midnight, $9.50-20). All the meats here are smoked in house and come stacked high on sandwiches like the Smokehouse Club, a rich take on the classic club sandwich, with smoked ham, smoked turkey, and smoked bacon. There are also the popular barbecued meats (pulled pork, tri-tip, sausage, and chicken) in sandwiches or on plates. Bon Ton's decor is all about music, from its battery of guitars hanging above the piano to a few framed platinum records on the wall.

French

After putting Carmel's Casanova Restaurant on the map as their chef, Didier Dutertre opened his own restaurant a block up from Cannery Row: **Bistro Moulin** (867 Wave St., 831/333-1200, www.bistromoulin.com, daily 5pm-10pm, $19-29). The menu is classic European through and through with items including escargot, moules frites (steamed mussels and fries), and coq au vin. If it's a weekend, you will want to make a reservation; Bistro Moulin is a small restaurant with limited seating.

Mediterranean

The owner of the small **Paprika Café** (309 Lighthouse Ave., 831/375-7452, Mon. and Wed.-Sat. noon-8pm, $7-13) will take your order, cook your food, ring you up, and then do the dishes. This one-man operation whips up tasty falafels, kebabs, hummus, and gyros. The recommended item is the unique and flavorful garlic chicken pita wrap; just make sure you have some breath mints after the meal.

Mexican

Just feet away from pricier Cannery Row restaurants is ★ **Papa Chevo's** (299 Cannery Row, 831/372-7298, http://papachevos.com, Mon.-Wed. 7am-10pm, Thurs.-Sun. 7am-11pm, $3.50-14), a superb and unassuming taco shop. The tacos are fine, but a couple menu items make this spot worth checking out. One is the chile relleno burrito, where a whole battered chile relleno is stuffed into a tortilla with lettuce, rice, and enchilada sauce. The other is their glorious breakfast burrito (eggs, potatoes, cheese, and your choice of breakfast meat) that is served at all hours. They also have outposts in Seaside (1760 Fremont Blvd., 831/393-1610, Mon.-Thurs. 6am-midnight, Fri.-Sat. 6am-1am, Sun. 7am-midnight) and Marina (3038 Del Monte Blvd., 831/884-9545, Mon.-Thurs. 6am-midnight, Fri.-Sat. 6am-2am, Sun. 7am-midnight) that are open late for the college crowd.

Pizza

Gianni's Pizza (725 Lighthouse Ave., 831/649-1500, Mon.-Thurs. 3:30pm-10pm, Fri.-Sun. 11am-11pm, $6-25) is a classic old-school pizza joint with giant pies delivered to tables draped in red-and-white-checkered tablecloths. Begin with breadsticks and a side of ranch or marinara sauce for dipping. Then move onto pizza pies the size of small tires. Their Big Wheel (a few pepperoni slices, a few Hawaiian slices, a few veggie slices and a few slices of cheese) is the call for a table that can't agree on toppings. They serve sodas with free refills and pitchers of beer to wash it all down.

Seafood

For a South Pacific spin on seafood, head to ★ **Hula's Island Grill & Tiki Room** (622 Lighthouse Ave., 831-655-4852, www.hulastiki.com, Fri.-Sat. 11:30am-10pm, Sun. 4pm-9pm, Mon. 4pm-9:30pm, Tues.-Thurs. 11:30am-9:30pm, $12-23). With surfing movies playing on the TVs and tasty tiki drinks, Hula's is Monterey's most fun casual restaurant with tasty and sometimes imaginative food. In addition to fresh fish and a range of tacos, the menu has land-based fare like Jamaican jerk chicken. If you're on a budget, Hula's has seriously long happy hours (Sun.-Mon. 4pm-6pm, Tues. all day, Wed.-Sat. 2pm-6pm) where you can score tiki drinks and pupus (appetizers) for just six bucks a pop.

The C Restaurant & Bar (831/375-4800, daily 6:30am-10pm, $29-58) is the restaurant in the fancy Intercontinental The Clement Monterey. The focus here follows the Monterey Bay Aquarium's Seafood Watch Program, which suggests seafood with less of an impact on the environment. The C serves breakfast, lunch, and dinner with breakfast items like huevos rancheros and omelets, all with tasty seafood ingredients. To experience the stellar views and food of The Clement without having to drop too much money, try The C Bar's superb happy hour (Sun.-Thurs. 4pm-7pm), where small plates, libations, and a fine cheeseburger are half price.

Opened in 1968 before Monterey's tourism boom, ★ **The Sardine Factory** (701 Wave St., 831/373-3775, Sun.-Thurs. 5pm-10:30pm, Fri.-Sat. 5pm-11pm, $26-59) is the area's iconic seafood and steakhouse. Its abalone bisque was served at one of President Ronald Reagan's inaugural dinners, and part of Clint Eastwood's 1971 directorial debut *Play Misty for Me* was filmed in the restaurant. This place oozes old-school cool, from the piano player tickling the ivories by the bar to the stunning glass-domed conservatory. The menu has pasta, steak, and seafood including wild abalone medallions, an item not found in many area restaurants.

Dine on seafood while staring at the sea within **Schooners Coastal Kitchen & Bar** (400 Cannery Row, 831/372-2628, www.schoonersmonterey.com, daily 6:30am-11pm, $24-42). Suspended off the Monterey Plaza Hotel & Spa over the bay, Schooners dishes include the Tails to Share dish for two that features prawns, king crab legs, baked oysters, and grilled swordfish. On a sunny day, Schooners's deck is a great place for a sipper and a snack.

The Fish Hopper (700 Cannery Row, 831/372-8543, www.fishhopper.com, Sun.-Thurs. 10:30am-9pm, Fri.-Sat. 10:30am-10pm, $18-40) is located on a busy block of Cannery Row. Jutting out over the bay, The Fish Hopper sets its sights on seafood including pasta with lobster, scallops, prawns, and crab.

For an informal seafood meal in the Cannery Row area, walk up a couple of blocks to the **Sea Harvest Fish Market & Restaurant** (598 Foam St., 831/646-0547, daily 11am-8pm, $10-21). Purchase raw seafood to cook at home or let them cook some up for you. The grilled salmon sandwich with fries or coleslaw is a deal at $10. They also have a north Monterey County location in Moss Landing (2420 Hwy. 1, Moss Landing, 831/728-8686, Sun.-Thurs. 9am-8pm, Fri.-Sat. 9am-9pm) that is right on Elkhorn Slough.

Steakhouse

Monterey is definitely a seafood town, but

there is a place to get a tasty cut of beef in Cannery Row. Located next to The Sardine Factory, the ★ **Whaling Station** (763 Wave St., 831/373-3778, Sun.-Thurs. 5pm-9pm, Fri.-Sat. 5pm-10:30pm, $24-58), a Monterey institution since 1970, is that place. Before you order, you can beef up on your beef knowledge as the waiters show off different cuts of meat on a tray and answer questions about the best qualities of each piece. The options include a tasty New York steak, beef Wellington, and a red wine-braised beef short rib. The Dijon-crusted rack of lamb is not a bad order either. There are also seafood and pasta possibilities including lobster fettuccine and salmon. Start off with the decadent prime rib egg rolls if you are hungry or a Caesar salad tossed at your table for something lighter. This is an unabashedly decadent establishment where the steamed broccoli comes with hollandaise sauce and the spinach sides come studded with chunks of bacon. Not in the mood for a full meal amid the white tablecloths in the dining room? Cozy up to the bar where you can order a steak sandwich or a burger made with ground filet mignon from the moderately priced bar menu.

Sushi

Fresh seafood and creative rolls make ★ **Crystal Fish** (514 Lighthouse Ave., 831/649-3474, Fri. 5pm-10pm, Sat. 1pm-10pm, Sun. 1pm-9:30pm, Mon.-Thurs. 5pm-9:30pm, entrees $14-27, rolls $4-13) the Monterey go-to for sushi. There's not a lot of ambience, but there are a lot of rolls, including fresh salmon, tuna, eel, octopus, and calamari, accentuated by sauces like creamy avocado, mango, wasabi, and miso. Unusual ingredients include lemon slices, asparagus, and eggplant.

Vegetarian

An inspired concept done well, **El Cantaro** (791 Foam St., 831/646-5465, www.elcantarovegan.com, Sun.-Thurs. 10am-9pm, Fri. 9am-3:30pm, $4-12) serves vegan Mexican food. Vegetables and vegan imitation meat (including a vegan tuna fish) fill out tortas, burritos, mole dishes, and chilaquiles. It's good stuff, but a tad bit pricier than other local taquerias.

Information and Services

A recommended first stop in Monterey is the **Monterey Visitors Center** (401 Camino El Estero, 888/221-1010, www.seemonterey.com, summer Mon.-Sat. 9am-6pm, Sun. 10am-5pm, winter Mon.-Sat. 9am-5pm, Sun. 10am-4pm). Located on the edge of Lake Estero, the two-room building has an impressive library of pamphlets. The main room has a staffed information desk and an interactive touch screen that visitors can utilize. The back room focuses on local lodging with maps and lodging directories. Below information on the accommodations, there are phones that are set up to ring the front desks of area hotels, motels, and B&Bs to check availability and pricing.

The **Monterey Peninsula Chamber of Commerce** (30 Ragsdale Dr., Ste. 200, http://montereychamber.com, 831/648-5360, Mon.-Fri. 9am-5pm) can also provide helpful information, though it is located a few miles east of downtown Monterey off Highway 68.

The local daily newspaper is the **Monterey County Herald** (www.montereyherald.com). The **Monterey County Weekly** (www.montereycountyweekly.com) is a popular free weekly with a comprehensive listing of the area's arts and entertainment events.

The Monterey **post office** (565 Hartnell St., 831/372-4063, www.usps.com, Mon.-Fri. 8:30am-5pm, Sat. 10am-2pm) is conveniently located a couple blocks east of downtown Monterey.

For medical needs, the **Community**

Hospital of the Monterey Peninsula (CHOMP, 23625 Holman Hwy., 831/624-5311 or 888/452-4667, www.chomp.org) provides emergency services to the area.

Transportation

Most visitors drive into Monterey via scenic Highway 1. Inland, U.S. 101 allows access into Salinas from the north and south. From Salinas, Highway 68 travels west into Monterey.

Monterey has its own airport: the **Monterey Regional Airport** (MRY, 200 Fred Kane Dr., 831/648-7000, www.montereyairport.com). The airport connects the city to San Francisco, San Diego, Los Angeles, Phoenix, and Las Vegas with 40 flights a day. Downtown Monterey and Cannery Row are just a five-mile taxi ride away.

A lot of visitors to Monterey fly into Bay Area airports. The **San Francisco International Airport** (SFO, Hwy. 101, San Francisco, 800/435-9736 or 650/821-8211, www.flysfo.com) can be just two hours away if traffic cooperates. **Mineta San José Airport** (SJC, 1701 Airport Blvd., San Jose, 408/392-3600, www.flysanjose.com) is an hour and 15 minutes to an hour and a half away from Monterey. The **Monterey Airbus** (831/373-7777, www.montereyairbus.com, one way $35-50 pp) provides bus transportation from San Francisco and San Jose airports to downtown Monterey and the nearby city of Marina.

For a more leisurely ride, **Amtrak's *Coast Starlight* train** (11 Station Place, Salinas, daily 8am-10pm, www.amtrak.com) travels through Salinas. **Greyhound** (19 W. Gabilan, Salinas, 831/424-4418, www.greyhound.com, daily 5am-11:30pm) offers service into Monterey from Salinas.

Once in Monterey, take advantage of the free **WAVE** bus (Waterfront Area Visitor Express, 831/899-2555, www.monterey.org, late May-late June daily 10am-7pm, late June-early Sept. Mon.-Fri. 10am-7pm, Sat.-Sun. and holidays 10am-8pm) that loops between downtown Monterey and the aquarium. **Monterey-Salinas Transit** (888/678-2871, www.mst.org, $1.25-2.50) has routes through Monterey.

Pacific Grove

Sandwiched between historic Monterey and exclusive Pebble Beach, and close to major attractions like the Monterey Bay Aquarium, Pacific Grove makes a fine base for exploring the peninsula. It's also worth a visit for its colorful turn-of-the-20th-century Victorian homes and its striking strand of coastline. The town has chosen "America's Last Hometown" as its nickname; it may make you nostalgic for small-town living. Founded in 1875 as a Methodist summer retreat, this quiet city is not the place to go for a night of carousing. But Pacific Grove's downtown is perfect for a relaxing afternoon of strolling among the yellow, purple, and green Victorian homes and cottages on Lighthouse Avenue. (It's worth noting that there's a different Lighthouse Avenue in adjacent Monterey.)

For those who don't want to pay the entrance fee to drive Pebble Beach's 17-Mile Drive, Pacific Grove's "Poor Man's 17-Mile Drive" winds around a piece of coastal real estate between Lover's Point Park and Asilomar Beach that's almost as striking. Start on Ocean View Boulevard by Lover's Point and continue onto Sunset Drive to get the full experience. In the springtime, flowering ice plant right along the road adds a riot of color to the landscape.

Pacific Grove

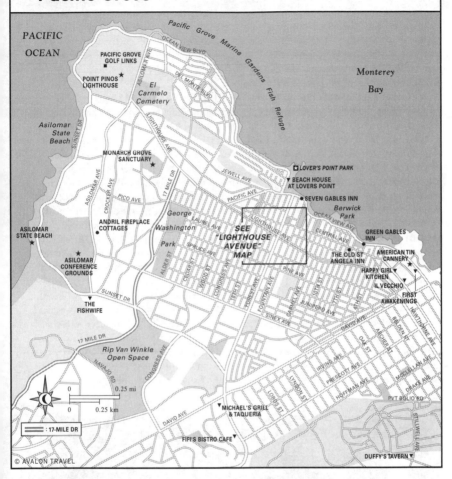

SIGHTS
★ Lover's Point Park

It is no surprise that the aptly named **Lover's Point Park** (Ocean View Blvd. and 17th St., 831/648-3100, www.ci.pg.ca.us) is one of the area's most popular wedding sites. A finger of land with a jumble of rocks at its northernmost point, Lover's Point offers expansive views of the interior section of the Monterey Bay.

The scenic spit of land is home to a large lawn, a shallow children's pool, a picnic area, restrooms, a beach volleyball court, and the Beach House Restaurant, which is perched on an envious spot with a fine bay view. The park also has a sheltered pocket beach that is ideal for a dip or wading on Pacific Grove's infrequent hot days. A kelp forest right offshore offers a superb spot for snorkelers to get a feel for Monterey Bay's impressive underwater ecosystem.

During summer months there is an old-fashioned hamburger stand above the beach and a vendor that rents kayaks, bikes, and snorkeling equipment.

Point Pinos Lighthouse

Surrounded by a golf course, **Point Pinos Lighthouse** (80 Asilomar Ave. between Lighthouse Ave. and Del Monte Ave., 831/648-3176, www.pointpinoslighthouse. com, Thurs.-Mon. 1pm-4pm, adults $2, children $1) has the distinction of being the oldest continuously operating lighthouse on the West Coast. It was one of the first eight lighthouses built on the West Coast, starting operations in 1855. Point Pinos is also notable for the two female lighthouse keepers who served there during its long history. The light was automated in 1975, but it is still an active aid to local marine navigation. Lighthouse lovers and appreciators of the past will enjoy walking through the building's two floors and cellar.

Monarch Grove Sanctuary

Pacific Grove is also known as "Butterfly Town U.S.A." An impressive migration of monarch butterflies descends on the town each year. Tucked in a residential area, the small **Monarch Grove Sanctuary** (Ridge Rd. between Lighthouse Ave. and Short St., 831/648-5716, www.ci.pg.ca.us, free) offers stands of eucalyptus and pine trees that are cloaked with colorful insects during the migration period (October-February).

The best time to visit the sanctuary is in the early afternoon, when sunlight illuminates the butterflies on the trees and docents are around to answer your questions. Just don't get too close to any of our flying friends, because anyone who molests a butterfly will be slapped with a hefty $1,000 fine.

Asilomar State Beach

One of the Monterey Peninsula's most popular beaches, **Asilomar State Beach** (Sunset Dr., 831/646-6440, www.parks.ca.gov) draws beachgoers, walkers, and surfers. The beach itself is a narrow one-mile-long strip of coastline with a boardwalk trail on the dunes behind it. You can keep walking on the trail into nearby Pebble Beach, an easy, cost-free way to get a taste of that exclusive community.

Right across Sunset Drive, visitors can explore the **Asilomar Dunes Natural Preserve** and the **Asilomar Conference Grounds** (800 Asilomar Ave., 831/372-8016, www.visitasilomar.com). The dunes preserve is 25 acres of restored sand dune ecosystem that can be accessed via a quarter-mile-long boardwalk. The conference grounds are shaded by Monterey pines and studded with Arts and Crafts-style structures designed by Hearst Castle architect Julia Morgan. Even if

a resident of the Monarch Grove Sanctuary

you are not staying overnight on the grounds or participating in a conference, you can enjoy the facilities, including the Phoebe A. Hearst Social Hall, which has pool tables, a fireplace, and some comfy seats. **Ranger-guided tours** of the grounds are available by calling 831/646-6443. The one-hour tours focus on four aspects of the grounds: architecture, the living dunes, the forest, and the coast.

To reach Asilomar, take the Route 68 West exit off Highway 1 and turn left on Sunset Drive.

Pacific Grove Museum of Natural History

Nature enthusiasts visiting the area should stop into the **Pacific Grove Museum of Natural History** (165 Forest Ave., 831/648-5716, www.pgmuseum.org, Tues.-Sun. 10am-5pm, adults $9, children, students, and military $6), which will help them identify the animal and plant species they encounter while on the Monterey Peninsula. The museum feels of a past era, with its mounted and stuffed animals, but it does provides a fairly comprehensive overview of the region's biodiversity. One room is dedicated to our feathered friends and includes 300 mounted birds found around the county, including the gigantic California condor. Other rooms highlight large terrestrial mammals (mountain lions, bears) and whales. With this being Butterfly Town U.S.A., there's a space devoted to the monarch butterfly. Out front is a life-sized gray whale statue, while out back is a native plant garden that includes an impressive jade boulder that was found on the Big Sur coast.

ENTERTAINMENT AND EVENTS
Cinema

Downtown Pacific Grove has its own small-town movie theater: the **Lighthouse Cinemas** (525 Lighthouse Ave., 831/643-1333, www.sregmovies.com), with four screens showing first-run movies.

Art Galleries

For over four decades, the **Pacific Grove Art Center** (568 Lighthouse Ave., 831/375-2208, www.pgartcenter.org, Wed.-Sat. noon-5pm, Sun. 1pm-4pm) has showcased the work of emerging artists in four galleries, including paintings, photos, sculptures, mixed media, and other artistic endeavors.

The **Lisa Coscino Gallery** (216 Grand Ave., 831/646-1939, www.lisacoscino.com, Tues.-Sat. 11am-5pm) gives exposure to the work of up-and-coming artists from all over the country, with an emphasis on California-based artists.

Festivals and Events

If you want a wild night out on the town, you're not going to get it in Pacific Grove. But there are a couple of family-friendly annual events in "America's Last Hometown." Recalling another era, Pacific Grove's **Good Old Days** (831/373-3304, www.pacificgrove. org, Apr.) is a weekend of good clean fun every April that includes a parade, a quilt show, pony rides, and live entertainment.

For over 70 years, the kids of Pacific Grove have been getting dressed up like butterflies at the **Butterfly Parade and Bazaar** (www. pacificgrove.org, first Sat. of Oct.), which welcomes the wintering monarch butterflies to the area every fall.

Ever wanted to try a triathlon? **The Triathlon at Pacific Grove** (831/373-0678, www.tricalifornia.com, Sept.) is a great event for a first-timer. They have an entry-level triathlon in which competitors swim 0.25 miles, bike 12.4 miles, and run 2 miles. For the more experienced, there's an Olympic-distance triathlon where you'll attempt to complete a 1.5-kilometer swim, a 40-kilometer bike ride, and a 10-kilometer run.

Pacific Grove's many bed-and-breakfasts get done up in Victorian-era holiday decor during the annual **Christmas at the Inns** (831/373-3304, www.pacificgrove.org/events, early Dec.).

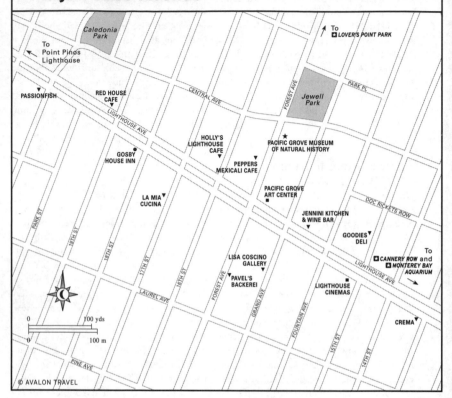

Lighthouse Avenue

Caledonia Park

To
Point Pinos
Lighthouse

To
LOVER'S POINT PARK

PASSIONFISH

RED HOUSE CAFE

CENTRAL AVE

FOREST AVE

Jewell Park

PARK PL

LIGHTHOUSE AVE

HOLLY'S
LIGHTHOUSE
CAFE

PACIFIC GROVE MUSEUM
OF NATURAL HISTORY

GOSBY
HOUSE INN

PEPPERS
MEXICALI CAFE

PACIFIC GROVE
ART CENTER

LA MIA
CUCINA

DOC RICKETS ROW

JENNINI KITCHEN
& WINE BAR

PARK ST

19TH ST

18TH ST

17TH ST

16TH ST

GOODIES
DELI

To
CANNERY ROW and
MONTEREY BAY
AQUARIUM

LISA COSCINO
GALLERY

LIGHTHOUSE AVE

PAVEL'S
BACKEREI

FOREST AVE

GRAND AVE

LIGHTHOUSE
CINEMAS

LAUREL AVE

0   100 yds

0   100 m

FOUNTAIN AVE

15TH ST

14TH ST

CREMA

PINE AVE

© AVALON TRAVEL

SHOPPING

A canning factory no more, the **American Tin Cannery** (125 Oceanview Blvd., 831/372-1442, www.americantincannery.com, daily 10am-6pm) is an indoor mall with discount outlets for national brands including Bass, Pendleton, and Van Heusen. You can also take a break from shopping at an indoor black light miniature golf course or get delicious handmade organic ice cream from **Kai Lee Creamery** (Ste. 128, 831/402-0627, http://kaileecreamery. com). Despite the good deals available within this former cannery, the cavernous space and its shops are frequently empty. In the summer of 2015, a proposal was made to transform the American Tin Cannery into a major luxury hotel with a fine dining restaurant.

SPORTS AND RECREATION

Scuba Diving and Snorkeling

Some of the best scuba diving and snorkeling spots on the Monterey Peninsula lie off Pacific Grove. **Lover's Point Park** (Ocean View Blvd. and 17th St., novice to advanced, 10-40 feet) has a protected cove and kelp forest right off its shores. The cove's protected sandy beach makes an easy entry point for scuba divers and snorkelers who want to explore the kelp forest. Just a few blocks away is **Otter Cove** (Ocean View Blvd. and Sea Palm Ave., novice to advanced, 10-60 feet) at the intersection of Ocean View Boulevard and Sea Palm Avenue. It's a dive spot that is best during days of calm seas. One of the highlights is an underwater pinnacle that rises from 50 feet to just 18 feet below the surface. Another notable site is the nearby **Coral Street Cove** (Coral St. and Ocean View Blvd., advanced, 20-50 feet), which is known for its fish populations. If you need equipment, visit **Bamboo Reef** (614 Lighthouse Ave., 831/372-1685, www.bambooreef.com, Mon.-Fri. 9am-6pm, Sat.-Sun. 7am-6pm), **Aquarius Dive Shop** (2040 Del Monte Ave., 831/375-1933, www. aquariusdivers.com, Mon.-Fri. 9am-6pm, Sat.-Sun. 7am-6pm), or **Breakwater Scuba** (225 Cannery Row, 831/717-4546, http:// breakwaterscuba.com, Mon.-Fri. 9am-6pm, Sat.-Sun. 7am-6pm) in nearby Monterey.

Surfing

During the summer and fall, clean swells produce fun waves at **Asilomar State Beach** (Sunset Dr., 831/646-6440, www.parks. ca.gov), making it one of the peninsula's most popular surf spots. Winter produces big, often dangerous swells, so stay out of the water during that time of year. To get there, take the Route 68 West exit off Highway 1 and turn left on Sunset Drive.

During big swells, **Lovers Point** (Ocean View Blvd. and 17th St.) turns into a nice left. There are some rocks in the lineup so it is probably best to go out with someone who knows the break on your first outing.

Sunshine Freestyle (443 Lighthouse Ave., Monterey, 831/375-5015, http://sunshinefreestyle.com, Mon.-Sat. 10am-6pm, Sun. 11am-5pm, surfboard rental $30/day, wetsuit rental $15/day) and **On the Beach** (693 Lighthouse Ave., Monterey, 831/646-9283, http://onthebeachsurfshop.com, Sun.-Thurs. 10am-6pm, Fri.-Sat. 10am-7pm, surfboard rental $30/day, wetsuit rental $15/day) rent boards and wetsuits in nearby Monterey.

Golf

The **Pacific Grove Golf Links** (77 Asilomar Blvd., 831/648-5775, www.playpacificgrove. com, daily sunrise-sunset, Mon.-Thurs. $46, Fri.-Sun. and holidays $52) doesn't have the acclaim of the nearby Pebble Beach courses, but it's located on a similarly gorgeous length of coastline just a few miles away.

ACCOMMODATIONS

Pacific Grove is known for its bed-and-breakfasts, many located within old Victorian buildings. There are also a few hotels, motels, and the Asilomar Conference Grounds.

Under $150

The ★ **Gosby House Inn** (643 Lighthouse Ave., 800/527-8828, www.gosbyhouseinn. com, $120-260) has been taking care of visitors since the 1880s. Today the white-and-yellow Queen Anne-style Victorian, which sits right on downtown Pacific Grove's main street, is a welcome cross between a boutique hotel and B&B. Amenities include free Wi-Fi and flat screens in every room but one. Yet the inn's old photos, antiques, and complimentary breakfast are the kind of features that make B&Bs the favorite kind of accommodation for some travelers. The main house has 22 rooms, some with gas fireplaces. The two deluxe rooms available in the adjacent Carriage House each have a balcony, a gas fireplace, a roomy tile bathroom, and a nice-sized soaking tub that allows even a six-foot individual to stretch out.

$150-250

Staying overnight at the ★ **Asilomar Conference Grounds** (804 Crocker Ave., 831/372-8016, www.visitasilomar.com, $190-335) can feel a bit like going back to summer camp. There are lots of common areas on the 107 acres including the Phoebe Apperson Hearst Social Hall, where visitors can relax by a roaring fire or play pool at one of two billiards tables. There is a real range of accommodations here from historic rooms to family cottages to modern rooms with a view of nearby Asilomar Beach. The rooms with an ocean view and a fireplace are definitely recommended for those who don't mind spending a little more money. Note that all the rooms here lack TVs and telephones. It's an incentive for you to head outdoors. This frequently overlooked state park-owned lodging hosts a multitude of conferences, so expect to see corporate types with laminated conference badges walking through the forests of Monterey pine, Monterey cypress, and coast live oaks alongside the roaming herds of semi-wild deer.

Right across the street from the Asilomar Conference Grounds, the **Andril Fireplace Cottages** (569 Asilomar Ave., 831/375-0994, www.andrilcottages.com, $200-675) are a cluster of cabins surrounded by pine forest. Most of the 1-5-bedroom structures have their own kitchens, private decks and, as the name promises, fireplaces. There are also three basic motel-style units. Outdoors are a whirlpool tub, Ping-Pong table, and some barbecue grills.

Before becoming a bed-and-breakfast in 1983, ★ **The Old St. Angela Inn** (321 Central Ave., 831/372-3246, www.oldstangelainn.com, $162-289) was a rectory and then a convent. This B&B spoils its guests with cozy accommodations, a friendly staff, and terrific food. The nine homey rooms have pine antiques, live plants, and comfortable beds. The Whale Watch room has a nice balcony where you can try and catch a glimpse of the namesake marine mammal during migration season. Downstairs are common areas that are comfy but not stuffy. Out back is a brick patio with tables, chairs, a fire pit, and a waterfall fountain. Despite all these fine amenities, one of the best features of The Old St. Angela Inn is its food. The afternoon teatime includes wine, a dessert, and an appetizer. (Hope for the indulgent pesto brie in a puff pastry!) The scrumptious breakfast includes yogurt, granola, muffins, and a hot sweet or savory item. All of it, including the yogurt, is made in house. Pick up one of the inn's cookbooks when you check out so that you can make some of its recipes at home.

Pacific Grove's Ocean View Boulevard has a handful of stunning Queen Anne Victorian buildings perched over the ocean. One of the finest and most notable is the dark

Gosby House Inn

green-and-white **Green Gables Inn** (301 Ocean View Blvd., 800/722-1774 or 831/375-2095, www.greengablesinnpg.com, $155-295). The main building, which was built 1888, has a downstairs common area with multiple nooks offering full-window ocean views. For Victorian-era enthusiasts, the main building is the place to stay with its impressive throwback feel and antique furnishings. The Gable Room has a ladder that allows you to climb into an attic-like gable. Behind the main inn is the Carriage House, which has five spacious rooms all with a gas fireplace, jetted tub, and ocean views. More reasons to stay at the Green Gables include an afternoon wine-and-appetizer serving, a morning breakfast buffet, and a quartet of bikes that can be borrowed for a spin on the nearby Monterey Bay Coastal Recreational Trail.

Over $250

The most striking bed-and-breakfast on the coast of Pacific Grove, the **Seven Gables Inn** (555 Ocean View Blvd., 831/372-4341, www.

sevengablesinn.com, $289-699) is perched just feet away from Lover's Point. Decorated with antique furniture and artwork, the Seven Gables Inn is for those who want to step back in time and experience ornate Victorian- and Edwardian-style lodging. Impressively, every single room has superb ocean views.

FOOD
American
Crema (481 Lighthouse Ave., 831/324-0347, http://cremapg.com, daily 7am-4pm, $7-15) is a gourmet comfort food restaurant housed in a multilevel building that feels like someone's house. Dine on oversized burgers or chicken sandwiches beside a fireplace, a cupboard, or a piano at this breakfast, lunch, and weekend brunch spot. They also have some interesting intoxicants including a stout beer float (stout beer, ice cream, and espresso) and weekend pitchers of mimosas and sangria. The downstairs floor is a coffee shop that serves Santa Cruz's Verve Coffee.

The stellar restaurant location on Lover's Point was vacant for years until the **Beach House** (620 Ocean View Blvd., 831/375-2345, www.beachhousepg.com, daily 4pm-9pm, $13-58) opened there in 2013. It has superb views of the bay and a heated and covered outdoor deck with an even better look down on the water. One way to experience the views and the casual California cuisine is to come for the Beach House's popular Sunset Supper Menu, a daily special where if you are seated by 5:30pm and order by 6pm, you can order one of six entrees for just $10. Make a reservation for a table during the Sunset Supper times so that you don't miss out on this superb promotion.

The **Red House Café** (662 Lighthouse Ave., 831/643-1060, Mon. 8am-2:30pm, Tues.-Sun. 8am-2:30pm and 5pm-9pm, $11-23) is easy to find. It is in a red Victorian building with a wraparound porch right on Pacific Grove's main drag. They serve up breakfast, lunch, dinner, and weekend brunch.

Bakeries
Pavel's Backerei (219 Forest Ave., 831/643-2636, Tues.-Fri. 7am-6pm, Sat. 7am-3pm) is one of the best bakeries on the Monterey Peninsula. They do pastries, croissants, cinnamon rolls, and giant glazed donuts that you can eat in the small indoor seating area or out front.

Breakfast
Located in one end of the cavernous American

the comfortable Old St. Angela Inn

Tin Cannery shopping mall, ★ **First Awakenings** (125 Oceanview Blvd., 831/372-1125, www.firstawakenings.net, Mon.-Fri. 7am-2pm, Sat.-Sun. 7am-2:30pm, $6-12) serves up oversized versions of classic breakfast fare including huevos rancheros, eggs Benedict, crepes, and omelets. Locals are fond of this spot, frequently voting it the county's top breakfast spot. On sunny days, you can dine outside on the large patio, surrounded by the sounds of nearby Monterey Bay. With the aquarium just feet away, it's a great place to fuel up for a day of viewing Monterey's sealife.

Holly's Lighthouse Café (602 Lighthouse Ave., 831/372-7006, www.hollyslighthousecafe.com, Wed.-Mon. 7am-2pm, $8-13) does great breakfasts in downtown P.G. Their griddle menu items include carrot cake pancakes and cinnamon-raisin French toast, but they also do savory fare like chicken-fried steak and eggs.

French
★ **Fifi's Bistro Café** (1188 Forest Ave., 831/372-5325, www.fifisbistrocafe.com, Mon.-Thurs. 11:30am-2:30pm and 5pm-8:30pm, Fri. 11:30am-2:30pm and 5pm-9pm, Sat. 5pm-9pm, Sun. 11am-2:30pm and 5pm-8:30pm, $18-31) celebrates French country cuisine in a space just east of downtown Pacific Grove. Inside, real flowers are placed on the tables, and wine bottles comprise a major part of the restaurant's decor. Do not miss Fifi's French onion soup, a true thing of wonder served with a delectable melted cheese crust. The dinner menu includes a stable of set entrées, including goat cheese-stuffed chicken breast in a mushroom sauce, as well as dinner specials that change every few days. This is a place to spoil yourself with great food and great wine. If you really enjoyed the wine you drank with dinner, purchase another bottle to go: Fifi's sells their Old World and New World wines so that you can enjoy them in your hotel or at home.

Italian
Travel to Italy without leaving the peninsula at **La Mia Cucina** (208 17th St., 831/373-2416, http://joerombi.com, Wed.-Sun. 5pm-close, $21-29). The professional, well-dressed waitstaff serves dishes like hand-rolled ravioli and eggplant Parmesan. Don't miss the arancini (fried rice balls) appetizer!

★ **Il Vecchio** (110 Central Ave., 831/324-4282, Fri. noon-1:30pm and 5pm-9:30pm, Sat. 5pm-9:30pm, Sun. 5pm-9pm, Mon.-Thurs. noon-1:30pm and 5pm-9pm, $13-22) is a new Pacific Grove favorite, but the name Il Vecchio, meaning "the old," refers to traditional Italian fare like gnocchi with pesto. They make their pasta every day and offer traditional Italian takes on meats and seafood. Mondays are Piatti at Vecchio (5pm-9pm), where you can sample three popular dishes in smaller portions for $18. At the weekday Lunch for the Workers Special (Mon.-Fri. noon-1:30pm) diners get a salad and two pastas for just $9.

Mediterranean
The ★ **Jeninni Kitchen & Wine Bar** (542 Lighthouse Ave., 831/920-2662, Thurs.-Tues. 4pm-close, $18-30) has elevated Pacific Grove's dining scene since opening in 2013. The menu changes frequently but the Wagyu bullfighter's steak and the eggplant fries are favorites. Eat in the dining area in the front of the building or walk up a few stairs to the bar area to try small plates, wines, and craft beers.

Mexican
A certain ingredient shows up everywhere at the very popular **Peppers Mexicali Café** (170 Forest Ave., 831/373-6892, www.pepperspg.com, Mon. and Wed.-Thurs. 11:30am-9pm, Fri.-Sat. 11:30am-10pm, Sun. 4pm-9pm, $10-20). Posters of peppers adorn the walls of the narrow dining room and adjacent bar, while plastic peppers hang from the doorway between the two usually crowded rooms. The pepper also makes many appearances on the menu, whether it's as a citrus habanero marinade on the chicken or the roasted red pepper that tops the grilled snapper. This is not straight-up Mexican food, as evidenced by

items like the winning Jamaican curry prawns with mango salsa. They also serve up glasses and pitchers of margaritas.

A healthy, California-style take on Mexican food is done at the popular **Michael's Grill & Taqueria** (1126 Forest Ave., 831/647-8654, www.michaelsgrillandtaqueria.com, Mon.-Sat. 10am-9pm, Sun. 10am-8pm, $11-30). At Michael's there are shades of Cajun cooking in the blackened chicken and blackened shrimp that are used in burritos and tostadas. Whether you order a fajita platter, a burrito, or a fajita salad, you will get a tasty, stomach-stuffing meal. They also have locations in **Marina** (265 Reservation Rd., 831/884-2568, daily 11am-8:30pm) and **Salinas** (321 Main St., 831/754-8917, Mon.-Sat. 10am-8pm).

Quick Bites

Part canning operation and part café, **Happy Girl Kitchen** (173 Central Ave., 831/373-4475, http://happygirlkitchen.com, Mon.-Sat. 7:30am-3pm, Sun. 7:30am-2pm, $3-10) has an urban hipster feel that might make Portlanders or Bay Area folks feel at home. The café has a very basic menu of items including toast with homemade jam, a sandwich of the day, and PB&J with milk. Within the shop (daily 7am-5pm), canned goodies like

Meyer lemon marmalade and honeyed mandarin oranges are sold. Or take one of their classes on canning, pickling, or fermenting so that you can preserve your own foodstuffs.

Stop into **Goodies Deli** (518 Lighthouse Ave., 831/655-3663, http://goodiesdeli. blogspot.com, Mon.-Sat. 9:30am-4pm, $7-8) for a hearty sandwich. Thirty-two options include classics like Philly cheesesteaks and BLTs, as well as alternative choices like hot tofu and teriyaki chicken. The dining area is a bit sterile, so grab your sandwich to go for a picnic at nearby Lover's Point.

Seafood

One of the Monterey Peninsula's most lauded seafood restaurants is ★ **Passionfish** (701 Lighthouse Ave., 831/655-3311, www.passionfish.net, Sun.-Thurs 5pm-9pm, Fri.-Sat. 5pm-10pm, $16-36), which is on a mission to spread the gospel about sustainable seafood. The top of their menu is adorned with a quote by Robert Redford about the importance of defending our natural resources, and every bill comes with a copy of the Monterey Bay Aquarium's Seafood Watch Guide. Passionfish does great food, especially creative and flavorful sustainable seafood. Their menu starts with a nice scallop appetizer and goes

the outdoor seating area at Happy Girl Kitchen

on to entrées that may include seared albacore tuna in a bacon sauce or basil-stuffed rainbow trout. They are also known for their extensive, moderately priced wine list. In addition to the very fine food and wine, the knowledgeable waitstaff here could teach a course on seafood, and the atmosphere is just right.

The Fishwife (1996 1/2 Sunset Dr., 831/375-7107, www.fishwife.com, Sun.-Thurs. 11am-9pm, Fri.-Sat. 11am-10pm, $12-22) occupies a fine spot out of downtown Pacific Grove near Asilomar Beach. A lot of their seafood entrées have a Caribbean twist. They also have a Seaside location (789 Trinity Ave., 831/394-2027, daily 11am-9pm).

Markets

It took a while, but now Pacific Grove has its own farmers market. The **Pacific Grove Certified Farmers' Market** (Central Ave. and Grand Ave., http://everyonesharvest.org/farmers-markets/pacific-grove, summer Mon. 3pm-7pm, winter Mon. 3pm-6pm) sets up in front of Jewell Park on Mondays.

INFORMATION AND SERVICES

To pick up pamphlets on Pacific Grove's sights and lodging options, stop in at the **Pacific Grove Tourist Information Center** (100 Central Ave., 831/324-4668, www.pacific-grove.org, daily 10am-5pm). Pacific Grove has its own banks, restaurants, and a **post office** (680 Lighthouse Ave., 831/373-2271, www.usps.com, Mon.-Fri. 9am-4:30pm, Sat. 10am-1pm).

For medical needs, the **Community Hospital of the Monterey Peninsula** (CHOMP, 23625 Holman Hwy., 831/624-5311 or 888/452-4667, www.chomp.org) provides emergency services to the area. It is actually located closer to Pacific Grove than Monterey.

TRANSPORTATION

Most visitors drive into Pacific Grove via scenic Highway 1. From Highway 1, take the Route 68 west exit to downtown Pacific Grove.

Northern Monterey County

North of Monterey are the coastal cities of Seaside, Marina, and Moss Landing. Seaside is a working-class community with some great inexpensive restaurants, while Marina is home to a couple of coastal state parks. Both cities were once home to the sprawling Fort Ord, a decommissioned base that now hosts students from California State University, Monterey Bay (CSUMB) instead of U.S. Army troops. Moss Landing is the northernmost town on the Monterey County coast. It has a working fishing harbor and long, sandy beaches.

SEASIDE

Seaside is the working-class community directly north of Monterey on the Monterey Bay. The city was very important to the residents of the U.S. Army's Fort Ord, which closed

down in 1994. Now it is worth seeking out for its long beach and many worthwhile ethnic restaurants.

Nightlife

Craft beer lovers from all over the Monterey Peninsula head to **Post No Bills** (600 Ortiz Ave., Sand City, 831/324-4667, www.postno-bills.net, Mon.-Thurs. 3pm-close, Fri.-Sun. 1pm-close), which is actually located in the tiny town of Sand City that is surrounded by Seaside. This warehouse-like building with street art on the walls feels like something that would be in a hip part of the San Francisco Bay Area. They have 17 interesting craft beers on tap along with a few fridges stocked with cold beer that you can take off site. Post No Bills doesn't serve food, but you can bring in a meal from one of Seaside's eateries.

Golf

Initially constructed for Fort Ord's soldiers by a general, the **Bayonet & Black Horse Golf Courses** (1 McClure Way, 831/899-7271, www.bayonetblackhorse.com, greens fees adults $40-135, seniors $75-95, children 17 and under $35) are two Seaside courses that have been visited by golf pros like Arnold Palmer and Jack Nicklaus. Bayonet was designed by a left-hander and has narrow fairways. Black Horse is the course you want to play if you like long, rolling fairways and views of the bay.

Accommodations

The **Embassy Suites Monterey Bay** (1441 Canyon Del Rey, 831/393-1115, http://embassysuites3.hilton.com, $265-307) has 225 bedroom and living room suites located in a tower two blocks from the beach. The tall, yellowish building also has an indoor swimming pool, a fitness center, and a unique open-air atrium lobby.

Food

CLASSIC AMERICAN

Seaside has a plethora of worthy inexpensive restaurants that are worth seeking out if you don't mind leaving Monterey. **Googie Grill** (1520 Del Monte Blvd., 831/392-1520, daily 8am-9pm, $13-25) has a memorably silly name, but these guys take their comfort food seriously. The breakfast menu includes beignets, Benedicts, and biscuits drenched in gravy, but the best of the batch is arguably the corned beef hash topped with two eggs and hollandaise sauce. Lunch and dinner is eclectic, with everything from fish tacos to meatloaf and Danish meatballs.

CAFÉS

The Press Club at The Weekly (1123 Fremont Ave., 831/394-5656, daily 6am-4pm) is a juice bar, coffee shop, art gallery, performance venue, and space celebrating journalism started by longtime area newspaper the *Monterey County Weekly*. The juice bar side of things is operated by the **Perfectly Pressed Juice Bar** (www.perfectlypressedjuice.com) of Salinas.

The coffee made at the **Acme Coffee Roasting Co.** (485 Palm Ave., Ste. B, 831/393-9113, www.acmecoffeeroasting.com, Mon.-Fri. 6:30am-3pm, Sat. 7am-3pm) is revered locally and served everywhere from unassuming bakeries to Big Sur's fancy Sierra Mar Restaurant. Head to an alley in Seaside to get a great cup of coffee at its source. The coffee bar is just a counter in an open garage, but it's so popular that it hosts a pool of locals on weekend mornings.

CAJUN

The folks behind **Ferdi's Creole Restaurant** (740 Broadway Ave., 831/394-2244, Mon.-Fri. 10:30am-2pm, $5-11, cash only) don't make it easy to get their flavor-filled New Orleans cuisine. The restaurant, which is split into a to-go side and a sit-down side, is only open a few hours a week and doesn't take credit cards. It is worth seeking out for its uniquely smoky gumbo, sandwiches on crusty bread, and curries. The sampler platter is a good way to go because you get to try small bowls of gumbo, jambalaya, and rice and beans.

ITALIAN

Gusto (1901 Fremont Blvd., 831/899-5825, www.gustopizzeriapasta.com, daily 11:30am-2:30pm and 4:30pm-9pm, $10-18) is a fine new addition to Seaside's varied dining scene. Gusto puts very reasonable prices on its pizzas and pastas, which include creative numbers like a rich short rib ravioli dish and classics like a wholly satisfying spaghetti and meatballs. This lively restaurant also serves wine and beer.

MEXICAN

There are many superb Mexican restaurants in Seaside, and one worth mentioning is **La Tortuga** (1257 Fremont Blvd., 831/899-8429, daily 6am-10pm, $6.50-15.50). The menu here is big and varied, but the tortas (Mexican sandwiches) are a definite highlight. The wide range of tortas includes breaded beef, chile relleno, and eggs-and-cactus versions.

★ **Mi Tierra** (1000 Broadway Ave., 831/394-8113, daily 7am-9pm, $5-9) is a neighborhood Mexican supermarket with a superb taqueria in the back. Walk past slabs of chicharrón and whole fried tilapia under a glass case on your way to a small window and grill. The tacos are a tasty, inexpensive treat at $1.50 a pop. The best one is the al pastor, which comes with crunchy pork, chunks of pineapple, sprigs of cilantro, and a splash of salsa on a little tortilla bed.

SUSHI

Harumi (1760 Fremont Blvd., Ste. H4, 831/899-9988, http://sushiharumi.com, Mon.-Thurs. 11am-2:30pm and 5pm-9pm, Fri. 11am-2:30pm and 5pm-10pm, Sat. noon-2:30pm and 5pm-10pm, Sun. noon-2:30pm and 5pm-9pm, rolls $3-15) is a large place with a large menu. The extensive sushi menu includes baked rolls and ingredients like deep-fried soft-shell crab and Japanese squash. With pitchers of beer on tap, the long bar can be a fun place to post up.

Transportation

Seaside is adjacent to Monterey and very easy to reach by car. Take Del Monte Avenue northeast out of downtown Monterey until you arrive in Seaside, or jump on Highway 1 and take the Fremont Street or Canyon del Rey Boulevard exits into Seaside.

MARINA

The city of Marina is eight miles north of Monterey on Monterey Bay. A large part of Fort Ord was located in Marina. The former U.S. Army base is now the home of California State University, Monterey Bay; the Fort Ord Dunes State Park; and the Fort Ord National Monument. The community is also known for its sweeping sand dunes, long beach, and its inexpensive restaurants and shops. With the land of the former fort still being developed, Marina has a lot of potential that it has not reached yet.

Marina State Beach

At **Marina State Beach** (end of Reservation Rd., 831/649-2836, www.parks.ca.gov, 8am-30 minutes after sunset, free), sand dunes give way to an expansive surf-slammed beach. The seemingly ever-present winds here make it a popular place for hang gliding and kite flying. There's a parking lot, bathrooms, and picnic tables for people who want to check out this beach known for its raw beauty.

Fort Ord Dunes State Park

The home to a U.S. Army post from 1917 to 1994, the dunes north of Monterey are a part of one of California's newest parks, **Fort Ord Dunes State Park** (831/649-2836, www.parks.ca.gov, 8am-30 minutes after sunset, free). Walk along a four-mile road past remnants of the military past or head down to the remote beach for a stroll. The restored dunes, which had 700,000 pounds of contaminated materials removed before opening to the public, are home to threatened and endangered plant and animal species including Monterey spineflower, Menzies' wallflower, dune gilia, and the black legless lizard. The main section of the park has a parking lot, interpretive panels, and a coastal viewpoint along with a trail to the south heading to the beach.

To reach Fort Ord Dunes State Park from Monterey, head north on Highway 1 and take the Lightfighter Drive exit. Turn left onto 2nd Avenue and then take another left on Divarty Street. Take a right on 1st Avenue and follow the signs to the park entrance at the 8th Street Bridge over Highway 1.

Fort Ord National Monument

A large section of former Fort Ord land became the **Fort Ord National Monument** (831/394-8314, www.blm.gov, daily dawn-dusk) in 2012. This 7,200-acre swath of land east of Marina and Seaside has 86 miles of rugged trails used by hikers, horseback riders, and wildflower enthusiasts, though it is primarily loved by mountain bikers.

Sports and Recreation
HIKING
Just north of Marina, the landscape gives way to open fields, rolling sand dunes, and vacant beaches. The **Salinas River National Wildlife Refuge** (Del Monte Ave., www.fws.gov, daily dawn-dusk) offers an entry point into this undeveloped area. The 367-acre refuge has two trails: the **River Trail** (1.2 miles round-trip, easy) and the **Beach Trail** (1.6 miles round-trip, easy). A worthwhile adventure that involves a shipwreck adds about another 1.5 miles round-trip to the Beach Trail. Take the Beach Trail out to the beach and then walk north for another 15-20 minutes, where you'll come upon a rusting barge beached in the sand and the surf. It hit the shore in 1983 and now serves as a perch for local fishermen. If the waves are not too big, you can hop up onto its rusting deck and walk around. Just be careful. To reach the Salinas River National Wildlife Refuge, take the Del Monte Boulevard exit north of Reservation Road off Highway 1. Go left as it becomes a dirt road between fields. It can be muddy and rutted in winter so don't attempt this during rugged conditions if you don't have four-wheel drive. There's an undeveloped parking lot at the end of the road.

Fort Ord Dunes State Park (831/649-2836, www.parks.ca.gov, 8am-30 minutes after sunset, free) has four miles of carless roads that are nice for hiking, running, and biking.

HORSEBACK RIDING
Marina is home to the **Marina Equestrian Center** (California Ave. and 9th St., 831/521-6168, www.marinaequestrian.org, Wed.-Sun. by appointment, private hour-long lesson $50, semiprivate hour-long lesson $40), a public park operated by the Marina Equestrian Association. Lessons are available by calling 831/392-5267.

The **Monterey Bay Equestrian Center** (831/663-5712, www.montereybayequestrian.com, $70pp/one-hour ride, $85pp/1.5-hour ride) can help you achieve your romantic dream of riding a horse on the beach. The center takes riders out on the sands between Marina and Moss Landing.

ROLLER SKATING
Water City Skate (2800 Second Ave., 831/384-0414, www.watercityskate.com, public skate times Sat. 2pm-5pm and 7pm-10pm, Sun. 1pm-4pm, admission $6, skate rental $3) is a big blue building on the former Fort Ord that houses a skating rink. Come on the weekends to get your skate on or show up for a Monday-night lesson (Mon. 5pm-6pm, $10/one drop-in lesson, $75/10 weeks of lessons). It's also where the **Monterey Bay Derby Dames** (www.montereybayderbydames.org), a league of female roller derby competitors, have their bouts. Check their website for a schedule.

Accommodations
Just a few sandy steps from Marina State Beach is the **Sanctuary Beach Resort** (3295 Dunes Dr., 831/883-9478 or 877/944-3863, www.thesanctuarybeachresort.com, $225-390). All of the guestrooms and suites are as close to the beach as you'll get in a Monterey County accommodation. Enjoy your own private patio or balcony to watch the sunset and a gas fireplace for when the sun goes down. An unexpected amenity is that your stay includes use of a private golf course to travel around the resort grounds. There's also an on-site heated pool and spa.

Food
BREAKFAST
There are few truly inexpensive sit-down restaurants in the Monterey area, and Marina's **Tommy's Restaurant** (204 Cypress Ave., 831/582-9503, Mon.-Sat. 7am-2pm, $1-6) is one of them. Who else can offer a two-egg-, hash brown-, and toast breakfast for 99 cents? Tommy's is a dream for budget-conscious diners and throwback breakfast place aficionados. The service is clipped, efficient, and friendly, while the food is basic but a great deal for the price. The breakfast menu includes egg

dishes, pancakes, and fried rice plates. Dine in a truly unique environment with working-class folk and local college students.

BREWPUBS

Marina has its own brewpub, the **English Ales Brewery** (223 A Reindollar Ave., 831/883-3000, http://englishalesbrewery.com, daily noon-11pm, $6-12), which brews six flagship ales on-site including the Fat Lip Amber Ale and the 1066 Pale Ale. Marina is a low-key town, and this brewpub feels like a neighborhood pub (including special member mugs hanging on the ceiling overhead). The food here includes burgers, sandwiches, and salads.

CAFÉS

The family-owned and -operated **Coffee Mia** (250 Reservation Rd., Ste. E, 831/384-0148, Mon.-Fri. 5am-5pm, Sat. 5am-3pm, Sun. 8am-2pm, $4-6) makes coffee dripped to order. They also serve café-style breakfast and lunch items, all dished up in a popular space filled with mosaic tile-topped tables. The breakfast recommendation here is the egg volcano, a mountain of egg, meat, and cheese topped with an explosion of salsa, sour cream, and avocado.

SANDWICHES

The **Wild Thyme Deli & Café** (445 Reservation Rd., 831/884-2414, www.wildthymedeli.com, Mon.-Sat. 10am-5:30pm, $5-12) is a great place to stock up on picnic supplies. They have a range of premade pasta salads behind the counter and some terrific sandwiches like the smoked chicken panino with chicken, smoked mozzarella, basil pesto and more.

STEAK AND SEAFOOD

There's nothing quite like the **Kula Ranch Island Grill & Sushi Bar** (3295 Dunes Dr., 831/883-9479, Mon. 4pm-9pm, Tues.-Thurs. and Sun. 11:30am-9pm, Fri.-Sat. 4pm-10pm, $14-27) in Marina. It offers a causal atmosphere, a nice outdoor patio, some tropical drinks, and a menu that goes all over the place from steak to sushi to pastas. The bar side of the restaurant is a fun place to watch some sports or have a happy hour drink, though the service is spotty. The Hawaiian nachos on the appetizer menu are an interesting dish of chicken, cheese, peanut sauce, and sour cream atop wonton strips in lieu of tortilla chips.

VIETNAMESE

Marina's **Noodle Bar** (215 Reservation Rd., Ste. E, Wed.-Mon. 11am-8pm, $5.50-8.50)

The cheapest breakfast in Marina can be found at Tommy's Restaurant.

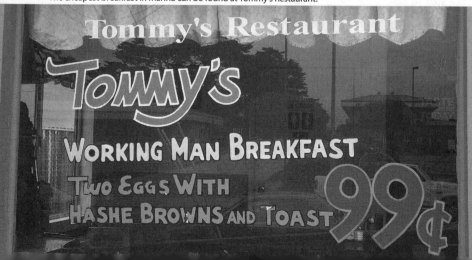

serves large plates of fresh Vietnamese food at very reasonable prices. They do phos (soups), dry noodle bowls, sautéed noodle dishes, and fried rice plates. A large sweet-and-sour chicken with fried rice costs just $6.50 and can last you for two meals. This little restaurant in a strip mall is very popular so expect to wait for a table on weekend evenings. They have an even smaller spot in Seaside (1944 Fremont Blvd., 831/392-0210, Mon.-Sat. 11am-8pm).

Transportation

Marina is a 10-minute drive north from Monterey on Highway 1. Just hop on the highway for eight miles and then exit at Del Monte Boulevard or Reservation Road.

MOSS LANDING

Located in the center of Monterey Bay, 25 miles south of Santa Cruz and 15 miles north of Monterey, Moss Landing is a picturesque, working fishing village; it helps if you can ignore the smokestacks of the towering Moss Landing Power Plant. The main drag, Moss Landing Road, has a scattering of antique stores and art galleries, and the Moss Landing Harbor is home to a fleet of fishing vessels. To the south of the harbor's mouth, Salinas River State Beach offers miles of wild, undeveloped shoreline. North of the inlet, Zmudowski State Beach is popular with local surfers during the winter months. Offshore, the Monterey Submarine Canyon is one of North America's largest submarine canyons. It's the reason that the Moss Landing Marine Laboratories and Monterey Bay Aquarium Research Institute have local addresses. The Moss Landing Chamber of Commerce website (www.mosslandingchamber.com) offers visitor information.

★ Elkhorn Slough

Elkhorn Slough is the second-largest section of tidal salt marsh in California after San Francisco Bay. The estuary hosts an amazing amount of wildlife that includes marine mammals and over 340 bird species, which makes it one of the state's best birding spots. The best way to explore the slough is by kayak, where you can view rafts of lounging sea otters and a barking rookery of California sea lions from water level. Located in Moss Landing's North Harbor, which connects to the slough, **Monterey Bay Kayaks** (2390 Hwy. 1, 831/373-5357, www.montereybaykayaks.com, Nov.-Feb. daily 8:30am-5pm, Mar.-late May 8:30am-6pm, late May-early Sept. daily 8:30am-7pm, guided tours $60-85, kayak rental $30-35/day, SUP rental $30/two hours) has kayak rentals as well as a range of guided tours from a two-and-a-half-hour paddle up the slough to monthly full-moon tours. While paddling a kayak is the recommended way to view the slough, the **Elkhorn Slough Safari** (Moss Landing Harbor, Dock A, 831/633-5555, www.elkhornslough.com, adults $38, children $28, seniors $35) is a possibility for those who wish to take a 1.5- to 2-hour tour of the estuary by boat. Check the website for current tour times.

Entertainment and Events

NIGHTLIFE

The **Moss Landing Inn** (7902 Hwy. 1, 831/633-9803, http://wenchilada.com, daily noon-close) is not a place to spend the night, but rather a dive bar where you can spend a few hours getting acquainted with the local characters. It's connected to The Whole Enchilada restaurant and offers live music on weekends.

FESTIVALS AND EVENTS

The success of reality TV shows like *Antiques Roadshow* and *American Pickers* have people scouring yard sales and antique shops for collectibles. On the last Sunday of July, Moss Landing is flooded with these enthusiasts for the annual **Moss Landing Antique Street Fair** (831/633-4501, www.mosslandingchamber.com). The giant outdoor antique market has over 200 booths selling collectibles, while other booths nearby serve local foods like fried fish and artichokes.

Shopping

Moss Landing it known for antique stores like the **Cottage By the Sea** (7981 E. Moss Landing Rd., 831/633-9909, Wed.-Mon. 11am-5pm) and **Hamlin Antiques** (8071 Moss Landing Rd., 831/633-3664, www.hauteenchilada.com, Thurs.-Tues. noon-5pm). It's also home to a growing arts community. Behind the Haute Enchilada Café, the **Haute Enchilada Gallery** (7902 Moss Landing Rd., 831/633-3743, www.hauteenchilada.com, daily 11am-5pm) has multiple rooms filled with sculptures, watercolors, woodworks, and ceramic items. Housed in the former post office, the aptly named **Old Post Office Gallery** (7981 Moss Landing Rd., 831/632-0488, Tues.-Sun. 11am-5pm) features visual arts including lots of landscape paintings.

Driftwood (8071-B Moss Landing Rd., 831/632-2800, www.driftwoodstore.com, Sun.-Thurs. noon-5pm, Fri.-Sat. 11am-6pm) bills itself as an "artisan gift boutique." Expect hipster-approved jewelry, home furnishings, and candles.

Sports and Recreation
BEACHES

Just north of Moss Landing's harbor, **Moss Landing State Beach** (Jetty Rd., 831/649-2836, www.parks.ca.gov) and **Zmudowski State Beach** (20 miles north of Monterey on Hwy. 1, 831/649-2836, www.parks.ca.gov) stretch for miles. They're mostly enjoyed by locals who fish, surf, or ride horses on the beach. To get there, take Struve Road and turn onto Giberson Road.

Just south of Moss Landing is the **Salinas River State Beach** (Potrero Rd., 831/649-2836, www.parks.ca.gov), which doesn't get as many visitors as other area beaches. Expect some serenity among a few horseback riders or anglers.

WHALE-WATCHING

For a glimpse of marine mammals in the wild, from gray whales to orcas, catch a ride with **Sanctuary Cruises** (7881 Sandholt Rd., 831/917-1042, www.sanctuarycruises.

com, adults $50, children 12 and under $40). Running on biodiesel, the 43-foot ocean vessel *Sanctuary* takes passengers out daily for 4-5-hour cruises. **Blue Ocean Whale Watch** (7881 Sandholt Rd., 877/229-9142, www.blueoceanwhalewatch.com, $50) also heads out into the bay for four-hour whale-watching expeditions.

Accommodations and Camping

With its nautical decor, the ★ **Captain's Inn** (8122 Moss Landing Rd., 831/633-5550, www.captainsinn.com, $199-265) is the perfect place to spend an evening in the fishing village. The inn offers rooms in two buildings: a historic structure that was once the site of the Pacific Coast Steamship Company and the Boathouse, where every room has a superb view of the nearby tidal marsh. The Boathouse rooms are recommended for animal lovers and nautical enthusiasts. Wildlife watchers might be able to catch a glimpse of marine mammals or birds in the nearby tidal marsh, while maritime fans can climb into bed sets crafted out of boats or boat parts. Wake up to a home-cooked breakfast that can be bagged if you are on the go.

Seeking solitude and miles of nearly empty coastline? The **Monterey Dunes Company** (407 Moss Landing Rd., 831/633-4883 or 800/553-8637, www.montereydunes.com, $345-690) rents 2-4-bedroom homes on the beach south of Moss Landing. Guests also have access to the development's tennis courts, swimming pool, saunas, and hot tub.

The **Moss Landing KOA Express** (7905 Sandholt Rd., 831/633-6800 or 800/562-3390, $68-75) has almost 50 RV sites right in the Moss Landing Harbor area.

Food
AMERICAN

Housed in a distinct red-and-white building, the **Moss Landing Café** (421 Moss Landing Rd., 831/633-3355, www.mosslandingcafe.com, Sun.-Thurs. 6:30am-3pm, Fri.-Sat. 6:30am-3pm and 5pm-8:30pm, $6-15) does home-style breakfasts and lunches that utilize area ingredients, whether artichokes or seafood. The breakfast menu has some unique meetings of terrestrial and ocean items in dishes like the crab omelet, the fish and eggs, and an omelet with bacon, veggies, and your choice of oysters or squid. The Cajun fish sandwich with avocado salsa is a winner. They also do dinner on the weekends.

LATIN AMERICAN

Part art gallery, part eatery, fanciful **Haute Enchilada Café & Galleries** (7902 Moss Landing Rd., 831/633-5843, www.hauteenchilada.com, Mon.-Thurs. 11am-9pm, Fri.-Sun. 9am-9pm, $17-26) is bursting with color. The menu includes items such as Peruvian empanadas and skirt steaks in Oaxacan black bean sauce.

MEXICAN

The Whole Enchilada (7902 Hwy. 1, 831/633-3038 http://wenchilada.com, daily 11:30am-9pm, $10-24) does seafood with a Mexican slant. Dine on seafood enchiladas, Mexican-style cioppino, or chile relleno stuffed with crab, shrimp, and cheese in the brightly colored dining room or outdoor patio.

SEAFOOD

As a harbor town, Moss Landing is probably best known for its seafood restaurants. The most popular is ★ **Phil's Fish Market** (7600 Sandholt Rd., 831/633-2152, www.philsfishmarket.com, Sun.-Thurs. 10am-8pm, Fri.-Sat. 10am-9pm, $9-23), which is known for its cioppino—a hearty Italian American seafood stew that includes clams, mussels, fish, Dungeness crab, prawns, and scallops. A heaping bowl comes with salad and garlic bread. Another worthwhile order is the blackened sea scallops cooked with lemon butter and capers. This informal market/eatery has a bluegrass band playing on some nights.

THAI

Moss Landing even has a great place to get Thai food with the **Lemon Grass Restaurant** (413 Moss Landing Rd., 831/633-0700, Tues.-Fri. 11am-3pm and 4pm-9pm, Sat.-Sun. 11am-9pm, $11-22). There are the typical pad Thais and curries, but there's also a roasted Cornish game hen and a seafood stir-fry with squid, scallops, shrimp, and mussels on the menu.

MARKETS

The **Whole Enchilada Marketplace** (7990 Hwy. 1, 831/632-2628, http://wenchilada.com, Mon.-Sat. 7am-8pm, Sun. 8am-8pm) is a great place for a snack and supplies if you are passing through Moss Landing or staying there for an evening. The market has fresh seafood, wine, beer, and unique sodas. A deli inside serves smoothies, sandwiches, and wraps. This market even has a wine bar inside that does complimentary wine tastings (Fri. 4pm-7pm).

Transportation

Moss Landing is a 20-mile drive from Monterey that under good traffic conditions should take about 20 minutes. Take Highway 1 north from Monterey. The highway switches from four lanes to two between Marina and Moss Landing so expect some traffic congestion if you are traveling on a summer day or holiday weekend. Take a left on Moss Landing Road to travel to the heart of the fishing community.

Carmel

Carmel began as an artists' colony. The region's landscape seems to have been created by those artists: fanciful curlicue cypress trees, artfully arranged rocks, and a white sand beach as blank as a canvas.

This most beautiful and glamorous of the Monterey Peninsula's communities has drawn important admirers throughout time, from Father Junipero Serra, who preferred the Carmel Mission to all of his California missions, to film icon Clint Eastwood, who was mayor of Carmel-by-the-Sea in the late 1980s.

More upscale than their neighbors, Carmel-by-the-Sea and Pebble Beach have long been vacation destinations for the well-heeled. Carmel-by-the-Sea has long been known as a quiet community with a predominately older crowd, but in recent years younger residents have opened bars and restaurants that have given the town a welcome jolt of youthful energy. Indulge with a locally made fine wine or a round of golf on Pebble Beach's sacred greens. Even if you can't manage to overnight in the area, make sure to visit Carmel Beach, the Carmel Mission, and nearby Point Lobos State Natural Reserve, which has been called the "Crown Jewel of the California State Park System." Pebble Beach's 17-Mile Drive is a great drive that winds through a wealthy coastal enclave.

Adjacent Carmel Valley is more unassuming, but this sunny rural valley is home to some of the best wineries, a few high-end resorts, some great hiking, and something that the Carmel coast doesn't have in the summer: abundant sunshine.

PLANNING YOUR TIME

The primary sights of Carmel can be explored in a day, though a weekend is recommended to best experience the fruits of the local wineries.

The town of Carmel-by-the-Sea is a very charming and walkable coastal city, suitable for an overnight stay—though there are no hostels or inexpensive lodging options. The stunning white sand beach and its European village-like downtown are worth your time. History buffs should check out the Carmel

---

Previous: Carmel Beach; Carmel Mission; **Above:** the pool deck at Carmel Valley Ranch.

Look for ★ to find recommended
sights, activities, dining, and lodging.

Highlights

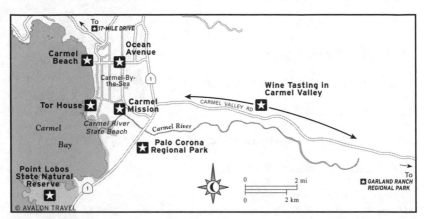

★ **Ocean Avenue:** The main thoroughfare of Carmel-by-the-Sea recalls a European town with its busy sidewalks, charming cafés, and cute boutiques (page 88).

★ **Carmel Mission:** One of the most authentically restored of all the state's missions offers a working chapel and lovely grounds (page 90).

★ **Tor House:** The stunning stone home of poet Robinson Jeffers and its adjacent Hawk Tower are monuments to the man's creative spirit. They still offer inspiration today and fine views of Carmel's coastline (page 90).

★ **Point Lobos State Natural Reserve:** The crown jewel of California's impressive state park system has pocket coves, tidepools, forests of Monterey cypress, and diverse wildlife (page 91).

★ **Palo Corona Regional Park:** Only accessible with a permit, this stunning park has sweeping views of the Carmel coast from Inspiration Point (page 91).

★ **Carmel Beach:** One of the finest beaches on Monterey Bay, this is a great place for a stroll, a picnic, or catching a wave (page 92).

★ **17-Mile Drive:** This drive through Pebble Beach passes by mansions, beaches, golf courses, and the famed Lone Cypress (page 107).

★ **Wine Tasting in Carmel Valley:** Carmel Valley's laid-back atmosphere makes for a fun day of tasting locally produced and bottled wines (page 112).

★ **Garland Ranch Regional Park:** This large county park offers some of the best hikes in Monterey County (page 115).

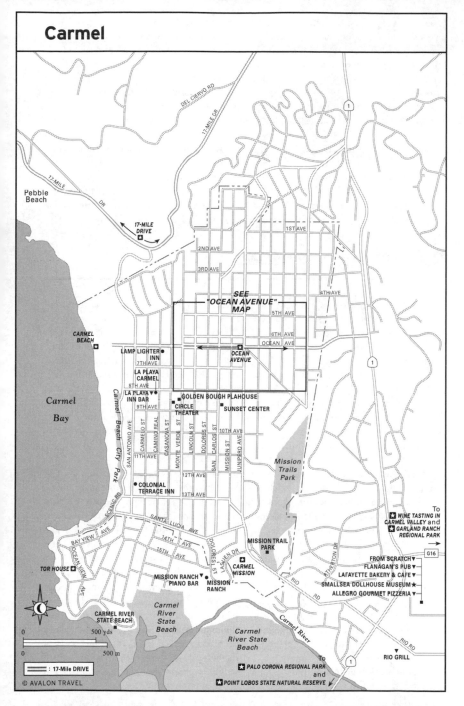

Carmel

© AVALON TRAVEL

Mission, one of the best in the state. Literature lovers should take a tour of the Tor House. Explore the windswept cypress trees, colorful tidepools, and easy trails of Point Lobos State Natural Reserve just three miles south of town.

Pebble Beach is the place to stay if you are a golf fanatic or want to splurge on lodging. Here, it's all about catering to wealthy vacationers. The 17-Mile Drive is one of the region's most popular attractions, with exceptional natural scenery and stunning mansions to gawk at.

Carmel Valley is more rustic, relaxed, and spread out. It is also the epicenter of the area's growing wine industry and the region's most consistently sunny spot. Carmel Valley has the region's finest wineries and some laid-back tasting rooms. There's also some stellar hiking to be had at Garland Ranch Regional Park, and Carmel Valley Road (G-16) is one of the best scenic drives around.

CA-1 of Highway 1 connects Carmel-by-the-Sea to Monterey. Carmel Valley Road (G-16) winds east from Carmel-by-the-Sea into the more rustic Carmel Valley. Pebble Beach can be accessed from Carmel-by-the-Sea and Pacific Grove. Expect to pay the $10 entrance fee if you are not spending the evening at one of Pebble Beach's upscale lodges.

Carmel-by-the-Sea

There are no addresses in Carmel-by-the-Sea (frequently referred to as simply Carmel). There are lots of trees and no streetlights, and street signs are wooden posts with names written vertically, to be read while walking along the sidewalk, rather than driving down the street. There's little to do at night. These are a few clues as to how this village facing the Pacific Ocean maintains its lost-in-time charm.

Formerly a Bohemian enclave where local poets George Sterling and Robinson Jeffers hung out with literary heavyweights such as Jack London and Mary Austin, Carmel-by-the-Sea is now a popular vacation spot for the moneyed, the artistic, and the romantic. People come to enjoy the small coastal town's almost European charm: strolling its sidewalks and peering into the windows of upscale shops and art galleries, which showcase the work of sculptors, plein air painters, and photographers. Between the galleries are some of the region's most revered restaurants. The main thoroughfare, Ocean Avenue, slopes down to Carmel Beach, one of the finest on the Monterey Peninsula.

The old-world charms of Carmel can make it a little confusing for drivers. Because there are no addresses, locations are sometimes given via directions, for example: on 7th Avenue between San Carlos and Dolores Streets; or the northwest corner of Ocean Avenue. The town is compact, laid out on a plain grid system, so you're better off getting out of your car and walking anyway. Expect to share everything from Carmel's sidewalks to its restaurants with our canine friends. Carmel is very pro-pup.

SIGHTS
★ Ocean Avenue
With its wide, clean sidewalks, posh stores, bakeries, and restaurants, **Ocean Avenue** has a European feel. The main street of downtown Carmel-by-the-Sea can be crowded with humans and their dogs during summer and on holidays, but it is worth a stroll to get a taste of Carmel's unique personality. The road is four lanes wide with a tree-lined median separating the east- and west-traveling traffic. West of Lincoln Avenue, Ocean Avenue slopes toward the sea at a grade that recalls a ski run. At the end of Ocean Avenue is one of the best places to access Carmel Beach. Paid parking via meters is enforced daily 8am-7pm at $2 per hour.

Dog-Friendly Carmel

Grasing's Coastal Cuisine

Carmel-by-the-Sea has been called the most dog-friendly town in the nation, and with good reason. Dogs are allowed to run off-leash on the fine sands of Carmel Beach. Carmel Plaza has a drinking fountain for dogs, and even Carmel's most upscale boutiques put out dog bowls in front of their shops for passing dogs.

Many local hotels welcome dogs, though most add a nightly cleaning fee. **Cypress Inn** (Lincoln and 7th Ave., 831/624-3871 or 800/443-7443, www.cypress-inn.com, $245-595), **Coachman's Inn** (San Carlos St. and 8th Ave., 831/624-6421, www.coachmansinn.com, $225-350), **Tradewinds Carmel** (Mission St. and 3rd Ave., 831/624-2776, www.tradewinds.com, $250-550), **Lamp Lighter Inn** (Ocean Ave. and Camino Real, 831/624-7372 or 888/375-0770, www.carmellamplighter.com, $185-450), and the **Hofsas House** (San Carlos St. between 3rd and 4th Aves., 831/624-2745 or 800/221-2548, www.hofsashouse.com, $145-400) can accommodate your pooch for nightly fees running $20-30.

Your dog can dine with you at a lot of local restaurants, but this might mean you have to eat outdoors on a patio. **Carmel Belle** (Doud Craft Studios, Ocean Ave. and San Carlos St., 831/624-1600, www.carmelbelle.com, Mon.-Tues. 8am-5pm, Wed.-Sat. 8am-8pm, Sun. 8am-6pm, $6-25), **Casanova** (5th Ave. between Mission St. and San Carlos St., Mon.-Thurs. 11:30am-3pm and 5pm-10pm, Fri.-Sat. 5pm-10:30pm, $23-49), **Grasing's Coastal Cuisine** (6th St. and Mission St., 831/624-6462, http://grasings.com, daily 11am-3pm and 5pm-9pm, $25-62), **Katy's Place** (Mission and 6th Ave., 831/624-0199, www.katysplacecarmel.com, daily 7am-2pm, $10-20), **La Balena** (Junipero St. between 5th Ave. and 6th Ave., 831/250-6295, http://labalenacarmel.com, Tues.-Wed. 5pm-10pm, Thurs.-Sun. 11:30am-3:30pm and 5pm-10pm, $21-33), and **Tommy's Wok** (San Carlos St. between Ocean and 7th Ave., 831/624-8518, Tues.-Sun. 11:30am-2:30pm and 4:30pm-9pm, $10-16) are all dog-friendly options. **Terry's Lounge** (inside the Cypress Inn, Lincoln and 7th Ave., 831/624-3871, www.carmelterrys.com, Sun.-Thurs. noon-11pm, Fri.-Sat. noon-midnight) is a terrific dog-friendly bar with seating indoors and outside in a courtyard that resembles that of a Mediterranean villa.

Ocean Avenue

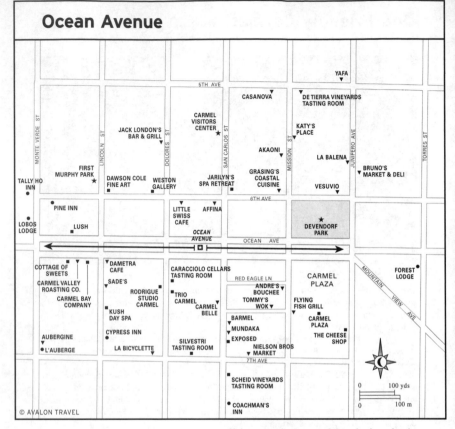

© AVALON TRAVEL

★ Carmel Mission

San Carlos Borromeo de Carmelo Mission (3080 Rio Rd., 831/624-1271, www.carmelmission.org, daily 9:30am-7pm, adults $6.50, seniors $4, children $2) was Father Junípero Serra's favorite among his California mission churches. He lived, worked, and eventually died here, and visitors today can see a replica of his cell. A working Catholic parish remains part of the complex, so please be respectful when taking the self-guided tour. The rambling buildings and courtyard gardens show some wear, but enough restoration work has gone into the church and living quarters to make them attractive and eminently visitor-friendly. The Carmel Mission has a small memorial museum in a building

off the second courtyard, but don't make the mistake of thinking that this small and outdated space is the only historical display. In fact, the "museum" runs through many of the buildings, showing a small slice of the lives of the 18th- and 19th-century friars. The highlight of the complex is the church with its gilded altar front, its shrine to the Virgin Mary, the grave of Junípero Serra, and an ancillary chapel dedicated to his memory. Round out your visit by walking out into the gardens to admire the flowers and fountains and to read the grave markers in the small cemetery.

★ Tor House

Local poet Robinson Jeffers penned nature poems to the uncompromising beauty of Carmel Point and nearby Big Sur. He built this rugged-looking castle on the Carmel coast in 1919. He named it **Tor House** (26304 Ocean View Ave., 831/624-1813, www.torhouse.org, tours Fri.-Sat. 10am-3pm, adults $10, students $5) after its rocky setting, and he added the majestic Hawk Tower a year later.

The Tor House Foundation has volunteer docents that do tours of the property. Tours include a walk through the original home, which was hand built by Jeffers with giant stones. The poet once hosted luminaries like Ansel Adams, Charlie Chaplin, Edna St. Vincent Millay, and Dylan Thomas within the dining room, which offers fine views of Carmel Point and Point Lobos. The highlight of the tour is a visit to **Hawk Tower,** a four-story stone structure crowned with an open-air turret. Climb up a hidden staircase (not for the claustrophobic) or opt for the outside staircase to reach stunning views of Jeffers's property and the natural beauty that inspired his best work.

★ Point Lobos State Natural Reserve

Said to be the inspiration behind the setting of Robert Louis Stevenson's *Treasure Island*, **Point Lobos State Natural Reserve** (CA-1, three miles south of Carmel, 831/624-4909, www.parks.ca.gov and www.pointlobos.org, winter daily 8am-30 minutes after sunset, spring-fall daily 8am-7pm, $10/vehicle) is a wonderland of coves, hills, and jumbled rocks. The reserve's **Cypress Grove Trail** winds through a forest of antler-like Monterey cypress trees that are cloaked in striking red algae. Point Lobos also offers a lesson on the region's fishing history in the **Whaler's Cabin** (daily 9am-5pm, staff permitting), a small wooden structure that was built by Chinese fishermen in the 1850s. Half of the reserve is underwater, open for scuba divers who want to explore the 70-foot-high kelp forests located just offshore. The parking lots in Point Lobos tend to fill up on crowded weekends, but the reserve allows people to park on nearby Highway 1 and walk in to visit the park during these times.

★ Palo Corona Regional Park

Palo Corona Regional Park (200 yards south of Carmel River Bridge off Hwy. 1, 831/372-3196, www.mprpd.org, daily sunrise-sunset, free, reservation access permit required) is a stunning 4,350-acre park that offers sweeping views of the coastline from Pebble Beach to Point Lobos. It is also an important habitat for plant and animal

Tor House and Hawk Tower

species that include rare amphibians like the California red-legged frog and the tiger salamander. The property was acquired in 2004 by a partnership of nonprofit and government agencies. The Monterey Peninsula Regional Park District runs the park and allows just 21 people to visit the property daily. Access permits are available online (www.mprpd.org) or by phone (831/372-3196, ext. 2). The 1.3-mile hike to **Inspiration Point** is a must-do for its terrific vistas.

BEACHES
★ Carmel Beach

Found at the end of Carmel-by-the-Sea's Ocean Avenue, **Carmel Beach** (Ocean Ave., 831/624-4909, http://ci.carmel.ca.us/carmel, daily 6am-10pm) is one of the Monterey Bay region's best beaches. Under a bluff dotted with twisted, skeletal cypress trees, it's a long, white, sandy beach that borders a usually clear blue-green Pacific. In the distance to the south, Point Lobos juts out from the land like a pointing finger, while just north of the beach, the green-as-billiard-table-felt golf courses cloak the grounds of nearby Pebble Beach. Like most of Carmel, Carmel Beach is very dog-friendly. On any given day, all sorts of canines fetch, sniff, and run on the white sand.

One of the best places to access the beach is at the west end of Ocean Avenue. There's a parking lot here, along with four beach volleyball courts, a wooden observation deck, and restrooms.

For surfers, Carmel Beach is one of the Monterey area's most consistent breaks. It's also the annual site of the Sunshine Freestyle Surfabout, the only surf contest in Monterey County.

Carmel River State Beach

When Carmel Beach gets overrun, **Carmel River State Beach** (Carmelo Rd., 831/649-2836, www.parks.ca.gov, daily 8am-30 minutes after sunset) makes a great alternative. Actually, this mile-long beach is even better if you are a birder or scuba diver. The north end of the beach is the site of the Carmel River Lagoon and Wetlands Natural Preserve, where the Carmel River pools up before it reaches the ocean. Here, birders can see a range of birds from great blue herons to warblers. Monastery Beach is a very popular dive spot located at the southern end of the park. While it's great for advanced divers, the water

the view from Palo Corona Regional Park

offshore gets very deep very fast, making it a dangerous place for other ocean activities.

WINE TASTING

The town of Carmel has tasting rooms in its downtown area, even though the vineyards are in the nearby Carmel Valley or Santa Lucia Highlands. Visit the Carmel Chamber of Commerce website (www.carmelcalifornia. org) for a downloadable map of Carmel-by-the-Sea's tasting rooms.

In the sleek **Caraccioli Cellars Tasting Room** (Dolores St. between Ocean Ave. and 7th Ave., 831/622-7722, www.caracciolicellars. com, Mon.-Thurs. 2pm-7pm, Fri.-Sat. 11am-10pm, Sun. 11am-7pm, tasting $10-15), visitors taste wines made from pinot noir and chardonnay grapes. Caraccioli also pours a brut and a brut rosé that you can enjoy on the wooden slab bar.

The family-owned **De Tierra Vineyards Tasting Room** (Mission St. and 5th Ave., 831/622-9704, www.detierra.com, summer Tues.-Thurs. 2pm-8pm, Fri.-Sun. noon-8pm, winter Tues.-Thurs. 2pm-7pm, Fri.-Sun. noon-8pm, tasting $10-15) has a range of wines, including a rosé, Syrah, merlot, chardonnay, red blend, Riesling, and a pinot noir. A chalkboard lists a cheese and chocolate plate menu. This is a place for great wine, good snacks, and occasional entertainment.

Grammy-winning composer Alan Silvestri has scored everything from the TV series *CHiPs* and the movie *Forrest Gump* to the 2014 series *Cosmos*. He also makes wine in Carmel Valley, which can be sampled in the **Silvestri Tasting Room** (7th Ave. between Dolores St. and San Carlos St., 831/625-0111, www.silvestrivineyards.com, daily noon-7pm, tasting $10-15).

At Scheid Vineyards, Al Scheid and his employees take winemaking seriously, utilizing 10 vineyards in inland Monterey County from north of Soledad south to the county line. The estate vineyards produce 38 varietals of grapes but keep the best to themselves to make wines like their popular claret and 50/50, a cabernet sauvignon-Syrah mix

that starts with a peppery kick before smoothing out. Sample their wares at the **Scheid Vineyards Carmel-by-the-Sea Tasting Room** (San Carlos St. and 9th Ave., 831/656-9463, www.scheidvineyards.com, Sun.-Thurs. noon-6pm, Fri.-Sat. noon-7pm, tasting $10-20), a clean, friendly space. There's a large map behind the counter that shows where all of the Scheid vineyards are located. A few large photographs on the wall show the vineyards and the winemaking process. They also have a location on the River Road Wine Trail (1972 Hobson Ave., Greenfield, 831/386-0316, daily 11am-5pm, tasting $5-10) that has an outdoor deck, a demo vineyard, and a bocce ball court.

Sample contemporary art, three wine labels (Peleria Wines, Mesa Del Sol Vineyards, Ian Brand & Family Winery), and olive oil at **Trio Carmel** (Dolores St. between Ocean Ave. and 7th Ave., 831/250-7714 or 800/860-3024, www. triocarmel.com, Sun.-Thurs. 11am-5pm, Fri.-Sat. 11am-6pm, tasting $9.50-15). Their Syrah and zinfandel are highly rated.

ENTERTAINMENT AND EVENTS

The events and entertainment in Carmel tend to center around either art or food. This town loves its haute culture, so you won't find too many sports bars or generic movie theaters here. Instead, enjoy classical music, a wealth of live theater, and a glass of wine in the mild evenings.

Bars and Clubs

Carmel's once nearly nonexistent nightlife gained a pulse with the opening of **Mundaka** (San Carlos St. and 7th Ave., 831/624-7400, Sun.-Wed. 5:30pm-9:30pm, Thurs.-Sat. 5:30pm-10pm), a Spanish-style tapas bar that attracts Carmel's younger crowd with live music and DJs. Many shirts have been ruined here by drinking wine from one of Mundaka's *porróns*, glass wine pitchers with a spout that allows you to pour wine into your mouth from above your head. Mundaka has proved so successful that the owners opened **Barmel** (San Carlos St. between Ocean Ave. and 7th Ave.,

831/626-3400, daily 2:30pm-midnight) next door. Barmel has live music from Thursday to Saturday with a DJ following on weekend nights.

Located upstairs in Carmel's The Barnyard Shopping Center, **Flanagan's Pub** (3772 The Barnyard Shopping Center, 831/625-5500, http://flanaganscarmel.com, daily 11:30am-2am) is a cozy drinking establishment with two fireplaces, a dartboard, a pool table, and a jukebox. There are eight beers on tap that you can enjoy indoors or out on the dog-friendly deck.

Carmel's dive bar is **Sade's** (Lincoln St. and Ocean Ave., 831/624-0787, daily 11am-2am, cash only). It's an intimate place with most seating placed around a U-shaped bar. In a place this small, you are bound to make some friends. Sade's accepts cash only.

For old-fashioned fun, head to the **Mission Ranch Piano Bar** (The Restaurant at Mission Ranch, 26270 Dolores St., 831/625-9040, www.missionranchcarmel.com, daily 4pm-11:30pm) for the nightly piano bar sing-along from 8pm to 11:30pm. It's possible you might spot owner Clint Eastwood joining in.

The **La Playa Inn Bar** (La Playa Carmel, Camino Real at 8th Ave., 831/293-6100, www.laplayahotel.com, daily 2pm-10pm) has one of the best drink deals in the area if not the country. On Sundays from 5pm to 5:10pm, well drinks are sold for just 10 cents a pop. Enjoy it while taking in the memento-laden bar area.

Live Music

Classical music aficionados will appreciate the dulcet tones of the musicians who perform for **Chamber Music Monterey Bay** (831/625-2212, www.chambermusicmontereybay.org). This society brings talented ensembles and soloists in from around the world to perform on the lovely Central Coast. One night you might find a local string quartet, and on another night you'll get to see and hear a chamber ensemble. (String quartets definitely rule the small stage and intimate theater.) At its shows, all of which are performed at the

Sunset Cultural Center (San Carlos St. at 9th Ave., 831/620-2048, www.sunsetcenter.org), Chamber Music Monterey Bay reserves up-front seats for children and their adult companions. The Sunset Cultural Center is a state-of-the-art performing center with over 700 seats that hosts a true range of events and artistic endeavors, including rock shows, dance recitals, classical music concerts, and theater performances. Recent performers have included LeAnn Rimes, Philip Glass, and Buddy Guy.

Theater

Despite its small size, Carmel has a handful of live theater groups. In a town that defines itself by its love of art, theater arts don't get left out. Don't hesitate to ask the locals what's playing where when you're in town.

The **Pacific Repertory Theater** (831/622-0100, www.pacrep.org, adults $15-39, seniors $15-28, students, teachers, and military $10-15, children $7.50) is the only professional theater company on the Monterey Peninsula. Its shows go up all over the region, most often in the **Golden Bough Playhouse** (Monte Verde St. and 8th Ave.), the company's home theater. Other regular venues include the **The Forest Theater** (Mountain View St. and Santa Rita St.) and the **Circle Theater** (Casanova St. between 8th and 9th Aves.) within the Golden Bough complex. The company puts on dramas, comedies, and musicals both new and classic. You might see a work of Shakespeare or a classic like *Fiddler on the Roof,* or maybe enjoy your favorite songs from *The Fantasticks,* or sing along to the newer tunes of *Hairspray!* Check the website for upcoming shows, and buy tickets online or over the phone to guarantee you'll get seats while you're in town.

Each fall, PacRep puts up the **Carmel Shakespeare Festival** (www.pacrep.org), a short showing of Shakespeare that's good enough to draw the notice of Bay Area theater snobs. Check the website for information on this year's shows and the venues.

Located in a quiet residential area, the **Carl**

Cherry Center for the Arts (4th Ave. and Guadalupe St., 831/624-7491, http://carlcherrycenter.org, Mon.-Fri. 11am-4pm) was the former home of a Carmel artist and her inventor husband. When they passed away, they left the building to the city with the provision that it would be a place that carries on Carmel's artistic tradition. The one-room gallery hosts rotating exhibits, while the 50-seat theater has infrequent plays and events.

Local artists display their fine art within the Sunset Cultural Center's **Marjorie Evans Gallery** (Sunset Cultural Center, San Carlos St. at 9th Ave., 831/620-2040, www.sunsetcenter.org, Mon.-Fri. 9:30am-5:30pm). The exhibits change every month.

Festivals and Events

Relais & Chateaux is an international collection of gourmet restaurants and luxury hotels. In 2014, they debuted the **Relais & Chateaux GourmetFest** (831/622-5909, www.gourmetfestcarmel.com, Mar.) in Carmel. The event brings chefs from Relais & Chateaux together with winemakers for dinners, demos, and mushroom hunts.

In a town famed for art galleries, one of the biggest events of the year is the **Carmel Art Festival** (Devendorf Park at Mission St., www.carmelartfestival.org, May). This four-day event celebrates visual arts in all media with shows by internationally acclaimed artists at galleries, parks, and other venues all across town. This wonderful festival also sponsors here-and-now contests, including the prestigious plein air (outdoor painting) competition. Visitors get a rare opportunity to witness the artists outdoors, engaging in their creative process as they use the Carmel scenery for inspiration. Round out your festival experience by bidding on paintings at the end-of-event auction. You can get a genuine bargain on original artwork while supporting both the artists and the festival. Perhaps best of all, the Carmel Art Festival is a great place to bring your family—a wealth of children's activities help even the youngest festivalgoers become budding artists.

Carmel is a big food and wine town, so it is no surprise that the Monterey County Vintners and Growers Association's largest annual event takes place in Carmel-by-the-Sea. The **Winemaker's Celebration** (Dolores St. between Ocean Ave. and 7th Ave., 831/375-9400, www.montereywines.org, May) finds over 100 Monterey County wines being poured and sampled downtown. There are also winemaking and grape-growing demonstrations.

Monterey County has its fair share of surfers, but the area's only annual surf contest is the **Sunshine Freestyle Surfabout** (Carmel Beach, 831/375-5015, http://sunshinefreestyle.com, early June). It is only open to local competitors, but the weekend-long event is fun to watch and a beach party springs up around it.

For a more classical experience, one of the most prestigious festivals in Northern California is the **Carmel Bach Festival** (831/624-1521, www.bachfestival.org, July). For 15 days each July, Carmel-by-the-Sea and its surrounding towns host dozens of classical concerts. Naturally the works of J. S. Bach are featured, but you can also hear renditions of Mozart, Vivaldi, Handel, and other heavyweights of Bach's era. Choose between big concerts in major venues or intimate performances in smaller spaces with only a small audience between you and the beautiful music. Concerts and recitals take place literally every day of the week—budget-conscious music lovers can just as easily enjoy the festival in the middle of the week as on the weekends.

During the summer, the **Forest Theater** (Mountain View St. and Santa Rita St., 831/626-1681, www.foresttheaterguild.org, $7) puts on its popular **Films in the Forest** series. Under the stars and trees, movie lovers can take in classics like *Singin' in the Rain* or more recent releases like *War Horse*. It's okay to bring in a bottle of wine or some snacks to sample during the flicks. Be sure to also pack a blanket to soften the blow of the theater's wooden bench seats. Visit the Forest Theater website for the summer film schedule.

The **Carmel International Film Festival**

(831/624-1521, http://carmelfilmfest.com, Oct.) lures debut movies and Hollywood stars to Carmel and the adjacent communities in October. The 2015 lineup included critical favorites *Nightcrawler*, *Whiplash*, and *The Homesman*.

Another entry into Carmel's annual food and wine events is **A Taste of Carmel** (831/624-2522 or 800/550-4333, www.carmel-california.org, Oct.), which showcases the region's wines and cuisine.

SHOPPING
Downtown

Shopping is a sport in Carmel, and Carmel-by-the-Sea offers a lot of upscale shopping opportunities on Ocean Avenue from high-end national retailers like Tiffany & Co. to locally owned shops.

It is easy to spend an afternoon poking into Carmel's many art galleries, browsing everything from the classical mythical sculptures at **Dawson Cole Fine Art** (Lincoln St. and 6th Ave., 800/972-5228, www.dawsoncolefineart.com, Mon.-Sat. 10am-6pm, Sun. 10am-5:30pm) to the playful paintings of a blue dog on display at **Rodrigue Studio Carmel** (Dolores St. between Ocean Ave. and 7th Ave., 831/626-4444, http://georgerodrigue.com, Mon.-Sat. 10am-6pm, Sun. noon-5pm). One of the best galleries in town is the **Weston Gallery** (6th Ave., 831/624-4453, www.westongallery.com, Tues.-Sun. 10:30am-5:30pm), which highlights the photographic work of 20th-century masters including Ansel Adams, Diane Arbus, Robert Mapplethorpe, and Edward Weston. A tiny art gallery owned by two local photographers, **Exposed** (Carmel Square, San Carlos St. and 7th Ave., 831/238-0127, http://galleryexposed.blogspot.com, Sat. 1pm-3pm or by appointment) is worth a peek even if you are just peering into its windows when it is closed.

When your head starts spinning from all the art, head to **Carmel Plaza** (Ocean Ave. and Mission St., 831/624-1385, www.carmel-plaza.com, Mon.-Sat. 10am-6pm, Sun. 11am-5pm), which offers lots of ways to part with your money. This outdoor mall has luxury fashion shops like Tiffany & Co. as well as the hip clothing chain Anthropologie. But don't miss locally owned establishment **The Cheese Shop** (831/625-2272, www.thecheeseshopinc.com, Mon.-Sat. 10am-6pm, Sun. 11am-5:30pm), which sells delicacies like cave-aged Gruyère cheese that you can pair with a local wine.

Carmel Plaza

The Tiniest Town

The small town of Smallsea has everything that you'd ever need including a post office, a brewery, a dance hall, a bookstore, a barbershop, and a variety of other businesses. But there's a catch: You'd have to be about as tall as a pencil to take up residence in the replica English town.

The creation of Diane and Howard Binberg, the **Smallsea Dollhouse Museum** (The Barnyard Shopping Center, Ste. F-22, Carmel, 831/250-7666, www.smallseamini.com, Wed.-Sat. noon-5pm, adults $2) is a miniature metropolis of 52 dollhouse-sized buildings populated with about 2,500 doll-sized figures. This tiny town, which is meant to resemble an Edwardian English town circa 1900-1905, is located within a suite inside The Barnyard Shopping Center.

Smallsea is built to 1:12 scale, meaning that every inch of the town represents one foot in our world. It makes for some amazingly intricate details, including silverware made of real silver, replica newspapers the size of small stamps, and fake produce no larger than a pencil eraser.

The scenes and situations are always changing in Smallsea, whether it's a bar fight outside the tavern or an elderly lady placing some flowers on a churchyard grave. Though the whole town is no larger than a city apartment, it is big on ideas and details.

Worth a browse is the eclectic **Carmel Bay Company** (Ocean Ave. and Lincoln St., 831/624-3868, www.carmelbaycompany.com, daily 10am-5pm), which features copper armoires and a fascinating collection of vintage photographic prints.

For the environment lover in your life, pick up natural milk-based paint or books like *The Gorgeously Green Diet* at **Eco Carmel** (San Carlos St. and 7th Ave., 831/624-1222, www.ecocarmel.com, Mon.-Sat. 10am-6pm, Sun. 11am-5pm). If you carry your purchases out without a bag, you get a 25-cent token that you can donate to one of three rotating nonprofits.

Inside handmade cosmetic store **Lush** (Ocean Ave., 831/625-5874, www.lush.com, Sun.-Thurs. 10am-6pm, Fri.-Sat. 10am-7pm), blocks of rough-cut soaps resemble cheeses (but with a different smell). Part of an international chain, Lush does colorful bath, shower, body, and hair supplies.

The **Cottage of Sweets** (Ocean Ave. between Monte Verde and Lincoln Sts., 831/624-5170, http://cottageofsweets.com, daily 10am-10pm) is a stunning little Carmel structure with moss on the roof and ivy running up its exterior. Inside, it's a sweet tooth's dream with homemade fudge, imported candies, and over 50 kinds of licorice.

The Barnyard Shopping Center

Just east of Highway 1 is **The Barnyard Shopping Center** (24600 Carmel Rancho Ln., www.thebarnyard.com, Mon.-Sat. 10am-6pm, Sun. 11am-5pm). Its multistory buildings are home to over 45 merchants and eight locally owned restaurants. Shop here for everything from riding apparel to home furnishings. It is also home to the unique **Smallsea Dollhouse Museum** (The Barnyard Shopping Center, Ste. F-22, Carmel, 831/250-7666, www.smallseamini.com, Wed.-Sat. noon-5pm, adults $2).

The Crossroads Shopping Center

The Crossroads Shopping Center (243 Crossroads Blvd., 831/625-4106, www.thecrossroadscarmel.com, Mon.-Sat. 10am-6pm, Sun. noon-5pm) is the southernmost place to shop in Carmel before Highway 1 heads into the wilds of Big Sur. Local businesses like **Lula's Chocolates** (831/626-3327, www.lulas.com, Mon.-Sat. 10am-6pm, Sun. noon-5pm) and **River House Books** (831/626-2665, www.riverhousebookscarmel.com, Mon.-Sat. 10am-6pm, Sun. noon-5pm) populate the shopping center, along with a few restaurants like longtime favorite

Rio Grill (101 Crossroads Rd., 831/625-5436, www.riogrill.com, Mon.-Sat. 11:30am-10pm, Sun. 11:30am-3pm and 4pm-10pm). It's also a good place to stock up on supplies before continuing to Big Sur, with a 24-hour Safeway grocery store.

SPORTS AND RECREATION
Parks

Devendorf Park (Ocean Ave. and Junipero Ave., 831/624-3543) is downtown Carmel-by-the-Sea's best public place. This block-long park features a grassy lawn rimmed by live oaks, benches, and monuments honoring U.S. servicepeople. It's the site of many Carmel-by-the-Sea events including the city's Fourth of July celebration, a Halloween parade, and an annual tree-lighting ceremony. It is also home to one of downtown's only public restrooms.

First Murphy Park (Lincoln St. and 6th Ave., 831/624-4447, www.carmelheritage.org) is owned by the city but maintained by the Carmel Heritage Society. The small park's primary feature is a 1902 home built by prominent Carmel architect Michael Murphy. The parcel also has a few benches, a native plant garden, some public art, and a public restroom topped by a wooden deck with views down to the ocean.

Surfing

Carmel Beach (Ocean Ave., 831/624-4909, daily 6am-10pm) has some of the area's most consistent beach breaks. Being a beach break, the sand bars shift, so the best spot on the beach frequently changes. The waves are usually at their finest from spring to late summer. The winds blow out a lot of area breaks in the spring, but Carmel Beach really comes alive during this time of year. In early summer, Carmel Beach is the venue for Monterey County's only annual surf contest, the **Sunshine Freestyle Surfabout** (831/375-5005, www.sunshinefreestyle.com). This is a great place to see the best surfers in the area in action and to experience a fun beach party, especially if it's sunny out.

Contact **Carmel Surf Lessons** (831/915-4065, www.carmelsurflessons.com) if you want to learn to surf at Carmel Beach. To rent a board, head to Monterey's **Sunshine Freestyle Surf & Sport** (443 Lighthouse Ave., Monterey, 831/375-5015, www.sunshinefreestyle.com, Mon.-Sat. 10am-6pm, Sun. 11am-5pm, surfboard rental $30/day, wetsuit rental $15/day) or **On the Beach** (693 Lighthouse Ave., Monterey, 831/646-9283, http://onthebeachsurfshop.com, Sun.-Thurs. 10am-6pm, Fri.-Sat. 10am-7pm, surfboard rental $30/day, wetsuit rental $15/day).

Scuba Diving

Just south of Carmel-by-the-Sea is a famed expert dive spot that one local has called the "Taj Mahal of local diving." The site is **Monastery Beach** (10-100 feet, expert), which is a beach dive off the southern end of Carmel River State Beach. It is best to enter on the north or south end of the beach, because the middle can have a strong current. (Do not attempt an entry during large swells!) The appeal of this dive is its dense sea life along with the fast-dropping, underwater Carmel Canyon offshore. You can dangle your fins above a wall that drops steeply more than 100 feet. The beach is right off Highway 1, 2.5 miles south of the road's intersection with Carmel Valley Road.

Point Lobos State Natural Reserve (CA-1, three miles south of Carmel, 831/624-4909, www.pointlobos.org, winter daily 8am-30 minutes after sunset, spring-fall daily 8am-7pm, diving permit $20-30) is known for its stunning terrestrial features, but there is a lot going on underwater as well. The reserve has the **Whaler's Cove** (20-45 feet, novice) and **Bluefish Cove** (40-100 feet, advanced) sites for divers. Whaler's is a beach dive easily accessible from the parking lot, while a boat or kayak is recommended to reach the deeper Bluefish Cove. Dive reservations can be made from two months to one day in advance. Two divers are required per reservation.

Hiking

Point Lobos State Natural Reserve (CA-1, three miles south of Carmel, 831/624-4909, www.parks.ca.gov and www.pointlobos.org, winter daily 8am-30 minutes after sunset, spring-fall daily 8am-7pm, $10/vehicle) has wonderful hikes. The hikes here involve little elevation gain but reward hikers with views of stunning coves, offshore marine life, and unique onshore vegetation. One of the best trails is the **Cypress Grove Trail** (Sea Lion Point parking lot, 0.8 miles round-trip, easy). This loop goes out on a finger of land with superb coast views, but the main attraction is the grove of wonderfully twisted Monterey cypress trees. That strange rust color on some of the tree branches? That is an algae that has carotene, the same pigment that causes carrots to have their orange coloring.

To view marine life, opt for the **Sea Lion Point Trail** (Sea Lion Point parking lot, 0.6 miles round-trip, easy). It offers vantage points to see a large sea lion colony on an offshore rock as well as the occasional sea otter backstroking through the kelp. The **South Shore Trail** (Bird Island parking lot, one mile, easy) is a nice stroll along the reserve's south shore. There are views of the unique coastal geology that Edward Weston captured in his famous photos, as well as tidepools where you might be able to spot sea stars, anemones, and crabs.

A nice place for an easy hike in Carmel proper can be found at the **Mission Trail Park** (Rio Rd. and Ladera Dr., http://ci.carmel.ca.us). This 35-acre parcel of canyon and woods has five miles of hiking trails. A trail runs the whole length of the park, connecting eastern downtown to the Carmel Mission area.

Palo Corona Regional Park (200 yards south of Carmel River Bridge off Hwy. 1, 831/372-3196, www.mprpd.org, daily sunrise-sunset, free, reservation access permit required) has one of the best hikes in the Carmel area: the Palo Corona Trail's **Inspiration Point Hike** (1.3 miles, moderate). Access must be done in advance by securing a free access permit online (www.mprpd.org) or by phone (831/372-3196, ext. 2). The park allows just 21 visitors a day. The hike to Inspiration Point begins by passing through ranchland where cattle may be grazing. Then the dirt road winds up a hill that rises quickly from sea level like a wave. It offers views of the coastline framed by oak trees cloaked in lace lichen before arriving at a saddle with a redwood bench and picnic table. This is Inspiration Point, and it is worth spending some time here. To add a little more to your hike, continue on the Palo Corona Trail another 0.3 miles (0.6 miles round-trip) to **Animas Pond.** The endangered California red-legged frog calls this ecosystem home.

GUIDED HIKES

Explore the beautiful parkland around Carmel with an experienced guide by signing up for a two- to three-hour guided hike with **Hike Carmel!** (831/760-6270, www.hikecarmel.com, hikes start at $75 pp). This outfit with knowledgeable leaders takes interested parties to Garland Ranch Regional Park in Carmel Valley, Point Lobos State Natural Preserve in Carmel, and Garrapata State Park in Big Sur. They'll even pick you up for your hike.

Spas

Carmel-by-the-Sea is as good place as any to get a spa treatment. **Kush Day Spa** (Morgan Court, Lincoln St. between 7th Ave. and Ocean Ave., 831/626-4100, www.kushincarmel.com, daily 9am-6pm, massages $100-155) is owned by a husband-and-wife team. They do massages (Swedish to cranial sacral therapy), facials, and waxing services.

Jarilyn's Spa Retreat (Vandervort Ct., Ste. E, San Carlos St. between Ocean Ave. and 7th Ave., 831/238-0977, www.jarilynsparetreat.com, Mon.-Sat. by appointment, facials $60-210) is the place for facials, whether you get a pure gold mask or an antiaging treatment with acai berries.

ACCOMMODATIONS
$150-250

Lobos Lodge (Monte Verde St. and Ocean Ave., 831/624-3874, www.loboslodge.com, $175-345) sits right in the midst of downtown Carmel-by-the-Sea, making it a perfect spot from which to dine, shop, and admire the endless array of art in this upscale town. Each of the 30 rooms and suites offers a gas fireplace, a sofa and table, a bed in an alcove, and enough space to stroll about and enjoy the quiet romantic setting. All but two of the rooms have a patio or balcony where you can enjoy the product of a local vineyard outside. In the morning, guests are treated to a continental breakfast and a newspaper.

The Bavarian-inspired, locally owned **Hofsas House** (San Carlos St. between 3rd and 4th Aves., 800/221-2548, www.hofsashouse.com, $145-400) offers surprisingly spacious rooms in a quiet neighborhood within easy walking distance of downtown Carmel. If you have a crew, Hofsas House has family suites for rent with two bedrooms and two bathrooms. If you can, get an oceanview room with a patio or balcony and spend some time sitting outside looking over the town of Carmel out toward the serene (from a distance) Pacific waters. The property also has a heated swimming pool, a sauna, and continental breakfast for guests.

Just two blocks from the beach, the ★ **Lamp Lighter Inn** (Ocean Ave. and Camino Real, 831/624-7372 or 888/375-0770, www.carmellamplighter.com, $185-450) has 11 rooms located in five blue-and-white cottages. The units have a comfortable, beachy decor befitting their location. The cottages encircle a nice courtyard area that has two fire pits, which are perfect for hanging out with old friends or making new ones. Guests are treated to an afternoon wine-and-cheese reception and a morning continental breakfast that they can enjoy in the courtyard. This is a pet-friendly property, and two of the units even have fenced-in backyards.

Located in a neighborhood just a block from Carmel Beach, **Colonial Terrace Inn**

By The Sea (San Antonio Ave. between 12th and 13th Aves., 831/624-2741, www.thecolonialterrace.com, $219-400) is the best place in the small town to fall asleep to the white noise of breaking waves. In addition to superb ocean views from the property, Colonial Terrace has a nice brick courtyard surrounded by blooming flowers that guests can enjoy on the area's warmer days.

Tally Ho Inn (Monte Verde St. and 6th Ave., 831/624-2232, www.tallyho-inn.com, $199-359) seeks to conjure a feeling of the English countryside with its flowers, gardens, and fireplaces. The units all have private decks and marble bathrooms. Spend a little more for a room with a fireplace or Jacuzzi tub.

You'll figure out that the **Pine Inn** (Ocean Ave. and Lincoln St., 831/624-3851 or 800/228-3851, www.pineinn.com, $179-359) was built in a different time when you enter the hotel lobby, which has wood paneling and is decorated with antiques. Constructed in 1889, the inn has unique rooms including some with marble bathrooms and Jacuzzi tubs. A breakfast buffet is served to guests on weekday mornings. The complex is home to a handful of shops and **Il Fornaio** (831/622-5100, www.ilfornaio.com, Mon.-Thurs. 8am-9pm, Fri. 8am-10pm, Sat. 9am-10pm, Sun. 9am-9pm, $12-34), an Italian restaurant.

Coachman's Inn (San Carlos St. and 8th Ave., 831/624-6421, www.coachmansinn.com, $225-350) is a small downtown motel with 30 clean, well-appointed rooms. The rooms were recently refurbished with new carpeting and bedding, and they all include large flat screens, mini-fridges, microwaves, and Keurig coffeemakers. Some also have gas fireplaces and jetted spa tubs. A stay includes access to a gated patio that has a hot tub, sauna, and exercise bike. The inn's staff serves wine and appetizers in the afternoon along with a buffet-style breakfast in the morning.

There are no TVs or telephones at the **Sea View Inn** (El Camino Real between 11th and 12th Aves., 831/624-8778, http://seaviewinncarmel.com, $180-295) to distract you from the sounds of the nearby ocean just three

the ornate entrance at the Cypress Inn

others have old-fashioned wood-burning models.

Over $250

Touted by *Architectural Digest*, ★ **Tradewinds Carmel** (Mission St. and 3rd Ave., 831/624-2776, www.tradewinds.com, $250-550) brings a touch of the Far East to California. Inspired by the initial proprietor's time spent in Japan, the 28 serene hotel rooms are decorated with Asian antiquities and live orchids. Outside, the grounds feature a water fountain that passes through bamboo shoots and horsetails along with a meditation garden, where an oversized Buddha head overlooks a trio of cascading pools. A stay comes with continental breakfast that includes French pastries and fruit.

The landmark Carmel-by-the-Sea hotel the ★ **Cypress Inn** (Lincoln St. and 7th Ave., 831/624-3871 or 800/443-7443, www.cypress-inn.com, $245-595) welcomes both human and dog guests in a white, ornate Mediterranean-inspired building. The property is co-owned by actress, singer, and animal rights activist Doris Day. Her influence is notable throughout the hotel, from her movie posters adorning the walls downstairs to the fact that every one of the inn's rooms is dog-friendly. This is one of the most pro-pup hotels in the whole state: There are dog cookies at the front desk, water bowls are situated around the hotel, and dog beds and towels are provided by request. The rooms all come with complimentary cream sherry, fruit, and snacks for guests, while some also have fireplaces and/or jetted tubs. Human visitors are also treated to a breakfast in the morning that includes several hot items. In the standout Tower Suite, a multilevel unit, the bedroom is located in a tower with views of the sea.

The ★ **Forest Lodge** (Ocean Ave. at Torres St. and Mountain View Ave., 831/624-7372, www.carmelforestlodge.com, $255-375), with its trees and several terraces, feels like it's in the middle of a park. It's in a tranquil location, yet Ocean Avenue is just a few feet down the hill. The six units are in three different

blocks away. The eight guestrooms are all done up differently. The ground-floor common area includes a living room, breakfast room, porch, and garden.

Outside of downtown Carmel, **Mission Ranch** (26270 Dolores St., 831/624-6436, www.missionranchcarmel.com, $165-380) is a sprawling old ranch complex with views of sheep-filled pastures and Point Lobos in the distance. If you get a glimpse of Mission Ranch's owner, it might just make your day: It's none other than Hollywood icon and former Carmel-by-the-Sea mayor Clint Eastwood. On the grounds is a restaurant with a nightly sing-along piano bar that is popular with Carmel's silver-haired crowd.

The **Carmel River Inn** (26600 Oliver Rd., 831/624-1575 or 800/882-8142, http://carmel-riverinn.com, $229-269) has two sets of accommodations on its 10 acres near the Carmel River: inn rooms and cottages. The inn rooms have basic amenities including mini-fridges and coffeemakers. Some of the one- or two-bedroom cottages have gas fireplaces, while buildings that have seen extraordinary figures pass through, including Albert Einstein and photographer Edward Weston. The uniquely decorated units all have fridges, microwaves, and complimentary items like cream sherry. The Forest Lodge is ideal for larger parties and families: Even the smallest unit, the Garden House, has two bedrooms.

L'Auberge Carmel (Monte Verde St. and 7th Ave., 831/624-8578, www.laubergecarmel. com, $430-725) is a luxurious hotel located in a former apartment building dating to the 1920s. Every one of its 20 rooms is unique, and all have radiant floor heating in the bathrooms and in-room espresso machines. The rooms are decorated in a French country style and include striking black-and-white photos of the coast by Carmel photographer Helmet Horn. A stay includes a fully prepared breakfast and valet services. This is the kind of place where the staff tries to accommodate your every request.

South of downtown Carmel-by-the-Sea, the **Tickle Pink Inn** (155 Highland Dr., 831/624-1244, www.ticklepinkinn.com, $329-629) is located in the Carmel Highlands, which is otherwise known as the gateway to Big Sur. The inn's cutesy name comes from the couple that used to reside in the inn: California state senator Edward Tickle and his wife Bess Tickle. All of the 35 rooms and suites have balconies (except for one, which has a bay window). Seventeen units also warm guests with in-room fireplaces. Other amenities include an outdoor hot tub, an evening wine-and-cheese reception, and an expanded continental breakfast with homemade pastries.

The initial structure at ★ **La Playa Carmel** (El Camino Real at 8th Ave., 831/293-6100 or 800/582-8900, www.laplayahotel.com, $219-479) was a mansion built for a member of the Ghirardelli family by a renowned landscape painter in 1905. Though La Playa underwent an extensive remodel in 2012, it still has many features from an earlier era including its dark, wood-walled bar, a stained glass window, and a tiled staircase. Beginning with check-in, you'll feel at home when you are handed a welcoming glass of champagne or sangria and take in the cozy lobby with its gas fireplace. Half of the 75 classic and cozy rooms look out on nearby Carmel Beach, Pebble Beach, and Point Lobos, and the beach is only two blocks away. La Playa's grounds are worthy of exploration, from the collection of newspapers in the library to the heated outdoor pool and the oversized chessboard and pieces in the courtyard. The staff will treat

La Playa Carmel

you to an afternoon wine reception, an evening dessert of fresh baked cookies served with cold milk, and a champagne breakfast that includes made-to-order omelets and waffles. La Playa Carmel is easily one of the best places in town for spoiling yourself.

FOOD
American
Grasing's Coastal Cuisine (6th Ave. and Mission St., 831/624-6462, http://grasings.com, daily 11am-3pm and 5pm-9pm, $25-62) serves the creations of Chef Kurt Grasing in a cute cottage atmosphere that is quintessential Carmel. Begin by flipping through the impressive 42-page wine list in which cabernets, pinots, and Burgundies are well represented. The dinner menu has a chophouse section, featuring fine steaks from Nebraska. The other entrées include farm-raised Monterey Bay abalone and a tasty paella studded with prawns, clams, mussels, and spicy sausage in a tomato broth over orzo and vegetables. In the high-ceilinged dining room, waiters in vests and ties serve guests, while the outdoor patio is dog-friendly. Save room for the subtle but worthwhile apple-caramel bread pudding.

The **Rio Grill** (101 Crossroads Blvd., 831/625-5436, www.riogrill.com, Mon.-Sat.

11:30am-10pm, Sun. 11:30am-3pm and 4pm-10pm, $12-39) has been luring diners to the Crossroads Shopping Center for decades. The grill's menu includes inventive fare like duck chilaquiles and stuffed poblano pepper. The popular happy hour (Mon.-Fri. 4pm-6:30pm, Sun. 4pm-10pm) offers a taste of the restaurant's cuisine in the bar, which is decorated with murals of local luminaries.

Breakfast
Katy's Place (6th Ave. and Mission St., 831/624-0199, www.katysplacecarmel.com, daily 7am-2pm, $10-20) serves gigantic, classic breakfasts such as Denver omelets and biscuits and gravy, inside or outside on a redwood-shaded deck. This longtime local favorite also has some unique eggs Benedict combinations including the Benedict Romanoff, with smoked salmon and caviar, and a Hawaiian version with bacon and pineapple.

★ **Carmel Belle** (Doud Craft Studios, Ocean Ave. and San Carlos St., 831/624-1600, www.carmelbelle.com, Mon.-Tues. 8am-5pm, Wed.-Sun. 8am-9pm, $6-25) is a little eatery with a big attention to detail. In the open section of an indoor mall, Carmel Belle serves up creative fare for breakfast and lunch, including an open-faced breakfast sandwich

a tasty sandwich at Carmel Belle

featuring a slab of toast topped with a poached egg, thick strips of bacon, a bed of arugula, and wedges of fresh avocado. Its slow-cooked Berkshire pork sandwich with red onion-currant chutney is a perfect example of what can happen when savory meets sweet. Dinner (Wed.-Sun. only) features a choice of two main items and three side items.

The **Little Swiss Café** (6th Ave. and Dolores St., 831/624-5007, Mon.-Sat. 7:30am-3pm, Sun. 8am-2pm, $10-13) is a perennial local go-to for breakfast. Grab a booth and gaze at the murals covering the walls. You might notice something is off when you spot a penguin or the Eiffel Tower hidden in the European countryside. The café favorites include blintzes and egg Benedicts.

From Scratch Restaurant (3626 The Barnyard Shopping Center, 831/625-2448, http://fromscratchrestaurant.com, daily 8am-2:30pm, $7-16) has been featured on the Food Network's *Diners, Drive-ins and Dives*. Start your day in The Barnyard Shopping Center with pancakes, a skillet platter, or an omelet. Or stop in for lunch when wraps, soups, salads, and a crustless quiche of the day are served.

Bakeries and Coffee Shops

Run by a French master baker and a French pastry chef, **Lafayette Bakery** (3672 The Barnyard Shopping Center, Ste. E22, 831/915-6286, www.lafayettebakery.com, Mon.-Sat. 7am-6pm, Sun. 7am-4pm) can tempt as much as any Paris bakery. The delectable goods, including artisan breads, pastries, and baguette sandwiches, are showcased at the counter.

The **Carmel Valley Coffee Roasting Co.** (Ocean Ave. between Lincoln St. and Monte Verde St., 831/626-2913, www.carmelcoffee-roasters.com, Sun.-Thurs. 6am-6pm, Fri.-Sat. 6am-7pm) is a great place to get caffeinated during a walk around Carmel-by-the-Sea. The brick-floored café has a few seats and tables on an upper level at which to drink or eat a pastry or premade sandwich. There are two other locations in Carmel, at the Crossroads Shopping Center (246 Crossroads Shopping Center,

831/626-8784, Mon.-Fri. 6:30am-5pm, Sat.-Sun. 7am-5pm) and at The Barnyard Shopping Center (3720 The Barnyard, 831/620-0844, Mon.-Fri. 6am-6pm, Sat. 7am-5pm, Sun. 7am-4pm).

Chinese

For an authentic hole-in-the-wall locals' dining experience, seek out **Tommy's Wok** (San Carlos St. between Ocean Ave. and 7th Ave., 831/624-8518, Tues.-Sun. 11:30am-2:30pm and 4:30pm-9pm, $10-16). You can dine in or take out items like the moo shu pork. It's often crowded.

French

If the international feel of Carmel-by-the-Sea has put you in the mood for European food, have dinner at the quaint French eatery **La Bicyclette** (Dolores St. at 7th Ave., 831/622-9899, www.labicycletterestaurant.com, daily 8am-11am, 11:30am-3:30pm, and 5pm-10pm, $14-28). The dinner menu changes nightly, but always includes wood-fired pizzas. Owned by the same family, **Casanova** (5th Ave. between Mission St. and San Carlos St., Mon.-Thurs. 11:30am-3pm and 5pm-10pm, Fri.-Sat. 5pm-10:30pm, $23-49) oozes romance. This charming Carmel fixture does a dinner menu that focuses on rustic French and Italian cuisine with a touch of Belgian influence as well. Expect pastas along with a small range of meat and seafood entrées. The restaurant built a special room to house a table that artist Vincent Van Gogh once dined on.

One of Carmel's famed French restaurants is **Andre's Bouchee** (Mission St. between Ocean Ave. and 7th Ave., 831/626-7880, Wed.-Sun. 11:30am-2pm and 5:30pm-9:30pm, Mon.-Tues. 5:30pm-9:30pm, $26-36). Inside the brick building, Chef Jacques Zagouri serves indulgent French staples including escargot, duck confit, and pan-seared sweetbreads.

L'Escargot (Mission St. and 4th Ave., 831/620-1942, www.escargot-carmel.com, daily 5:30pm-11:30pm, $17-38) is a fine French restaurant. The menu often includes indulgent favorites like rack of lamb, roasted duck breast, and chicken in a black truffle Madeira cream sauce. The wine list skews French and Californian.

Italian

On paper, **Vesuvio** (6th Ave. and Junipero St., 831/625-1766, http://chefpepe.com/restaurants/vesuvio, daily 4pm-11pm, $16-32) is an Italian restaurant, with dishes like cannelloni, gnocchi, and wood-oven pizzas, but there's a lot more going on. There's a popular rooftop bar with fire pits, heat lamps, and love seats. There's also a great eight-ounce burger topped with bunches of caramelized onions, oozing cambozola cheese, and a chipotle aioli on a house-made roll. It can be ordered as a "Grown-up Happy Meal" with fries and a well cocktail or glass of wine.

At popular **La Balena** (Junipero St. between 5th and 6th Aves., 831/250-6295, http://labalenacarmel.com, Tues.-Wed. 5pm-10pm, Thurs.-Sun. 11:30am-3:30pm and 5pm-10pm, $21-33), a farm-to-kitchen Italian restaurant, it's difficult to secure a reservation. Menu items change, but may include fresh-made pastas and an osso buco. The fried half-chicken entrée, available on Sundays and Tuesdays, is a local favorite.

Mediterranean

While **Dametra Café** (Ocean Ave. at Lincoln St., 831/622-7766, www.dametracafe.com, daily 11am-11pm, $12-28) has a wide-ranging international menu that includes an all-American cheeseburger and Italian dishes like spaghetti alla Bolognese, it's best to go with the lively restaurant's signature Mediterranean food. The Greek chicken kebab entrée is a revelation, with two chicken and vegetable kebabs drizzled with a distinct aioli sauce, all served over yellow rice and with a Greek salad. The owner and his staff have been known to serenade evening diners.

Come into ★ **Yafa** (5th Ave. and Junipero St., 831/624-9232, www.yafarestaurant.com, daily 5pm-10pm, $14-30), and you'll feel like you have suddenly become a member of a giant Mediterranean family. Owner and manager Ben Khader and his father will make you feel utterly welcome as you enter this popular one-room restaurant. The restaurant makes dining fun, with occasional eruptions of singing, dancing, and clapping. The menu includes pastas (lamb ravioli, lobster ravioli) along with Mediterranean classics (Moroccan chicken, lamb kebabs). Try the Aleppo Kefta platter, starring a tasty ground beef-and-lamb kebab mixture.

Carmel-by-the-Sea's lively Dametra Café

Pizza

Allegro Gourmet Pizzeria (3770 The Barnyard Shopping Center, 831/626-5454, Sun.-Thurs. 11am-9:30pm, Fri.-Sat. 11am-10pm, $7-30) doesn't just serve up your standard slice of pie. There are some inspired creations here, including a chicken Thai peanut pie and the O Sole Mio, with cream cheese, mozzarella, avocado, sun-dried tomato, and sweet red onion.

Seafood

The **Flying Fish Grill** (Mission St. between Ocean Ave. and 7th Ave., 831/625-1962, http://flyingfishgrill.com, daily 5pm-10pm, $26-37) serves Japanese-style seafood with a California twist in the Carmel Plaza open-air shopping mall. Entrées include rare peppered ahi and black bean halibut. You might even be able to score a market-priced meal of Monterey abalone. Whatever you order, you'll dine in a dimly lit, wood-walled establishment.

Sushi

★ **Akaoni** (Mission St. and 6th Ave., 831/620-1516, Tues.-Sun. 5:30pm-8:30pm, $7-40) is a superb hole-in-the-wall sushi restaurant. Sit at the bar or at one of the few tables,

if you can get in. The menu includes tempura-fried oysters, soft-shell crab rolls, and *unagi donburi* (eel bowl). Look at the daily specials on the whiteboard for the newest seafood, including items flown in from Japan. For adventurous diners, the live Monterey spot prawn is the freshest seafood you'll ever eat.

Tapas

Affina (San Carlos St. and 6th Ave., 831/915/4756, Mon. 5:30pm-11pm, Tues.-Sun. 11:30am-4pm and 5:30pm-11pm, $17-45) has injected a dose of cool into Carmel's dining scene. The corner restaurant has a white grand piano and a popular wraparound bar. Old black-and-white movies are projected above the piano for ambience. The menu may include fried chicken, pork shoulder, or baby octopus.

Markets

★ **Bruno's Market & Deli** (6th Ave. and Junipero St., 831/624-3821, www.brunosmar-ket.com, daily 7am-8pm) is the place to pick up supplies for a Carmel Beach picnic. They have great made-to-order sandwiches, and if there is a long line at the counter, they have a batch of premade sandwiches including meatloaf, turkey, and sausage in a fridge across

The Nielson Bros. Market has a great wine shop.

from the deli case. Bruno's also has a good selection of sodas and juices to wash it all down.

Nielsen Bros. Market (7th Ave. and San Carlos St., 831/624-6441, daily 8am-7pm) is the market to stop at if you are looking to buy fine wines or rare liquors. The wine room has local labels and sometimes hosts a wine consultant. The market makes sandwiches and has basic goods.

INFORMATION AND SERVICES

You'll find the **Carmel Visitors Center** (San Carlos St. between 5th and 6th Aves., 831/624-2522 or 800/550-4333, www.carmelcalifornia.org, daily 10am-5pm) right in the middle of downtown Carmel-by-the-Sea.

For more information about the town and current events, pick up a copy of the weekly *Carmel Pine Cone* (www.pineconearchive.com), the local newspaper. It also has a (possibly unintentionally) funny police log.

The nearest major medical center to Carmel-by-the-Sea and the Carmel Valley is in nearby Monterey: the **Community Hospital of the Monterey Peninsula** (23625 Holman Hwy., Monterey, 831/624-5311, www.chomp.org).

TRANSPORTATION

If you've made it to Monterey by car, getting to Carmel is a piece of cake. The quick and free way to get to Carmel from the north or the south is via Highway 1. From Highway 1, take Ocean Avenue into the middle of downtown Carmel. A more expensive but more beautiful route is via Pebble Beach's 17-Mile Drive.

As you read the addresses in Carmel-by-the-Sea and begin to explore the neighborhoods, you'll realize something interesting. There are no street addresses. (Some years ago Carmel residents voted not to enact door-to-door mail delivery, thus there is no need for numeric addresses on buildings.) So you'll need to pay close attention to the street names and the block you're on. Just to make things even more fun, street signs can be difficult to see amid the mature foliage, and a dearth of streetlights can make them nearly impossible to find at night. If you can, show up during the day to get the lay of the land before trying to navigate after dark.

Pebble Beach

Located between Pacific Grove and Carmel, the gated community of Pebble Beach lays claim to some of the Monterey Peninsula's best and highest-priced real estate. Pebble Beach is famous for the scenic 17-Mile Drive and its collection of high-end resorts, restaurants, spas, and golf courses owned by the Pebble Beach Company, a partnership that includes golf legend Arnold Palmer and film legend Clint Eastwood. In February, Pebble Beach hosts the annual AT&T Pebble Beach National Pro-Am, a charity golf tournament that pairs professional golfers with celebrities.

SIGHTS
★ 17-Mile Drive

The best way to take in the stunning scenery of Pebble Beach is the **17-Mile Drive.** But don't get too excited yet—long ago, the all-powerful Pebble Beach Corporation realized that the local scenery is also a precious commodity, and began charging a toll ($10/vehicle). The good news is that when you pay the fee at the gatehouse, you receive a map of the drive that describes the parks and sights that you will pass along the winding coastal road: the much-photographed Lone Cypress, the beaches of Spanish Bay, and Pebble Beach's golf course, resort, and housing complex. If you're in a hurry, you can get from one end of the 17-Mile Drive to the other in 20 minutes. But go slowly and stop often to enjoy the natural beauty of the area (and get your money's worth). There are plenty of turnouts where you can stop to take photos of the iconic cypress trees and stunning coastline. You can picnic at many of the beaches, most of which have basic restroom facilities and ample parking lots. The only food and gas to be had are at the Inn at Spanish Bay and the Lodge at Pebble Beach.

ENTERTAINMENT AND EVENTS

If you dream of watching Bill Murray or Kevin Costner play golf—and who doesn't?—plan a trip to Pebble Beach in February for the **AT&T Pebble Beach National Pro-Am** (831/649-1533, www.attpbgolf.com, Feb., event prices vary). This almost weeklong tournament pairing pro golfers with Hollywood celebrities is the biggest annual event in Pebble Beach and arguably the whole Monterey Peninsula.

The biggest epicurean event on the peninsula is the annual **Pebble Beach Food & Wine** (866/907-3663, www.pbfw.com, Apr., event prices vary). Hobnob with celebrity chefs from your favorite cooking shows and restaurants during four days of wine tastings, cooking demos, and indulgent dinners.

The **Concours d' Elegance** (831/622-1700 or 877/693-0009, www.pebblebeachconcours. net, Aug., event prices vary) is a showcase of upscale and rare automobiles, held on the 18th hole of the Pebble Beach Golf Links. Former *Tonight Show* host and car enthusiast Jay Leno almost always attends this annual event.

SPORTS AND RECREATION

Biking

Traveling the **17-Mile Drive** by bike means you don't have to pay the $10 vehicle admission fee. It's also a great bike route. Cyclists can enjoy the smells and sounds of the spectacular coastline in a way that car passengers just can't. Expect fairly flat terrain with lots of twists and turns, and a ride that runs . . . about 17 miles. Foggy conditions can make this ride a bit slick in the summer, but spring and fall weather are perfect for pedaling.

Bay Bikes (3600 The Barnyard Shopping Center, 831/655-2453, www.baybikes.com, Sun.-Mon. 10am-5pm, Tues.-Fri. 10am-6pm, Sat. 9am-6pm, bike rentals $8-16/hr, $24-48/ four hours) in Carmel is the closest place to rent a bike to tool around 17-Mile Drive. The options include cruisers, hybrid bikes, road bikes, and tandems.

Golf

There's no place for golfing quite like Pebble Beach. Golf has been a major pastime here since the late 19th century; today avid golfers come from around the world to tee off inside the gated community. You can play courses trodden by the likes of Tiger Woods and Jack Nicholson, pause a moment before you putt to take in the sight of the stunning Pacific Ocean, and pay $200 or more for a single round of golf.

One of the Pebble Beach Resort courses, the 18-hole, par-72 **Spyglass Hill** (1700 17-Mile Dr., 800/654-9300, www.pebblebeach. com, $395) gets its name from the Robert Louis Stevenson Novel *Treasure Island*. Don't be fooled—the holes on this beautiful course may be named for characters in an adventure novel, but that doesn't mean they're easy. Spyglass Hill boasts some of the most challenging play in this golf course-laden region. Expect a few bogeys, and tee off from the championship level at your own (ego's) risk.

Another favorite with the Pebble Beach crowd is the famed 18-hole, par-72 **Poppy Hills Golf Course** (3200 Lopez Rd., 831/622-8239, www.poppyhillsgolf.com, $210). Though it's not managed by the same company, Poppy Hills shares amenities with Pebble Beach golf courses. Expect the same level of care and devotion to the maintenance of the course and your experience as a player.

The **Pebble Beach Golf Links** (1700 17-Mile Dr., 800/877-0597, www.pebblebeach. com, $495) has been called nothing short of the nation's best golf course by *Golf Digest*. The high ranking might have something to do with the fact that some of the fairways are perched above the Pacific Ocean. The course has hosted six men's championships and is one of three courses utilized during the popular AT&T Pro-Am.

Less pricey to play than the Pebble Beach Golf Links course, **The Links at Spanish Bay** (2700 17-Mile Dr., 831/647-7495 or 800/877-0597, $155-270) is located on some of Pebble Beach's native sand dune habitat. Due to the environmental sensitivity of the grounds, the course caps the amount of players and spectators on the greens.

Spas

Of course there's a spa in Pebble Beach, named **The Spa at Pebble Beach** (1518 Cypress Dr., 831/649-7615 or 800/877-0597, www.pebblebeach.com, daily 8:30am-7:30pm, massages $165-470). They have specialty massages for golfers before or after a day on the greens.

Kayaking and Stand-Up Paddleboarding

Pebble Beach's **Stillwater Cove** (adjacent to The Beach & Tennis Club) on the south end of 17-Mile Drive is a terrific place to kayak or stand-up paddleboard. There is a public boat launch here to get your craft in the water. Offshore is an island that blocks swells, and there is a kelp forest behind it. To the north is Pescadero Point, while Arrowhead Point is to the south. **Adventures By the Sea** (831/372-1807, www.adventuresbythesea.com, $85 pp) and **Monterey Bay Kayaks** (800/649-5357, www.montereybaykayaks.com, $120 pp) do guided tours of Stillwater Cove. To bring in your own kayak or SUP, you'll have to pay the Pebble Beach admission fee and then head to the coastal access ramp. It's a good idea to make a parking reservation (831/625-8536, free) in advance.

ACCOMMODATIONS

You need to drop some serious money to stay in Pebble Beach. Expect luxury amenities at **The Lodge at Pebble Beach** (1700 17-Mile Dr., 831/647-7500 or 800/654-9300, www.pebblebeach.com, $790-1,070), located by the 18th hole of the Pebble Beach Golf Links. Most rooms and suites have wood-burning

fireplaces as well as private patios or balconies. Some of the high-end rooms have their own spas. A stay also includes access to The Beach & Tennis Club, which has a heated outdoor pool, a whirlpool spa, and a tennis pavilion.

Like The Lodge at Pebble Beach, **The Inn at Spanish Bay** (2700 17-Mile Dr., 831/647-7500 or 800/654-9300, www.pebblebeach.com, $670-3,060) has rooms with fireplaces and decks or patios. There's also a fitness center and tennis pavilion on site.

A favorite of the luxury crowd, **Casa Palmero** (1518 Cypress Dr., 831/647-7500 or 800/877-0597, www.pebblebeach.com, $940-2,990) has just 24 rooms on its Mediterranean-style estate. The units all have large soaking tubs and wood-burning fireplaces for a romantic mood. Amenities include a billiards table, a library, and an outdoor heated pool.

FOOD

To experience the luxury of Pebble Beach without dropping your savings on a night's stay, consider having lunch, dinner, or a drink in the exclusive community before heading back to less expensive lodging in nearby Pacific Grove or Monterey.

The Hawaiian fusion cuisine of celebrity chef Roy Yamaguchi takes center stage at **Roy's at Pebble Beach** (The Inn at Spanish Bay, 2700 17-Mile Dr., 831/647-7423, www.pebblebeach.com, daily 6:30am-10pm, $26-78). Island-inspired dishes include seafood and sushi, all with an Asian flair. Another option at The Inn at Spanish Bay is **Peppoli** (The Inn at Spanish Bay, 2700 17-Mile Dr., 831/647-7433, www.pebblebeach.com, daily 5:30pm-10pm, $20-100). Head here for a hearty Italian dinner of gnocchi with black truffle cream sauce or seared local halibut.

If you want to experience Pebble Beach in a low-key way, **The Tap Room** (The Lodge at Pebble Beach, 1700 17-Mile Dr., 831/625-8535, daily 11am-11:30pm, $17-52) is your place. This wood-walled bar serves burgers, bratwurst, Wagyu beef filet mignon, and fresh Maine lobster (the prime rib chili is also worth your time). The Tap Room has 14 beers on tap at an inflated price ($10.75), yet it will all be money well spent if you end up spending the afternoon drinking with Bill Murray, an occasional customer.

Golfers might not need to know much more than that **The Bench Restaurant** (The Lodge at Pebble Beach, 1700 17-Mile Dr., 800/654-9300, daily 10am-10pm, $18-31) overlooks the famed 18th hole of the Pebble Beach Golf Links. The chef employs wood-roasting and open-flame cooking techniques to create wood-fired Brussels sprouts and grilled steaks.

Pebble Beach newcomer **Porter's in the Forest** (3200 Lopez Rd., 831/622-8240, http://poppyhillsgolf.com/porters, daily 6am-7pm,

$13-25) is beside the Poppy Hills Golf Course in Pebble Beach. It serves ingenious twists on typical clubhouse fare with items like a Korean Philly cheesesteak and short rib fries, braised ribs, and a Muenster cheese au gratin over French fries. They serve breakfast, lunch, and a twilight menu.

GETTING THERE

There are several gates to get into Pebble Beach including three in Pacific Grove and one in Carmel. Admission to Pebble Beach is $10 if you aren't staying here. You can get the fee waived if you are going in to dine at a Pebble Beach restaurant. Just make a reservation and tell the guard at the entry gate that you have one.

Carmel Valley

When the Carmel coastline gets socked in with summer fog, locals flock inland to the reliably sunny Carmel Valley. But locals aren't the only people making their way to this corridor through the Santa Lucia Mountains. Carmel Valley is becoming known as a burgeoning but still unassuming wine region due to its tasty cabernet sauvignons, merlots, and other reds.

The landscape changes quickly as you leave the coast: You'll see the mountains rising above you, and the land is dotted with farms, ranches, and orchards. Thirteen miles east of Highway 1 is the unincorporated Carmel Valley Village. This small strip of businesses hugging Carmel Valley Road includes a collection of wineries, tasting rooms, restaurants, and even an Old West saloon.

SIGHTS
Earthbound Farm

Today one of the largest purveyors of organic produce in the United States, Earthbound Farm began at the **Earthbound Farm's Farm Stand** (7250 Carmel Valley Rd., 831/625-6219, www.ebfarm.com, Mon.-Sat.

8am-6:30pm, Sun. 9am-6pm). This 2.5-acre farm and roadside stand offers visitors easy access to the company's smallish facility in the Carmel Valley. Drive up to the farm stand and browse a variety of organic fruits, veggies, and flowers. Outdoors, you can ramble into the fields, checking out the chamomile labyrinth and the kids' garden (yes, your kids can look *and* touch). Select and harvest your own fresh herbs from the cut-your-own-herb garden, or leave the cooking to the experts and purchase delicious prepared organic dishes at the farm stand. If you're interested in a more in-depth guided tour of the farm, check the website for a schedule of walks, which will take you, a group, and an expert guide—perhaps a chef or famous local foodie—out into the fields for a look at what's growing and how to use it.

Carmel Valley Village

The social and business center of Carmel Valley is the **Carmel Valley Village,** an unincorporated business district 13 miles inland from the junction of Carmel Valley Road and Highway 1. This is the easiest place to go wine tasting without doing a lot of driving, as there

Carmel Valley

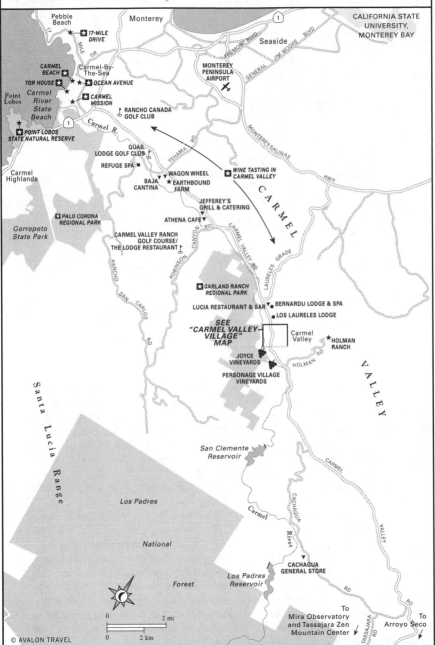

Pebble Beach

Monterey

CALIFORNIA STATE UNIVERSITY, MONTEREY BAY

Seaside

★ 17-MILE DRIVE

MILE DR

FREMONT BLVD

GENERAL

JIM MOORE BLVD

CARMEL BEACH ★
TOR HOUSE ★
Carmel-By-The-Sea

★ OCEAN AVENUE

MONTEREY PENINSULA AIRPORT

Point Lobos

★ CARMEL MISSION

★ RANCHO CANADA GOLF CLUB

Carmel River State Beach

Carmel R.

TEHAMA RD

MONTEREY-SALINAS HWY

★ POINT LOBOS STATE NATURAL RESERVE

QUAIL LODGE GOLF CLUB

REFUGE SPA ■

★ WINE TASTING IN CARMEL VALLEY

Carmel Highlands

BAJA CANTINA ▼
★ WAGON WHEEL
★ EARTHBOUND FARM

C A R M E L

JEFFEREY'S GRILL & CATERING ▼

ATHENA CAFE ▼

CANYON RD

CARMEL VALLEY RD

★ PALO CORONA REGIONAL PARK

Garrapata State Park

CARMEL VALLEY RANCH GOLF COURSE/ THE LODGE RESTAURANT ▼

ROBINSON

LAURELES GRADE

RANCHO SAN CARLOS RD

★ GARLAND RANCH REGIONAL PARK

LUCIA RESTAURANT & BAR

● BERNARDU LODGE & SPA
● LOS LAURELES LODGE

SEE "CARMEL VALLEY VILLAGE" MAP

Carmel Valley

★ HOLMAN RANCH

V A L L E Y

JOYCE VINEYARDS

PERSONAGE VILLAGE VINEYARDS

HOLMAN RD

S a n t a   L u c i a   R a n g e

San Clemente Reservoir

CARMEL

Los Padres

Carmel

CACHAGUA

National

CACHAGUA VALLEY RD

Los Padres Reservoir

Forest

CACHAGUA River

▼ CACHAGUA GENERAL STORE

N

0   2 mi
0   2 km

TASSAJARA RD

RD

To Mira Observatory and Tassajara Zen Mountain Center

To Arroyo Seco

© AVALON TRAVEL

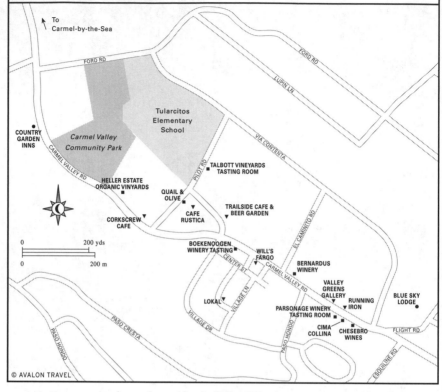

are six tasting rooms on the southeast side of the village just feet away from one another. There are also several fine restaurants and a classic Western tavern called the Running Iron Restaurant & Saloon.

★ Wine Tasting

The Carmel Valley's tiny size necessarily limits the number of vineyards and wineries that can set up shop there. But this small, charming wine region makes for a perfect wine-tasting day trip from Carmel, Monterey, or even Big Sur. Small crowds, light traffic, and meaningful tasting experiences categorize this area, which still has many family-owned wineries. You'll get personal attention and delicious wines, all in a gorgeous green setting.

One fun way to get around the Carmel Valley Village's wineries is to hitch a ride on the **Happy Trails Wagon Tour** (831/970-8198, Wed.-Sun. noon-4pm). Cowboy Pete pulls a 10-passenger wagon behind an antique tractor to wineries and restaurants in the immediate area.

The **Bernardus Winery** (5 W. Carmel Valley Rd., 831/298-8021 or 800/223-2533, www.bernardus.com/winery, daily 11am-5pm, tasting $12-20) sits on a vineyard estate that also hosts a connected luxurious lodge and gourmet restaurant. Bernardus creates a small list of wines. The grapes growing all around you go into the pride of the winery: the Bordeaux-style blended red Marinus Vineyard wine. Other varietals (chardonnay, pinot noir, and sauvignon blanc) come from cool coastal vineyards. If you're interested and lucky, you might also get to sip some small-batch vintages of single-vineyard wines that are available only in the tasting room.

On the other end of the spectrum, tiny **Parsonage Village Vineyard** (19 E. Carmel Valley Rd., 831/659-7322, www.parsonagewine.com, daily 11am-5pm, tasting $10) has a tasting room that sits in a little strip of shops, the space glowing with light that bounces off the copper of the bar. The space also is home to a display of quilts. At the bar, you'll taste wonderful Syrahs, hearty cabernet sauvignons, and surprisingly deep and complex blends—the Snosrap (that's Parsons spelled backwards) table wine is inexpensive for the region and incredibly tasty. If you find a vintage you love at Parsonage, buy it then and there since they sell out of many of their wines every year.

Just a few feet away from Parsonage is the tasting room for **Chesebro Wines** (19 E. Carmel Valley Rd., Ste. D, 831/659-2125, www. chesebrowines.com, Thurs.-Fri. 1pm-5pm, Sat.-Sun. and holidays noon-5pm, tasting $10). A former Bernardus Winery employee, Mark Chesebro makes chardonnays, pinot noirs, Grenache rosés, and vermentino, their signature white wine. These wines are smart and affordable.

In the same strip of wineries, **Cima Collina** (19 E. Carmel Valley Rd., Ste. A, 831/620-0645, http://cimacollina.com, summer Sun.-Tues. noon-6pm, Wed.-Sat. noon-7pm, winter daily noon-6pm, tasting $5) has a tasting room that looks like a farmhouse with a front porch. Inside, enjoy pinot noir, chardonnay, sauvignon blanc, pinot blanc, and Cima Collina wines that are only available in the tasting room, like the Howlin' Good Red.

Another smaller, well-regarded Carmel winery is the **Heller Estate Organic Vineyards** (69 W. Carmel Valley Rd., 831/659-6220, www.hellerestate.com, daily 11am-5pm, tasting $11-15). Heller is a completely organic winery that uses natural methods, including predatory wasps, to get rid of vineyard insect pests rather than resorting to chemical-laden sprays. After visiting the tasting room, sit outdoors in Heller's sculpture garden while enjoying a bottle in the Carmel Valley sun.

Folktale Winery and Vineyards (8940 Carmel Valley Rd., 831/293-7500, www.folktalewinery.com, summer 11am-8pm, winter 11am-7pm, tasting $20) has taken over the former Chateau Julien property and promised to liven up the local wine scene. They aim to be "an extension of your backyard"

Chesebro Wines tasting room

with bocce, horseshoes, and corn hole. The winery has even teamed up with local radio station KRML to put on concerts in their barrel room.

Talbott Vineyards (25 Pilot Rd., 831/659-3500, www.talbottvineyards.com, daily 11am-5pm, tasting $10-15) utilizes two vineyards 18 miles apart to produce their chardonnays and pinot noirs. At the Carmel Valley tasting room, they pour six of their chardonnays and six of their pinot noirs alongside an impressive collection of vintage motorcycles. There's another tasting room near Salinas (1380 River Rd., 831/675-0942, Thurs.-Mon. 11am-4:30pm, tasting $10-15).

Boekenoogen Vineyard & Winery (24 W. Carmel Valley Rd., 831/659-4215, www.boekenoogenwines.com, daily 11am-5pm, tasting $8-10) was a cattle ranch before it became a winery. Their tasting room offers pinot noirs, chardonnays, and Syrahs, as well as a garden patio for those sunny Carmel Valley afternoons.

ENTERTAINMENT AND EVENTS
Bars

While many of Carmel Valley's ranches are being transformed into vineyards, **The**

Running Iron Restaurant and Saloon (24 E. Carmel Valley Rd., 831/659-4633, www.runningironrestaurantandsaloon.com, Mon.-Fri. 11am-2am, Sat. 10am-2am, Sun. 9am-2am) keeps the region's cowboy past alive. This watering hole's Old West style includes branding irons and other cowboy paraphernalia hanging from the ceiling and the walls. In addition to serving beer, wine, and liquor, the Running Iron offers an extensive food menu with seafood, burgers, steaks, and ribs.

The **Valley Greens Gallery** (16 E. Carmel Valley Rd., 831/620-2985, www.valleygreensgallery.com, Sun.-Mon. and Wed.-Thurs. noon-8pm, Fri.-Sat. noon-11pm) pairs culture and craft beer in Carmel Valley Village. The beer part of the equation showcases four craft beers on tap that rotate weekly, along with over 60 more brews in bottles and cans. Get a beer and then wander around the space to take in the local art on the walls. The gallery also puts on all sorts of fun events, including painting classes, live music, movie nights (first Wed. of the month), and Open Vinyl Nights (Sun.), where folks can bring in their own records to be played.

Festivals and Events

In June, Carmel Valley Village shows off

Cima Collina's tasting room

its local wines and locally produced art at the daylong **Carmel Valley Art & Wine Celebration** (831/659-4000, www.carmel-valleychamber.com, June, free).

SHOPPING

Taste something besides wine at **The Quail & Olive** (3 Pilot Rd., 831/659-4288, www.quailandolive.com, Wed.-Mon. 11am-5pm). This specialty food store allows you taste their balsamic vinegars and olive oils. Olive oils come in rosemary, basil, truffle, and bacon versions.

SPORTS AND RECREATION
★ Garland Ranch Regional Park

The 4,462-acre **Garland Ranch Regional Park** (700 W. Carmel Valley Rd., 831/372-3196, www.mprpd.org, daily sunrise-sunset, free) allows hikers to take in all sorts of natural ecosystems from oak woodlands to redwood forests. With the park's elevation ranging 200-2,000 feet above sea level, it is also a great place to get a workout, and boasts the best **hiking trails** in Carmel Valley. The **Lupine Loop** (1.4 miles, easy) is a level, dog-friendly trail that circles around a flat part of the park. On the other end of the spectrum, the **Snively's Ridge Trail-Sky Loop** (6 miles, difficult) involves a very steep hike up to a ridge that offers views of the ocean and mountains. The **Mesa Trail** (1.6 miles, moderately strenuous) climbs to a saddle with valley views and a small pond.

Golf

If you want to play golf in the sun, head out to Carmel Valley. The **Quail Lodge Golf Club** (8505 Valley Greens Dr., 831/624-2888, www.quaillodge.com, $100-150) has an 18-hole course with 10 lakes, as well as an academy to improve your game. Two 18-hole courses at **Rancho Canada Golf Club** (4860 Carmel Valley Rd., 800/536-9459, www.

ranchocanada.com, $20-70) wind back and forth over the Carmel River.

Spas

After an exhausting day of wine tasting in Carmel Valley, unwind at **Refuge Spa** (27300 Rancho Carlos Rd., 831/620-7360, www.refuge.com, daily 10am-10pm, admission $44, treatments $109-125). Sprawled over two acres in the shadow of the Santa Lucia Mountains, this adult water park includes warm waterfalls tumbling into soaking pools and two kinds of cold plunge pools: one that is comparable to the body-shocking temperature of a mountain stream in the Sierra, and the other close to the chilling temp of the nearby Pacific Ocean. Don't miss the eucalyptus steam room, where a potent minty cloud of steam will purge all of your body's impurities.

Swimming

When summer fog takes over the Monterey Peninsula, locals head inland to the almost-always sunny Carmel Valley, at least in part because the region provides several places to take a dip. The **Los Laureles Lodge** (313 W. Carmel Valley Rd., 831/659-2233, http://loslaureles.com, May-Oct. entrance fee $8) has a pool and bar that can be quite a scene on warm days.

For river swimming, head to **The Bucket,** a fabled Carmel Valley swimming hole in the Carmel River. It's nicknamed the Bloody Bucket, either because visitors have cut their feet on the jagged rocks or as a reference to a tavern that once existed nearby—regardless, it's a good idea to wear footwear here. It can be found by going 13 miles east on Carmel Valley Road from the junction of Carmel Valley Road and Highway 1. Look for a place to park after passing the Camp Stephanie road sign on Carmel Valley Road. Then walk down Carmel Valley Road and look for a hole in the fence just before the Stone Pine sign. Duck through the fence and descend on the path to the Carmel River.

Off-Roading

Learn how to drive over piles of rocks and navigate steep trail ascents in a four-wheel drive vehicle at the **Land Rover Experience Driving School** (Quail Lodge & Golf Club, 8000 Valley Greens Dr., 831/620-8854, www.quaillodge.com, daily 9am-5pm, driving lessons $250/hour, $1,200 full day) at the Quail Lodge & Golf Club. The driving instructor can also teach you about winching, vehicle recovery, and expedition travel.

ACCOMMODATIONS
Under $150

There's plenty of space to absorb Carmel Valley's sunshine at the ★ **Blue Sky Lodge** (10 Flight Rd., 831/659-2256, www.blueskylodge.com, $119-413), whether on your unit's private patio or sundeck or in the lodge's courtyard, which has a pool, a lawn, a multi-person hot tub, table tennis, and lots of lounge chairs. The units have thick carpeting and are a bit dated, but in a charming, retro-chic way. Six of the rooms also have kitchens. Behind the pool is a comfy common room with a fireplace, an extensive library, a piano, a lot of houseplants, and a computer for guest use. The Blue Sky Lodge's location can't be beat—it is just a few hundred feet up from Carmel Valley Village and its many tasting rooms.

Hosting guests on and off since 1915, the former ranch at **Los Laureles Lodge** (313 W. Carmel Valley Rd., 831/659-2233, www.loslaureles.com, $130-285, three-bedroom house $650) can put you up in a guestroom, a honeymoon cottage, or a three-bedroom house. Enjoy the property's restaurant, saloon, and, most of all, its swimming pool and adjacent pool bar.

$150-250

For folks who come to Carmel Valley to taste wine, hike in the woods, and enjoy the less-expensive golf courses, **Country Garden Inns** (102 W. Carmel Valley Rd., 831/659-5361, www.countrygardeninns.com, $181-199) offers a perfect spot to rest and relax. Actually composed of two inns, the Acacia and the Hidden Valley, Country Garden's small B&Bs offer violet and taupe French Country-style charm in the guestrooms, as well as a pool, a self-serve breakfast bar, and strolling gardens. Rooms run from romantic king-bed studios up to big family suites; most sleep at least four people (with daybeds in the window nooks).

the unique grounds of Blue Sky Lodge

Golfers may opt to stay at the **Quail Lodge & Golf Course** (8205 Valley Greens Dr., 831/624-2888, $195-870), which is known for its 18-hole championship golf course. The renovated guestrooms and suites all have an outdoor patio or balcony. All stays include a continental breakfast buffet.

Carmel Valley Lodge (8 Ford Rd., 831/659-2261, www.valleylodge.com, $189-389) offers up 31 guest units, all with a patio or deck. Start your day healthily with a complimentary raw vegan breakfast and then spend some time in the seasonal outdoor pool and hot tub.

Over $250

To truly spread out and relax, book a stay at the 500-acre ★ **Carmel Valley Ranch** (1 Old Ranch Rd., 831/625-9500, www.carmelvalleyranch.com, $400-600). The units here are all spacious suites ranging 650-1,200 square feet with fireplaces and decks to take in the valley views and wild turkeys trotting through the grounds. With rooms this nice you may be tempted to stay inside, but Carmel Valley Ranch has so many outdoor activities that it feels like an upscale summer camp. An activity calendar comes with your stay and includes everything from a beekeeping class to horseback riding and nightly s'mores roasting over an open fire. At **Spa Aiyana** (831/626-2586, Sun.-Thurs. 9am-7pm, Fri.-Sat. 9am-8pm, massages $145-280), masseurs use lavender grown on-site in their treatments. The **Carmel Valley Ranch Golf Course** (resort guests $160, non-guests $175) is an 18-hole course that winds into the hills. Don't miss the amazing saltwater swimming pool long enough for laps and the infinity hot tub overlooking some beautiful oak trees and the resort's vineyard.

The **Bernardus Lodge & Spa** (415 W. Carmel Valley Rd., 831/658-3400, www.bernarduslodge.com, $475-965) has luxury guestrooms with high-end features like two-person soaking tubs, oversized patios, and limestone fireplaces. The property has other notable features, including an outdoor heated pool, two tennis courts, a croquet lawn, and a fitness room that is open 24 hours daily.

FOOD
American

Valley Kitchen (Carmel Valley Ranch, 1 Old Ranch Rd., 831/626-2599, www.carmelvalleyranch.com, daily 7am-10pm, $15-46) truly takes advantage of its location on the sprawling Carmel Valley Ranch. Executive chef Tim Wood utilizes ingredients from the ranch's garden, henhouse, and apiary. He even uses sea salt that's dried and flavored on-site. The restaurant has floor-to-ceiling windows overlooking the adjacent pool deck. Be seated at a table for a dinner that may include a fresh line-caught fish of the day. Or just cozy up to the U-shaped stone bar and graze on what might be the standout menu item: their signature honey-chili chicken wings. Even if you aren't staying at the Carmel Valley Ranch, the wings and the atmosphere make Valley Kitchen worth a trip.

The **Corkscrew Café** (55 W. Carmel Valley Rd., 831/659-8888, daily 11:30am-9pm, $22-32) honors its namesake with a permanent collection of the wine-opening devices. The food utilizes ingredients from an organic garden and includes dinner entrées like wood-fired whole trout or rib eye steak.

The frequently sunny Carmel Valley is a great place to dine al fresco. With a large outdoor dining area, **Café Rustica** (10 Del Fino Pl., 831/659-4444, www.caferusticacarmel.com, Tues.-Sun. 11am-2:30pm and 5pm-9pm, $13-30) is known for its nightly fish specials and herb-roasted half chicken.

The creative menu at **Lokal** (13762 Center St., 831/659-5886, Wed. 8am-3pm, Thurs.-Sun. 8am-3pm and 6pm-9pm, $14-26) takes advantage of the valley's farms and wines. The ever-changing menu by chef Brendan Jones utilizes fresh, locally sourced ingredients in a wide range of creations. The wine list leans heavily toward bottles produced just miles away. Sit at a candlelit table or the long bar made from the 1967 Monterey Pop Festival's stage.

Far out in eastern Carmel Valley, dining is a real adventure at the **Cachauga General Store** (18840 Cachauga Rd., 831/659-1857, Mon. 6pm-11pm, Sun. 10am-noon, $20-30). Chef Michael Jones serves upscale cuisine on Sunday mornings and Monday evenings only, in a rustic atmosphere complete with live country music. The service here can be very hit or miss, but the food and the ambience is memorable.

The ★ **Lucia Restaurant & Bar** (Bernardus Lodge & Spa, 415 W. Carmel Valley Rd., 831/658-3400, www.bernarduslodge.com, daily 7am-11am, 11:30am-2:30pm, and 5pm-9pm, $21-62, chef's tasting menu $95) opened in 2015, taking the place of the Bernardus Lodge's Marinus and Wicket's Bistro. Led by revered local chef Cal Stamenov, Lucia truly utilizes the nearby land, using herbs from the garden out front and serving wines created from the adjacent vineyard. The menu starts with worthwhile items like a creamed spinach appetizer (once only a holiday menu option). Meat-centric dishes includes brick-oven pizzas, Hudson Valley foie gras, prime beef, and a smoked duck stew. A favorite entrée is the grilled king salmon steak wrapped in pancetta with asparagus spears. It's one of the better pieces of fish around. Oenophiles and others should consider wine pairings, including the superb Bernardus Pisoni pinot noir and the Bernardus Ingrid's chardonnay. The knowledgeable and friendly staff will properly guide you. The dining room puts the focus on the vineyard out front with a counter looking toward the vines and an outdoor terrace. This is a great place to get a feel for what makes Carmel Valley special.

Breakfast

Carmel Valley has two fine breakfast places that are worth a drive from the coast. ★ **Jeffrey's Grill & Catering** (112 Mid Valley Center, 831/624-2029, www.jeffreysgrillandcatering.com, Tues.-Sat. 7am-3pm, Sun. 7am-2:30pm, $7-15) serves creative

egg dish at Jeffrey's Grill & Catering

breakfast plates from an inconspicuous space in a Carmel Valley strip mall. The menu includes sausages served with apple fritters and an omelet with sweet pasilla peppers countered by salty ham. The weekend specials go more outside the box with smoked turkey hash and grilled lamb served with eggs.

A famed Carmel Valley breakfast spot is the **Wagon Wheel Restaurant** (7156 Carmel Valley Rd., 831/624-8878, daily 6:30am-2pm, $8-12). This down-home place is decorated with horseshoes, ropes, and other Western knickknacks. The menu includes hearty three-egg dishes and oatmeal pancakes.

The **Trailside Café** (3 Del Fino Pl., 831/298-7453, http://trailsidecafecv.com, daily 8am-9pm, $9-18) used to reside on Monterey's Coastal Recreation Trail but now it's in Carmel Valley with a focus on beer (12 beers and a cider on tap) and a dinner menu. They do a classic breakfast with omelets, Benedicts, and beignets. Dine or drink in the beer garden, dining room, or out front on the sunny patio.

Steakhouses

★ **Will's Fargo** (16 W. Carmel Valley Rd., 831/659-2774, http://wfrestaurant.com, Sun.-Thurs. 4:30pm-9pm, Fri.-Sat. 4:30pm-10pm, $15-35) was a tea room, a roadhouse, and a restaurant called The Carousel before it became, in 1959, the place it is now. This place has a great Old West atmosphere, complete with longhorns and cow skulls. The interior includes a bar with a fireplace and a dining room. The executive chef at unassuming Will's Fargo has worked in Michelin one-star and two-star restaurants. The steaks (prime Angus top sirloin, filet mignon, Kansas City, and porterhouse) are served a la carte, and you choose from sides like quail, lobster tail, bacon, and vegetables. It's possible to enjoy a full meal off the appetizer menu in the bar while soaking up the ambience. The steak bites showcase tender and tasty meat, while the half Cobb salad has all the trademark ingredients over chopped lettuce.

Mediterranean

Carmel Valley has a great little Mediterranean restaurant with **Athena Café** (315 Mid Valley Center, 831/624-3056, www.athenacafecarmel.com, $12-28). It's a one room eatery decorated with faux vines in a strip mall, but it serves Greek salads, gyros, lamb kebabs, and a small burger menu at dinner.

Mexican

Sip a wide range of tasty, intoxicating margaritas on the large wooden deck at ★ **Baja Cantina** (7166 Carmel Valley Rd., 831/625-2252, www.carmelcantina.com, Mon.-Fri. 11:30am-11pm, Sat.-Sun. 11am-midnight, $13-20). Catch a sports game on one of the big-screen TVs and enjoy the car memorabilia covering the walls. The menu includes hearty Americanized Mexican cuisine, like rosemary chicken burritos and wild mushroom and spinach enchiladas. Even the nachos are worthwhile—they have so much baked cheese that they resemble a casserole.

INFORMATION AND SERVICES

Call or visit the website of the **Carmel Valley Chamber of Commerce** (831/659-4000, http://carmelvalleychamber.com) for basic information before arriving. Most services are available in nearby Carmel-by-the-Sea, but the unincorporated community of Carmel Valley has a **post office** (11 Via Contenta, 831/659-8839, www.usps.com, Mon.-Fri.

Will's Fargo

CARMEL
CARMEL VALLEY

9am-4:30pm) and a **Safeway** (104 Mid Valley Center, 831/624-4600, daily 24 hours).

The nearest major medical center to Carmel Valley is in nearby Monterey: the **Community Hospital of Monterey** (23625 Holman Hwy, Monterey, 831/624-5311, www. chomp.org).

TRANSPORTATION

To get to Carmel Valley, take Highway 1 to Carmel Valley Road, which is a major intersection with a stoplight. Take Carmel Valley Road east for 13 miles to the Carmel Valley Village, where most of the area's restaurants and wineries are located.

Salinas

Look for ★ to find recommended
sights, activities, dining, and lodging.

Highlights

★ **National Steinbeck Center:** Learn about Nobel Prize-winning author John Steinbeck and his relationship to Salinas at this multimedia museum (page 125).

★ **River Road Wine Trail:** Take in stunning views of Salinas Valley as you sip fine pinot noirs and chardonnays along this unassuming wine route (page 127).

★ **Tassajara Zen Mountain Center:** Naturally occurring hot springs and a unique Zen Buddhist retreat make this remote mountain spot worth seeking out (page 132).

★ **Pinnacles National Park:** One of the nation's youngest national parks, Pinnacles offers trails, crags, caves, and lots of wildlife-viewing opportunities (page 133).

★ **Mission San Juan Bautista:** Located on a scenic town square, Mission San Juan Bautista is the largest of California's missions (page 136).

★ **Fremont Peak State Park:** A 3,169-foot summit draws people for its superb views of the Monterey Bay and the night sky (page 137).

Salinas Valley is one of the country's most productive agricultural regions. Its hub, Salinas, is a small city dominated by agriculture. To literature lovers, it's known as the hometown of Pulitzer Prize-winning author John Steinbeck.

Salinas is more unassuming than the nearby cities of the Monterey Peninsula and has a significant population of farmers, cowboys, field laborers, and blue-collar workers. The best way to get a feel for Salinas's small town ambience is to spend a little time in Oldtown, where Main Street is lined with local businesses. Steinbeck fans should spend some time at the illuminating National Steinbeck Center and the Steinbeck House, where the author lived during the early part of his life.

Outside of Salinas, inland Monterey County offers many worthy attractions and unique experiences that are spread throughout the region's hotter, drier interior. On the eastern side of Salinas Valley is the country's newest national park, Pinnacles National Park, which has caves and jagged rock formations perfect for climbers and hikers alike. The western side of the valley is lined with some of the county's best vineyards and tasting rooms, especially along the River Road

Wine Trail. You can also enjoy solitude at the remote Mission San Antonio de Padua, climb the 5,856-foot Junipero Serra Peak, or reflect in an Eastern inspired setting at the Tassajara Zen Mountain Center.

Just north of the county line, the historic town of San Juan Bautista may look familiar to film fans: The historic downtown and mission were the setting of many pivotal scenes in Alfred Hitchcock's masterpiece *Vertigo*. Nearby, 3,169-foot Fremont Peak in Fremont Peak State Park offers one of the area's best views of the Monterey Bay as well as some of the Central Coast's finest stargazing.

Be aware that Salinas and inland Monterey are almost always hotter than the Pacific Ocean-cooled peninsula. Bring lots of water and plenty of sunscreen.

PLANNING YOUR TIME

Salinas is Monterey County's largest city and a popular attraction for fans of writer John

---

Previous: Pinnacles National Park; Mission San Antonio de Padua; **Above:** The Steinbeck House.

Salinas and Vicinity

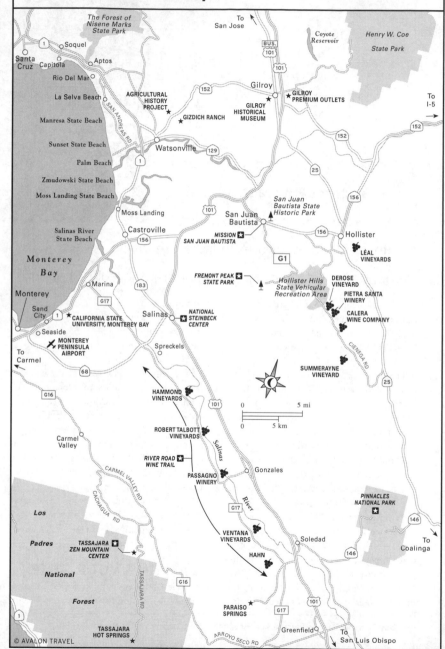

The Forest of Nisene Marks State Park

Coyote Reservoir

Henry W. Coe State Park

To San Jose

Santa Cruz

Soquel

Capitola

Aptos

Rio Del Mar

La Selva Beach

Manresa State Beach

Sunset State Beach

Palm Beach

Zmudowski State Beach

Moss Landing State Beach

Salinas River State Beach

Monterey Bay

AGRICULTURAL HISTORY PROJECT

GIZDICH RANCH

Gilroy

GILROY HISTORICAL MUSEUM

GILROY PREMIUM OUTLETS

To I-5

Watsonville

Moss Landing

Castroville

San Juan Bautista

San Juan Bautista State Historic Park

Hollister

MISSION SAN JUAN BAUTISTA

LÉAL VINEYARDS

G1

FREMONT PEAK STATE PARK

Hollister Hills State Vehicular Recreation Area

DEROSE VINEYARD

PIETRA SANTA WINERY

CALERA WINE COMPANY

CIENEGA RD

Marina

G17

Monterey

Sand City

Seaside

CALIFORNIA STATE UNIVERSITY, MONTEREY BAY

MONTEREY PENINSULA AIRPORT

Salinas

NATIONAL STEINBECK CENTER

To Carmel

68

Spreckels

SUMMERAYNE VINEYARD

G16

Carmel Valley

HAMMOND VINEYARDS

Salinas

ROBERT TALBOTT VINEYARDS

RIVER ROAD WINE TRAIL

PASSAGNO WINERY

Gonzales

0   5 mi
0   5 km

CARMEL VALLEY RD

CACHAGUA RD

Los

Padres

National

Forest

TASSAJARA ZEN MOUNTAIN CENTER

TASSAJARA RD

G16

VENTANA VINEYARDS

HAHN

River

G17

PINNACLES NATIONAL PARK

146

To Coalinga

Soledad

146

PARAISO SPRINGS

G17

TASSAJARA HOT SPRINGS

Greenfield

To San Luis Obispo

ARROYO SECO RD

© AVALON TRAVEL

Steinbeck. The best place to visit in Salinas is its Oldtown area, where the National Steinbeck Center is located. There are chain hotels in Salinas, but you can find better (albeit more expensive) lodging on the Monterey Peninsula.

Inland Monterey is pretty spread out, so it doesn't make sense to try and get to everything in a couple of days. Instead, focus on what area sounds the most interesting. The Eastern Los Padres is a great place for outdoor enthusiasts. Fort Hunter Liggett is for those that treasure out-of-the-way places. A superb day can be made by hiking in Pinnacles National Park and then visiting the tasting rooms of the River Road Wine Trail while heading back to Monterey or Salinas. San Juan Bautista is in neighboring San Benito County, and is worth an afternoon of exploration for people interested in early California history. Gilroy makes a fine stopping point on trips between Monterey and the Bay Area.

Salinas

Salinas is the major city of the Salinas River Valley, a fertile agricultural region dubbed the "Salad Bowl of the World." The Monterey County seat's other claim to fame is as the hometown of Nobel Prize-winning author John Steinbeck, which explains why the local library, an elementary school, and a produce company are named after him. The Oldtown Salinas area situated around Main Street has the city's best restaurants, shops, and the National Steinbeck Center.

It's best to confine your visit to Oldtown Salinas due to crime in other parts of the city. Avoid East Salinas, where a lot of the city's gang violence occurs.

SIGHTS
★ National Steinbeck Center

The **National Steinbeck Center** (1 Main St., 831/775-4721, www.steinbeck.org, daily 10am-5pm, adults $15, seniors and students $9, youth 13-17 $8, children 6-12 $6) utilizes multimedia displays that employ sight, sound, and even touch to tell the story of Salinas's most popular son, famed writer John Steinbeck. The permanent exhibit includes

The National Steinbeck Center pays tribute to Salinas's most famous native son.

Oldtown Salinas

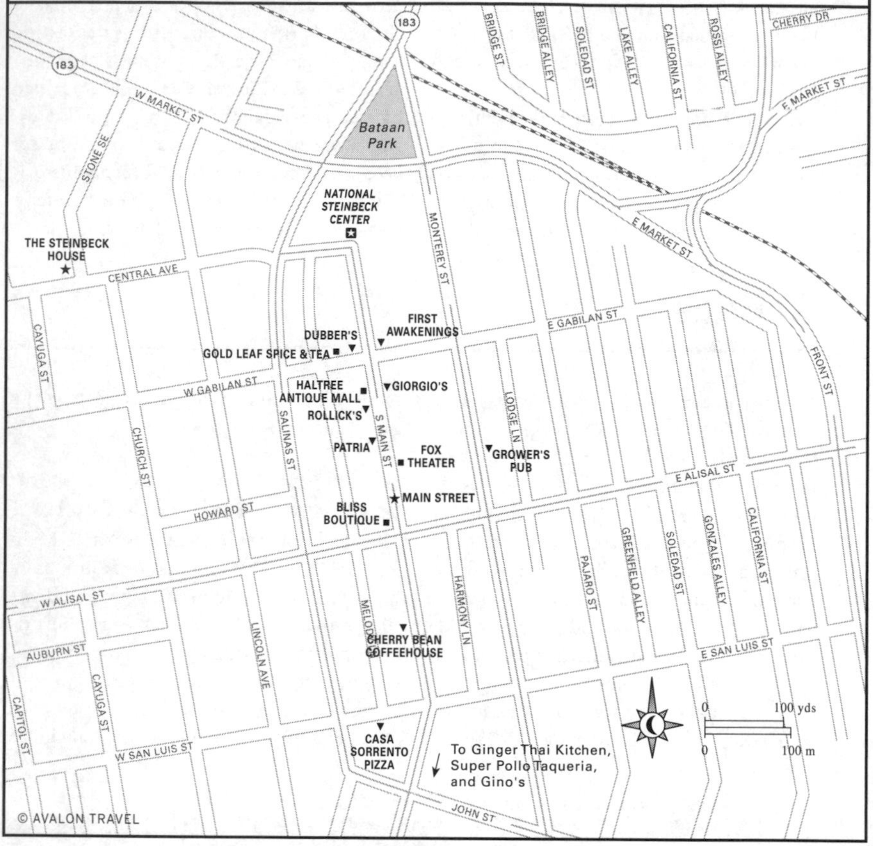

Map labels: 183, 183, W MARKET ST, STONE SE, Bataan Park, BRIDGE ST, BRIDGE ST, SOLEDAD ST, LAKE ALLEY, CALIFORNIA ST, ROSSI ALLEY, CHERRY DR, E MARKET ST, E MARKET ST, NATIONAL STEINBECK CENTER, MONTEREY ST, THE STEINBECK HOUSE, CENTRAL AVE, CAYUGA ST, FIRST AWAKENINGS, E GABILAN ST, FRONT ST, DUBBER'S, GOLD LEAF SPICE & TEA, W GABILAN ST, HALTREE ANTIQUE MALL, GIORGIO'S, ROLLICK'S, CHURCH ST, SALINAS ST, S MAIN ST, PATRIA, FOX THEATER, GROWER'S PUB, LODGE LN, MAIN STREET, E ALISAL ST, BLISS BOUTIQUE, HOWARD ST, GREENFIELD ALLEY, SOLEDAD ST, GONZALES ALLEY, CALIFORNIA ST, PAJARO ST, W ALISAL ST, HARMONY LN, MELON, E SAN LUIS ST, AUBURN ST, CAYUGA ST, LINCOLN AVE, CHERRY BEAN COFFEEHOUSE, CAPITOL ST, CASA SORRENTO PIZZA, To Ginger Thai Kitchen, Super Pollo Taqueria, and Gino's, W SAN LUIS ST, JOHN ST, 0 100 yds, 0 100 m, © AVALON TRAVEL

lengthy book passages, photos, footage from film adaptations, and sets mocked up to resemble scenes from the author's novels, lending insight into the life of the author of the American classics *The Grapes of Wrath*, *East of Eden*, *Cannery Row*, and *Of Mice and Men*. Much of the museum showcases Steinbeck's relationship with Salinas and the surrounding region. A highlight is the camper that Steinbeck used to journey across America and write the 1962 travelogue *Travels with Charley*.

Main Street

Main Street is the main thoroughfare of **Oldtown Salinas** (http://oldtownsalinas.

com) and the best section of town to visit. Lined with local shops, restaurants, and historic buildings, Main Street feels like it has been the same for decades (probably why the 2001 film *Bandits,* starring Bruce Willis, Billy Bob Thornton, and Cate Blanchett filmed scenes here). The National Steinbeck Center is located at the north end of the one-way street.

The Steinbeck House

A yellow Victorian in downtown Salinas, **The Steinbeck House** (132 Central Ave., 831/424-2735, http://steinbeckhouse.com, gift shop Tues.-Sat. 11am-3pm) is where John Steinbeck was born and spent his early years.

There is no museum here, but rather a restaurant (Tues.-Sat. 11:30am-2pm, $12-14) that serves lunch five days a week. The interior is still decorated with Steinbeck family photos. Visit the cellar-level gift shop, where *The Steinbeck House Cookbook* is sold alongside novels by the famed author.

Another way to experience the house is to get a **tour** (Tues.-Sat. 10am-11am and 2pm-3pm, donations appreciated) of the main floor and cellar. Stop in for the brief (15-20 minutes) docent-guided tour before or after the weekday lunch service. You do not have to dine in the house to take the tour. More complete 30-45 minute tours (June-Sept., first Sun. of the month noon-3pm, $10/person, $20/family) take place on the first Sunday of the month during the summer.

★ River Road Wine Trail

Just 10 miles south of Salinas, the **River Road Wine Trail** (www.riverroadwinetrail.com) runs about 40 miles down to Soledad, comprising a collection of wineries in the Santa Lucia Highlands, a region known for its chardonnays and pinot noirs. The drive along River Road and Foothill Road makes for a scenic back-road excursion, and the tasting rooms rarely get too crowded, meaning the employees will have more time to interact and answer your questions. Allot about half a day to explore the wine trail—it's a perfect afternoon adventure.

It's worth heading another 15 minutes south to the spacious **Hahn Winery Tasting Room** (37700 Foothill Dr., 831/678-4555, www.hahnwinery.com, daily 11am-5pm, tasting $15) for its superb outdoor deck and its emphasis on wines not readily available in the marketplace. Like other River Road wineries, the chardonnays and pinot noir are the focus. Sip your wine at the long bar, on the deck for stellar views of Salinas Valley and the Gabilan Mountains, or opt for an **ATV Adventure Tour** (1.5 hours, daily 10:30am and 1:30pm, $45), which includes a trip to the vineyard's highest point, a stop at the wine cellar, and a tasting in the winery's VIP room.

Head to the **Paraiso Vineyards Boutique & Tasting Room** (38060 Paraiso Springs Rd., 831/678-0300, www.paraisovineyards.com, Thurs.-Mon. 11am-5pm, tasting $15) for its pinot noir, deck with great views, and outdoor fire pit. Stop by the boutique and pick up home decor and fashion accessories before you go.

The Steinbeck House

ENTERTAINMENT AND EVENTS
Nightlife

Oldtown Salinas has a sports bar in **Dubber's** (172 Main St., 831/679-0256, Sun.-Thurs. 11:30am-midnight, Fri.-Sat. 11:30am-1am). The walls are decorated with sports gear and flat-screen TVs for taking in your favorite team's game. Watch all the action while sipping one of the eight beers on tap.

Casa Sorrento Pizzeria (393 Salinas St., 831/757-2720, www.casasorrento.com, daily 11am-close) is a Salinas pizza joint that gets some impressive musicians, including reggae, rap, and country acts, to perform frequently. Past performers have included The Mighty Diamonds, Shock G, and Pato Banton. Performances take place on the large stage in an equally large, open room. Grab a drink from the full bar before settling in for the show. Check their website for upcoming events.

The **Fox Theater** (241 Main St., 831/758-8459 or 888/825-5484, www.foxtheater-salinas.com) has occupied a sweet spot in Oldtown since 1921. It was closed for some time, but reopened in 2007 with a show by comedian George Lopez. It now hosts cumbia bands, comedians, and the occasional rock group. The Fox has three different bars and balcony seating.

Festivals and Events

Salinas honors its most famous export every even year with the **Steinbeck Festival** (National Steinbeck Center, 1 Main St., 831/775-4721, www.steinbeck.org, May). The weekend-long celebration of the author's life includes talks, tours, parties, and panel discussions.

The **California Rodeo Salinas** (Salinas Sports Complex, 1034 N. Main St., 831/775-3100 or 800/549-4989, www.carodeo.com, July, $7-55) is one of the city's biggest events and the largest professional rodeo in California. For four days every July, over 700 cowboys and cowgirls come to Salinas to compete in bull-riding events. There's also live music, parties, and mutton busting, where children (ages 4-7, under 60 pounds, $25) take part in a sheep-riding competition.

Every fall, the sky above Salinas fills with aerobatic planes and skydivers for the annual **California International Airshow** (Salinas Municipal Airport, 30 Mortensen Ave., 844/647-7469, www.salinasairshow.com, Sept., $10-35 per day). Come see legendary flight demonstration teams like the

SALINAS
SALINAS

Dubber's, a sports bar in Oldtown Salinas

U.S. Navy Blue Angels and the U.S. Air Force Thunderbirds soar through the air. All proceeds from this two-day event benefit local charities.

SHOPPING

Oldtown Salinas

Oldtown Salinas (831/758-0725, http://oldtownsalinas.com), based around Main Street, is a pleasant place to shop, with easy parking and restaurants scattered throughout. The **Halltree Antique Mall** (202 Main St., 831/757-6918, www.halltreeantiquemall.com, Mon.-Fri. 10am-5:30pm, Sat.-Sun. 10:30am-5pm), in a large building that was a gentleman's club and then a bank, has 22 antiques vendors. There's a little of everything sold here, from coins and jewelry to furniture and kitchenware, all divided across vendor spaces that are about 15 feet by 20 feet.

Head to **Gold Leaf Spice & Teas** (8 1/2 Gabilan St., 831/753-7700, www.goldleafspiceandteas.com, Tues.-Fri. 10am-5pm, Sat. 9am-3pm) to taste teas, olive oils, and balsamic vinegars. This one-room shop/tea lounge has a multitude of canisters of tea and "sniffer jars" to take in the many spices for sale. Their most popular item is matcha, a powdered green tea.

For women's contemporary clothing, try **Bliss Boutique** (266 Main St., 831/757-4055, Mon.-Fri. 11am-7pm, Sat. 10am-5:30pm, Sun. noon-4pm).

Northridge Mall

Sprawling **Northridge Mall** (796 Northridge Mall, 831/449-7226, http://shop-northridge-mall.com, Mon.-Sat. 10am-9pm, Sun. 11am-7pm, some store and restaurant hours may vary) is home to Best Buy, Macys, Sears, Big 5 Sporting Goods, and more. You can also catch a film here at the **Century 14** (350 Northridge Mall, 831/449-4168, www.cinemark.com).

Farmers Markets

Salinas is known for its agriculture, so it comes as no surprise that the city hosts five farmers markets a week in peak season. The single year-round market is the **Downtown**

Salinas Saturday Farmers Market (Gabilan St. between Main St. and Salinas St., Sat. 9am-2pm). The seasonal markets are the **Alisal Farmers Market** (632 E. Alisal St., June-Sept. Tues. 11am-4pm), the **Natividad Farmers Market** (1441 Constitution Blvd., May-Oct. Wed. 11am-3:30pm), the **Salinas Thursday Farmers Market** (E. Alisal St. and S. Pearl St., July-Oct. Thurs. 9am-4pm), and the **Salinas Valley Memorial Market** (Salinas Valley Memorial Hospital, 450 E. Romie Lane, May-Oct. Fri. 2pm-6pm).

SPORTS AND RECREATION

Parks

Toro Park (501 Monterey-Salinas Hwy. 68, 831/755-4895, www.co.monterey.ca.us, daily 8am-dusk, $8/vehicle, $2/pedestrian) is a great place to recreate just six miles from downtown Salinas. The 4,756-acre park has hiking, biking, and horseback-riding trails, softball fields, volleyball courts, and horseshoe pits. Take a steep, challenging hike on the **Ollason Peak Loop** (9 miles round-trip, strenuous, 1,650 foot elevation gain), which climbs to the 1,800 foot summit of Ollason Peak.

FOOD

Breakfast

There is no better place to start a day in Salinas than at ★ **First Awakenings** (171 Main St., 831/784-1125, www.firstawakenings.net, daily 7am-2pm, $9-12). Menu options include a carnitas scramble, frittatas, eggs Benedict, and huevos rancheros. They also have a Pacific Grove location (125 Oceanview Blvd., 831/372-1125, Mon.-Fri. 7am-2pm, Sat.-Sun. 7am-2:30pm).

Coffee Shops

Oldtown Salinas has two coffee shops. **Rollick's** (210 Main St., 831/422-1760, http://rollicks.com, Mon.-Thurs. 6:30am-6:30pm, Fri. 6:30am-7pm, Sat. 7:30am-6pm, Sun. 7:30am-4:30pm) is known for their Mexican mochas. They offer use of their Internet-enabled computers with a purchase. **Cherry**

Bean Coffeehouse (332 Main St., 831/424-1989, www.cherrybeancoffeehouse.com, Mon.-Fri. 5:30am-7pm, Sat.-Sun. 6:30am-6pm) roasts their own beans and attracts a more alternative crowd. Cherry Bean's walls are decorated with the works of local artists.

European

★ **Patria** (228 Main St., 831/424-5555, daily 11:30am-2pm and 3pm-close, $10-38) is not the kind of restaurant you might expect in unassuming Salinas. The interior has a rustic European feel due to its artwork, exposed wooden beams, and antler chandelier hanging in the foyer. The kitchen is run by a German chef, who offers items like spaetzle and jaeger schnitzel on the dinner menu. Patria also has a serious Italian influence exemplified by its house-made pastas and pizzas. Try the caramelized onion and thyme pizza with loads of smoked bacon, goat cheese, and a bacon béchamel sauce.

Italian

Founded in 1975 by an Italian immigrant, ★ **Gino's** (1410 S. Main St., 831/422-1814, www.ginosfamilyrestaurantgroup.com, Mon.-Thurs. 11am-3pm and 5pm-9pm, Fri. 11am-3pm and 5pm-10pm, Sat. 5pm-10pm, $9-30)

is a Salinas institution, set in a multiroom building with a patio. The food here is hearty home-style Italian, like pasta, pizza, chicken Parmesan, and abalone-style calamari picatta. The appetizer meatballs braised in a spicy tomato garlic sauce are a good place to start. This family-friendly restaurant is where locals come for special occasions.

Giorgio's (201 Main St., 831/800-7573, www.201complex.com, Tues.-Thurs. 11am-8:30pm, Fri.-Sat. 11am-9:30pm, Sun. 8am-8:30pm, $11-28) is the anchor restaurant of 201 Main, a former bank renovated into a restaurant and market complex. Giorgio's boasts a chic illuminated bar and a modern Italian menu of pizza, pasta, fish, and meat.

Mexican

Salinas has some great inexpensive Mexican restaurants, one of which is **Super Pollo Taqueria** (1237 S. Main St., 831/424-4930, Mon.-Fri. 8am-7:30pm, Sat. 8am-4pm, $6-12). This unassuming eatery is short on ambience, but its food is widely loved. It's known for its burritos, including breakfast, carne asada, carnitas, and chicken versions.

Steakhouses

Grower's Pub (227 Monterey St.,

Patria, Oldtown Salinas

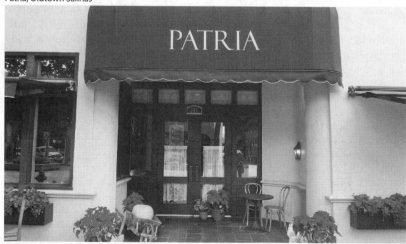

831/754-1488, www.growerspub.com, Mon.-Thurs. 11am-9pm, Fri. 11am-10pm, Sat. 4pm-10pm, $12-27) is on the fancier side of Salinas's dining options, and one of the priciest restaurants in town. This white-tablecloth place is a throwback to another era, from its 1940s bar to its popular slow-roasted prime rib.

Thai

At **Ginger Thai Kitchen** (1104 S. Main St., 831/422-8424, www.gingerthaikitchen.com, Mon.-Fri. 11am-2:30pm and 4pm-9pm, Sat.-Sun. noon-9pm, $9-17), expect tasty Thai classics including curries, noodle dishes, and rice plates. There are options for vegetarians like soy vegetarian duck. Cool off from the spicy dishes with beer or a California wine.

INFORMATION AND SERVICES

For information on Salinas, stop into Oldtown's **Salinas 411** (222 Main St., 831/435-4636, www.salinas411.org, daily 9am-7pm). Their website has information about restaurants, lodging, and attractions, along with a Salinas-centric smartphone app. Salinas has three **post offices:** at 100 West Alisal Street (831/758-1204, www.usps.com, Mon.-Fri. 8:30am-5pm), 303 North Sanborn Road (831/757-7704, Mon.-Fri. 9am-4:30pm), and 1011 Post Drive (831/770-7145, Mon.-Fri. 8:30am-5pm, Sat. 9am-4pm).

TRANSPORTATION

Salinas is 20 miles from Monterey; the drive takes about 30 minutes if CA-68 is not backed up. It is not a good idea to drive from Monterey to Salinas around 5pm, when two-lane CA-68 gets crowded with commuters. From Monterey, take CA-1 north, then merge right onto CA-68 and head east. The highway becomes South Main Street as it enters Salinas.

Inland Monterey County

At 1.5 times the size of the state of Delaware, Monterey County is a big place. While the Monterey Peninsula and the Big Sur coast get most of the area's visitors, the inland portion of the county and its neighboring region boast a burgeoning wine country, an uncrowded national park, and a few out-of-the-way gems worth seeking out.

EASTERN LOS PADRES NATIONAL FOREST

The western side of Los Padres National Forest is in Big Sur, and thus receives many visitors. The eastern portion of Los Padres has worthwhile destinations with fewer people. Compared to the coast, it's hotter and drier here during summer, so bring ample water.

Los Padres Reservoir

The Los Padres Dam on the Carmel River is responsible for the **Los Padres Reservoir.**

The area is worthwhile for hikers and backpackers who want to experience the Carmel River Valley. A good day hike is the **Carmel River Trail to Danish Creek** (5.6 miles round-trip, moderate, 300-foot elevation gain), which meanders along the western edge of the Los Padres Reservoir before reaching Danish Creek.

GETTING THERE

Los Padres Reservoir is about an hour drive from Monterey. Head south out of Monterey on CA-1 and turn left on Carmel Valley Road. Turn right on Tassajara Road, then take another right on Cachagua Road. Finally, take a left on Nason Road and follow it almost two miles to the reservoir.

The drive from Salinas is also about an hour. Head south on South Main Street and stay on it as it becomes CA-68. Continue east, then turn left on Laureles Canyon Road, which takes you over the mountain. Turn left on Carmel Valley Road, then turn right on Tassajara Road. Take another right on Cachagua Road. Finally, take a left on Nason Road and follow it to the reservoir.

★ Tassajara Zen Mountain Center

Tucked on the eastern edge of Los Padres National Forest, **Tassajara Zen Mountain Center** (39171 Tassajara Rd., 831/659-2229 or 800/743-9362, www.sfzc.org, late Apr.-mid-Sept. daily 9am-9pm, day use adults $30, children $12) is known for its naturally occurring hot springs and is where Buddhist scholars study in a monastic setting. Run by the San Francisco Zen Center, Tassajara is closed to the public from late September to early April so that students can study, meditate, and work in peace. During the summer, the grounds are open for daily and overnight visits. The primary attractions here are the Japanese-style bathhouses that offer access to the hot springs. (During daytime hours, men and women must use separate bathhouse facilities.) Day guests are also welcome to hike the grounds, dip into the outdoor pool, or take in the center's Asian-inspired buildings. There are also shared dorm rooms and private cabins ($105-407) available for those who want to spend the night in this tranquil setting. A stay includes three vegetarian meals a day. The center is reached by driving a windy, mountainous, unpaved road for 14 miles. The road is not navigable to vehicles with automatic transmissions and low clearance. First-timers are advised to secure a seat in the eight-person passenger van (daily 10:30am and 1:15pm based on demand, $57/round-trip pp) that leaves from Jamesburg, which is about 15 miles south of Carmel Valley.

GETTING THERE

The Tassajara Zen Mountain Center is more than an hour's drive from Monterey. Head south out of Monterey on CA-1 and turn left on Carmel Valley Road, which you continue on for about 20 miles. Then turn right on Tassajara Road and stay on it for just over a mile before taking a slight left. The last four miles are unpaved and steep.

From Salinas, head south on South Main Street and stay on it as it becomes CA-68. From CA-68, turn left on Laureles Canyon Road. On the other side of the mountain, turn left on Carmel Valley Road. Turn right on Tassajara Road and stay on it for about a mile before taking a slight left.

Arroyo Seco Recreation Area and Campground

When it gets hot out, people come in droves to the **Arroyo Seco Recreation Area** (47600 Arroyo Seco Rd., 831/674-5726, picnic area daily 8am-6pm, gorge area daily 8am-midnight, $10/vehicle) for the deep, cold pools of the Arroyo Seco River. There are swimming holes right upon entering the area but a better option is to hike one mile up Indian Mary Road (closed to vehicular traffic) to reach the **Arroyo Seco Gorge.** The deep pool of this stunning gorge is surrounded by rocky cliffs.

Spend the night at one of the 50 RV or tent sites at **Arroyo Seco Campground** (831/674-5726, www.recreation.gov, developed campsites $25-40, primitive campsites $20-40) if you want multiple swimming days. Some sites here are able to be reserved in advance (877/444-6777), while others are first come, first served. The campground can accommodate RVs, but there are no hookups. Developed sites have access to showers and flush toilets, while the primitive sites have just vault toilets.

This is a popular spot for day trips. On summer weekends the day-use parking areas are known to fill up.

GETTING THERE

The trip to Arroyo Seco takes a good 1.5 hours from Monterey. Take CA-1 out of the coastal city before heading east on CA-68. Exit at Speckels Boulevard and follow the roadway until it turns into Harris Street. Turn right on Abbott Street and continue to US-101 South. After about 20 miles, exit at Arroyo Seco

Road. Take Arroyo Seco Road for another 20 miles.

Arroyo Seco is just an hour from Salinas. Drive south on US-101 for almost 30 miles and exit at Arroyo Seco Road. Take Arroyo Seco Road for about 20 miles.

★ PINNACLES NATIONAL PARK

Pinnacles National Park (5000 Hwy. 146, 831/389-4485, www.nps.gov/pinn, west entrance daily 7:30am-8pm, $10/vehicle, $5/person on foot or bicycle) is made up of naturally occurring castles of rock spires, towers, walls, canyons, and caves that rise up above the Gabilan Mountains on the east side of Salinas Valley. A natural wonder created by volcanic activity, Pinnacles had been a national monument since 1908, until it was elevated to national park status in 2013. This stunning 26,000-acre park has over 30 miles of hiking trails along with rock faces that are popular with climbers and some of the world's largest talus caves, which are created when boulders become lodged in narrow canyons. Pinnacles is home to wildlife like California condors, Townsend's big eared bats, California red-legged frogs, 100 species of wildflower, and 400 bee species.

Pinnacles National Park can be accessed on both its western and eastern sides via Highway 146, though the highway does not traverse the park. For visitors coming from Monterey or Salinas, the west side of the park is about 45 minutes closer. The western side has the shortest trails to the Balconies Caves and the High Peaks area. It also hosts the **West Pinnacles Visitor Contact Station** (831/389-4427, ext. 4487, Sat.-Sun. and holidays 9am-4:30pm, some weekdays staff permitting). The eastern side of the park has numerous trailheads, the **Pinnacles Visitor Center** (831/394-4485, daily 9:30am-5pm), and **Pinnacles Campground** (2400 CA-146, Pacines, 877/444-6777, www.recreation.gov, $23 tent site, $36 RV site), which is the only campground in the national park.

Hiking

Pinnacles has over 30 miles of hiking trails that traverse the park. They are the only way to reach unique features like the High Peaks, the Balconies Caves, and Bear Gulch Reservoir. One of the best ways to experience the geology of Pinnacles is to do the west side's **Juniper Canyon Loop** (Chaparral Trailhead, 4.3 miles round-trip, strenuous, 1,215 feet elevation gain). Begin on the Juniper Canyon Trail

fantastic rock formations at Pinnacles National Park

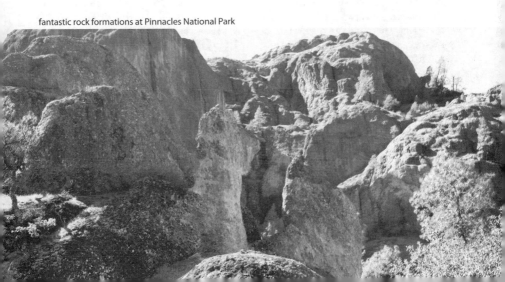

and climb 2,605-foot Scout Peak, where you may spot a condor soaring overhead. Then the hike gets exciting as you traverse a steep and narrow section of the High Peaks Trail. This 0.7-mile portion climbs across the rock-strewn ridgeline via steps carved into the rock with handrails for support. It's almost like a beginner's version of Yosemite's famed Half Dome hike.

Another worthwhile hike from the west side is the **Balconies Cliffs-Balconies Cave Loop** (Chaparral Trailhead, 2.4 miles round-trip, easy to moderate, 100-foot elevation gain). The highlight here is a 0.4-mile section that passes through the talus caves. Bring a flashlight!

From the east side, hikers can reach the Balconies Caves via the **Old Pinnacles Trail** (Old Pinnacles Trailhead, 5.3 miles round-trip, moderate, no elevation gain). A more intense hike from this end of the park is the **Condor Gulch-High Peaks Loop** (Bear Gulch Day Use Area, 5.3 miles round-trip, strenuous, 1,300-foot elevation gain).

Accommodations

Visitors to Pinnacles can pitch a tent at the **Pinnacles Campground** (2400 CA-146, Pacines, 877/444-6777, www.recreation.gov, $23 tent site, $36 RV site), though it is only accessible from the park's east side. The sites have picnic tables and fire rings, while some RV sites have electrical hookups.

On the western side, the **Inn at the Pinnacles** (32025 Stonewall Canyon Rd., 831/678-2400, www.innatthepinnacles.com, $235-260) is just outside the park entrance in an area lined with vineyards. The luxury bed-and-breakfast has six suites, each with with a gas fireplace, wet bar, gas barbecue, and whirlpool tub.

Getting There

The drive from Monterey to Pinnacles National Park's west side takes just over an hour. Take CA-68 east out of the Monterey Peninsula and exit at Spreckels Boulevard. Spreckels Boulevard turns into Harris Road.

Take a right onto Abbott Street and then go south on US-101. Exit in Soledad and take CA-146 east for 10 windy miles until you reach the park.

The park's west side is 45 minutes from downtown Salinas. Simply take US-101 south to Soledad. Then head east on CA-146 until you reach the park.

The drive from Monterey to the park's eastern side is longer and more involved. Expect it to take an hour and a half. Take CA-1 north before hopping east onto CA-156, then go north on US-101. Take Highway 156 east until Hollister. Then turn right on San Juan Road, which becomes 4th Street. Turn right onto San Benito Street and then left on Nash Road, which becomes Tres Pinos Road. From there, take a right on CA-25 until it reaches CA-146, then head into the park.

The park's east side is just over an hour drive from Salinas. Take US-101 north from Salinas and get off at the San Juan Bautista/Hollister exit (Highway 156 East). Follow CA-156 east until you reach Hollister. Then turn right on San Juan Road, which becomes 4th Street. Turn right onto San Benito Street and then left on Nash Road, which becomes Tres Pinos Road. From there, take a right on CA-25 until reaching CA-146, then head into the park.

FORT HUNTER LIGGETT AREA

Fort Hunter Liggett is a 165,000-acre U.S. Army Reserve training facility located in a scenic oak-dotted valley. Though much of the region is closed to the public, there are a few worthy, off-the-beaten-track sites, including a quiet mission, a former William Randolph Hearst ranch house-turned-hotel, and Monterey County's tallest peak. All visitors to Fort Hunter Liggett must have a valid driver's license, vehicle registration, and proof of insurance to pass through the base.

Hearst Hacienda Lodge

The **Hearst Hacienda Lodge** (10 Infantry Rd., 831/386-2262, http://fhlfmwr.com,

$50-200) is a historic gem of southern Monterey County. The Mission Revival-style complex with its unique dome tower was designed by Hearst Castle architect Julia Morgan for William Randolph Hearst. The newspaper magnate used the lodge as a ranch headquarters for his employees and a place to entertain guests including Spencer Tracy, Clark Gable, and Errol Flynn. The lodge is now in the National Register of Historic Places. Overnight options range from Cowboy Rooms with shared bathrooms to suites with two bedrooms and a fully equipped kitchen. Each room comes with breakfast foods stored in the fridge so that you won't have to leave the base for your first meal. The **Hearst Hacienda Lounge** (Wed.-Sat. 5pm-11pm) is the place to grab a beer or cocktail in the complex.

Mission San Antonio de Padua

The third mission founded by Junipero Serra in 1771, **Mission San Antonio de Padua** (end of Mission Rd., 831/385-4478, http://missionsanantonio.net, daily 10am-4pm, adults $5, children under 12 $3) is a quiet place that hasn't changed much since California's early days. This remote mission once had a

water-powered gristmill, a tannery, and a lumber storage facility. Today the 86-acre site retains its chapel and adjacent courtyard, along with a Salinan Indian cemetery and a museum showcasing artifacts from the mission era and early California times.

Junipero Serra Peak

At 5,857 feet, **Junipero Serra Peak** is the tallest peak in Monterey County and the Santa Lucia Mountain Range. The **Santa Lucia Trail** (12 miles round-trip, difficult) offers a way to reach the top with a steep, switchbacked 3,724-foot climb. The summit is home to a dilapidated tower and several places where you can get fine views of the region. Snow frequently blankets the mountain in winter. To reach the trailhead from Fort Hunter Liggett, take a left on Del Venturi Road, which becomes Milpitas Road. Follow it until you enter Los Padres National Forest. Continue until you see the trailhead and small parking area.

Getting There

It is an hour and 40-minute drive from Monterey to the Fort Hunter Liggett area. Take CA-1 out of the coastal city for a half

secluded Mission San Antonio de Padua

mile before hopping on CA-68 East for 7.5 miles. Exit at Spreckels Boulevard and follow that road 1.6 miles until it turns into Harris Street. Continue on Harris 2 miles, then turn right on Abbott Street and go 2 miles to US-101 South. Keep on the highway for 39 miles and then exit at Jolon Road/County Highway G14. Continue down Jolon Road for 17.5 miles before taking a right on Mission Road, which goes into the base. Remember you must have a valid driver's license, vehicle registration, and proof of insurance to drive into Fort Hunter Liggett.

From Salinas, the drive to Fort Hunter Liggett is an hour and 15 minutes. Take US-101 south out of Salinas and exit at Jolon Road/County Highway G14. Continue down Jolon Road for 17.5 miles before taking a right on Mission Road, which goes into the base.

SAN JUAN BAUTISTA

Located in the San Juan Valley between Salinas and Gilroy, San Juan Bautista is a small, scenic city dotted with historic landmarks. There is much to recommend here for California history enthusiasts, including Mission San Juan Bautista, San Juan Bautista State Historic Park, and one of the only Spanish plazas left in the state. A block away from the historic park, the town's 3rd Street is lined with historic structures that house antique stores, restaurants, and gift shops.

The hillside adjacent to the mission is the former site of the Camino Real, a 600-mile trail connecting the California missions, while below the rise is visible evidence of the San Andreas Fault, which has caused many of the state's earthquakes. If San Juan Bautista looks familiar, it's because the town and mission played a prominent role in Alfred Hitchcock's masterpiece *Vertigo*.

★ Mission San Juan Bautista

Dedicated in 1812, **Mission San Juan Bautista** (406 2nd St., 831/623-4528, www.oldmissionsjb.org, daily 9:30am-4:30pm, adults $4, seniors $3, students $2, children 5 and under free) boasts the state's largest mission chapel, which is three aisles wide. After the 1906 San Francisco earthquake, sections of the mission, including the side walls of the chapel, had to be replaced. Upon entering the chapel, look for the impressive and ornate main altar, which holds six statues. Also keep an eye out for the cat door that's carved

Mission San Juan Bautista

into the Guadalupe Chapel's blue door. Cats were kept on the mission grounds and allowed to enter the chapel to control the mouse population.

The padre's former living quarters now serve as the complex's museum, with a model of the grounds along with a collection of vestments. Adjacent to the church is a cemetery that is thought to be the final resting place of over 4,000 Native American, Spanish, Mexican, and American people. The mission was the setting of the climax in Hitchcock's *Vertigo*, though the bell tower depicted in the film was a painting, as the mission's original bell tower had been torn down.

San Juan Bautista State Historic Park

San Juan Bautista State Historic Park (2nd St. at Mariposa St. and Washington St., 831/623-4881, www.parks.ca.gov, daily 10am-4:30pm, adults $3, children under 16 free) is composed of the buildings that rim the town's plaza, which give a feel for what life was like here back in the late 1800s. Start your tour of the park in the Plaza Hotel, a former 18-room lodging establishment with fully furnished re-creations of the hotel's dining room, private card room, parlor, saloon, and a guestroom.

The Castro-Breen Adobe, adjacent to the hotel, uses old photos and interpretive displays to detail two of the town's prominent early families that resided in the building. Across 2nd Street and overlooking the plaza is the Plaza Stable, which shelters a fleet of stagecoaches, wagons, and carriages. Other buildings of interest include the blacksmith shop, the Zanetta House, the jail, and the settler's cabin.

The park puts on several events a year, including an antique firearm display, Dutch cooking demonstrations, living-history days, and a special *Vertigo* event with tours, dinner, and a screening of the film on the Plaza Lawn. Check the website for dates. Be on the lookout for strange occurrences while wandering

through the park's old buildings; it is said that many ghosts reside on the premises. It's possible to experience the park in just one or two hours.

★ Fremont Peak State Park

Eleven miles south of San Juan Bautista, **Fremont Peak State Park** (San Juan Canyon Rd. off Hwy. 156, 831/623-4255, www.parks.ca.gov, daily 8am-30 minutes after sunset, $6/vehicle) has one of the best views of the Monterey Bay area from its 3,169-foot mountaintop, letting visitors take in both the Salinas and San Benito Valleys. Drive close to the summit and then hike 0.5 miles (one way, moderate) for the best views.

Fremont Peak offers more than a look down below. The state park is one of the best places in the region for stargazing. It has an **observatory** (www.fpoa.net, programs April-Oct. Sat. 8pm or 8:30pm) with a 30-inch diameter telescope that hosts summer astronomy programs on Saturday nights. In addition, there is a **campground** (800/444-7275, www.reserveamerica.com, $25) with 25 primitive sites.

Nightlife

Mom & Pop's Saloon (205 3rd St., 831/623-2393, Mon.-Thurs. 11am-8pm, Fri.-Sat. 10am-2am, Sun. 10am-9pm) is a cash-only bar on San Juan Bautista's main business street. A small stage is barely big enough to host the rock and blues trios that perform on weekends. A friendly clientele (that look like extras from the TV show *Sons of Anarchy*) crowd the long wooden bar, while others play pool on the saloon's billiards table.

Performing Arts

Theater company **El Teatro Campesino** (705 4th St., 831/623-2444, www.elteatrocampesino.com) began with members performing skits on flatbed trucks and union halls to highlight the plight of farmworkers during the 1965 Delano Grape Strike. In 1971 the theater company, led by Luis Valdez (the playwright who wrote *Zoot Suit* and directed the 1987 film *La Bamba*), moved to San Juan Bautista. Today the company does original productions like the annual *La Virgen del Tepeyac,* performed during the holiday season, which is about Our Lady of Guadalupe.

Shopping

San Juan Bautista is home to many antique shops. **Aggie's Porch** (37 Mariposa St., 831/623-4753, Fri.-Sun. 11am-5pm and by appointment) is a two-room Victorian with a range of antiques, from vintage furniture to old anchovy tins. A block away from Aggie's is **Fat Willy's Antiques** (603 4th St., 831/801-7375, Fri.-Sun. 10am-4pm), which specializes in furniture from the 1800s and 1900s.

The Guatemalan Boutique (302 3rd St., 831/623-1117, Wed.-Sun. 11am-5pm) breaks away from the antiques scene and sells lovely handcrafted items and folk art from Mexico and Guatemala.

Recreation

If off-roading is your thing, head for the hills. Specifically, the **Hollister Hills State Vehicular Recreation Area** (7800 Cienega Rd., 831/637-8186, www.parks.ca.gov, daily dawn-dusk, $5/vehicle), which has over 150 miles of trails created for four-wheel-drive vehicles, ATVs, and motorcycles. The Upper Ranch area caters to four-wheel drives and motorcycles, while the Lower Ranch is just for motorbikes and ATVs. Hollister Hills also has seven **campgrounds** (first come, first served, $10).

Accommodations

There are just two lodging options in San Juan Bautista. The **Hacienda de Leal** (410 The Alameda, 831/623-4380, www.haciendadeleal.com, $175-350) is a boutique hotel with 42 rooms and suites. All rooms have hardwood floors and custom-made wood furniture along with iPhone docking stations and flat-screen TVs. There is also a nice courtyard area with a fountain and a pet playground. All guests are treated to a continental breakfast in the morning.

The other option in town is the **Posada De San Juan** (310 4th St., 831/623-4030, www.posadadesanjuanbautistaca.com, $125-275). A stay in one of the 34 rooms includes a light breakfast in the morning. This Spanish-style hotel has hosted the likes of Clint Eastwood, Linda Ronstadt, and Cheech Marin. Some of the rooms have fireplaces and soaking tubs.

Food

JJ's Homemade Burgers (100 The Alameda, 831/623-1748, Mon.-Sat. 11am-8pm, Sun. 11am-7:30pm, $11-15) is a throwback burger joint with modern prices. All of the burgers here are made with beef from the Central Valley's Harris Ranch. Options include bacon cheeseburgers, Hawaiian burgers, and the El Jefe Burger, topped with bacon, avocado, jack cheese, grilled onions, and jalapeños. Dine inside under biker decor or out front on the patio. Get your photo on the wall if you can complete the JJ's Burger Challenge: Consume a four-patty burger, fries, and a milkshake in 20 minutes or less.

Vertigo Coffee (81 4th Ave., 831/623-9533, www.vertigocoffee.com, Tues.-Fri. 7am-7pm, Sat.-Sun. 8am-7pm) is a great place for a pick-me-up while exploring San Juan Bautista. Vertigo roasts their beans in-house and makes drip coffee, espresso, and Americanos. They also have a small menu of sandwiches, salads, pizzas, and calzones.

The Happy Rooster (313 3rd St., 831/623-4126, daily 7am-8:30pm, $14-27) does Italian food and more at its location on San Juan Bautista's main drag. The favorite dinner menu items are chicken marsala, cheese ravioli in Alfredo sauce, and a 20-ounce cowboy steak.

On a sunny afternoon, it's hard to beat dining in the outdoor courtyard and garden at **Jardines De San Juan** (115 3rd St., 831/623-4466, Sun.-Thurs. 11:30am-9pm, Fri.-Sat. 11:30am-10pm, $7-20). The menu includes Mexican staples like tacos, tostadas, and burritos, while regional specialties are served on Friday, Saturday, and Sunday nights. They also do some interesting margaritas, including a spicy mango version and an avocado one.

Also known as "the Basque restaurant," the **Basque Maxtain Extea Basque Restaurant** (206 4th St., 831/623-4472, www.thebasquerestaurant.com, Wed.-Thurs. 4pm-9pm, Fri. noon-9pm, Sat.-Sun. 11am-9pm, $14-22) offers a unique dining experience in San Juan Bautista. The owners and chef are Basque natives that do traditional Spanish cuisine from tapas to lamb stew. Go for a family-style meal (adult lunch $18, adult dinner $18-22, child lunch or dinner $11), which includes soup, salad, fries, rice, meat, house wine, coffee, and the dessert of the day.

Transportation

San Juan Bautista is just outside of Monterey County, a 35-minute drive from downtown Monterey. Head north on CA-1 and then east on CA-156. The two-lane highway dead-ends into US-101. Head north on US-101 and then turn off on the CA-156 exit toward San Juan Bautista and Hollister. Take CA-156 east for two miles before taking a left towards San Juan Bautista's downtown area.

The town is a 25-minute drive from nearby Salinas. Take US-101 north and take the CA-156 exit toward San Juan Bautista and Hollister. Take CA-156 east for two miles before taking a left towards San Juan Bautista's downtown area.

GILROY

Gilroy is located in Santa Clara County, 16 miles south of San Jose. It is known as the "Garlic Capital of the World" due to the pungent crop that you can sometimes smell while passing through the city on Highway 101, and it hosts the annual Gilroy Garlic Festival. The city is the home of the Gilroy Gardens Family Theme Park and the Gilroy Premium Outlets. Gilroy makes for a nice place to stop while traveling between Monterey and the Bay Area, as it's about the halfway point between the two destinations.

Gilroy Gardens Family Theme Park

The **Gilroy Gardens Family Theme Park** (3050 Hecker Pass Hwy., 408/840-7100, www.gilroygardens.org, Mon.-Fri. 11am-5pm, Sat.-Sun. 10am-5pm, adults $52, children $42) is a family-friendly amusement park featuring

San Juan Bautista's Vertigo Coffee

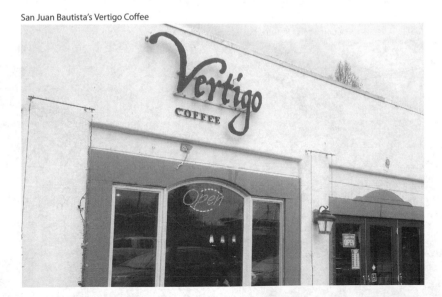

the Quiksilver Express Mine Coaster. The other rides include a carousel, a raft that floats through gardens, and a swing around a giant mushroom. The theme park is also known for its Circus Trees, which have been shaped and grafted to resemble hearts and chain-link fences. Ticket discounts are available online.

Festivals and Events

Gilroy is known as "The Garlic Capital of the World," and the annual **Gilroy Garlic Festival** (Christmas Hill Park, 7050 Miller Ave., 408/842-1625, http://gilroygarlicfestival.com, July, adults $20, children and seniors $10) celebrates the flavorful plant over a summer weekend. Be adventurous and try garlic ice cream or other gourmet foods. Events include cook-offs, craft-making, live music, and the crowning of Miss Gilroy Garlic. Be aware that if you are traveling through Gilroy during this weekend, there will be major traffic jams on Highway 101.

Shopping

Beyond garlic, Gilroy is known for its sprawling outlet mall that draws shoppers from all over Central California. The **Gilroy Premium Outlets** (681 Leavesley Rd., Suite 175, 408/842-3729, www.premiumoutlets.com, Mon.-Sat. 10am-9pm, Sun. 10am-7pm) has 145 outlet stores ranging from preppy clothes retailer Abercrombie & Fitch to surfwear company Volcom. You can also pick up shoes from Timberland, necklaces from Kay Jewelers, and cookware from Le Creuset.

Food

Gilroy is home to an In-N-Out Burger, but if you'd rather have a burger at a local joint, try the **Café 152 Burger Co.** (8401 Church St., 408/767-2055, http://cafe152burgerco.com, daily 11am-8pm, $5-9). The options here hinge around quarter-pound and third-pound Angus beef burgers. This being Gilroy, the Big Roy Burger is stuffed with roasted garlic and caramelized onions.

Another fast option is **Barbecue 152** (8295 Monterey Rd., 408/842-4499, daily 11:30am-9pm, $7-25). It has a classic barbecue joint menu of meat (pulled pork, ribs, tri-tip, chicken, and spicy hot links) and sides (potato salad, coleslaw, and beans).

The **Garlic City Café** (7461 Monterey St., 408/847-7744, Sun.-Mon. 8am-3pm, Tues.-Sat. 8am-3pm and 5pm-9pm, $7-13) utilizes the city's favorite edible plant in its calamari steak

The Gilroy Premium Outlets offer over 100 different stores.

sandwich and its pasta. The signature soup is none other than cream of garlic.

Getting There

It takes 45 minutes to travel from Monterey to Gilroy, and closer to 1.5 hours on a summer or holiday weekend. Take CA-1 north out of Monterey and hop on CA-156 going east. Take the two-lane road to US-101, then head north for about 20 miles until you hit Gilroy.

Driving from Salinas to Gilroy can take just 30 minutes. Get on US-101 heading north and travel 25 miles until you reach the city limits.

Santa Cruz

There's no place like Santa Cruz. Even in the left-leaning Bay Area, you won't find another town that has embraced cultural experimentation, radical philosophies, and progressive politics quite like this little beach city.

Santa Cruz has made out-there ideas into a kind of municipal cultural statement. Everyone does their own thing: Surfers ride the waves, nudists laze on the beaches, tree-huggers wander the redwood forests, tattooed and pierced punks wander the main drag, and families walk their dogs along West Cliff Drive.

Most visitors come to Santa Cruz to hit the Boardwalk and the beaches. Locals and UC Santa Cruz students tend to hang downtown on Pacific Avenue and stroll on West Cliff. Local food qualifies as a hidden treasure, with myriad international cuisines represented and enjoyed.

The West Side is the section of town northwest of the San Lorenzo River that includes the boardwalk, Steamer Lane, West Cliff Drive, and the university, and it tends toward families with children. The East Side has fewer attractions, but offers a vibrant surf scene situated around Pleasure Point.

Outside Santa Cruz proper, several tiny towns blend into appealing beachside suburbia. Aptos and Capitola lie to the south along the coast. They've each got their own shopping districts, restaurants, and lodgings, as well as charming beaches, which can be as foggy, as crowded, or as nice to visit as those of their northern neighbors.

Up north, on the coast, the West Side's buildings quickly give way to scenic coastal bluffs dotted with attractions like Wilder Ranch State Park, the tiny town of Davenport, and Año Nuevo State Park, with its gigantic elephant seals.

The redwood-forested Santa Cruz Mountains are home to the quirky communities of Felton, Ben Lomond, and Boulder Creek. It's also a great place to take a walk in the forest, at Big Basin Redwoods State Park or Henry Cowell Redwoods State Park.

Previous: Cowell's Beach; wave breaking off a beach in Santa Cruz; **Above:** Sempervirens Falls in Big Basin Redwoods State Park.

Look for ★ to find recommended
sights, activities, dining, and lodging.

Highlights

the city's eclectic characters to strut their stuff (page 147).

★ **Santa Cruz Surfing Museum:** Perched above Santa Cruz's most well-known break, Steamer Lane, this one-room museum honors the seaside city's most popular pastime (page 151).

★ **Surfing in Santa Cruz:** The shape and direction of Santa Cruz's coastline means that there is a near-constant parade of waves suitable for surfers of all abilities (page 157).

★ **Wilder Ranch State Park:** Just north of Santa Cruz, the buildings recede to stunning coastal terraces. Wilder Ranch State Park provides a great way to experience this region whether you are a hiker or mountain biker (page 172).

★ **Davenport:** Nine miles north of Santa Cruz, this small coastal community is surrounded by terrific beaches with sea stacks offshore (page 172).

★ **Año Nuevo State Park:** See nature in action at this park, where one of the world's largest groups of elephant seals congregate (page 174).

★ **Roaring Camp Railroads:** Experience the redwood forests of the Santa Cruz Mountains via train at this popular attraction (page 175).

★ **Big Basin Redwoods State Park:** California's first state park amazes with its towering coast redwoods and many hiking trails (page 177).

★ **Santa Cruz Beach Boardwalk:** One of the state's last beach boardwalks, this amusement park is a blast of throwback fun with its iconic wooden roller coaster, arcade, and summer beach concerts (page 146).

★ **Pacific Avenue:** Santa Cruz's liveliest street is packed with the city's best restaurants, shops, and bars. It also serves as a runway for

Santa Cruz and Vicinity

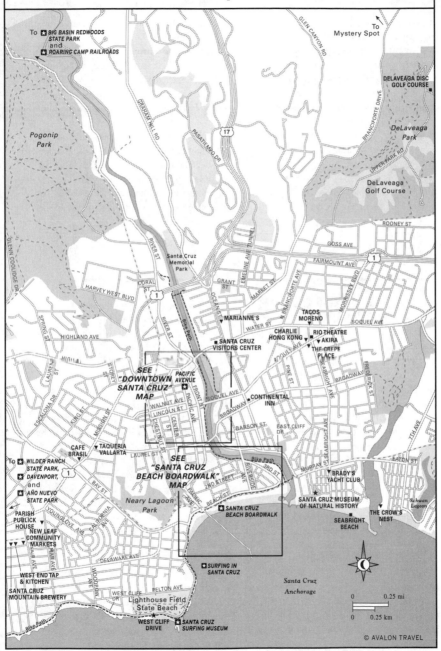

To Mystery Spot

To ⚑ BIG BASIN REDWOODS STATE PARK
and
⚑ ROARING CAMP RAILROADS

GLEN CANYON RD

DELAVEAGA DISC GOLF COURSE

Pogonip Park

PASATIEMPO DR

GRAHAM HILL RD

BRANCHFORTE DRIVE

DeLaveaga Park

UPPER PARK RD

17

DeLaveaga Golf Course

GLENN COOLIDGE DR

RIVER ST

Santa Cruz Memorial Park

ROONEY ST

GOSS AVE

EMELINE AVE TUNNEL

FAIRMOUNT AVE

1

HARVEY WEST BLVD

CORAL

GRANT ST

OCEAN ST

MARKET ST

N BRANCHFORTE AVE

MORRISSEY BLVD

SOQUEL AVE

SPRING ST

HIGHLAND AVE

1

MARIANNE'S

WATER ST

TACOS MORENO

CHARLIE HONG KONG

RIO THEATRE

AKIRA

SOQUEL AVE

SEABRIGHT AVE

FREDRICK ST

SANTA CRUZ VISITORS CENTER

THE CREPE PLACE

LAUREL ST

HIGH

Bike Path

PINE ST

BROADWAY

7TH AVE

ESCALONA DR

KING ST

MISSION ST

STOREY ST

SEE "DOWNTOWN SANTA CRUZ" MAP

PACIFIC AVENUE

FRONT ST

PACIFIC AVE

SOQUEL AVE

BROADWAY

CONTINENTAL INN

WALNUT AVE

LINCOLN ST

CENTER ST

CHESTNUT ST

BARSON ST

EAST CLIFF DR

CAFE BRASIL

TAQUERIA VALLARTA

LAUREL ST

SEE "SANTA CRUZ BEACH BOARDWALK" MAP

3RD ST

Bike Path

RIVERSIDE

MURRAY ST

BRADY'S YACHT CLUB

EATON ST

To ⚑ WILDER RANCH STATE PARK,
⚑ DAVENPORT, and
⚑ AÑO NUEVO STATE PARK

1

BAY ST

BEACH ST

PACIFIC

Neary Lagoon Park

SANTA CRUZ BEACH BOARDWALK

SANTA CRUZ MUSEUM OF NATURAL HISTORY

Schwan Lagoon

THE CROW'S NEST

PARISH PUBLICK HOUSE

NEW LEAF COMMUNITY MARKETS

YOUNGLOVE AVE

CALIFORNIA ST

MESA AVE

DELAWARE AVE

SEABRIGHT BEACH

WEST END TAP & KITCHEN

SANTA CRUZ MOUNTAIN BREWERY

WOODROW AVE

SURFING IN SANTA CRUZ

Santa Cruz Anchorage

PELTON AVE

WEST CLIFF DR

Lighthouse Field State Beach

0   0.25 mi

0   0.25 km

Bike Path

WEST CLIFF DRIVE

SANTA CRUZ SURFING MUSEUM

© AVALON TRAVEL

PLANNING YOUR TIME

Santa Cruz is ideal for a two- to three-day trip. In that amount of time, you can enjoy the rides of the Santa Cruz Beach Boardwalk, go surfing, explore downtown's Pacific Avenue, and head into the Santa Cruz Mountains to experience redwood forests or travel north on the coast for secluded beaches and elephant seals.

Summers can be particularly crowded in Santa Cruz due to masses of people from San Jose and the Bay Area traveling to the city for the boardwalk and beaches. During this time, parking can be a real nightmare, especially since many residential areas near the beach have resident-only parking. On summer days when Monterey is socked in with fog, the sun is often shining in Santa Cruz.

Consider visiting Santa Cruz in the off-season, when hotel room prices are a lot more affordable. Note that the boardwalk is closed in the off-season, and many restaurants and other businesses in the area have reduced hours.

Highway 1 connects Santa Cruz to Monterey and Carmel. During the morning and evening rush hours, this part of Highway 1 can be jammed, especially the southbound section from the Highway 17/Highway 1 junction down to the 41st Avenue exit.

Highway 9 connects Santa Cruz to the mountain towns of Felton, Ben Lomond, and Boulder Creek, and it can be closed in the winter for long periods due to slides. Highway 17, traversing the mountains en route to San Jose and Silicon Valley, is a steep, windy road that sees lots of accidents.

Sights

★ SANTA CRUZ BEACH BOARDWALK

The **Santa Cruz Beach Boardwalk** (400 Beach St., 831/423-5590, www.beachboardwalk.com, Memorial Day-Labor Day daily, Labor Day-Nov. and Dec. 26-Memorial Day Sat.-Sun. and holidays, check website for hours, individual rides $3-6, all-day pass $32, parking $6-15), or just "the Boardwalk" as it's called by locals, has a rare appeal that beckons to young children, too-cool teenagers, and adults of all ages.

The amusement park rambles along each side of the south end of the Boardwalk; entry is free, but you must buy either per-ride tickets or an unlimited-ride wristband. The Giant Dipper is an old-school wooden roller coaster that opened back in 1924 and is still giving riders a thrill after all this time. The Double Shot shoots riders up a 125-foot tower with great views of the bay or inland Santa Cruz before free-falling straight down. In summertime, a log ride cools down guests hot from hours of tromping around. The Boardwalk also offers several toddler and little-kid rides.

At the other end of the Boardwalk, avid gamesters choose between the lure of prizes from the traditional midway games and the large arcade. Throw baseballs at things, try your arm at Skee-Ball, or take a pass at a classic or newer video game. The traditional carousel actually has a brass ring you (or your children) can try to grab.

After you've worn yourself out playing games and riding rides, you can take the stairs down to the broad, sandy beach below the Boardwalk. It's a great place to flop down and sun yourself, or brave a dip in the cool Pacific surf. Granted, it gets a bit crowded in the summertime. But you've got all the services you could ever want right here at the Boardwalk, plus the sand and the water (and the occasional strand of kelp). What could be more perfect?

During the summer, the Boardwalk puts on free Friday-night concerts on the beach featuring retro acts like hair metal band Warrant and 1980s New Wave band A Flock of Seagulls. See the website for a complete schedule of upcoming acts.

SANTA CRUZ WHARF

The half-mile-long **Santa Cruz Wharf** (21 Municipal Wharf, 831/420-6025, www.ci.santa-cruz.ca.us, parking $1/hour up to four hours, $2/hour after four hours) claims to be the longest wooden wharf in the coastal United States. Built in 1914, it was originally used for commercial purposes. Today it's used for recreational purposes, including fishing, strolling, and sightseeing, with both pedestrian and vehicle lanes. At the western end there are places to observe the sea lions hanging out on the pilings below. Docents from the nearby Seymour Discovery Center lead 30-minute **nature tours** (831/459-3800, http://seymourcenter.ucsc.edu, spring-summer Sat.-Sun. 1pm and 3pm, free) of the pier.

★ PACIFIC AVENUE

The center of downtown Santa Cruz is **Pacific Avenue,** stretching nine blocks from Water Street to Laurel Street. The vibrant, two-lane road is lined with many of the city's finest restaurants, shops, bars, and entertainment options, including the three-screen, art deco Del Mar Theatre. At the northern end is a handsome clock tower. The sidewalks are often jammed with shoppers, street performers, panhandlers, and sightseers.

For information on Santa Cruz, stop by the **Downtown Information Kiosk** (1130 Pacific Ave., K2, www.downtownsantacruz.com, May-Oct. Sun.-Thurs. 11am-6pm, Fri.-Sat. 11am-8pm, Nov.-April Sun.-Thurs. 11am-5pm, Fri.-Sat. 11am-7pm).

NATURAL BRIDGES STATE PARK

At the tip of the West Side, **Natural Bridges State Park** (2531 West Cliff Dr., 831/423-4609, www.parks.ca.gov, daily 8am-sunset, $10) used to have three coastal arches right offshore; today only one arch remains. This picturesque state park has a beach that falls back deeply, crossed by a creek that feeds into the sea. An inconsistent break makes surfing at Natural Bridges fun on occasion, while the near-constant winds bring out windsurfers nearly every weekend. Hardy sun-worshippers brave the breezes, bringing out their beach blankets, umbrellas, and sunscreen on rare sunny days (usually in late spring and fall). Back from the beach, a wooded picnic area has tables and grills. Beyond the picnic tables, the park has a monarch butterfly preserve, where the migrating insects take over the eucalyptus grove during the fall and winter.

Tidepools range out to the west side of the

Santa Cruz Beach Boardwalk

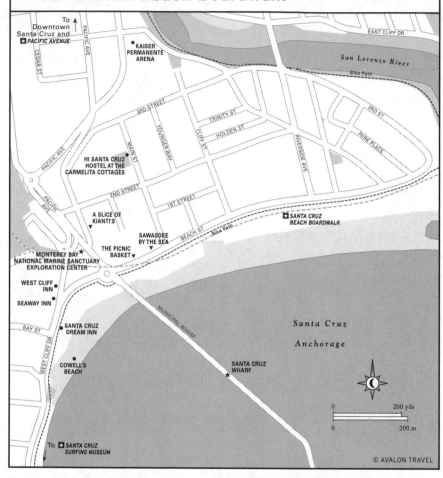

Santa Cruz Beach Boardwalk

To Downtown Santa Cruz and ⚡ PACIFIC AVENUE

EAST CLIFF DR

San Lorenzo River

Bike Path

CEDAR ST

PACIFIC AVE

KAISER PERMANENTE ARENA

3RD STREET

TRINITY ST

3RD ST

PACIFIC AVE

YOUNGER WAY

MAIN ST

CLIFF ST

HOLDEN ST

RIVERSIDE AVE

PARK PLACE

HI SANTA CRUZ HOSTEL AT THE CARMELITA COTTAGES

2ND STREET

1ST STREET

A SLICE OF KIANTI'S

BEACH ST

⚡ SANTA CRUZ BEACH BOARDWALK

SAWASDEE BY THE SEA

Bike Path

THE PICNIC BASKET

MONTEREY BAY NATIONAL MARINE SANCTUARY EXPLORATION CENTER

WEST CLIFF INN

SEAWAY INN

BAY ST

WEST CLIFF DR

SANTA CRUZ DREAM INN

MUNICIPAL WHARF

Santa Cruz Anchorage

SANTA CRUZ WHARF

COWELL'S BEACH

SANTA CRUZ WHARF

To ⚡ SANTA CRUZ SURFING MUSEUM

0   200 yds
0   200 m

© AVALON TRAVEL

beach. You can access them by a somewhat scrambling short hike (0.25-0.5 miles) on the rocky cliffs. These odd little holes filled with sea life aren't like most tidepools—many are nearly perfectly round depressions in the sandstone cliffs worn away by harder stones as the tides move tirelessly back and forth. To avoid causing harm, don't touch the delicate residents of these pools. Rangers offer **guided tours** (year-round at low tide) of the tidepools. Visit the visitors center for the current tour schedule.

MONTEREY BAY NATIONAL MARINE SANCTUARY EXPLORATION CENTER

Opened in 2012, the **Monterey Bay National Marine Sanctuary Exploration Center** (35 Pacific Ave., 831/421-9993, Wed.-Sun. 10am-5pm, free) teaches visitors about the protected waters off Santa Cruz and Monterey. Just across the street from Cowells Beach and the Santa Cruz Wharf, this two-story facility built and operated by the National Oceanic and Atmospheric Administration (NOAA) has exhibits on the water quality, geology, and marine life of the continental United States' largest marine sanctuary. Highlights include a 15-minute film screened upstairs and an interactive exhibit where visitors get to control a remote operational vehicle (ROV) with an attached camera in a large aquarium. The downstairs has a gift shop with books, T-shirts, and postcards. The center also practices environmental sensitivity: The building is built from mostly recycled or reused construction waste and runs on solar power.

SANTA CRUZ MISSION STATE HISTORIC PARK

Believe it or not, weird and funky Santa Cruz started out as a mission town. **Santa Cruz Mission State Historic Park** (144 School St., off Mission St. and Emmett St., 831/425-5849, www.parks.ca.gov, Mon. and Thurs.-Sat. 10am-4pm, Sun. noon-4pm, free) was one of the later California missions, dedicated in 1791. Today, the attractive white building with its classic red-tiled roof welcomes visitors to its active Holy Cross church and historical museum. The park's accessible buildings are not the original complex built by the Spanish fathers in the 18th century. Instead, they're a

replica that was built in the 1930s. One of the better museum exhibits relates the story of the local Ohlone and Yokuts peoples. After touring the complex and grounds, be sure to stop in at the Galeria, which houses the mission gift shop and a stunning collection of religious vestments—something you won't see in many other California missions.

SANTA CRUZ MUSEUM OF ART & HISTORY

A block off Pacific Avenue, the **Santa Cruz Museum of Art & History** (705 Front St., 831/429-1964, www.santacruzmah.org, Tues.-Thurs. and Sat.-Sun. 11am-5pm, Fri. 11am-9pm, adults $5, seniors and students $3) showcases contemporary art alongside Santa Cruz County's history. Rotating exhibition topics have included the Grateful Dead as well as old surfboards. There's an outdoor sculpture garden on the museum's rooftop.

LONG MARINE LABORATORY

While the Monterey Bay Aquarium down the road in Monterey provides the best look into the nearby bay, the **Long Marine Laboratory** (100 Shaffer Rd., 831/459-3800, http://seymourcenter.ucsc.edu, Sept.-June

Monterey Bay National Marine Sanctuary Exploration Center

Downtown Santa Cruz

© AVALON TRAVEL

Tues.-Sun. 10am-5pm, July-Aug. daily 10am-5pm, adults $8, seniors, students, and children $6) is a worthwhile stop for people interested in sea creatures and marine issues. The large, attractive complex at the end of Delaware Avenue sits right on the edge of the cliff overlooking the ocean—convenient for the research done primarily by students and faculty of UCSC. Your visit will be to the **Seymour Marine Discovery Center,** the part of the lab that's open to the public. You'll be greeted outside the door by a full blue whale skeleton that's lit up at night. Inside, instead of a standard aquarium setup, you'll find a marine laboratory similar to those used by scientists elsewhere in the complex. The aquariums showcase fascinating creatures including monkey face eels and speckled sand dabs, while displays highlight environmental issues like shark finning. Kids particularly love the touch tanks, while curious adults enjoy checking out the seasonal tank that contains the wildlife that's swimming around outside in the bay *right now.*

If you've never been to Long/Seymour before, the best way to introduce yourself to the lab is to take a tour. Tours run at 1pm, 2pm, and 3pm each day; sign up an hour in advance to be sure of getting a slot.

UNIVERSITY OF CALIFORNIA, SANTA CRUZ

The **University of California, Santa Cruz** (1156 High St., 831/459-0111, www.ucsc.edu) might be the single most beautiful college campus in the country. Set in the hills above downtown Santa Cruz, the classrooms and dorms sit underneath groves of coast redwood trees, among tangles of ferns and vines that are home to woodland creatures. The Office of Admissions (Cook House, Mon.-Fri. 9am-4pm) provides **self-guided tour maps.** Or just find a parking lot and wander out into the woods like the students do, looking for a perfect circle of trees to sit and meditate within.

The UCSC campus has some other natural wonders: caves, which are located in a gulch behind Porter and Kresge Colleges. **Porter Cave** is the easiest to find and the best for beginning spelunkers. Enter the subterranean chamber by descending down a 20-foot steel ladder. The cave can get quite muddy, so wear clothes you don't mind getting dirty. To find the cave, go behind Porter College and follow the trail across the meadow and into the trees. Then head right alongside Empire Grade Road. Look for a concrete block that marks the cave opening. Bring a flashlight.

Deadheads and fans of 1960s counterculture have another reason to visit UCSC: the **Grateful Dead Archive** (second floor of McHenry Library, Steinhart Rd., http://library.ucsc.edu). Artifacts from the popular rock band are displayed in the library's Dead Central Gallery, while visitors can peruse items in the reading room.

★ SANTA CRUZ SURFING MUSEUM

Just feet away from Santa Cruz's best-known surf spot, Steamer Lane, the tiny **Santa Cruz Surfing Museum** (1701 West Cliff Dr., 831/420-6289, www.santacruzsurfingmuseum.org, July 4-Labor Day Wed.-Mon. 10am-5pm, Labor Day-July 3 Thurs.-Mon. noon-4pm, donation requested) is housed within a still-operating lighthouse. Opened in 1986, it is the world's first museum dedicated to the water sport. Run by the Santa Cruz Surfing Club Preservation Society, the one-room museum has pictures of Santa Cruz's surfing culture from the 1930s to the present. One haunting display on shark attacks includes a local surfboard with bite marks from a great white shark.

THE MYSTERY SPOT

Klamath has the Trees of Mystery, Leggett has its drive-through tree, and Santa Cruz has its own kitschy tourist trap: **The Mystery Spot** (465 Mystery Spot Rd., 831/423-8897, www.mysteryspot.com, summer Mon.-Fri. 10am-6pm, Sat.-Sun. 9am-8pm, winter Mon.-Fri. 10am-4pm, Sat.-Sun. 10am-5pm, adults $6, children under 3 free, $5 parking). It's a tiny piece of land just outside of Santa Cruz where gravity fails. Balls can roll uphill and people can stand off the side of a wall. It may be an area of spatial distortion where the laws of physics don't apply . . . or it may be a collection of optical illusions. Regardless, it has a sweet gift shop that sells the near-iconic Mystery Spot bumper sticker and other necessities like thong underwear.

SANTA CRUZ MUSEUM OF NATURAL HISTORY

Housed in a former library within the city's Seabright neighborhood, the **Santa Cruz Museum of Natural History** (1305 East Cliff Dr., 831/420-6115, Tues.-Sat. 10am-5pm, adults $4, seniors and students $3, children free) began with donations from a collector and an Indian artifact enthusiast. Exhibit topics include the indigenous people of the Monterey Bay region and the area's plant and animal diversity, with a live honeybee display and a live snake. Outdoors, there is a garden that imparts sustainable gardening techniques and information about native plants.

Surf City

There's a plaque outside the Santa Cruz Surfing Museum that explains how three Hawaiian princes introduced surfing to California in 1885. Apparently, they rode redwood planks from a nearby lumber mill on waves at the mouth of the San Lorenzo River in Santa Cruz.

While Santa Cruz's claim as the birthplace of surfing on the mainland is not disputed, the popular surfing town calling itself "Surf City" has raised the hackles of Southern California's Huntington Beach, which also likes to have its tourist T-shirts adorned with "Surf City." In 2006, Huntington Beach was awarded exclusive use of the title "Surf City" by the U.S. Patent and Trademark Office and went after Santa Cruz beachwear stores that sold T-shirts with the words "Santa Cruz" and "Surf City."

Despite Huntington Beach's aggressive legal action, the residents of Santa Cruz might have the last laugh. In 2009, *Surfer Magazine* proclaimed Santa Cruz as "The Real Surf City, USA" in a piece about the best surf towns. To Huntington Beach's chagrin, it didn't even make the magazine's top 10 list.

Entertainment and Events

BARS AND CLUBS

Lovers of libations should grab a drink at **Red Restaurant & Bar** (200 Locust St., 831/425-1913, www.redsantacruz.com, daily 3pm-1:30am), located upstairs in the historic Santa Cruz Hotel Building. Creative cocktails include signature creations like the Jean Grey, a mix of house-infused Earl Grey organic gin, lemon, and simple syrup. They also have a nice selection of 30 craft and Belgian beers on tap. With its dark wood paneling and burgundy barstools, Red feels like an old speakeasy. It also serves a comprehensive late-night menu until 1am for those who need some food to soak up their alcohol.

Hopheads and other beer fans should make their way to the **Lupulo Craft Beer House** (233 Cathcart St., 831/454-8306, www.lupulosc.com, Sun.-Thurs. 11:30am-10pm, Fri.-Sat. 11:30am-10:30pm). A small spot with a hip industrial feel, Lupulo has 16 rotating craft beers on tap and over 100 types of bottled beer (which can also be taken to go). A small-bites menu features tacos, salads, and sandwiches. This husband-and-wife-owned business also conducts brewing demos, tastings, and other events.

Located in an alley, popular Irish pub **The**

Poet & The Patriot (320 Cedar St., 831/426-8620, daily 1pm-2am) was opened by a Santa Cruz politician and playwright. The bar has two main rooms, including one where there is live music 3-4 times per week and another one that has four regulation dartboards. Framed Irish mementos decorate the walls and banners hang from the ceiling. On the first Sunday of the month at 3pm, the pub hosts a Celtic music jam.

On the West Side, the **Santa Cruz Mountain Brewery** (402 Ingalls St., 831/425-4900, www.scmbrew.com, daily 11:30am-10pm) serves their organic brews in a taproom and outdoor beer garden. There are always seven of their flagship beers on tap, including an IPA and 2-3 seasonal brews. They also serve typical pub food. On Monday nights, they screen films in the beer garden. Another drinking establishment on the West Side is the **Parish Publick House** (841 Almar Ave., www.polaro.com/parish, daily 11am-2am), which serves 16 beers on draft and pub grub from its space in a strip mall.

The Jury Room (712 Ocean St., 831/426-7120, daily 6am-2am), a dive bar just east of downtown, is a local favorite for its cheap drinks, free pool, and jukebox filled with

The Rio Theatre hosts concerts, movies, and other events.

The Catalyst (1011 Pacific Ave., 831/423-1338, www.catalystclub.com), right downtown on Pacific Avenue, hosts a variety of reggae, rap, and punk acts from Snoop Dogg to Agent Orange. Be sure to check the calendar when you buy tickets—some shows are 21 and over. The 800-person main concert hall is a standing-room-only space, while the balconies offer seating. The bar sits downstairs adjacent to the concert space. The vibe tends to be low-key, but it depends on the night and the event. The new Catalyst Atrium, a smaller room in the same building, snags some superb national touring bands. You can buy tickets online or by phone; purchasing in advance is recommended, especially for national acts.

Named one of the greatest jazz venues in the world by *DownBeat* magazine, the **Kuumbwa Jazz Center** (320 Cedar St., 831/427-2227, http://kuumbwajazz.org) is a 200-seat treasure. It puts on 120 intimate concerts a year aided by a superb sound and lighting setup. Past performers have included Bobby Hutcherson, Pharaoh Saunders, Christian McBride, and David Grisman.

The **Crow's Nest** (2218 East Cliff Dr., 831/476-4560, www.crowsnest-santacruz.com) is as a venue for all kinds of live music acts. Rock, soul, reggae, and funk bands typically play Tuesday-Saturday. Sundays are live comedy evenings, and Tuesdays are reggae jam nights.

A former 1940s movie house, the **Rio Theatre** (1205 Soquel Ave., 831/423-8209, www.riotheatre.com) hosts everything from film festivals to performances by international touring acts like Ladysmith Black Mambazo and Built to Spill. Check the theater's website for a full list of upcoming events.

A short drive south of downtown, **Moe's Alley** (1535 Commercial Way, 831/479-1854, www.moesalley.com) draws nationally touring rock, reggae, blues, funk, and jam bands to its venue every night of the week except for Mondays. Depending on the show, Moe's can accommodate an audience of 300-350 people.

punk rock songs. It's also got creepy cred: It was once the hangout of 1970s serial killer Edmund Emil Kemper.

The Crepe Place (1134 Soquel Ave., 831/429-6994, http://thecrepeplace.com, Mon.-Thurs. 11am-midnight, Fri. 11am-1am, Sat.-Sun. 9am-midnight) has recently emerged as a hangout for the hipster crowd, who are drawn in by the high-profile indie rock acts and popular Bay Area bands that perform in its intimate front room. They also have outdoor seating and a comprehensive menu of creative crepes.

There aren't any boats at **Brady's Yacht Club** (413 Seabright Ave., 831/425-9854, daily 10am-2am), a welcoming dive bar in the Seabright neighborhood where friendly locals might be playing a game of pool or dice. The bar is cluttered with knickknacks, and branches and Christmas lights hang in the rafters. They have some beer on tap and a deal on Moscow mules (vodka, ginger beer, and lime juice) served in a copper mug for just $6. Cash only.

Hitchcock's Santa Cruz

Famed film director Alfred Hitchcock had a deep connection to the Santa Cruz area. It began in earnest when Hitchcock bought a 200-acre estate in the Santa Cruz Mountains near Scotts Valley in 1940 as a second home. From then on, the Santa Cruz area was part of his work. In the 1941 film *Suspicion,* the Santa Cruz coastline stands in for the English countryside. It's rumored that the mansion in his 1960 masterpiece *Psycho* was based on the former Hotel McCray, which is now the Sunshine Villa senior living facility on Beach Hill. The town of Santa Cruz is even mentioned in *The Birds* as the place that the strange phenomena in the film first occurred. Today, the former Hitchcock estate is the Heart O' the Mountain Winery. Unfortunately, it is not open to the public.

CINEMA

Santa Cruz has two great downtown movie theaters: **The Nickelodeon** (210 Lincoln St., 831/426-7500 or 831/426-7507, http://thenick. com), a classic art house movie theater, and the art deco **Del Mar Theatre** (1124 Pacific Ave., 831/426-7500 or 831/469-3224, http:// thenick.com), which dates back to 1936. Both screen independent features, foreign films, and the occasional big-budget flick. The Del Mar also frequently shows a slate of midnight movies. Check the website for details.

COMEDY

For a good laugh in Santa Cruz, the **Crow's Nest** (2218 East Cliff Dr., 831/476-4560, www. crowsnest-santacruz.com, Sun. 9pm, $7) hosts a weekly stand-up comedy show. Because the show runs on Sunday nights, the Crow's Nest takes advantage of the opportunity to hire big-name comics who have been in San Francisco or San Jose for weekend engagements. This lets folks see headliners in a more casual setting for a fraction of the cost of the big-city clubs. The Crow's Nest, with its great views out over the Pacific, also has a full bar and restaurant. You can enjoy drinks and dinner while you get your giggle on.

THEATER

When the long-running Shakespeare Santa Cruz went belly up in 2013, the nonprofit **Santa Cruz Shakespeare** (The Sinsheimer-Stanley Festival Glen, UCSC Performing Arts Center, Meyer Dr., 831/460-6396, www.

santacruzshakespeare.com, July-Aug., adults $40-52, seniors and military $36-48, children 18 and under $16, previews $20) was formed in 2014 so Bard lovers could still get their fix. Recent productions, presented in the Sinsheimer-Stanley Festival Glen, have included *Much Ado About Nothing*, *Macbeth*, and the Shakespeare-inspired *The Liar.*

The **Jewel Theatre Company** (Center Stage, 1001 Center St., 831/425-7506, www. jeweltheatre.net) is the only Santa Cruz County troupe that produces plays throughout the year. You might be able to catch something like George Bernard Shaw's *Saint Joan* or a world premiere of a local playwright's work. Plays are mounted at the 89-seat Center Stage building.

FESTIVALS AND EVENTS

Every winter when the rains start and the mushrooms emerge, Santa Cruz celebrates with three days of fun(gi) at the **Fungus Fair** (Louden Nelson Community Center, 301 Center St., 831/684-2275, http://ffsc.us, Jan., $5-10). The festivities include talks, cooking demonstrations, a dinner, and displays of different types of mushrooms.

Watch surf kayakers and stand-up paddleboarders compete on the giant winter swells at **Santa Cruz Paddlefest** (Steamer Lane, 925/818-6058, http://santacruzpaddlefest. com, Mar., free), which unfolds over three days in March. The event includes a stand-up paddleboard race from Cowell's Beach to the Santa Cruz Harbor and back, along with a popular SUP and surf kayaking competition at Steamer Lane. Crowds gather on West Cliff Drive to catch the action. Food trucks and merchandise booths set up along the cliffside.

The Santa Cruz Blues Festival filled the Aptos Village Park every Memorial Day Weekend with blues acts and fans for 20 years before calling it quits in 2014. Thankfully, in 2015, the **Santa Cruz American Music Festival** (Aptos Village Park, 100 Aptos Creek Rd., www.santacruzamericanmusic-festival.com, Memorial Day weekend, adults single day $65-75, adult two days $120-130, children single day $25) stepped into the void with an inaugural lineup that included Bonnie Raitt, Los Lonely Boys, Big & Rich, and others.

Woodies were pre-1950s cars with partial wood bodies that are associated with early surf culture. **Woodies on the Wharf** (Santa Cruz Wharf, 21 Municipal Wharf, 831/420-5273, www.santacruzwoodies.com, June, free) finds more than 200 of these cool cars and trucks displayed on the wharf for a day in late June.

Watch Santa Cruz's best surfers rip apart waves at the **O'Neill Coldwater Classic** (Steamer Lane, www.oneill.com/cwc, Oct., free). The winner of the two-day surf contest gets bragging rights and a coveted yearlong sponsorship from O'Neill.

The four-day **Santa Cruz Film Festival** (http://santacruzfilmfestival.org, Nov.) has brought movies large and small to town including *Chasing Mavericks*, *Frank*, and *Doomsdays*. Most movies are screened in the Rio Theatre (1205 Soquel Ave.), but some are screened at other venues across the city.

Shopping

PACIFIC AVENUE

For a small city, Santa Cruz has a bustling downtown, centered on **Pacific Avenue,** which extends from Water Street to Laurel Street for about nine blocks. At the northern end, shoppers peruse antiques, clothing, and kitchenware. In the middle, you can grab a cappuccino, a cocktail, or a bite to eat in one of the many independent eateries. At the (slightly seedy) south end, visitors can

O'Neill Surf Shop in downtown Santa Cruz

purchase body jewelry or tattoos. The sidewalks are often jammed with shoppers, street performers, panhandlers, and sightseers. It's a good idea to park in one of the structures a block or two off Pacific Avenue and walk from there.

Book Shop Santa Cruz (1520 Pacific Ave., 831/423-0900, www.bookshopsantacruz. com, Sun.-Thurs. 9am-10pm, Fri.-Sat. 9am-11pm) is a superb independent bookstore that hosts regular readings by literary heavy hitters like Jonathan Franzen and Daniel Handler.

Santa Cruz's Jack O'Neill is credited with making cold-water surfing possible with the invention of the wetsuit. His **O'Neill Surf Shop** (110 Cooper St., 831/469-4377, www. oneill.com, Sun.-Thurs. 10am-8pm, Fri.-Sat. 10am-9pm) specializes in surfboards, brand-name clothing, and, of course, wetsuits. If your trip to California has gotten you hooked on riding the waves, and you just have to invest in your own equipment, O'Neill can be a good place to start. You can also buy a T-shirt or some sweats here—handy if you didn't pack quite right for Central Coast summer fog. There's also another location in Capitola (1115 41st Ave., 831/475-4151, Mon.-Fri. 9am-8pm, Sat.-Sun. 8am-8pm).

If you're wanting to buy clothes in Santa Cruz, chances are you're looking for a secondhand store. This town has plenty of them. One of the largest of these sits only a block off Pacific Avenue—the aptly if redundantly named **Thrift Center Thrift Store** (504 Front St., 831/429-6975, Mon.-Sat. 9am-8pm, Sun. 10am-6pm). This big, somewhat dirty retail space offers a wide array of cheap secondhand clothes. You'll need to hunt a bit to find that one perfect vintage item, but isn't that the fun of thrift shopping?

Camouflage (1329 Pacific Ave., 831/423-7613, www.shopcamouflauge.com, Mon.-Thurs. 11am-9pm, Fri.-Sat. 11am-10pm, Sun. 11am-7pm) is an independent, family-owned, and women-friendly adult store. The first room contains mostly lingerie and less-shocking items. Dare to walk through the narrow black-curtained passage and you'll find the *other* room, which is filled with grown-up toys designed to please women of every taste and proclivity.

Stop by **Streetlight Records** (939 Pacific Ave., 888/648-9201, www.streetlightrecords. com, Sun.-Mon. noon-8pm, Tues.-Thurs. 11am-9pm, Fri.-Sat. 11am-10pm) to pick up the latest music for your drive down the coast. With records and turntables making a serious comeback, Streetlight is also the place in Santa Cruz to find new and used vinyl.

Sports and Recreation

BEACHES

Natural Bridges State Park (2531 West Cliff Dr., 831/423-4609, www.parks.ca.gov, daily 8am-sunset, $10) is one of Santa Cruz's best, but the city also boasts two other excellent beaches. Lots of beginning surfers rode their first waves at **Cowell's Beach** (350 West Cliff Dr.). This West Side beach sits right at a crook in the coastline and features a reliable small break that lures new surfers by the dozens.

At the south end of Santa Cruz, down by the harbor, beachgoers flock to **Seabright Beach** (East Cliff Dr. at Seabright Ave., 831/427-4868, www.santacruzstateparks.org, daily 6am-10pm, free) all summer long. This miles-long stretch of sand, protected from the worst of the winds by the surrounding cliffs, is a favorite retreat for sunbathers and loungers. While there's little in the way of snack bars, permanent volleyball courts, or facilities, you can still have a great time at Seabright. There is a lot of soft sand to lie in, plenty of room to play football or set up your own volleyball net, and, of course, easy access to the chilly Pacific Ocean. There's no surfing here—Seabright has a shore break that delights skim-boarders, but makes wave riding impossible.

★ SURFING

The coastline of Santa Cruz has more than its share of great surf breaks. The water is cold, demanding full wetsuits year-round, and the shoreline is rough and rocky. But that doesn't deter the hordes of locals who ply the waves every day they can.

The best place for beginners is **Cowell's** (stairs at West Cliff Dr. and Cowell's Beach). The waves rarely get huge here, so they provide long, mellow rides, perfect for surfers just getting their balance. Because the Cowell's break is acknowledged as the newbie spot, the often-sizeable crowd tends to be polite to newcomers and visitors.

Visitors who know their surfing lore will want to surf the more famous spots along the Santa Cruz shore. **Pleasure Point** (between 32nd Ave. and 41st Ave.) encompasses a number of different breaks. You may have heard of **The Hook** (steps at 41st Ave.), a well-known experienced longboarder's paradise. But don't mistake The Hook for a beginner's break; the locals are protective of the waves here and aren't always friendly toward inexperienced newcomers. The break at **36th and East Cliff** (steps at 36th Ave.) can be a better place to go on weekdays—on the weekends, the intense crowding makes catching your own wave a challenge. Up at **30th and East Cliff** (steps at 36th Ave.), you'll find shortboarders catching larger, long peeling sets if there is a swell in the water. When the point breaks are crowded, consider **26th Avenue,** a rare beach break in town. Parking is easiest at nearby Moran Lake Park off East Cliff Drive.

The most famous break in all of Santa Cruz can also be the most hostile to newcomers. **Steamer Lane** (West Cliff Dr. between Cowell's and the Santa Cruz Surfing Museum) has a fiercely protective crew of locals. But if you're experienced and there's a swell coming in, Steamer Lane can have some of the best waves on the California coast.

Yes, you can learn to surf in Santa Cruz

despite the distinct local flavor at some of the breaks. Check out either **Club Ed Surf School and Camps** (831/464-0177, www.club-ed.com, beginner group lesson $90 pp, private lessons $120/hour) or the **Richard Schmidt School** (849 Almar Ave., 831/423-0928, www.richardschmidt.com, 2-hour class $90 pp, private lessons $100-150/hour) to sign up for lessons. Who knows, maybe one day the locals will mistake you for one of their own.

STAND-UP PADDLEBOARDING

The latest water-sports craze has definitely hit Santa Cruz. Stand-up paddleboarders vie for waves with surfers at Pleasure Point and can also be found in the Santa Cruz waters with less wave action. **Covewater Paddle Surf** (726 Water St., 831/600-7230, www.covewatersup.com, 2-hour lesson $65) conducts beginner stand-up paddleboarding (SUP) classes in the relatively calm waters of the Santa Cruz Harbor. They also rent SUPs (Mon.-Fri. $30, Sat.-Sun. $35).

HIKING AND BIKING

To walk or bike where the locals do, just head out to **West Cliff Drive.** This winding street with a full-fledged sidewalk trail running its length on the ocean side is the town's favorite walking, dog walking, jogging, skating, scootering, and biking route. Start at Santa Cruz Municipal Wharf and go 2.75 miles to Natural Bridges State Park (the west end of West Cliff). You'll pass the *To Honor Surfing* statue along with flowering ice plant and views of the ocean studded with sea stacks. Bring your camera if you're strolling West Cliff on a clear day—you won't be able to resist taking photos of the sea, cliffs, and sunset. Watch for fellow path-users, as it can get crowded.

To rent a bike for cruising West Cliff Drive, head over to **Pacific Ave Cycles** (320-322 Pacific Ave., 831/471-2453, daily 10am-6pm, hourly bike rental $8-15, daily bike rental $25-45). The small shop with single- and multiple-speed bikes for rent is just a few blocks east of the start of West Cliff Drive.

SANTA CRUZ
SPORTS AND RECREATION

DISC GOLF

For disc golfers, the **DeLaveaga Disc Golf Course** (DeLaveaga Park, 850 Branciforte Dr., http://delaveagadiscgolf.com, $2 parking) is like the Pebble Beach of disc golf courses, a famed place known by most who play the sport. Created in 1984 as a host site for the World Disc Championship, this 27-hole course still draws over 100 players a day. Its most famous hole is 26, which is a long 600 feet from tee box to basket. Many a disc has been lost here.

SAILING

You don't have to ride a surfboard to get into the waters off Santa Cruz. *Chardonnay II* (790 Mariner Park Way, 831/423-1213, https://chardonnay.cernesystems.com, adults $23-56, children $19-30) is a 70-foot sailboat with a large deck and seating area that does weekend sunset sails, whale-watching brunches, afternoon pizza parties, sushi parties, and more.

Another way to get onto the bay is through **Lighthall Yacht Charters** (Santa Cruz Harbor, 831/429-1970, www.lighthallcharters.com, two-hour sail $40 pp, private sail $240-300). They do two-hour outings and private charter sails on their fleet of three yachts, ranging 32-42 feet long. Passengers are free to bring their own food and drink on board. The skipper is highly knowledgeable about the area.

SPAS

It's hard to beat a hot-water soak after a day of surfing Santa Cruz's breaks or walking the city's vibrant downtown area. The **Tea House Spa** (112 Elm St., 831/426-9700, www.teahousespa.com, daily 11am-midnight, spa rooms $12-35/hour, massages $55-140) is a half-block off Pacific Avenue and offers private hot tubs with views of a bamboo garden. It's not a fancy facility, but the tubs will warm you up and mellow you out.

The **Well Within Spa** (417 Cedar St., 831/458-9355, http://wellwithinspa.com, daily 11am-midnight, spa rooms and outdoor spas $15-44/hour, massages $45-115) has indoor spa rooms and outdoor spas and offers massages.

SPECTATOR SPORTS

In 2012, Santa Cruz became home to the Santa Cruz Warriors, an NBA Development League team associated with the Golden State Warriors. The team plays in the **Kaiser Permanente Arena** (140 Front St., 831/713-4400, http://santacruz.dleague.nba.com,

the view along West Cliff Drive

tickets $17-160), a new indoor arena just west of downtown. The sporting facility, which can accommodate over 2,500 spectators, also hosts bouts for the **Santa Cruz Derby Girls** (www.santacruzderbygirls.org) and **UCSC basketball games** (http://goslugs.com).

Accommodations

Though there are no campgrounds in Santa Cruz proper, there are several near the beach in the Capitola and Aptos areas. The Santa Cruz Mountains also have camping opportunities at Henry Cowell Redwoods State Park and Big Basin Redwoods State Park. Most of these are so close to Santa Cruz that they make fine places to stay while exploring the city if you don't mind a bit of a drive.

Under $150

Staying at a hostel in Santa Cruz just feels right. And the **Hostelling International Santa Cruz Hostel at the Carmelita Cottages** (321 Main St., 831/423-8304, www.hi-santacruz.org, dorm beds $31, private rooms $48-113) offers the area's only real budget lodging. These historic renovated cottages are just two blocks from the Santa Cruz Boardwalk. They're clean, cheap, friendly, and also close to Cowell's Beach. The big,

homelike kitchen is open for guest use and might even be hiding some extra free food in its cupboards. Expect all the usual hostel-style amenities: a nice garden out back, an outdoor deck, free linens, laundry facilities, and a free Internet kiosk. The private rooms are a deal due to their size and cleanliness. The hostel is closed to guests from 11am to 5pm daily, meaning there is no access to guestrooms or indoor common areas. Guests are allowed to leave their luggage inside or in outdoor lockers. Another thing worth noting is the hostel's (basically unenforced) midnight curfew.

The ★ **Seaway Inn** (176 West Cliff Dr., 831/471-9004, www.seawayinn.com, $139-288) offers a night's stay in a great location across from Cowell's Beach for a moderate price, as beach accommodations go. The rooms are clean but not fancy, and the bathrooms are small. All have a shared patio or deck out front with chairs. The 18 units in

SANTA CRUZ
ACCOMMODATIONS

the Ocean Echo Inn & Beach Cottages

the main building have TVs with DVD players along with microwaves and mini-fridges. In addition, there are family suites that can accommodate up to five adults. Add in the complimentary breakfast (with make-your-own waffles) and the friendly staff, and you have a good place to stay by the beach without breaking the bank. The inn also consists of a nearby building that has five studio apartments ($148-298), each with a full kitchen. Pets are welcome in all units for a $15 fee.

Located among a strip of motels on Ocean Street, the **Continental Inn** (414 Ocean St., 831/429-1221, www.continentalinnsantacruz.com, $89-379) doesn't look like much from the outside. But inside, most of the rooms have hardwood floors, and all include a fridge and microwave. A stay includes continental breakfast and access to a pool and spa. It is also a short walk to Santa Cruz's downtown.

Escape the busy Boardwalk and downtown areas for the **Ocean Echo Inn & Beach Cottages** (410 Johans Beach Dr., 831/462-4192, www.oceanecho.com, $155-385), a secluded gem on the East Side. The inn is just 53 footsteps (the innkeepers' count) down to a locals' pocket beach known to some as Sunny Cove and to others as Johan's Beach. The inn's property is thought to have once been a farm,

and its water tower, chicken coop, and carriage house have all been converted into cozy cottages. There are 15 units at Ocean Echo, including cottages and inn rooms. Each is different and 11 of the 15 units have full kitchens. There are multiple outdoor decks on site, along with a Ping-Pong table and some grills for cooking out. A modest continental breakfast is set out in the morning.

$150-250

The four-room **Adobe on Green Street** (103 Green St., 831/469-9866, www.adobeongreen.com, $169-219) offers lovely bed-and-breakfast accommodations close to the heart of Santa Cruz. The location, within walking distance of downtown, lets you soak in the unique local atmosphere to your heart's content. A unifying decorative scheme runs through all four guestrooms— a dark and minimalist Spanish Mission style befitting Santa Cruz's history as a mission town. Each room has a queen bed, a private bath (two have whirlpool tubs), a small TV with a DVD player, and lots of other amenities that can make you comfortable even over a long stay. An expansive continental spread is set out in the dining room each morning 8am-10:30am. Expect yummy local pastries,

The opulent West Cliff Inn overlooks the wharf and boardwalk.

organic and soy yogurts, hard-boiled eggs, coffee, and juice.

The ★ **West Cliff Inn** (174 West Cliff Dr., 831/457-2200, www.westcliffinn.com, $210-350) is a gleaming white mansion topping the hill above Cowell's Beach and the Boardwalk. This three-story historic landmark was constructed in 1877 and was the first of the bluff's "Millionaires' Row" residences; it was transformed into an elegant inn in 2007. The nine rooms in the main house have stunning white marble bathrooms and some have oversized soaking tubs. If your room is on a higher floor, use the inn's dumbwaiter to transport your luggage. The more moderately priced and pet-friendly "Little Beach Bungalow" is behind the main house. All guests can fill up at a morning breakfast buffet and an afternoon wine-and-appetizer hour. The inn's veranda and second-floor balcony provide wonderful views.

In the residential East Side, **Bella Notte** (21305 East Cliff Dr., 877/342-3552, www.bellanotteinn.com, $199-279) is a Mediterranean boutique hotel with just 10 rooms. Mix a drink at your own wet bar with fridge. Some rooms also have a fireplace or soaking tub.

High up on a hilltop, the **Chaminade Resort & Spa** (1 Chaminade Ln., 831/475-5600, www.chaminade.com, $215-389) occupies an impressive 300 acres. Occupy your time at the fitness center, heated outdoor pool, tennis courts, hiking trails, or **The Spa at Chaminade** (831/465-3465, Mon.-Fri. 10am-8pm, Sat.-Sun. 9am-8pm, massages $120-190).

Over $250

The ★ **Santa Cruz Dream Inn** (175 West Cliff Dr., 831/426-4330, www.dreaminnsantacruz.com, $349-556) is in a location that cannot be beat. Perched over Cowell's Beach and the Santa Cruz Wharf, the Dream Inn has 165 rooms, all with striking ocean views and either a private balcony or a shared common patio. The rooms have a retro-chic feel that matches perfectly with the vibrant colors of the nearby Santa Cruz Boardwalk. On a sunny day, it would be difficult to ever leave the Dream Inn's sundeck, which is located right on Cowell's Beach. You can take in the action of surfers, stand-up paddleboarders, and volleyball players from the comforts of the deck's heated swimming pool or large multi-person hot tub. Or you could just relax on a couch or reclining chair while sipping a cocktail from the poolside bar.

The large pool deck at the **Hotel Paradox** (611 Ocean St., 831/425-7100, www.hotelparadox.com, $289-629) is the new boutique hotel's best asset. Take advantage of Santa Cruz's sunshine at the tempting pool and large hot tub that can accommodate a dozen or more. Waiters from the hotel restaurant Solaire deliver cocktails and food to those enjoying the deck from 11:30am to 5pm. The rooms are clean and modern with flat-screen TVs and Keurig coffeemakers. Opt for a unit on the ground floor with a small outdoor deck area, or choose a room higher up with a view of the pool action.

Food

Afghan

★ **Laili** (101 B Cooper St., 831/423-4545, http://lailirestaurant.com, Sun. and Tues.-Thurs. 11:30am-2:30pm, 5pm-9pm, Fri.-Sat. 11:30am-2:30pm, 5pm-10pm, $10-28) is in a sleek, modern building with an open kitchen and marbled bar that oozes style. This cuisine complements the space with artfully prepared dishes ranging from a cilantro Caesar salad to *bolani,* a vegan flatbread. Meals begin with a hefty serving of naan and dipping sauce. The filet mignon kebab, three tender pieces of meat with dipping sauces, is exceptional.

Asian Fusion

Street food is a hot culinary trend. Having

opened in 1998, **Charlie Hong Kong** (1141 Soquel Ave., 831/426-5664, www.charliehong-kong.com, daily 11am-11pm, $5-9) has been in the vanguard of this movement for over a decade. A casual eatery, Charlie Hong Kong does organic Asian street food including flavorful bowls, salads, soups, and Vietnamese sandwiches. There are lots of vegan dishes along with a range of gluten-free offerings by request. Eat at a counter indoors or on an outdoor patio under an awning.

Breakfast

A downtown breakfast favorite since 1985, **Zachary's** (819 Pacific Ave., 831/427-0646, Tues.-Sun. 7am-2:30pm, $5-12) makes everything in-house including their breads and rolls. Choose between favorites like the sourdough pancakes, the pesto scramble, and the corned beef hash and eggs. Zachary's is housed in a building that dates back to 1912. The restaurant has high ceilings and is decorated with a variety of plants.

There is almost always a line spilling out of ★ **Cliff Café** (815 41st Ave., 831/476-1214, daily 8am-12:30pm, $8-11). That's partly because this intimate café has just six tables. The other reason is because of the great service and superb omelets, tofu dishes, and pancakes. The pesto and Swiss cheese omelet with an addition of bacon (done extra crispy) is highly impressive.

Coffee and Bakeries

★ **Verve Coffee Roasters** (1540 Pacific Ave., 831/600-7784, www.vervecoffeeroasters.com, daily 6:30am-9pm) offers a hip, open space with lots of windows at the eastern edge of Pacific Avenue. They roast their own beans in the nearby Seabright neighborhood. After ordering your drink at the counter, look for a seat in this frequently crowded coffee shop. They also have locations on the East Side at 846 41st Avenue (831/475-7776, Mon.-Thurs. 6am-7:30pm, Fri. 6am-8:30pm, Sat. 7am-8:30pm, Sun. 7am-7:30pm) and 104 Bronson Street, Suite 19 (831/471-8469, daily 6am-5pm). If Verve's Pacific Avenue location is too packed, head across the street to **Lulu Carpenter's** (1545 Pacific Ave., 831/439-9200, www.lulucarpenters.com, daily 6am-midnight) for coffee. Lulu Carpenter's has the distinction of being the first business to reopen on Pacific Avenue after the 1989 Loma Prieta earthquake. They have other locations at 925 Soquel Avenue (daily 6am-6pm) and 118 Cooper St. (Mon.-Fri. 7am-7pm, Sat.-Sun. 8am-7pm).

Enjoy Afghan food at Laili.

Desserts

Santa Cruz has two favorite local ice cream shops. **Marianne's** (1020 Ocean St., 831/458-1447, www.lovemariannes.com, Sun.-Thurs. 10am-11pm, Fri.-Sat. 10am-midnight) has served scoops of butter brickle and other flavors since 1947. The **Penny Ice Creamery** (913 Cedar St., 831/204-2523, http://thepennyicecreamery.com, daily noon-11pm) is the newcomer, serving hipster-approved flavors like whiskey custard and orange star anise sorbet. Penny also has an East Side location at 820 41st Avenue (Sun.-Thurs. noon-9pm, Fri.-Sat. noon-10pm).

Gastropub

The **West End Tap & Kitchen** (334 Ingalls St., 831/471-8115, http://westendtap.com, Sun.-Thurs. 11:30am-9:30pm, Fri.-Sat. 11:30am-10pm, $10-24) creates food to pair with their fine craft beers and wines. Their 18 beers and four wines on tap can be enjoyed with salads, sandwiches, flatbreads, and entrées like gnocchi or a house-ground burger. West End is a hip, airplane hangar-like space where wooden barrels serve as both furniture and decor.

Hawaiian

The **Pono Hawaiian Grill** (120 Union St., 831/426-7666, www.ponohawaiiangrill.com, Sun.-Wed. 11am-10pm, Thurs.-Sat. 11am-11pm, $7-19) brings the culture and food of the Hawaiian Islands to Santa Cruz. The grill has traditional Hawaiian items like Kalua pork, teriyaki bowls, and a poke bar with 15 types of the raw salad, all made to order. The teriyaki beef and the Korean short ribs are recommended. On Friday nights, live musicians perform Hawaiian music starting at 6:30pm.

Markets

Any self-respecting hippie community should have a market that sells organic and natural foods. Santa Cruz's superb mini-chain, **New Leaf Community Market** (1101 Fair Ave., 831/426-1306, http://newleaf.com, daily 8am-10pm), offers a local alternative to Whole Foods. Stock up on groceries or grab a meal of sandwiches, smoothies, or the terrific chicken pesto quesadilla at the flagship Fair Avenue location on the West Side or at their locations downtown (1134 Pacific Ave., 831/425-1793, daily 8am-9pm) and 1210 41st Avenue (831/479-7987, daily 8am-9pm).

The nonprofit **Santa Cruz Community Farmers' Markets** (831/454-0566, www.santacruzfarmersmarket.org) runs three community markets in Santa Cruz with goods and food from over 100 farms and vendors. The **Downtown Farmers Market** (Cedar St. and Lincoln St., spring-summer Wed. 1:30pm-6:30pm, winter Wed. 1:30pm-5:30pm) operates a block north of Pacific Avenue, while the **Live Oak Farmers Market** (15th St. and East Cliff Dr., Sun. 9am-1pm) is staged in a strip mall parking lot on the East Side. Finally, the **Westside Market** (Western Dr. and Mission St., Sat. 9am-1pm) takes place on the western boundary of town.

Mexican

Santa Cruz has some great taquerias, but **Tacos Moreno** (1053 Water St., 831/429-6095, www.tacosmoreno.com, daily 11am-8pm, $6-11) may be the best, as evidenced by the locals lined up outside the nondescript eatery during lunch. Tacos Moreno serves just the basics: burritos, tacos, quesadillas, and beverages to wash them down. The standout item is the al pastor burrito supreme with crispy barbecued pork, cheese, sour cream, and guacamole, among other savory ingredients. They also have a second location near the Boardwalk (303 Beach St., 831/427-2200, daily 11am-8pm).

El Palomar (1336 Pacific Ave., 831/425-7575, http://elpalomarsantacruz.com, Mon.-Fri. 11am-3pm and 5pm-10pm, Sat.-Sun. 10am-3pm and 5pm-10pm, $13-27) is located in the dining room of an old luxury hotel. Enjoy shrimp enchiladas or chicken mole while mariachi bands rove around and play to diners. Jose's Special Appetizer ($17) can be a light meal for two, though don't forget to try El Palomar's tasty guacamole. Their informal taco bar is great for a quick bite and drink. It also has a happy hour (Mon.-Fri. 3pm-6pm).

Taqueria Vallarta (1101 Pacific Ave., 831/471-2655, Sun.-Thurs. 9am-10pm, Fri.-Sat. 9am-11pm, $4.50-11) has a Mexican food empire in Santa Cruz County, with three locations in Santa Cruz alone. Vallarta's dominance is due to their inexpensive but tasty menu. Their super quesadilla alone will fill you up, while the jumbo burrito with your choice of meat can easily stuff you silly for two meals. The other Santa Cruz locations include 893 41st Avenue (831/464-7022, daily 9am-11pm) and 1221 Mission Street (831/426-7240, Sun.-Wed. 9am-10pm, Thurs.-Sat. 9am-11pm).

New American

Assembly (1108 Pacific Ave., 831/824-6100, http://assembleforfood.com, Wed.-Thurs. 11:30am-9:30pm, Fri. 11:30am-10:30pm, Sat. 10am-10:30pm, Sun. 10am-9:30pm, $11-19) focuses on what they call "rustic Californian" food. For dinner, this might mean a burger, a plate of braised short rib tacos, or a chickpea bowl. Meals start off promising with tasty house-made bread and salted butter. Even the salads have a creative touch, with one bed of greens employing breadcrumbs in place of croutons. Assembly also has a truly inspired beer menu and a wine list that highlights local products. Dine at a private table or at one of the large communal tables for multiple parties, located under chandeliers made of antlers.

Right downtown, the **Soif Restaurant & Wine Bar** (105 Walnut Ave., 831/423-2020, www.soifwine.com, Sun.-Thurs. 5pm-9pm, Fri.-Sat. 5pm-10pm, entrées $19-25) has locally sourced sustainable and organic fare to go with your glass of red or white wine. Snack from the small-plate menu or sample some exotic cheeses. The entrées have an Italian tinge.

With its contemporary and warm interior, **Suda** (3910 Portola Dr., 831/600-7068, www.eatsuda.com, Sun.-Wed. 11:30am-9pm, Thurs.-Sat. 11:30am-10pm, $10-30) brings a downtown feel to the East Side. The menu splits the difference between comfort food (burgers, mac-and-cheese) and healthier California fare (lettuce wraps, a gluten-free vegetable bowl). It has a nice long bar along with a few high-top tables for sampling some of their classic and creative cocktails or one of the 22 beers on draft.

Pizza

An untold number of surfers have stopped by ★ **Pleasure Pizza** (4000 Portola Dr., 831/475-4002, http://pleasurepizzasc.com, daily 11am-10pm, $3-6) for a slice after a morning of surfing nearby Pleasure Point or The Hook. This unassuming shack is just a couple blocks from the waves. The large, tasty slices are served on paper plates in a somewhat dingy building decorated with old surfboards and local surfing photos. Surfing legend Jay Moriarity once worked here (as immortalized in the 2012 film about his life, *Chasing Mavericks*). On Tuesdays, slices of cheese pizza go for just $2. There is also a downtown location (1415 Pacific Ave., 831/600-7859, Sun.-Wed. 11am-10pm, Thurs.-Sat. 11am-12:30am).

Right on bustling Pacific Avenue, **Kianti's Pizza & Pasta Bar** (1100 Pacific Ave., 831/469-4400, www.kiantis.com, Mon.-Fri. 11am-10pm, Sat.-Sun. 10am-10pm, $13-21) draws in crowds with individual and family-size servings of pastas, pizzas, and salads. Pizza toppings range from traditional Italian ingredients to more creative options (one pie is covered with seasoned beef, lettuce, tomato, avocado, and tortilla chips). People are also drawn in by Kianti's full bar and outdoor seating area right on Pacific Avenue. They also have a location near the Boardwalk called **A Slice of Kianti's** (46 Front St., 831/469-4421, summer daily 11am-7pm, winter Fri.-Sun. 11am-5pm).

Bantam (1010 Fair Ave., Ste. J, 831/420-0101, www.bantam1010.com, Mon.-Thurs. 5pm-9pm, Fri.-Sat. 5pm-9:30pm, $11-20) has a small menu dominated by thin-crust wood-fired pizza. Unique ingredients, including spicy honey and a chickpea crust, abound at this hipster-ish space decorated with subway tiles and reclaimed wood.

Sandwiches

Operating out of a kiosk downtown, **Press Juices & Sandwiches** (1520 K1 Pacific Ave., 831/466-9195, daily 10am-5:30pm, $4-6.50) is small in size, but its sandwiches are big in flavor. Options include a three-cheese grilled cheese, roast pork, and leek-and-spinach sandwiches. They also make Brazilian fruit drinks out of exotic fruits like acerola, cupuaca, and graviola. Seats and tables for customers circle the kiosk.

Zoccoli's (1534 Pacific Ave., 831/423-1711, www.zoccolis.com, Mon.-Sat. 8am-6pm, Sun. 10am-6pm, $6-8) is an old-fashioned Italian deli that serves warm sandwiches, soups, green salads, and pasta salad from behind a long case. The breaded chicken pesto sandwich with roasted red peppers and Swiss cheese is hard to beat.

Just feet from the corndog-slinging Boardwalk is ★ **The Picnic Basket** (125 Beach St., 831/427-9946, http://thepicnicbasketsc.com, late May-early Sept. daily 7am-9pm, early Sept.-late May Mon.-Thurs. 7am-4pm, Fri.-Sun. 7am-9pm, $3-9), a casual eatery with a simple menu of tasty, locally sourced goodness. The attention to detail here shines through even on a deceptively simple turkey, cheese, and avocado sandwich. Other options include breakfast dishes, salads, mac-and-cheese, and even local beer and wine. Dine inside or out front, where you can take in the sounds of the bustling Boardwalk.

Seafood

Hula's Island Grill (221 Cathcart St., 831/426-4852, www.hulastiki.com, Tues.-Thurs. 11:30am-10pm, Fri.-Sat. 11:30am-11pm, Sun. 11:30am-9:30pm, $12-23) has a fun surf theme that fits perfectly with Santa Cruz's culture. Surfing movies play on loop and paraphernalia covers the walls while diners enjoy a diverse menu featuring seafood as well as burgers, bowls, tacos, and curries. They also have a Monterey location.

South American

Cafe Brasil (1410 Mission St., 831/429-1855, www.cafebrasil.us, daily 8am-3pm, $6-11) serves up the Brazilian fare its name promises. Painted jungle green with bright yellow and blue trim, you can't miss this totally Santa Cruz breakfast and lunch joint. In the morning, the fare runs to omelets and Brazilian specialties, including a dish with two eggs topping a steak. Lunch includes pressed sandwiches, meat and tofu dishes, and Brazilian house specials.

Sushi

When locals who love their sushi get that craving for raw fish, they head for **Shogun Sushi** (1123 Pacific Ave., 831/469-4477, Mon.-Wed. noon-2:30pm and 5pm-9pm, Thurs.-Fri. noon-2:30pm and 5pm-10pm, Sat. 3pm-10pm, rolls $5-17). Right on Pacific Avenue, Shogun serves big fresh slabs of *nigiri*. They also have an interesting collection of sushi rolls including the "Saketemp Roll," which is a large, multicolored combination of shrimp tempura, cucumber, avocado, green onion, mayo, and smoked salmon. The fish served here is some of the freshest you'll find in this seacoast city. Their meats and other dishes also please diners with fresh ingredients and tasty preparations. Do be aware that there's often a wait for a table in the evenings, especially on weekends.

South of downtown, **Akira** (1222 Soquel Ave., 831/600-7093, http://akirasantacruz.com, daily 11am-11pm, rolls $10-17) is a modern sushi bar with interesting creations. Some of the rolls here employ unconventional ingredients like skirt steak, Sriracha sauce, and spicy truffled shoestring yams. They also serve more typical items including Philly rolls, spider rolls, and spicy tuna rolls. This being Santa Cruz, skateboard art decorates some of the walls. At happy hour (daily 4pm-6pm and 9:30pm-10:30pm), diners can snack on appetizers and enjoy beer, sake, or wine.

Thai

Just feet from the Boardwalk, **Sawasdee**

By the Sea (101 Main St., 831/466-9009, www.sawasdeesoquel.com, Sun.-Thurs. 11am-9pm, Fri.-Sat. 11am-10pm, $7-18) does great Thai food in a restaurant with large windows that have views of the beach and wharf. The menu is long and daunting, but there are curries, noodle dishes, fried rice plates, salads, and soups. Downstairs is a bar with beers on tap and unique cocktails like a potent vodka-spiked Thai iced tea. The bar area also has a small (just four tables) outside deck that is perfect for a sunny afternoon. They have free parking (a rare thing for venues near the Boardwalk). Sawasdee is at the top of the hill at the corner of 1st Street and Main Street.

Information and Services

While it can be fun to explore Santa Cruz just by using your innate sense of direction and eye for the bizarre, those who want a bit more structure to their travels can hit the **Santa Cruz County Visitors Center** (303 Water St., Ste. 100, 800/833-3494, www.santacruz.org, Mon.-Fri. 9am-noon and 1pm-4pm, Sat.-Sun. 11am-3pm) for maps, advice, and information. Or stop by the **Downtown Information Kiosk** (1130 Pacific Ave., K2, www.downtownsantacruz.com, May-Oct. Sun.-Thurs. 11am-6pm, Fri.-Sat. 11am-8pm, Nov.-April Sun.-Thurs. 11am-5pm, Fri.-Sat. 11am-7pm) on Pacific Avenue.

The daily *Santa Cruz Sentinel* (www.santacruzsentinel.com) offers local news plus up-to-date entertainment information. The free weekly newspaper *Good Times* (www.gtweekly.com) is also filled with upcoming events.

The **post office** (850 Front St., 831/426-0144, www.usps.com, Mon.-Fri. 9am-5pm) is near Pacific Garden Mall.

Medical treatment is available at **Dominican Hospital** (1555 Soquel Ave., 831/462-7700, www.dominicanhospital.org).

Santa Cruz is wired. You'll be able to access the Internet in a variety of cafés and hotels. There are Starbucks locations here, and many indie cafés compete with their own (sometimes free) Wi-Fi.

Santa Cruz has plenty of banks and ATMs (including some ATMs on the arcade at the Boardwalk). Bank branches congregate downtown near Pacific Avenue. The West Side is mostly residential, so you'll find a few ATMs in supermarkets and gas stations, but little else.

Transportation

Visitors planning to drive or bike around Santa Cruz should get themselves a good map, either before they arrive or at the visitors center in town. Navigating the winding, occasionally broken-up streets of this oddly shaped town isn't for the faint of heart. CA-1, which becomes Mission Street on the West Side, acts as the main artery through Santa Cruz and down to Capitola, Soquel, Aptos, and coastal points farther south. You'll find that CA-1 at the interchange to CA-17, and sometimes several miles to the south, is often a parking lot. No, you probably haven't come upon a major accident or a special event; it's just like that a lot of the time.

CAR

If you're driving to Santa Cruz from Silicon Valley, you have two choices of roads. Most drivers take fast, dangerous Highway 17. This narrow road doesn't have any switchbacks and is the main truck route "over the hill." Most locals take this 50-mile-per-hour corridor fast—probably faster than they should. Each year, several people die in accidents on Highway 17. So if you're new to the road, keep to the right and take it slow, no matter what the traffic to the left of you is doing. Check traffic reports before you head out; Highway 17 is known to be one of the worst commuting roads in all of the Bay Area, and the weekend beach traffic in the summer jams up fast in both directions too.

For a more leisurely drive, you can opt for two-lane Highway 9. The tight curves and endless switchbacks will keep you at a reasonable speed, and you can use the turnouts to let the locals pass. On Highway 9, your biggest obstacles tend to be groups of bicyclists and motorcyclists, both of whom adore the slopes and curves of this technical driving road. The good news is that you'll get an up-close-and-personal view of the gorgeously forested Santa Cruz Mountains, complete with views of the valley to the north and ocean vistas to the south.

Parking

Parking in Santa Cruz can be its own special sort of horror. Downtown, head straight for the parking structures one block from Pacific Avenue on either side. They're much easier to deal with than trying to find street parking. The same goes for the beach and Boardwalk areas. At the Boardwalk, just pay the fee to park in the big parking lot adjacent to the attractions. You'll save an hour and a possible car break-in or theft trying to find street parking in the sketchy neighborhoods that surround the Boardwalk.

BUS

In town, the buses are run by the **Santa Cruz Metro** (831/425-8600 www.scmtd.com, adults $2 per ride, passes available). With routes running all around Santa Cruz County, you can probably find a way to get nearly anywhere you'd want to go on the Metro.

Capitola and Aptos

Just south of Santa Cruz, Capitola was founded as the vacation resort Camp Capitola in the late 1800s before becoming the seaside hamlet of Capitola-by-the-Sea around 1900. Said to be the Pacific Coast's oldest seaside resort town, Capitola has all the features you'd want in a small oceanside city including an esplanade, a wharf, and a sandy beach split by Soquel Creek. The few blocks that comprise downtown are scenic, with shops and restaurants worth visiting. Capitola also makes a fine base from which to explore the Santa Cruz coast.

Aptos is south of Capitola. This unincorporated area is home to the Forest of Nisene Marks State Park and Seacliff State Beach. At the state park is the epicenter of the 1989 Loma Prieta Earthquake. Seacliff is popular for its pier that leads out to a sunken concrete ship.

SIGHTS
New Brighton State Beach

One of the region's most popular sandy spots is **New Brighton State Beach** (1500 Park Ave., Capitola, 831/464-6330, www.parks. ca.gov, daily 8am-sunset, $10/vehicle). This forest-backed beach has everything: a strip of sand that's perfect for lounging and swimming, a forest-shaded campground for both tent and RV campers, hiking trails, and ranger-led nature programs. New Brighton can get crowded on sunny summer days, but it's nothing like the wall-to-wall people of the popular Southern California beaches. Call in advance to make camping reservations at this popular state park.

Seacliff State Beach

Seacliff State Beach (201 State Park Dr.,

Aptos, 831/685-6500, www.parks.ca.gov, daily 8am-sunset, $10/vehicle) is otherwise known as "the beach with the shipwreck." The concrete vessel SS *Palo Alto*, connected to the shore by a fishing pier, was once a floating attraction with a ballroom and restaurant before its hull cracked. The wreck is closed to the public but you can get close to it on the pier. The bluff-sheltered beach is a mile long, and has a **visitors center** (Wed.-Sun. 10am-4pm) with a model of the *Palo Alto* and a viewing tank filled with tidepool organisms.

The Forest of Nisene Marks State Park

Take a walk at **The Forest of Nisene Marks State Park** (four miles north of Aptos on Aptos Creek Rd., 831/763-7062, www.parks.ca.gov, daily sunrise-sunset, $8/vehicle), once the site of serious logging operations but now shaded by second-growth redwoods. Mountain bikers can ride up the fire road through the center of the park, while hikers can head out on more than 30 miles of hiking trails that take off from the roadway. One popular hike is the **Loma Prieta Grade Trail** (six miles round-trip), which follows an old railway bed up to the remnants of a lumber camp. Another point of interest within the park is the epicenter of the 1989 Loma Prieta Earthquake, which interrupted the World Series and caused the collapse of a section of San Francisco's Bay Bridge.

Manresa State Beach

One of the nicest stretches of beach in Santa Cruz County, **Manresa State Beach** (1445 San Andreas Rd., 831/761-1795, www.parks.ca.gov, $10/vehicle) draws beachgoers and surfers to its sandy shores. Advanced surfers are fond of the nice, less-crowded break at Manresa, especially in the summer. The large parking lot has restrooms and an outdoor shower. There's free parking in the residential area just south of the beach's entrance.

Sunset State Beach

Surrounded by agricultural fields, **Sunset State Beach** (201 Sunset Beach Rd., Watsonville, 831/763-7063, daily 8am-sunset, $10/vehicle) in southern Santa Cruz County feels like it is in the middle of nowhere despite being just 16 miles south of Santa Cruz. Pine trees shade the campground on the bluffs

scenic Capitola

above a truly wild beach. The oceanside picnic spots are pleasant if the wind isn't too bad.

ACCOMMODATIONS

The ★ **Monarch Cove Inn** (620 El Salto Dr., Capitola, 831/464-1295, www.monarchcove-inn.com, $200-400) is on a 2.5-acre property with manicured gardens, gurgling fountains, towering palm trees, a monarch butterfly sanctuary, and a marvelous view of Monterey Bay curving from Moss Landing to Monterey. The grounds were once a private retreat for two English families and then a resort that hosted noted guests such as Mary Pickford and Al Capone. The inn's Victorian mansion is divided into nine units along with two suites, all of which have private entrances. The Carriage House Cottage, with a full kitchen, private outdoor deck, private gazebo, and private hot tub, is one of two cottages available. A continental breakfast is delivered to guests each morning. Capitola is just a 10-minute walk away.

It's difficult to miss the **Capitola Venetian Hotel** (1500 Wharf Rd., Capitola, 831/476-6471, www.capitolavenetian.com, $245-529), the cluster of brightly colored Mediterranean-style buildings on Soquel Creek. This longtime Capitola fixture has one-, two-, and three-bedroom units, all with fully equipped kitchens. Some also have fireplaces.

For a vacation full of sun and sand, book one of the 283 suites at the **Seascape Beach Resort** (1 Seascape Beach Resort Dr., Aptos, 831/688-6800, $344-768), all of which have a kitchen and fireplace. The grounds include a pool, spa, fitness center, beach access, and two restaurants: **Sanderlings** (831/662-7120, www.sanderlingsrestaurant.com, Mon.-Fri. 6am-11am, 11:30am-2:30pm, 5:30pm-10pm, Sat.-Sun. 7am-2:30pm, 5:30pm-10pm, $19-59) and **Palapas** (831/662-9000, www.palapasrestaurant.com, daily 11:30am-9pm, $12-27).

Camping

Whether you want an inexpensive place to stay while exploring nearby Santa Cruz or just want to camp near a beach, the Santa Cruz state beach campgrounds in Capitola and Aptos fit the bill. The biggest and possibly best camping option is at **New Brighton State Beach** (1500 Park Ave., Capitola, 800/444-7275, www.reserveamerica.com, $35). There are over 100 campsites in a 93-acre

the outdoor deck at Capitola's Monarch Cove Inn

area situated on a bluff above the beach. Santa Cruz is just 6.5 miles away.

RV campers have 26 sites with full hookups and 37 non-hookup sites to choose from at **Seacliff State Beach** (201 State Park Rd., Aptos, 800/444-7275, www.reserveamerica.com, $55). Those without much to carry can opt for the 60 walk-in campsites at the **Manresa Uplands Campground** (205 Manresa Beach Rd., La Selva Beach, 800/444-7275, www.reserveamerica.com, $35) in Manresa State Beach.

Less than four miles from Manresa State Beach, **Sunset State Beach** (201 Sunset Beach Rd., Watsonville, 800/444-7275, www.reserveamerica.com, $35) is an underrated and worthy place to pitch a tent. It feels far from Santa Cruz, but the city is only a 20-minute drive north.

FOOD

The **Paradise Beach Grille** (215 Esplanade, Capitola, 831/476-4900, http://paradisebeachgrille.com, Mon.-Thurs. 11:30am-3:15pm and 4pm-9pm, Fri. 11:30am-3:15pm and 4pm-10pm, Sun. 11:30am-3:15pm and 5pm-9pm, $20-34) offers a prime location on Capitola's Esplanade, live music four days a week, and an outdoor deck hanging over Soquel Creek. Enjoy seafood, steak, pasta, and chicken entrées in a jungle-themed setting, complete with potted plants and furniture decorated with foliage prints.

The **Shadowbrook Restaurant** (1750 Wharf Rd., Capitola, 831/475-1511, www.shadowbrook-capitola.com, Mon.-Fri. 5pm-8:45pm, Sat. 4:30pm-9:45pm, Sun. 4:30pm-8:45pm, $22-34) is where to celebrate a special occasion. The adventure begins with a cable car ride down to the restaurant, which is perched on a steep slope above Soquel Creek. Entrées include a slow-roasted, bone-in pork prime rib, a one-pound surf-and-turf dish, and several vegetarian options. If you're staying within a three-mile radius of the restaurant, you can be shuttled to the restaurant in a 1950 Dodge (free, but tips are appreciated).

Reserve a ride when you make your dinner reservations.

Gayle's Bakery (Upper Village Shopping Center, 504 Bay Ave., Capitola, 831/462-1200, www.gaylesbakery.com, daily 6:30am-8:30pm, $4-17) is a lot more than a place to pick up baked goods. This 10,000-square-foot facility has a rotisserie and deli that serves salads, sandwiches, hot entrées, and nightly blue-plate specials.

In Aptos, **Cafe Sparrow** (8042 Soquel Dr., Aptos, 831/688-6238, www.cafesparrow.com, Sun.-Fri. 11:30am-2pm and 5:30pm-9pm, Sat. 11am-2pm and 5:30pm-9pm, $20-33) serves country French cuisine that's consistently tasty. Whatever you order, it will be fantastic. The seafood is noteworthy as are the steaks. Cafe Sparrow's kitchen prepares all the dishes with fresh ingredients, and the chef (who can sometimes be seen out in the dining room checking on customer satisfaction with the food) thinks up innovative preparations and creates tasty sauces. He's also willing to accommodate special requests and dietary restrictions with good cheer. For dessert, treat yourself to the profiteroles, which can be created with either ice cream or pastry cream.

Just inland from Capitola, in Soquel, **Café Cruz** (2621 41st Ave., 831/476-3801, www.cafecruz.com, Mon.-Fri. 11:30am-2:30pm and 3pm-close, Sat. 11:30am-2:30pm and 5:30pm-close, Sun. 5pm-close, $16-31) is a local favorite known for its rotisserie chicken. Watch the meat twirling away on the rotisserie as the cooks create the other entrées in the open kitchen. There's also a heated patio for those who want to head outdoors.

INFORMATION AND SERVICES

For information about the Capitola area, you can call the **Capitola Soquel Chamber of Commerce** (831/475-6522, www.capitolachamber.com) or visit their website. The Capitola **post office** (826 Bay Ave., Capitola, 831/475-5948, www.usps.com, Mon.-Fri. 9am-4:30pm, Sat. 10am-1pm) is available if you need to send a package or a postcard.

Excursion to Corralitos

Corralitos Brewing Company

Twenty miles south of Santa Cruz, tucked below the Santa Cruz Mountains, Corralitos is a community of vineyards and farmlands. Since 1957, Corralitos has been a mecca for meat eaters thanks to the **Corralitos Market & Sausage Company** (569 Corralitos Rd., 831/722-2633, Mon.-Sat. 8am-6pm, Sun. 9am-5pm) and its smoked sausages and marinated tri-tips, ribs, and chicken. The house-made sausages are their claim to fame, with flavors including the very popular "Cheezy Bavarian," a beef and pork sausage with chunks of sharp cheddar cheese. You can purchase hot sandwiches like the tasty tri-tip from the back counter.

The **Corralitos Brewing Company** (2536 Freedom Blvd., 831/728-2311, www.corralitosbrewingco.com, Wed.-Fri. 3pm-8pm, Sat.-Sun. 1pm-8pm, tasting flight $7.50) opened in 2015, providing a perfect place to get suds with your Corralitos Market sausages. This beautiful tasting room is attached to the owner's family's lumber store, which explains the interior filled with stunning woodwork—from redwood beams and madrone hardtops to Monterey pine floors and ceilings. The beer here is superb. The taproom has 10 draft beers brewed on-site, including a terrific red ale and their flagship IPA. On the front porch are barrel tables and wood-slab seats for those who would rather sip their suds outdoors.

If you prefer a pinot noir or chardonnay with your smoked sausage sandwich, head down the **Corralitos Wine Trail** (www.corralitoswinetrail.com). Here you can visit four family-owned wineries: **Windy Oaks Winery** (550 Hazel Dell Rd., 831/786-9463, www.windyoaksestate.com, Sat. noon-5pm), **Alfaro Family Vineyards** (420 Hames Rd., 831/728-5172, www.alfarowine. com, Sat. noon-5pm), **Nicholson Vineyards** (2800 Pleasant Valley Rd., 831/724-7071, www. nicholsonvineyards.com, Sat. noon-5pm), and **Pleasant Valley Vineyards** (600 Pleasant Valley Rd., 831/728-2826, www.pvvines.com, Sat. noon-5pm).

Corralitos is just a 20-minute drive from Santa Cruz. Head south out of town on CA 1 toward Watsonville. After about eight miles, exit onto Freedom Boulevard. Turn left on Freedom Boulevard and follow it for almost three miles. Then go straight on Hames Road for a half mile before turning right on Pleasant Valley Road, which you continue on for another half mile. Take the first left to get back on Hames Road and take it 1.5 miles. Then turn right on Corralitos Road to get into the heart of Corralitos.

TRANSPORTATION

The village of Capitola is just six miles south of Santa Cruz. Hop onto CA-1 and go south for almost five miles before exiting at Bay Avenue/Porter Street. Take a slight right onto Bay Avenue and continue for almost a half mile. Then take a right on Capitola Avenue and follow almost another half mile to the village.

Aptos is eight miles south of Santa Cruz. Take CA-1 about seven miles and exit on State Park Drive.

Northern Santa Cruz Coast

The northern coastal section of Santa Cruz is made up of agricultural lands, parks, open spaces, and secluded beaches dotted with sea stacks. Residents of this region have started calling this stretch of coastline the Slowcoast, due to its rural, unrushed attitude. Recently, there has been an effort to transform 5,800 acres of this coastline into the Santa Cruz Redwoods National Monument.

★ WILDER RANCH STATE PARK

North of Santa Cruz's city limits, the land on both sides of Highway 1 suddenly gives way to farmland perched atop coastal terraces. The best place to get a feel for this mostly undeveloped stretch of coastline is to visit **Wilder Ranch State Park** (1401 Coast Rd., 831/423-9703, www.parks.ca.gov, daily 8am-sunset, $10/vehicle). The park allows visitors to step back in time and discover what it was like to live on a ranch over 100 years ago at its many living-history demonstrations. Other annual events include gardening demonstrations and the Old-Fashioned Independence Day Celebration. For those who would rather check out the park's natural beauty in the present, the 2.5-mile **Old Cove Landing Trail** is a flat, easy hike out to the coastline, which is pocketed with sea caves and usually decorated with wildlife from elegant cormorants to harbor seals lazing on the coastal shelves.

The east side of the park is very popular with mountain bikers for its beginner to intermediate climbs with coastal views. The **Wilder Ridge Loop** provides a good introduction to the park's trails along with its coastal views. The **Enchanted Loop** traverses more technical terrain.

Getting There

Wilder Ranch State Park is less than a 10-minute drive from downtown Santa Cruz. Just get on Mission Street, which doubles as CA-1 through town, and head north. It is less than three miles north of town.

★ DAVENPORT

Nine miles north of Santa Cruz's West Side, the small community of Davenport (pop. 400) sits on the coastline's scenic bluffs. Right off Highway 1, Davenport has a few art galleries, cafés, and the Bonny Doon Vineyard Tasting Room. Across the street from town is a dirt pullout that offers access to Davenport Beach and some coastal headlands that are a great spot for whale-watching during winter. The region around Davenport is worth exploring for its stunning beaches, coastal cliffs, and unique sea stacks offshore.

Shark Fin Cove

Less than one mile south of Davenport on the west side of Highway 1 sits the aptly named Shark Fin Cove. This popular pull-off for photographers looks out over a small, vertical island that rises out of the sea like a shark fin. The formation is a remnant of the mudstone cliff that surrounds the adjacent beach.

Davenport Landing Beach

Santa Cruz County has a lot of fine beaches, and **Davenport Landing Beach** (Davenport Landing Rd.) is one of its best. Located almost two miles north of town on Davenport Landing Road, it is a scenic stretch of sand bookended by rocky terraces and looming headlands. Rumored to have once been a whaling port, this beach is popular with surfers, who like the right- and left-breaking waves on either side of the beach, and wind-surfers, who turn up for the afternoon winds. A sea cave with a large opening can be found on the north end of the beach and accessed during low tide. Facilities include pit toilets, a wheelchair-accessible ramp to the beach, and a swing set with a bench seat.

The beach is also the location of **American Abalone Farms** (245 Davenport Rd., www. americanabalone.net, Sat. 10am-2pm), an aquaculture business that raises California red abalone. Though the facility is not open for tours, on Saturdays they welcome people who want to purchase abalone.

Wine Tasting

One of the biggest and most colorful characters in California's winemaking scene is Randall Grahm, who began the Bonny Doon Vineyard in 1983. A three-time James Beard Award winner, Grahm makes wine from oddball grapes like his flagship Le Cigare Volant, a red Rhône blend of Grenache, mourvèdre,

Syrah, and Cinsault. In 2013, the **Bonny Doon Vineyard Tasting Room** (450 Hwy. 1, Davenport, 831/471-8031, www.bonnydoon-vineyard.com, winter Mon. and Wed.-Sun. 11am-5pm, summer Sun.-Thurs. 11am-5pm, Fri. 11am-6pm, Sat. 11am-7pm, tasting $10) opened in the bottom floor of a distinctive, two-story white building in Davenport. Inside, there's a long metal bar, a few picnic tables, and a living room-like sitting area with couches to lounge on while tasting Bonny Doon's flavorful wines.

Shopping

Occupying a classic 1954 Airstream trailer, **Slowcoast** (25 Swanton Rd., Davenport, www.slowcoast.org, summer daily 9:30am-6pm, winter daily 10:30am-5pm) is more than a shop selling artisan goods: It is also a celebration of the lifestyles of the northern Santa Cruz coast. Inside the Airstream, there are books, clothes, massage oils, homemade shampoo, and goat milk soap, all made by area artists and craftspeople. Outside is a fenced-in lot with picnic tables, perfect for getting in the Slowcoast frame of mind.

Food

In a small community, some businesses have

scenic Davenport Landing Beach

to be more than one thing. The **Whale City Bakery Bar & Grill** (490 Hwy. 1, 831/423-9009, www.whalecitybakery.com, Fri.-Wed. 6:30am-8pm, Thurs. 6:30am-9pm, $7-13) certainly fits this bill. It's a bakery, restaurant, bar, coffee shop, live music venue, and community gathering place. The menu items include burgers, sandwiches, and a few seafood options. On Thursday nights, they stay open later for live music performances.

Davenport Roadhouse (1 Davenport Ave., 831/426-8801, http://davenportroadhouse.com, Mon. 8:30am-3pm, Tues.-Fri. 8:30am-9pm, Sat. 8am-9pm, Sun. 8am-8:30pm, $10-28) is a gourmet option in little Davenport. The menu ranges from wood-fired pizzas to molasses-cured duck breast. They also have taco night on Tuesday and a Wednesday night fixed-price menu for two.

Another option is to pick your own fruit at the **Swanton Berry Farm** (25 Swanton Rd., Davenport, 831/469-8804, www.swantonberryfarm.com, daily 8am-6pm). April and May are the months for pick-your-own strawberries. Or stop by the stand and purchase a berry pie, soup, or strawberry drink.

Getting There

Davenport is a simple nine-mile drive north of Santa Cruz on CA-1. You'll see the buildings on your right and a large dirt pullout on the left.

RANCHO DEL OSO AND WADDELL BEACH

A section of Big Basin Redwoods State Park reaches the coastline at **Rancho Del Oso and Waddell Beach** (17 miles north of Santa Cruz on Hwy. 1, 831/427-2288, www.parks.ca.gov). The primary attraction of this inland section of the park is the **Rancho del Oso Nature and History Center** (3600 CA-1, 831/427-2288, http://ranchodeloso.org, Sat.-Sun. noon-4pm). The museum is housed within an old ranch house where one of President Herbert Hoover's relatives resided. The interactive exhibits examine the region's natural and cultural history.

the Bonny Doon Vineyard Tasting Room in Davenport

There is also a large deck with views of the ocean and Waddell Valley. To reach the center, take a right on the dirt road before the Waddell Creek Bridge and follow it inland to the structure.

The area around the center has six miles of road along Waddell Creek that are good for biking or hiking. For an overnight excursion, there are three **backpack trail camps** (831/338-8861, May-Oct., $15/night, $8 processing fee) within a short hike of the center. Bring protective containers or rope to keep your food safe from critters.

On the west side of the highway is **Waddell Beach.** This is one of the area's best places for windsurfing and kite surfing. It can be quite entertaining to watch the boarders carve across the sea and launch themselves into the sky.

★ AÑO NUEVO STATE PARK

Año Nuevo State Park (1 New Year's Creek Rd., Pescadero, 650/879-2025, www.

parks.ca.gov, daily 8:30am-sunset, $10/vehicle) is one of the California coast's truly wild places. The beach is one of the largest mainland breeding spots of the elephant seal—up to 10,000 seals can pile up in the sand here. Offshore, the giant marine mammals have overrun the abandoned buildings of Año Nuevo Island. Great white sharks circle the small island, waiting for an opportunity to snack on one of the seals. The only way to experience this stunning display of nature up close is by taking a **guided tour** (800/444-4445, $7) between December 15 and March 31. Other reasons to visit include a secluded cove and the Marine Education Center (daily 8:30am-4:30pm) with its exhibits, bookstore, and theater.

Getting There

Año Nuevo State Park is located in San Mateo County right above the Santa Cruz County/San Mateo County line. From Santa Cruz, Año Nuevo is a half-hour drive north on CA-1.

PIGEON POINT LIGHTHOUSE

On a secluded section of coast, the **Pigeon Point Lighthouse** rises 115 feet above its headlands perch and the crashing Pacific Ocean. Built in 1871, the structure is tied with Point Arena Lighthouse in Mendocino County for the title of tallest lighthouse on the West Coast. Even cooler: You can spend an evening on the grounds at the ★ **Pigeon Point Lighthouse Hostel** (210 Pigeon Point Rd. at Hwy. 1, 650/879-0633, www.norcalhostels.org/pigeon, dorm beds $25-28, private rooms $76-168). It has simple but comfortable accommodations, both private and dorm style. Amenities include three kitchens, free Wi-Fi, a fire pit, and beach access. But the best amenity of all is the cliff-top hot tub ($8/half hour).

Getting There

The Pigeon Point Lighthouse is located in San Mateo County and can be reached via a simple half-hour drive north up CA-1 out of Santa Cruz.

Santa Cruz Mountains

Less than 10 miles outside the city, the Santa Cruz Mountains feel a world away from Santa Cruz's bustling Pacific Avenue and Boardwalk. The mountains are cloaked in forests of coast redwoods and dotted with parks. Along Highway 9 and the San Lorenzo River are a string of scenic mountain towns starting with Felton, Ben Lomond, and Boulder Creek, the latter of which is just 13 miles from Santa Cruz. Boulder Creek is also the best of the bunch, with colorful storefronts and a few eateries lining Highway 9 amid a backdrop of forested mountain ridges.

SIGHTS
★ Roaring Camp Railroads

One of the best ways to experience the redwoods is to hop on a train at **Roaring Camp**

Railroads (5401 Graham Hill Rd., Felton, 831/335-4484 or 831/335-4400, www.roaringcamp.com). There are two train trips to choose from: The **Redwood Forest Steam Train** (year-round, adults $27, children $20, one hour and 15 minutes round-trip) and the **Santa Cruz Beach Train** (April-Sept., adults $29, children $23, three hours round-trip). Both of these trains chug through the towering redwood forests that cloak the Santa Cruz Mountains. Pulled by a diesel electric engine, the Beach Train passes through Henry Cowell Redwoods State Park and travels along the San Lorenzo River as it makes its way down to the Boardwalk. There's a one-hour layover at the Boardwalk before it climbs back up into the mountains. The Redwood Forest Steam Train is a narrow-gauge steam locomotive that billows impressive clouds of steam as it climbs Bear Mountain. Along the way, it offers close views of coast redwoods that are up to 1,800 years old. Both trains have a guide who narrates your journey over the clanking machinery of the locomotives. Passengers ride outdoors on open-air cars, so bring a sweater and sunblock.

Bigfoot Discovery Museum

Most people believe if Bigfoot lived anywhere, it would be in the dense forests of Northern California. The folks at **The Bigfoot Discovery Museum** (5497 Hwy. 9, Felton, 831/335-4478, http://bigfootdiscoveryproject.com, Wed.-Mon. 11am-6pm, donations appreciated) maintain that the hairy biped has also been seen in the Santa Cruz Mountains. This little red building with wooden Bigfoot carvings out front is an essential stop for conspiracy theorists and lovers of quirky attractions. Inside, there is information on local Bigfoot sightings, plaster footprints of what is said to be Bigfoot, and the iconic 1967 film footage of the beast striding across the screen, which plays on continuous loop. A fun section of the small museum is devoted to Bigfoot in popular culture, from its appearance on the label of Sierra Nevada Brewing Co.'s Bigfoot Ale to toys associated with the 1987 film *Harry and the Hendersons.*

Mount Hermon Redwood Canopy Tours

Experience the coast redwoods from way up high at the **Mount Hermon Redwood Canopy Tours** (Mount Hermon Conference Center, 17 Conference Dr., 831/430-4357, www.mounthermon.org, $89). Taking their lead from Costa Rica's popular rainforest canopy tours, these two-hour guided adventures involve traversing six zip lines and two sky bridges to gain a unique perspective on California's sky-scraping trees.

PARKS
Henry Cowell Redwoods State Park

Henry Cowell Redwoods State Park (101 N. Big Trees Park Rd., Felton, 831/335-4598, www.parks.ca.gov, daily sunrise-sunset, $10/vehicle) is the closest of the Santa Cruz Mountain parks to downtown Santa Cruz. Just over six miles away from the coastal city, the 4,650-acre park's highlight is a 40-acre stand of virgin coast redwoods that can be experienced via the **Redwood Grove Loop Trail** (trailhead by the nature center, 0.8

a Roaring Camp Railroads train gearing up for a trip through the redwoods

miles round-trip, easy, no elevation gain). Some unique natural features along the loop are the Fremont Tree, in whose burnt-out trunk Gen. John C. Fremont is said to have spent a night, and the albino redwood trees, which have white needles due to a lack of chlorophyll.

There's a section of the park worth visiting during warm days for the so-called **Garden of Eden,** a less crowded spot featuring deep pools of the San Lorenzo River and a nice beach. It's also known as a frequent nude sunbathing spot. To reach it, drive out of Santa Cruz three miles toward Felton on Highway 9. Look for the sign for the north entrance of the park, then drive into the dirt pullout on the right with the green metal gates. Park your vehicle and pass through the southern gate. Follow the trail downhill and take a right at the next fork. When you hit the train tracks, take a right and walk until you see the "No Campfire" and "No Alcoholic Beverages" signs. Follow the steep trail down to the river and the Garden of Eden.

★ Big Basin Redwoods State Park

There's no better place to experience the tall-as-a-tower ancient coast redwoods of the Santa Cruz Mountains than at **Big Basin Redwoods State Park** (21600 Big Basin Way, Boulder Creek, 831/338-8860, www.parks.ca.gov, daily 6am-sunset, $10/vehicle). These inspiring stands of trees, which can be as old as 2,000 years and as tall as 375 feet, inspired the creation of California's first state park in 1902. Decorating this 18,000-acre state park are multiple waterfalls, rock formations pocked with Native American mortar holes, and wildlife ranging from bright yellow banana slugs to stealthy coyotes.

Upon entering, the **visitors center** (daily 9am-5pm) is a good place to get your bearings. This one-room facility has free handouts along with exhibits on the parkland's native peoples, the area's logging practices, and an explanation on how the region was preserved.

HIKING

The best way to experience Big Basin is to head out on one of the park's 80 miles of trails or roads. An easy hike that is well worth a few minutes is the **Redwood Loop Trail** (trailhead at the parking lot across from Big Basin Headquarters, 0.5 miles, easy, no elevation gain). Take in trees as wide as dinner tables and as tall as the Statue of Liberty on this

Big Basin Redwoods State Park

flat, easygoing walk. Highlights include the Chimney Tree with its hollow interior and the Father of the Forest, an impressive specimen that shoots skyward 250 feet.

A little more involved is the **Sequoia Trail to Sempervirens Falls** (trailhead at parking area just south of Big Basin Headquarters, 1.7 miles one way, moderate, 300-foot elevation gain). Wander slightly up this shaded trail to an observation deck that provides a nice view of the 15-foot-high Sempervirens waterfall spilling into a green grotto. Be sure to walk a few hundred yards farther up the trail to Slippery Rock, a rocky hillside dimpled with Native American mortar holes. To make this a slightly longer loop, continue on the **Shadowbrook Trail,** creating a 4.7-mile hike that meanders above and crosses over a scenic stream at several points.

To see some more impressive falls, do the **Sunset Trail-Berry Creek Falls Trail-Skyline to Sea Trail** (trailhead across the road from Big Basin Headquarters, 10.5 miles round-trip, strenuous, 400-foot elevation gain). The hike passes by some of the largest old-growth redwoods in the park along the way to four waterfalls.

BACKPACKING

One way to really experience Big Basin Redwoods State Park is to embark on the **Skyline to Sea Trail** (reservations 831/338-8861, $8 reservation plus $15 campsite fee), a 30-mile backpacking hike that begins in Castle Rock State Park and spends most of its length within Big Basin on the way to Waddell Beach. For most people, this excursion takes two to three days. If you start at Castle Rock most of the hike will be downhill toward the ocean. Along the way, you'll pass through amazing redwood forests and by scenic waterfalls. Camping is only permitted in designated backcountry campgrounds.

Castle Rock State Park

Crowning the top of the Santa Cruz Mountains, **Castle Rock State Park** (15000 Skyline Blvd., 408/867-2952, daily 6am-sunset, $8/vehicle) is best known for its weathered sandstone rock formations that resemble giant slabs of Swiss cheese. Goat Rock is one of several destinations for the region's rock climbers. The 5,150-acre park also has 34 miles of hiking trails. The **Saratoga Gap and Ridge Trail Loop** (trailhead at main parking lot, 5.6 miles round-trip, moderate) hits most of the park's best sites including Goat Rock, Castle Rock Falls, and the Russell Point Overlook.

ACCOMMODATIONS

Cool off during the summer months by renting a cottage at the **Fern River Resort** (5250 Hwy. 9, Felton, 831/335-4412, www.fernriver. com, $98-269). These red cottages are scattered over a property located right on the San Lorenzo River. Among the choices are a studio cabin with a kitchenette or a two-bedroom unit with a full kitchen and a river view. There's an on-site spa available for guests, set within a wooden gazebo.

Jaye's Timberlane Resort (8705 Hwy. 9, Ben Lomond, 831/336-5479, www.jayestimberlane.com, $105-195) has 10 cabins spread across a seven-acre plot of land. All of the one- or two-bedroom units have full kitchens and some have fireplaces. Each one has its own private deck for taking in the forest. The grounds have a solar-heated pool, a horseshoe pit, and a Ping-Pong table.

Just 10 miles from Big Basin Redwoods State Park, the **Merrybrook Lodge** (13420 Big Basin Way, Boulder Creek, 831/338-6813, www.merrybrooklodge.net, $130-170) provides a place to relax after a day of hiking. Choose between the four motel rooms and the six cottages. Each of the cottages has a woodstove and fully equipped kitchen.

Camping

The Santa Cruz Mountains are an ideal place to pitch a tent. **Henry Cowell Redwoods State Park** (2591 Graham Hill Rd., Scotts Valley, 800/444-7275, www.reserveamerica. com, Apr.-Oct., $35) has 113 campsites in a section of the park that is a five-minute drive or 45-minute hike from Cowell's popular redwood grove. The campground closes during the winter.

Big Basin Redwoods State Park (21600 Big Basin Way, Boulder Creek, 800/44-7275, www.reserveamerica.com, drive-in campsites $35, hike-in, bike-in, and backpack-in campsites $6-15) has four major drive-in campgrounds open in the summer and one open in the winter. The largest is the Blooms Creek Campground. If you left your camping gear at home, rent a **tent cabin** (reservations 800/444-7275 or www.reserveamerica.com, information www.bigbasintentcabins.com, $85-105). Each tent cabin is perched on a wooden platform and has two double platform beds topped with mattress pads. They also have woodstoves.

FOOD

The Cremer House (6256 Hwy. 9, Felton, 831/335-3976, www.cremerhouse.com, Sun.-Thurs. 3pm-9pm, Fri.-Sat. 3pm-10pm, $13-20) is an alehouse and restaurant that opened in downtown Felton's oldest building in late 2014. The structure, dating back to 1874, is said to have possibly been a safe haven for prostitutes and illegal spirits (liquor) in the past. Today, it updates the old with a new sophistication. Smoked pork chops are served in skillets, while 21 draft beers are served out of a copper contraption. There is limited seating in the wooden interior and on a covered wraparound deck for diners who want a bit of mountain air.

The **Cowboy Bar & Grill** (6155 Hwy. 9, Felton, 831/335-2330, www.feltoncowboy.com, Mon. and Wed.-Sat 11am-9pm, Sun. 9am-9pm, $9-30) gives comfort food a creative spin. On tablecloths resembling spotted cowhides, this longtime Felton favorite serves a buffalo beef patty atop a pile of mashed potatoes, or pork on corn bread topped with cheese, cilantro, and a jalapeno glaze. They also do inventive cocktails from a full bar.

INFORMATION AND SERVICES

Felton has its own **post office** (6101 Gushee St., 831/335-8015, www.usps.com, Mon.-Fri. 9am-4pm, Sat. 11:30am-2pm). Boulder Creek has one, too, at 200 Lorenzo Street (831/338-4865, www.usps.com, Mon.-Fri. 9:30am-4pm).

The Cremer House restaurant in Felton

TRANSPORTATION

When Highway 9 is open, it's only a seven-mile drive from Santa Cruz to Felton on the mountainous road. It usually takes half an hour to get to Boulder Creek from Santa Cruz along a 15-mile stretch of the road. To avoid the windy bottom section of Highway 9, take CA-17 toward San Jose for just over three miles before exiting on Mt. Hermon Road. Then continue on that road for almost four miles before turning right on Graham Hill Road. After a quarter mile, Graham Hill Road hits Highway 9 in Felton.

Big Sur

Look for ★ to find recommended sights, activities, dining, and lodging.

Highlights

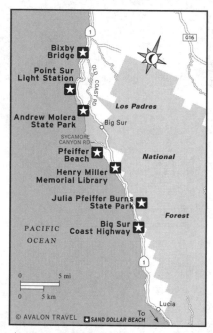

★ **Big Sur Coast Highway:** One of the most scenic drives in the world, Big Sur's Highway 1 passes redwood forests and crystal-clear streams and rivers while offering breathtaking, ever-present views of the coast (page 185).

★ **Bixby Bridge:** An architectural marvel and one of the world's most photographed bridges, Bixby Bridge dramatically spans a deep canyon with the Pacific as a backdrop (page 186).

★ **Point Sur Light Station:** One of California's most stunning lighthouses is perched atop a looming 360-foot-tall rock surrounded on three sides by ocean. Take a worthwhile three-hour tour to learn about its history, which includes shipwrecks and tethered chickens (page 187).

★ **Andrew Molera State Park:** This sprawling, lightly developed park that provides visitors access to a stunning stretch of coast and offers horseback riding, mountain biking, and hiking the Ridge Trail and Panorama Trail Loop (page 187).

★ **Pfeiffer Beach:** With rock formations offshore and purple sand, Pfeiffer Beach is one of Big Sur's most picturesque spots (page 188).

★ **Henry Miller Memorial Library:** Dedicated to preserving the idiosyncratic artistic spirit of former resident and acclaimed author Henry Miller, this quirky arts outpost is both bookstore and cultural center—and a great place to play a game of table tennis (page 189).

★ **Julia Pfeiffer Burns State Park:** This park's claim to fame is McWay Falls, an 80-foot waterfall that pours right into the Pacific. Lesser-known features such as Partington Cove and the Ewoldsen Trail are well worth your time (page 190).

★ **Sand Dollar Beach:** This is one of the largest stretches of sand on Big Sur's rugged coastline (page 192).

Big Sur is not a town, a rock, or a beach, but rather the stunning 90-mile stretch of coastline between Carmel and San Simeon. Highway 1, which runs through Big Sur, is one of the world's iconic coastal drives.

There is a lot to see off the precipitous roadway including skyscraping coast redwoods, waterfalls decorating cliff faces, steep mountains and their accompanying valleys, and rugged beaches that are as scenic as any along the California coast.

Big Sur is a collision of land and sea as well as a juxtaposition of vibrant colors: green hills, orange cliffs, and blue seas. It is a place for contemplation, recreation, relaxation, and rejuvenation. Even with Big Sur's rising popularity, it's still possible to find a peaceful parcel to take in the majesty of the natural world, whether it's whales moving and spouting off the coast like locomotives or California condors swirling above your head like campfire embers.

The range of restaurant and lodging options in Big Sur mirrors the gap between the area's towering peaks and deep canyon floors. Visitors can pitch a tent by the Big Sur River or opt to spend a night in one of Big Sur's famed luxury hotels, the Post Ranch Inn and the Ventana Inn. Or make a picnic with takeout food from the Big Sur Deli or watch the sunset drop from Nepenthe Restaurant's stunning outdoor deck.

The region has inspired all sorts of artists including risqué writer Henry Miller, beat icon Jack Kerouac, nature poet Robinson Jeffers, and indie rock frontman Ben Gibbard of Death Cab for Cutie, and most likely, it will inspire you too.

PLANNING YOUR TIME

Summer is the busy season for Big Sur, though its booming popularity makes it an increasingly year-round destination. Summer is when there can be frequent coastal fog. Away from the coast, the Big Sur Valley can offer some relief from the fog. Reservations are essential for hotels and campsites during the summer. Fall is the ideal time for a trip to the area, with warmer temperatures and fewer crowds.

Previous: the jagged peaks of the Big Sur backcountry; Bixby Bridge; **Above:** McWay Falls.

Big Sur

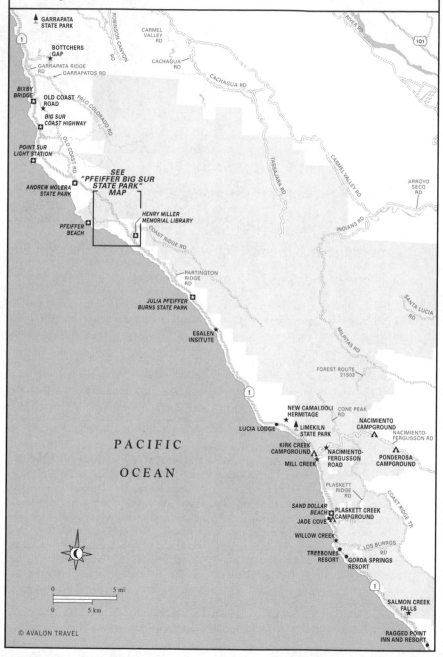

GARRAPATA
STATE PARK

BOTTCHERS
GAP

GARRAPATA RIDGE
RD
GARRAPATOS RD

ROBINSON CANYON
RD

CARMEL
VALLEY
RD

CACHAGUA
RD

CACHAGUA RD

RIVER RD

101

BIXBY
BRIDGE

OLD COAST
ROAD

BIG SUR
COAST HIGHWAY

PALO COLORADO RD

POINT SUR
LIGHT STATION

OLD COAST RD

ANDREW MOLERA
STATE PARK

PFEIFFER
BEACH

SEE
"PFEIFFER BIG SUR
STATE PARK"
MAP

HENRY MILLER
MEMORIAL LIBRARY

COAST RIDGE RD

TASSAJARA RD

CARMEL VALLEY RD

ARROYO
SECO
RD

INDIANS RD

PARTINGTON
RIDGE
RD

JULIA PFEIFFER
BURNS STATE PARK

ESALEN
INSITUTE

MILPITAS RD

SANTA
LUCIA
RD

FOREST ROUTE
21S03

1

PACIFIC

OCEAN

NEW CAMALDOLI
HERMITAGE

CONE PEAK
RD

LIMEKILN
STATE PARK

LUCIA LODGE

KIRK CREEK
CAMPGROUND

MILL CREEK

NACIMIENTO-
FERGUSSON
ROAD

NACIMIENTO
CAMPGROUND

NACIMIENTO-
FERGUSSON RD

PONDEROSA
CAMPGROUND

PLASKETT
RIDGE
RD

SAND DOLLAR
BEACH

JADE COVE

WILLOW CREEK

TREEBONES
RESORT

PLASKETT CREEK
CAMPGROUND

GORDA SPRINGS
RESORT

LOS BURROS
RD

COAST RIDGE TR

1

SALMON CREEK
FALLS

0   5 mi

0   5 km

RAGGED POINT
INN AND RESORT

© AVALON TRAVEL

Highway 1, the road in and out of Big Sur, is a twisting two-lane highway, with frequent construction and closures. Check the California Department of Transportation's website (www.dot.ca.gov) for information about closures and possible delays. If you are driving slower than most traffic on Highway 1, pull over into a pullout and allow the traffic to pass. To stop for photos, turn into the nearest pullout. Give the drivers behind you enough notice that you will be slowing down and turning.

A lot of people drive through Big Sur in a day, taking Highway 1 from Carmel to San Simeon and pulling off at the road's many turnouts to take in the views. Outdoors enthusiasts who want to get off the highway and really experience Big Sur will need at least a couple days. The Big Sur Valley (26 miles south of Carmel) is a good place to stay if you want both a great outdoors experience and amenities such as restaurants and lodging.

The valley is also home to Pfeiffer Big Sur State Park, which has over 200 campsites. The south coast of Big Sur—the stretch from Lucia to San Simeon—has significantly fewer amenities; there are a few campgrounds and the Treebones Resort.

A trip to Big Sur involves planning. It's a good idea to secure supplies and gas before entering Big Sur (at Carmel in the north or Cambria in the south). While Big Sur does have a few markets, you will pay higher prices for a smaller selection of goods. Definitely fill up your tank before heading into Big Sur. While there are a few gas stations on the 90-mile stretch of coastline, you will pay a premium for a gallon of gas. Gas stations in Big Sur have made headlines for having the most expensive gas in the nation.

Consider visiting famous and very popular attractions like Pfeiffer Beach, Nepenthe, and McWay Falls at off-peak hours to better enjoy them.

Sights

★ BIG SUR COAST HIGHWAY

Even if you're not up to tackling the endless hiking trails and deep wilderness backcountry of Big Sur, you can still get a good sense of the glory of this region just by driving through it. The **Big Sur Coast Highway,** a 90-mile stretch of Highway 1, is quite simply one of the most picturesque roads in the country. A two-lane road, Highway 1 twists and turns with Big Sur's jagged coastline, running along precipitous cliffs and rocky beaches, through dense redwood forests, over historic bridges, and past innumerable parks. In the winter, you might spot migrating whales offshore spouting fountains of air and water, while spring finds yucca plants feathering the hillsides and wildflowers coloring the landscape. Construction on this stretch of road was completed in the 1930s, connecting Cambria to Carmel. You can start out at either of these towns and spend a whole day making your way to the other end of the road. The road has plenty of wide turnouts set into picturesque cliffs to make it easy to stop to admire the glittering ocean and stunning wooded cliffs running right out to the water. There can be frequent highway delays due to road construction.

GARRAPATA STATE PARK

The 3,000-acre **Garrapata State Park** (Hwy. 1, 6.7 miles south of Rio Rd., 831/624-4909, www.parks.ca.gov, daily 8am-30 minutes after sunset, free) is Big Sur's northernmost park. Just three miles south of Point Lobos, the park includes the popular Soberanes Point and namesake Garrapata Beach.

At Soberanes Point, trails circle out onto headlands. Make the short climb to the top of Whalers Peak, a knob on the west side of the highway. More substantial hikes depart from the east side of the highway, including the strenuous Rocky Ridge Trail and the Soberanes Canyon Trail, which begins in a cacti-studded landscape and travels into a redwood canyon.

One of Big Sur's best and most easily accessed beaches, Garrapata Beach is just over two miles south of Soberanes Point. Pass through Gate 18 or Gate 19 to get down to the sand. The beach's southern side has some rocky coves and caves. Be careful of dangerous sleeper waves here.

★ BIXBY BRIDGE

You'll probably recognize the **Bixby Bridge** (CA-1, 5.5 miles south of Garrapata State Park) when you come upon it on CA-1 in Big Sur. The picturesque, cement, open-spandrel arched bridge is one of the most photographed bridges in the nation, and it has been used in countless car commercials over the years. The bridge was built in the early 1930s as part of the massive government works project that completed CA-1 through the Big Sur area, finally connecting the north end of California to the south. Today, you can pull out north of the bridge to take photos or just look out at the attractive span and Bixby Creek flowing into the Pacific far below. Get another great view of the bridge by driving a few hundred feet down the dirt Old Coast Road, which is located on the bridge's northeast side.

OLD COAST ROAD

Before the Bixby Bridge spanned the impressive Bixby Canyon, the **Old Coast Road** was the route that Big Sur locals used to get to Carmel. This 10-mile dirt road provides a scenic drive through ranchland and redwood forests with views of the coastline at either end. The road is best traversed with a four-wheel drive, though a confident driver with a two-wheel drive and some clearance can pull off this road during the dry summer months. Begin just north of Bixby Bridge where the Old Coast Road starts its trek inland. Stop after 100 yards or so for one of the best vantage points of Bixby Bridge, spread across the deep canyon like a giant spiderweb, with the blue Pacific as a backdrop. Continue on, eventually descending into a redwood forest along the Little Sur River. The road rises once again, offering great views of the Big Sur River Valley to the south, Andrew Molera State Park down below, and Point Sur to the north. The road returns to CA-1 across from Andrew Molera State Park. Be aware of local

Big Sur's curving coastline

traffic and expect to share the road with hikers and bikers.

★ POINT SUR LIGHT STATION

Sitting lonely and isolated out on its cliff, the **Point Sur Light Station** (CA-1, 6.7 miles south of Bixby Bridge, 831/625-4419, www.pointsur.org, Nov.-Mar. tours Wed. 1pm, Sat.-Sun. 10am, Apr.-June and Sept.-Oct. Wed. and Sat. 10am and 2pm, Sun. 10am, July-Aug. Wed. and Sat. 10am and 2pm, Thurs. 10am, Sun. 10am, adults $12, children $5) crowns the 361-foot-high volcanic rock Point Sur. It keeps watch over ships navigating near the rocky waters of Big Sur. It's the only complete 19th-century light station in California that you can visit, and even here access is severely limited. First lit in 1889, this now fully automated light station still provides navigational aid to ships off the coast; families stopped living and working in the tiny stone compound in 1974. But is the lighthouse truly uninhabited? Take one of the **moonlight tours** (call for information) to learn about the haunted history of the light station buildings.

You can't make a reservation for a Point Sur tour, so you should just show up and park your car off CA-1 on the west side by the farm gate.

Your guide will meet you there and lead you up the paved road 0.5 miles to the light station. Once there, you'll climb the stairs up to the light, explore the restored keepers' homes and service buildings, and walk out to the cliff edge. Expect to see a great variety of wildlife, from brilliant wildflowers in the spring to gray whales in the winter to flocks of pelicans flying in formation at any time of year. Dress in layers; it can be sunny and hot or foggy and cold, winter or summertime, and sometimes both on the same tour! Tours last three hours and require more than a mile of walking, with a bit of slope, and more than 100 stairs. If you need special assistance for your tour or have questions about accessibility, call 831/667-0528 as far in advance as possible of your visit to make arrangements.

★ ANDREW MOLERA STATE PARK

At 4,800 acres, **Andrew Molera State Park** (CA-1, 3.1 miles south of Point Sur Light Station, 831/667-2315, www.parks.ca.gov, day use 30 minutes before sunrise-30 minutes after sunset, $10/vehicle) is a great place to immerse yourself in Big Sur's coastal beauty and rugged history. Among its many assets is the Big Sur River, one of the area's best hikes (the

the iconic Bixby Bridge

Eight-Mile Loop), and a long, sweeping beach decorated with driftwood huts.

Today, the **Cooper Cabin,** which is off the Trail Camp Beach Trail, is a remnant from the park's past. The redwood structure built in 1861 is the oldest building standing on the Big Sur coast. The **Molera Ranch House Museum** (831/667-2956, http://big-surhistory.org, June 12-Sept. 1 Thurs.-Sun. 11am-3pm) displays stories of the life and times of Big Sur's human pioneers and artists as well as the wildlife and plants of the region. Take the road signed for horse tours to get to the ranch house. Next to the ranch house is the **Ventana Wildlife Society's Big Sur Discovery Center** (831/624-1202, www.ventanaws.org, Memorial Day-Labor Day Sat.-Sun. 10am-4pm). This is the place to learn about the successful reintroduction of the California condor to the region.

The park has numerous hiking trails, like the **Ridge Trail and Panorama Trail Loop,** which run down to the beach and up into the forest along the river. Many trails are open to cycling and horseback riding as well. Most of the park trails lie to the west of the highway.

PFEIFFER BIG SUR STATE PARK

The most developed park in Big Sur is **Pfeiffer Big Sur State Park** (CA-1, 2.7 miles south of Andrew Molera State Park, 831/667-2315, www.parks.ca.gov, day use 30 minutes before sunrise-30 minutes after sunset, $10/vehicle). It's got the Big Sur Lodge, a restaurant and café, a shop, an amphitheater, a somewhat incongruous softball field, plenty of hiking-only trails, and lovely redwood-shaded campsites. This park isn't situated by the beach; it's up in the coastal redwoods forest, with a network of roads that can be driven or biked up into the trees and along the Big Sur River. It is one of the best parks in the area to see Big Sur's redwoods and a great place to dip into the cool Big Sur River.

Pfeiffer Big Sur has the tiny **Ernest Ewoldsen Memorial Nature Center,** which features stuffed examples of local wildlife. It's open seasonally; call the park for days and hours. The historic **Homestead Cabin,** located off the Big Sur Gorge Trail, was once the home of part of the Pfeiffer family, who were the first European immigrants to settle in Big Sur. They ushered in Big Sur's reputation as a vacation destination by forming Pfeiffer's Ranch Resort on what is now the site of the Big Sur Lodge.

The **Nature Trail** (0.7 miles round-trip, no elevation gain, easy) leaves from the Big Sur Lodge and provides an introduction to the park's natural assets. Pick up a guide to do this self-guided tour from the end of the trail across from Day Use Lot No. 2. Learn about the park's plant life, including bay laurels, oaks, redwoods, and poison oak, along with information about forest fire damage and decomposition.

No bikes or horses are allowed on trails in this park, which makes it quite peaceful for hikers.

★ PFEIFFER BEACH

Big Sur has plenty of striking meetings of land and sea, but **Pfeiffer Beach** (end of Sycamore Canyon Rd., http://campone.com, daily 9am-8pm, $10/vehicle) is definitely one of the coastline's most picturesque spots. This frequently windswept beach has two looming rock formations right where the beach meets the surf, and both of these rocks have holes that look like doorways, allowing waves and sunlight to pass through. Occasionally, purple sand colors the beach; it is eroded manganese garnet from the bluffs above. It can be incredibly windy here some days.

For newcomers, getting to Pfeiffer Beach is a bit tricky. It is located at the end of the second paved right south of the Big Sur Station. Motorists (no motor homes) must then travel down a narrow, windy, two-mile road before reaching the entrance booth and the beach's parking lot. It's part of the adventure. This road gets very busy during the summer and on weekends. If you can, plan a trip to Pfeiffer Beach when it's less busy. Otherwise, the

Pfeiffer Big Sur State Park

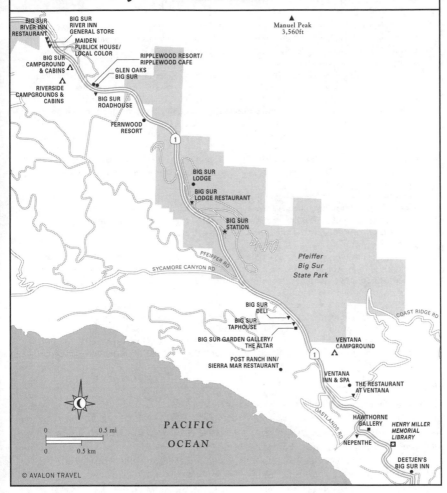

two-mile drive might take a lot longer than expected.

★ HENRY MILLER MEMORIAL LIBRARY

A number of authors have spent time in Big Sur, soaking in the remote wilderness and sea air to gather inspiration for their work. Henry Miller lived and wrote in Big Sur for 18 years, and his 1957 novel *Big Sur and the Oranges of Hieronymus Bosch* describes his time here. Today, the **Henry Miller Memorial Library** (48603 CA-1, between Nepenthe Restaurant and Deetjen's Big Sur Inn, 831/667-2574, www.henrymiller.org, daily 11am-6pm, free) celebrates the life and work of Miller and his brethren in this quirky community center, museum, coffee shop, and gathering place. What you won't find is a typical lending library or slicked-up museum. Instead, inside is a well-curated bookstore featuring the works of Miller as

Big Sur as the Writer's Muse

With so much beauty, it's no wonder that Big Sur has stirred the souls of many of the country's finest writers. Poet Robinson Jeffers was one of the first famous writers to pen praises to Big Sur's beauty. His poems, including "Bixby's Landing" and "The Place For No Story," aptly impart a feeling of the region's rugged character.

Big Sur-based novelist Lillian Bos Ross wrote firsthand about the challenges of living in the area with her Big Sur Trilogy beginning with 1942's *The Stranger,* a National Book Award winner that was later made into the 1974 film *Zandy's Bride* starring Gene Hackman and Liv Ullmann.

Henry Miller is the best known of the writers that spent significant time in Big Sur. He resided in the area from 1944 to 1962. His 1957 novel *Big Sur and the Oranges of Hieronymus Bosch* is a portrait of the region during the time he lived there. The **Henry Miller Memorial Library** (48603 CA-1, between Nepenthe Restaurant and Deetjen's Big Sur Inn, 831/667-2574, www.henrymiller.org, daily 11am-6pm) is a nonprofit arts center that celebrates the late author. It has framed photos of Miller along with a bookstore that sells some of the works that influenced the controversial writer.

Another heavyweight literary figure that spent time in the area and wrote about his experiences is Beat writer Jack Kerouac. His dark 1962 novel *Big Sur* goes into unflinching detail about a depressing, alcohol-soaked time that he spent in fellow writer Lawrence Ferlinghetti's Bixby Canyon cabin. The novel was adapted into a 2013 film of the same name starring Jean-Marc Barr and Kate Bosworth.

Other well-known writers have had Big Sur inform their careers to lesser extents. Gonzo journalist Hunter S. Thompson worked as a security guard at the hot springs that are now known as the Esalen Institute in 1961. His time there helped form the basis of his first feature article in a national magazine, titled "Big Sur: The Tropic of Henry Miller."

Richard Brautigan, who is best known for his 1967 novella *Trout Fishing in America,* was also inspired to write about Big Sur. His 1964 cult favorite novel *A Confederate General from Big Sur* sprung out of some time he spent visiting a friend on Big Sur's South Coast.

More recently, Thomas Steinbeck's 2002 *Down to a Soundless Sea* has seven stories, most of which are about Big Sur's early settlers. The author is the son of Nobel Prize-winning author John Steinbeck.

well as other authors like Jack Kerouac and Richard Brautigan, along with a crew of employees who are always worth striking up a conversation with. There is also a bookshelf devoted to literary works that influenced Miller; it includes novels by Joseph Conrad, Fyodor Dostoevsky, and others. The controversial writer was also a rabid table tennis player, so a table is available outside for those who'd like to play a game or work on their serve. Over the last few years, the library has become an important arts and music center for the Central Coast. The small redwood-shaded lawn hosts concerts and literary events. During summer, the library puts on an international short-film series every Thursday night. Check the library's website for a list of upcoming events.

★ JULIA PFEIFFER BURNS STATE PARK

One of Big Sur's best postcard-perfect views can be attained at **Julia Pfeiffer Burns State Park** (CA-1, 7.7 miles south of Henry Miller Memorial Library, 831/667-2315, www.parks.ca.gov, day use 30 minutes before sunrise-30 minutes after sunset, $10/vehicle). To get to it, the **Overlook Trail** runs only 0.66 miles round-trip along a level, wheelchair-friendly boardwalk. Stroll under CA-1, past the Pelton wheelhouse, and out to the **observation deck** to take in the stunning view of **McWay Falls.** The 80-foot-high waterfall cascades year-round off a cliff and onto the beach of a remote cove, where the water wets the sand and trickles out into the sea. The water of the cove gleams bright cerulean blue against the slightly off-white sand of the beach; it looks more like the South Pacific than California. Anyone with an ounce of love for the ocean will want to build a hut right there beside the waterfall. But you can't. In fact, the reason you'll look down on a pristine and empty stretch of sand is that there's no way down to the cove that is even remotely safe.

The waterfall once spilled right into the ocean, but that all changed after a giant landslide just north of the cove occurred in 1983. This massive slide of dirt and rock closed Highway 1 for almost a year. To reopen the road, eight million cubic yards of dirt and debris had to be pushed into the sea. Eventually, this sediment washed into McWay Cove and created the beach below McWay Falls.

Just past the waterfall observation deck on the same walkway are the ruins of the Brown family's Waterfall House. At one time, the home, which was built in 1940, had artwork by Degas, Dufy, and Gaugin hanging on its walls to go with its spectacular views of the waterfall. It was demolished in 1966, and now only the ruins of the home's walls and terraces remain.

Julia Pfeiffer Burns State Park has some of the best day hiking in the area. From the main entrance in the park, hikers can traverse the loop of **Ewoldsen Trail** with its views of redwoods and the coast. At an unmarked section of the park to the north, visitors can access Partington Cove and embark on the Tanbark Trail. The new Waters Trail connects the Ewoldsen Trail and the Tanbark Trail.

NEW CAMALDOLI HERMITAGE

Removed from society and its flood of sounds, the **New Camaldoli Hermitage** (62475 CA-1, 0.5 miles south of Lucia, 831/667-2456, www.contemplation.com) is located two miles above Highway 1 on a stunning Big Sur ridgeline. The 900-acre facility at 1,300 feet is home to a community of Roman Catholic monks who reside at the serene site for contemplation and prayer. New Camaldoli is named for a Tuscan hermitage founded by Saint Romauld in 1012. Day-use visitors are welcome to explore the public portions of the grounds, including the **New Camaldoli Hermitage Bookstore** (daily 8am-11:15am and 1:15pm-5pm), and attend the daily Eucharist (Mon.-Sat. 11:30am, Sun. 11am) in the chapel, where robed monks sing, speak, and meditate. Strategically placed benches around the

McWay Falls, Julia Pfeiffer Burns State Park

property allow visitors to take in the soothing sea and the enveloping silence.

LIMEKILN STATE PARK

The 716-acre **Limekiln State Park** (63025 CA-1, 805/434-1996, www.parks.ca.gov, daily 8am-sunset, $10/vehicle) is a small park with redwoods, an impressive waterfall, ruins from the region's rugged past, a nice beach on the stunning coastline, and a campground. The park is named for four limekilns located a half-mile from the coast in a redwood forest. These large rusted kilns can be accessed via the park's Limekiln Trail. For just three years beginning in 1887, the Rockland Lime and Lumber Company extracted and processed limestone rock deposits in these kilns using wood fires to purify the stones. Also worth hiking to is **Limekiln Falls,** a 100-foot-high waterfall that splashes down a rock face in two distinct prongs. The beach is a sandy stretch littered with boulders that has the Limekiln Creek Bridge as a backdrop. A single picnic table plopped in the sand provides a terrific place for a picnic lunch. The park also has a campground with 32 sites.

MILL CREEK

Mill Creek (CA-1, 2.2 miles south of Limekiln State Park, http://campone.com, daily 6am-10pm) is a Forest Service day-use area right off Highway 1. It is one of several places along Big Sur's south coast that provides easy access to the rocky coastline. Take a walk on the boulder-strewn beach or enjoy the small picnic area with its tables and raised grills. Add in the two pit toilets and fresh ocean air for a worthwhile driving break.

NACIMIENTO-FERGUSSON ROAD

The only road that traverses Big Sur's Santa Lucia Mountains, the **Nacimiento-Fergusson Road** (four miles south of Lucia) offers spectacular coastal views to those who are willing to wind up this twisty, paved, 1.5-lane road. Simply drive a few miles up to see an eyeful of the expansive Pacific Ocean or to

Limekiln Falls

get above Big Sur's summer fog. It also heads in and out of infrequent redwood forests on the way up. The road connects Highway 1 to U.S. 101, passing through Fort Hunter Liggett army base on its journey. The road is frequently closed during the winter months. Not recommended for those who get carsick.

★ SAND DOLLAR BEACH

Sand Dollar Beach (9.2 miles south of Lucia, http://campone.com, daily sunrise-sunset, $10/vehicle) is one of Big Sur's biggest and best beaches. On Big Sur's south coast, this half-moon-shaped beach is tucked under cliffs that keep the wind down. Though frequently strewn with rocks, the beach is a great place to plop down for a picnic or an afternoon in the sun. From the beach, enjoy a striking view of Big Sur's south coast mountains, including Cone Peak, rising like a jagged fang from a long ridgeline. A series of uncrowded beach breaks offer waves for surfers even during the flatter summer months. The area around the parking lot has picnic tables with raised grills, pit toilets, and a pay phone. If the parking lot is full, you can park on the dirt pullout to the south of the entrance.

JADE COVE

Jade Cove (CA-1, 0.7 miles south of Sand Dollar Beach, http://campone.com) is a rock-jumbled coastal indentation that is said to have a jade-veined underwater cave offshore. This is the place where jade diver Don Wobber found the giant boulder of jade that now resides at the Pacific Grove Museum of Natural History. It's possible to find jade at low tide on this rocky stretch of shore. Getting to the cove involves walking about 100 yards through an open field before descending down a steep rocky path, the bottom section of which is so steep that ropes have been set up to help people into and out of the cove.

WILLOW CREEK

Willow Creek (CA-1, 2.4 miles south of Jade Cove, http://campone.com, daily 6am-10pm), with its rugged, boulder-strewn beach, is one of the best places to find jade on Big Sur's south coast. This Forest Service day-use area is right off the highway and has a nice coastal overlook. If you have time, take the

steep, short road under the highway bridge and down to sea level. Here, you can wander among the rocks searching for naturally occurring chunks of jade at low tide. Or just stand in Willow Creek, whose water is strained through a series of rocks on its way to the sea. Straight offshore is Gorda Rock, a sea stack said to resemble a large woman. Willow Creek has two pit toilets.

SALMON CREEK FALLS

One of the southern portions of Big Sur's best natural attractions is **Salmon Creek Falls** (CA-1, 8.8 miles south of Willow Creek). Flowing year-round, a pair of waterfalls pour down rocks over 100 feet high, their streams joining halfway down. To get a great perspective of the falls, take an easy 10-minute walk over a primitive trail littered with rocks from the highway. The unmarked parking area is a pullout in the middle of a hairpin turn on Highway 1.

TOURS

One way to visit Big Sur is to let someone else do all of the work. **Big Sur Tours & More** (831/241-2526 or 831/657-9442, www.big surtoursandmore.com, $195-370) provides guided tours of the area in a Volvo or Rolls

Willow Creek

Royce. The tours start at two hours and can accommodate 2-4 people. Possible stops include Bixby Bridge, Nepenthe, and McWay Falls.

Big Sur Guides (831/594-1742, www.bigsurguides.com, private hikes $125 pp) is run by Stephen Copeland, who does all sorts of tours ranging from helicopter and whale-watching tours to art gallery tours along the Big Sur coast. He also does a daily guided hike from Ventana Inn & Spa (48123 CA-1, daily 11:30am, $75 pp) that lasts 2.5-3 hours.

Hiking

Only a small portion of Big Sur is accessible by car. Many of the region's best sights—waterfalls tucked into redwood canyons, remote beaches, expansive vistas from steep mountain peaks—can only be experienced on foot. Big Sur's hiking trails also provide an opportunity to see the little details that make the area special, from wildflowers splashed across hillsides to bright yellow banana slugs inching under dark redwood trees.

It should be noted that Big Sur hikes can be more of a challenge than expected due to the region's steep V-shaped mountains and accompanying sheer-walled canyons. In addition, summer and fall can see high temperatures on Big Sur's ridgelines. Be prepared with lots of water and a snack when heading out on a substantial day hike.

GARRAPATA STATE PARK

Garrapata State Park (Hwy. 1, 6.7 miles south of Rio Rd., 831/624-4909, www.parks.ca.gov, daily 8am-30 minutes after sunset) has most of the features that make Big Sur such a famed destination for outdoor enthusiasts: redwood trees, rocky headlands, pocket beaches, and ocean vistas from steep hills and mountains. Garrapata, which means "tick" in Spanish, includes Garrapata Beach, northern Big Sur's finest beach, and two miles of coastline. The two-mile round-trip **Soberanes Point Trail** to the west of the highway is a mild hike up and around the park's rocky headlands. Stroll along the beach, scramble up the cliffs for a better view of the ocean, or check out the seals, sea otters, and sea lions near Soberanes Point. In the wintertime, grab a pair of binoculars to look for migrating gray whales passing quite close to shore here.

For a more invigorating hike, connect the **Soberanes Canyon Trail** with the **Rocky Ridge Trail,** making a 4.5-mile loop. In Soberanes Canyon, you'll get a taste of a small redwood forest before climbing up to the outstanding coast views offered by 1,700-foot-high Rocky Ridge. In the spring months, the trail is littered with a profusion of wildflowers. A bench on the coastal side of Rocky Ridge offers a great place to catch your breath and take in the scenery. This is the same landscape that inspired nature poet Robinson Jeffers to pen his popular poem, "The Place For No Story."

Expect little in the way of facilities here—you'll park in a wide spot on Highway 1, and if you're lucky you might find a pit toilet open for use.

BOTTCHERS GAP

At the end of Palo Colorado Road, **Bottchers Gap** (Palo Colorado Rd., nine miles east of CA-1, $10/vehicle) is a campground and day-use area that offers entrance into the northern section of Big Sur's Ventana Wilderness. The **Skinner Ridge Trail to Mount Carmel** (9.6 miles round-trip, strenuous, 2,500-foot elevation gain) gets hikers to a summit with a 360-degree view. You'll pass through chaparral and oak as you climb to 4,185-foot Devil's Peak, and then continue another 0.8 miles up to 4,417-foot Mount Carmel. Make sure to clamber up the rock outcropping at the summit for full views of the Big Sur backcountry and Monterey Bay.

An easier hike via a gated road is the **Little Sur River Camp Hike** (5.6 miles round-trip, moderate, 1,200-foot elevation gain). Simply descend on the gated dirt road at the south end of Bottchers Gap to a camp on a small fork of the Little Sur River.

ANDREW MOLERA STATE PARK

Andrew Molera State Park (CA-1, 3.1 miles south of Point Sur Light Station, 831/667-2315, www.parks.ca.gov, day use 30 minutes before sunrise-30 minutes after sunset, $10/vehicle) has several hiking trails that run down to the beach and up into the forest along the river. The beach is a one-mile walk down the easy, multiuse **Trail Camp Beach Trail** (two miles round-trip, no elevation gain, easy). From there, climb out to the headlands on the **Headlands Trail** (0.5 miles round-trip, 30-foot elevation gain, easy) for a beautiful view of the Big Sur River emptying into the sea. In the distance you can also spot Pico Blanco, one of the region's most distinct mountains, rising like a pyramid from behind a ridgeline.

If you prefer to get a better look at the river, take the flat, moderate **Bobcat Trail** (5.5 miles round-trip, negligible elevation gain, easy) and perhaps a few of its ancillary loops. You'll walk right along the riverbank, enjoying the local microhabitats.

For a longer and more difficult trek up the mountains and down to the beach, take the eight-mile **Ridge Trail and Panorama Trail Loop** (eight miles round-trip, 1,000-foot elevation gain, moderate). This is one of the best coastal hikes in Big Sur. You'll start at the parking lot on the **Creamery Meadow Beach Trail,** then make a left onto the long and fairly steep **Ridge Trail** to get a sense of the local ecosystem. Then turn right onto the **Panorama Trail,** which has sweeping views of the coast, including Molera Point and Point Sur, as it runs down to the coastal scrublands. Be sure to take the small **Spring Trail** (0.2 miles round-trip, little elevation gain, easy) down a driftwood-littered gully to a scenic stretch of beach. Hike back out and take a left

connecting to the **Bluffs Trail,** which takes you back to Creamery Meadow along the top of a marine terrace.

A fairly short but steep hike that is never crowded is the **East Molera Trail** (three miles round-trip, 1,300-foot elevation gain, strenuous), which is located on the east side of Highway 1. From the main parking lot, walk to the white barn and take the tunnel under the road that leads to the trail. The trail is a steep series of switchbacks that climb up to a saddle with coast views to the west and a glimpse of the imposing, pyramid-shaped Pico Blanco to the east.

At the park entrance, you'll find bathrooms but no drinkable water and no food concessions.

PFEIFFER BIG SUR STATE PARK

For a starter walk at **Pfeiffer Big Sur State Park** (CA-1, 2.7 miles south of Andrew Molera State Park, 831/667-2315, www.parks.ca.gov, 30 minutes before sunrise-30 minutes after sunset, $10/vehicle), take a short stroll on the Valley View Trail to **Pfeiffer Falls** (1.5 miles round-trip, 200-foot elevation gain, easy). The trail passes through a redwood forest, crosses a creek, and then heads up into the hills. The burnt redwoods you'll see are from the 2008 Basin Complex Fire, the third-largest wildfire in the state's history. Eventually, the trail reaches a T-intersection. A right turn heads into a redwood-shaded canyon and ends at a view of the 60-foot waterfall spilling down a rock face. The **Valley View Overlook** (1 mile from trailhead and 0.5 miles from Pfeiffer Falls) peers down the Big Sur Valley to Point Sur in the distance.

The **Buzzard's Roost Trail** (three miles round-trip, 750-foot elevation gain, moderate) explores the portion of the park on the west side of Highway 1. Climb from the river's edge through redwoods and oak trees on the way up to the summit of Pfeiffer Ridge, where you'll have a view of the coastline. Other coastal hikes such as Molera's Eight-Mile Loop have better vistas.

For a longer, more difficult, and interesting hike that leaves the park and goes into the adjoining Ventana Wilderness, start at the Homestead Cabin and head to the **Mount Manuel Trail** (10 miles round-trip, 3,150-foot elevation gain, strenuous). From the Y-intersection with the Oak Grove Trail, it's four miles of sturdy hiking up a steep grade to Mount Manuel, a 3,379-foot peak that looms high over the Big Sur Valley. On summer days, during the trail's initial climb, it's possible to hear swimmers in the Big Sur Gorge below. The tallest point has some rocks and a view of the ocean behind Pfeiffer Ridge. Bring lots of water for this hike.

Need to cool off after hiking? Scramble out to the undeveloped **Big Sur River Gorge,** where the river slows and creates pools that are great for swimming. Relax and enjoy the water, but don't try to dive here. The undeveloped trail to the gorge can be found at the eastern end of the campground.

This is one of the few Big Sur parks to offer a full array of services. Before you head out into the woods, stop at the **Big Sur Lodge** restaurant and store complex to get a meal and some water, and to load up on snacks and sweatshirts. Between the towering trees and

the summer fogs, it can get quite chilly and somewhat damp on the trails.

BIG SUR STATION

One way to experience the Big Sur backcountry without heading out on an overnight trip is to hike from **Big Sur Station** (47555 CA-1, 0.6 miles south of Pfeiffer Big Sur State Park, 831/667-2315, daily 9am-4pm), the main ranger station for Big Sur. From the parking lot adjacent to Big Sur Station, take the **Pine Ridge Trail to Ventana Camp** (8.6 miles round-trip, 1,130-foot elevation gain, moderate, $5/vehicle). This excursion makes for a nice day hike that ends at a scenic section of the Big Sur River with opportunities for a swim. The Pine Ridge Trail is very popular due to the Sykes Hot Springs, which lie beyond Ventana Camp (also explaining why most people bypass the worthy Ventana Camp). The trail begins by switchbacking up a ridge out of the Big Sur Valley before leveling out as it passes over the Big Sur River Gorge. At 2.3 miles, the trail enters the Ventana Wilderness. Keep going almost four miles and look for a sign marking the Ventana Camp Trail Junction. Here, you'll take the spur trail down to Ventana Camp, a steep mile-plus descent down to the river. The trail continues to the

Mount Manuel, Pfeiffer Big Sur State Park

backcountry Ventana Camp, and, even better, a scenic section of the river downstream in which you can cool off.

COAST RIDGE ROAD

If you hike it far enough, **Coast Ridge Road** (two miles south of Big Sur Station, off CA-1) rewards with sweeping, unobstructed views of the Big Sur Valley and the Big Sur backcountry. Originating by the Ventana Inn & Spa, this gated dirt road is usually closed from November to May. Coast Ridge Road climbs fast, so within a few miles hikers can attain stunning views of the Big Sur River Valley, Point Sur, the massive monolith of Mount Manuel, and the rocky line of peaks known as the Ventana Double Cones. It is possible to do a satisfying out-and-back hike on the road, but another option is the **Coast Ridge Road to Terrace Creek Trail to Pine Ridge Trail Loop** (12.5 miles round-trip, 1,600-foot elevation gain, moderate), which combines Coast Ridge Road's open, sweeping views with the wooded Terrace Creek Trail and Pine Ridge Trail. It is best done as a shuttle hike, parking one car at the Big Sur Station Pine Ridge Trail lot and then driving to Coast Ridge Road to begin. (If you don't have two cars, you'll have to walk along CA-1 for the 1.7 miles between Big Sur Station and the start of Coast Ridge Road.)

To embark on the hike from Coast Ridge Road, hike up the gated roadway for four miles until you see Terrace Creek Trail departing down to the left. Take the tree-shaded trail down 1.5 miles to Terrace Creek Camp, which is located at the junction with Pine Ridge Trail. Take a left at the T-intersection to continue on Pine Ridge Trail; from there it's 5.3 miles to Big Sur Station.

The unmarked parking area for Coast Ridge Road is located on the drive up to the Ventana Inn & Spa. While driving toward the inn, look for the first big dirt pullout on your right. Park your vehicle here and walk up the paved road until you see a gated dirt road on the right. This is Coast Ridge Road.

JULIA PFEIFFER BURNS STATE PARK

If you're up for a longer hike after taking in McWay Falls within **Julia Pfeiffer Burns State Park** (CA-1, 7.7 miles south of Henry Miller Memorial Library, 831/667-2315, www.parks.ca.gov, day use 30 minutes before sunrise 30 minutes after sunset, $10/vehicle), go back the other way to pick up the **Ewoldsen Trail** (4.5 miles round-trip, 1,500-foot

the view from Coast Ridge Road

elevation gain, moderate). This trek takes you through McWay Canyon, where you'll see the creek and surrounding lush greenery as you walk. Some of Big Sur's finest redwoods are located here. Then you'll loop away from the water and climb up into the hills. One part of the trail is perched on a ridgeline where there is little vegetation growing on the steep hillside below. This is the site of a 1983 landslide that closed the highway below for a whole year. A quick detour can be made by taking the Overlook Trail, a short spur that goes to an open viewing area with a bench offering a glimpse of the sea spread out to the horizon. Be sure to bring water, as this hike can take several hours.

If you want to spend all day at Julia Pfeiffer Burns State Park, drive two miles north from the park entrance to the Partington Cove pullout and park along the side of the highway. On the east side of the highway, start out along the **Tanbark Trail** (6.4 miles round-trip, 1,900-foot elevation gain, strenuous). You'll head through redwood groves and up steep switchbacks to the top of the coastal ridge. Near the top is the Tin House, a dilapidated structure with a large concrete front porch still intact. It is said the former owner built it for his wife, and when she didn't like it, the house became a hangout for the owner and his friends. Return back down the trail or take the fire road, which descends steeply to the highway. Utilizing the fire road creates a loop hike, though this also means hiking a mile on Highway 1 to get back to your vehicle.

The west side of the road is where you pick up the **Partington Cove Trail** (two miles round-trip, 200-foot elevation gain, easy) an underrated walk that goes to a striking, narrow coastal inlet. It begins as a steep dirt road. It soon reaches a bridge over Partington Creek and continues through a 60-foot-long tunnel blasted into the rock. The trail arrives at a cove where John Partington used to ship out the tanbark trees that he had harvested in the canyon above. There is a bench at the end of the trail offering views of the cove and the coastline to the south. To reach the trailhead from the north, drive nine miles south of Pfeiffer Big Sur State Park on Highway 1. Look for a big bend in the road to the east with dirt pullouts on either side. Park here and then begin your hike where the gated road departs from the west side.

The 1.2-mile **Waters Trail** (1.2 miles one-way, negligible elevation gain, easy) is the newest hiking option in Julia Pfeiffer Burns State Park. This worthy addition to the park connects the Tanbark Trail to the Ewoldsen

hikers on Waters Trail in Julia Pfeiffer Burns State Park

Trail, traversing a piece of the park that was previously inaccessible. Begin either at the main park entrance—where you'll find the trailhead off the Ewoldsen Trail—or start from the Tanbark Trail. The path cuts across the hillside while offering postcard-worthy coastal views along most of its route. In the spring, this area is painted purple by fields of flowering lupine. Unless you use two cars, you will have to walk along the highway a short distance to return to your vehicle. This hike is worth all of the effort.

LIMEKILN STATE PARK

Limekiln State Park (63025 CA-1, 14.4 miles south of Pfeiffer Burns State Park, 805/434-1996, www.parks.ca.gov, daily 8am-sunset, $10/vehicle) has only one major trail, but it's worth your time. The **Limekiln Trail** (one mile round-trip, 170-foot elevation gain, easy) begins by heading up the canyon on the dirt road that passes the campground. After crossing Hare Canyon Creek on a footbridge, the trail travels up beside the scenic Limekiln Creek through a redwood forest standing in bright green puddles of ferns and sorrel. Up past a third bridge, the trail comes to the large, rusty kilns topped with tufts of vegetation.

On the way up or back, be sure to take the **Limekiln Waterfall Spur Trail** (0.5 miles round-trip, easy-moderate), located about 100 feet past the second bridge. The trail traverses the creek multiple times over logs and bridges made of planks of lumber. This half-mile round-trip detour leads to its namesake 100-foot waterfall, which splashes down a vegetation-cloaked rock face. On a warm day, duck your head under the left falls for an invigorating experience.

The **Hare Creek Trail** (one mile round-trip, 150-foot elevation gain, easy) includes a walk on the campground road before crossing the footbridge over Hare Creek. When the trail forks, the left fork becomes the Limekiln Trail and the right fork heads up a canyon where Hare Creek spills over rocks. The walk ends at a small waterfall.

NACIMIENTO-FERGUSSON ROAD AREA

Nacimiento-Fergusson Road (four miles south of Lucia) offers access to one of Big Sur's most stunning hikes, the Cone Peak Trail, as well as the rarely crowded **Mill Creek Trail** (three miles round-trip, 500-foot elevation change, moderate). The latter trail can be reached by driving up to a noticeable bend in Nacimiento-Fergusson Road about 0.8 miles from its junction with Highway 1. This trail goes up the namesake creekbed in a redwood forest and is best ended at the unofficial camp 1.5 miles up.

Cone Peak dominates the skyline of Big Sur's South Coast. This impressive mountain rises from sea level to 5,150 feet in just three miles. It is also the second-tallest peak in the Santa Lucia Mountains, about 700 feet shorter than nearby Junipero Serra Peak. Though it takes some mountain driving to get to its trailhead, the **Cone Peak Trail** (five miles round-trip, 1,150-foot elevation change, moderate) offers a moderate hike that pays big dividends. The trailhead can be reached by driving Nacimiento Fergusson Road seven miles from Highway 1 up to the dirt Coast Ridge Road. Take a left on Coast Ridge Road (also called Cone Peak Road by some), then drive six miles to a small parking area by the trailhead. The trail itself is exposed and climbs steadily. The astounding views from the top include Ventana Double Cone to the north and Junipero Serra Peak to the east. Most impressive is the view to the west, where mountains drop precipitously toward the sea. A defunct fire lookout crowns the peak and can be climbed for an even better view.

Coast Ridge Road is usually closed from November to May. Call the U.S. Forest Service Office in King City (831/385-5434) to make sure the road is open before departing. When Coast Ridge Road is closed, you can hike in on the dirt road, but it adds an extra 12 miles to your round-trip journey.

PACIFIC VALLEY AREA

Pacific Valley is a distinct, broad coastal terrace designated with a green-and-white sign just south of Mill Creek. The coastal terrace boasts headlands that poke into the sea like spread-out fingers. It's also home to to the lightly used **Prewitt Loop Trail** (12 miles round-trip, 1,500-foot elevation gain, strenuous). The trail does a long loop inland from the Pacific Valley coast. Past Stag Camp, four miles in, trail conditions deteriorate. Hardy hikers can continue up and then down to Pacific Valley Station, a Forest Service facility. It will be almost a mile's walk north back to the initial trailhead off Highway 1. This trail is most rewarding during wildflower season in spring. There is trailhead parking at a pullout off Highway 1. It is located 57 miles south of Carmel and 0.8 miles north of the Pacific Valley Ranger Station.

To explore the western edge of Pacific Valley, opt for the **Pacific Valley Bluffs Trail** (0.7 miles round-trip, no elevation gain, easy). Start across from the Pacific Valley Ranger Station and take the wooden steps over the fence line. The trail passes through an open meadow where cattle sometimes graze. It makes its way out to bluffs over the ocean and continues southwest before ending at a small sand dune.

RAGGED POINT

The **Ragged Point Cliffside Trail** (one mile round-trip, 300-foot elevation gain, moderate) originates on the edge of the Ragged Point Inn's property and descends down to a black sand beach. The bottom is also the base of the 300-foot **Black Swift Falls.** Those who aren't up for the steep climb can take in the region from a viewing platform on top of the cliff. Ragged Point Inn (19019 Hwy. 1, Ragged Point) is 85 miles south of Carmel and 20 miles north of San Simeon.

BACKPACKING

If you long for the solitude of backcountry camping, the **Ventana Wilderness** (www.fs.usda.gov) is ideal for you. This area comprises the peaks of the Santa Lucia Mountains and the dense growth of the northern reaches of Los Padres National Forest. It has 167,323 acres of steep V-shaped canyons and mountains that rise to over 5,000 feet. You'll find many trails beyond the popular day hikes of the state parks, especially as Big Sur stretches down to the south. Farther south in Big Sur, there's also the less visited **Silver Peak Wilderness** (www.fs.usda.gov), a 31,555-acre parcel on the southwest Big Sur coast. There are many points from which to access the wilderness in Big Sur. Check the Ventana Wilderness Alliance website (www.ventanawild.org) to find reports on trail conditions, and stop in at Big Sur Station to get the latest news on the backcountry areas.

Bottchers Gap

Bottchers Gap (end of Palo Colorado Rd., nine miles east of CA-1, $10/vehicle) offers access into the backcountry via trails to the Ventana Double Cone and the Little Sur River. There is a challenging multiday hike from here to the 4,853-foot **Ventana Double Cone** (30 miles round-trip, difficult), which has 360-degree views of the northern wilderness. It is best attempted during clear days in the winter or spring due to flies and heat in the summer. Hike the Skinner Ridge Trail past the junction to Mount Carmel and Devils Peak. Then continue on via the Big Pines Trail and the Ventana Trail. The suggested overnight spot is Pat Spring Camp, located seven miles from Bottchers Gap.

Pico Blanco Camp is one of the finest backcountry camps in the Ventana Wilderness. It is located under the striking 3,709-foot Pico Blanco—"blanco" refers to the mountain's white limestone—and above a section of the Little Sur River with a stunning little waterfall. The **Bottchers Gap to Pico Blanco Camp Hike** (14.8 miles round-trip, strenuous) begins by taking the gated road (Pico Blanco Road) down from Bottchers Gap. You'll pass through the Pico Blanco Boy Scout camp (not to be confused with Pico

Blanco Camp, your destination), which can be overrun with kids during the summer, before reaching the Little Sur Trail. Head west on the Little Sur Trail for 2.6 miles including one steep section known as Cardiac Hill to reach Pico Blanco Camp. If you have two cars, you can do a through-hike from **Bottchers Gap to Pico Blanco Camp to Old Coast Road** (12.4 miles). Park one vehicle at Bottchers Gap and another at the other end of the Little Sur Trail on Old Coast Road three miles in from the road's southern intersection with CA-1. The best way to hike the trail is to begin at Bottchers Gap and hike down to Old Coast Road.

Big Sur Station

The Pine Ridge Trail that originates from **Big Sur Station** (47555 CA-1, 0.6 miles south of Pfeiffer Big Sur State Park, $5/vehicle) is by far the most popular backcountry trail in Big Sur. The reason is **Sykes Hot Springs,** a cluster of warm mineral pools on the Big Sur River located 10 miles down the trail. The springs and the adjacent Sykes Camp get overrun with visitors on weekends, holidays, and during the summer. The camp and springs are not big enough to accommodate the amount of people that visit during busy periods, so expect crowded camps and jostling for the springs if you decide to come during these times. The camp and springs could be worth a visit if you can manage a trip during the offseason or midweek. The **Pine Ridge Trail to Sykes Camp** (20 miles round-trip, moderately strenuous) involves hiking in 12 miles on the frequently crowded trail. Despite its overuse, the hike to Sykes is a challenging one, so be prepared.

There are several other worthy backcountry campgrounds off the Pine Ridge Trail other than Sykes Camp. One is **Barlow Flat Camp** (14 miles round-trip, moderately strenuous), a large camp on a section of the Big Sur River that is dotted with swimming holes. Another is **Redwood Camp** (24 miles round-trip, moderately strenuous), a quiet camp in a forest with old-growth redwoods. Located

two miles past Sykes, Redwood Camp gets a lot less foot traffic.

The Pine Ridge Trail traverses the entire Ventana Wilderness, meaning those who want to truly immerse themselves in Big Sur's backcountry can attempt to backpack the entire **Pine Ridge Trail from China Camp to Big Sur Station** (24 miles one way, challenging). The hike will take two to three days. China Camp is on the far eastern end of the wilderness at almost 5,000 feet. Since the Big Sur Station trailhead is at 370 feet elevation, the China Camp trailhead is the best place to start a backpacking adventure across the whole length of the trail. The ends of the trail are more than 1.5 hours apart by car so this requires two cars or someone dropping you off on one end. The trail camps along the way include Divide Camp, Pine Ridge Camp, Redwood Camp, Sykes Camp, Barlow Flat Camp, Terrace Creek Camp, and Ventana Camp.

Kirk Creek Area

Less crowded than the Pine Ridge Trail, the **Vicente Flat Trail to Vicente Flat Camp** (10.6 miles round trip, moderately strenuous) heads up towards Cone Peak, the jagged mountain rising in the distance, while gaining sweeping views of the coast. It is on the South Coast of Big Sur across from the Kirk Creek Campground, which is four miles south of Lucia and 38 miles south of Pfeiffer Big Sur State Park on CA-1. The trail starts with switchbacks and climbs almost 2,000 feet along hillsides that are painted with wildflowers during the spring months. After 1.4 miles, the trail reaches a ridge with coast views. Continue on to Vicente Flat Camp with its large redwoods near Hare Creek. You can also do this as a grueling up-and-back day hike.

The **Cone Peak Loop** (15 miles round-trip, strenuous) offers a multiday backpacking trip that ascends the 5,150-foot Cone Peak from sea level. The loop leaves from the Kirk Creek area and travels up the Vicente Flat Trail to Vicente Flat Camp. It then utilizes the Stone Ridge Trail, the Gamboa Trail, the

Coast Ridge Trail, the Cone Peak Trail, Cone Peak Road, and the Vicente Flat Trail to make a circular route to and from the high peak. Overnight opportunities include the backpacking camps at Vicente Flat Camp, Goat Camp, Ojito Camp, and Trail Springs Camp.

Silver Peak Wilderness

The **Silver Peak Wilderness** is located on the south end of the Big Sur coast near the Monterey County-San Luis Obispo County border. It has waterfalls, redwoods, and fine coast views like the Ventana Wilderness, but it receives less foot traffic than its northern neighbor. One relatively easy way to experience the Silver Peak Wilderness is to embark on the **Salmon Creek Trail to Spruce Creek Camp** (four miles round-trip, moderate). The Salmon Creek Trailhead is off a noticeable turn on CA-1, eight miles south of Gorda and 27 miles south of Big Sur Station. After about 10 minutes on the trail, a spur trail heads to the left to get closer to the impressive Salmon Creek Falls. The main trail is to the right and continues upward, winding in and out of the creek canyon along the way. Spruce Creek Camp is situated at the intersection of Spruce Creek and Salmon Creek. If you still have energy, continue onto **Estrella Camp** (6.5 miles round-trip). The trail passes by some waterfalls on Salmon Creek on the way to the backcountry camp.

Sports and Recreation

HORSEBACK RIDING

You can take a guided horseback ride into the forests or out onto the beaches of Andrew Molera State Park with **Molera Horseback Tours** (831/625-5486, http://molerahorsebacktours.com, $48-84). Tours of 1-2.5 hours depart each day starting at 9am, 11am, 1pm, and 3:30pm. Call ahead to guarantee your spot or to book a private guided ride. Each ride begins at the modest corral area, from which you'll ride along multiuse trails through forests or meadows, or aside the Big Sur River, and down to Molera Beach. There you'll guide your horse along the solid sands as you admire the beauty of the wild Pacific Ocean.

Molera Horseback Tours are suitable for children over age six and riders of all ability levels; you'll be matched to the right horse for you. All but one of the rides go down to the beach. Tours can be seasonal, so call ahead if you want to ride in the fall or winter.

MOUNTAIN BIKING

It's possible to mountain bike in Big Sur, though you'll have to bring your own bike or rent one in Carmel. **Andrew Molera State Park** (CA-1, 3.1 miles south of Point Sur Light Station, 831/667-2315, www.parks.ca.gov, 30 minutes before sunrise-30 minutes after sunset, $10/vehicle) has a few trails open to bikes. One of the easiest is the **Creamery Meadow Trail** (two miles round-trip, easy) that goes along the side of its namesake meadow to the beach. Another more rigorous option is the **Ridge Trail** (6.4 miles round-trip, strenuous) that climbs 1,000 feet to views of the coast stretching north to Point Sur. Be aware that you may encounter hikers and horseback riders while riding.

Across the highway from Molera, the **Old Coast Road** offers lots of hill climbs for riders who want to break a sweat. The 10-mile road heads inland before reaching the coast again to the north of Bixby Bridge. Do a section or attempt the whole road.

The closest shop that rents bikes is **Bay Bikes** (3600 The Barnyard Shopping Center, Carmel, 831/655-2453, www.baybikes.com, Sun.-Mon. 10am-5pm, Tues.-Fri. 10am-6pm, Sat. 9am-6pm, bike rentals $8-16/hr, $24-48/four hours).

FISHING

No harbors offer deep-sea charters around Big Sur, but if your idea of the perfect outdoor vacation includes a rod and reel, you can choose between shore and river fishing. Steelhead run up the Big Sur River to spawn each year, and a limited fishing season follows them up the river into **Pfeiffer Big Sur State Park** and other accessible areas. Check with Fernwood Resort (831/667-2422, www.fernwoodbigsur. com) and the other lodges around Highway 1 for the best spots during the season of your visit.

The numerous creeks that feed into and out of the Big Sur River are home to their fair share of fish. The California Department of Fish and Game (www.dfg.ca.gov) can give you specific locations for legal fishing, season information, and rules and regulations.

If you prefer the fish from the ocean, you can cast off several of the beaches for the rockfish that scurry about in the near-shore reefs. **Garrapata State Beach** has a good fishing area, as do the beaches at **Sand Dollar.**

SCUBA DIVING

There's not much for beginner divers in Big Sur. Expect cold water and an exposure to the ocean's swells and surges. Temperatures are in the mid-50s in the shallows, dipping into the 40s as you dive deeper down. Visibility is 20-30 feet, though rough conditions can diminish this significantly; the best season for clear water is September-November.

The biggest and most interesting dive locale here is **Julia Pfeiffer Burns State Park** (CA-1, 12 miles south of Pfeiffer Big Sur State Park, 831/667-2315, www.parks.ca.gov, daily sunrise-sunset). You'll need to acquire a special permit at Big Sur Station and prove your experience to dive at this protected underwater park. The park, along with the rest of the coast of Big Sur, is part of the Monterey Bay National Marine Sanctuary. You enter the water from the shore, which gives you the chance to check out all the ecosystems, beginning with the busy life of the beach sands

before heading out to the rocky reefs and then into the lush green kelp forests.

Divers at access-hostile **Jade Cove** (CA-1, 0.7 miles south of Sand Dollar Beach) aren't usually interested in cute, colorful nudibranchs or even majestic gray whales. Jade Cove divers come to stalk the wily jade pebbles and rocks that cluster in this special spot. The semiprecious stone striates the coastline right here, and storms tear clumps of jade out of the cliffs and into the sea. Much of it settles just off the shore of the tiny cove, and divers hope to find jewelry-quality stones to sell for a huge profit.

If you're looking for a guided scuba dive of the Big Sur region, contact **Adventure Sports Unlimited** (303 Potrero St., Santa Cruz, 831/458-3648, www.asudoit.com).

BIRD-WATCHING

Many visitors come to Big Sur just to see the birds. The Big Sur coast is home to innumerable species, from the tiniest bushtits up to grand pelicans and beyond. The most famous avian residents of this area are no doubt the rare and endangered California condors. Once upon a time, condors were all but extinct, with only a few left alive in captivity and conservationists struggling to help them breed. Today, more than 60 of these birds soar above the trails and beaches of Big Sur. You might even see one swooping down low over your car as you drive down CA-1!

The **Ventana Wildlife Society** (VWS, www.ventanaws.org) watches over many of the endangered and protected avian species in Big Sur. As part of their mission to raise awareness of the condors and many other birds, the VWS offers bird-watching expeditions. Check their website for schedules and prices.

SPAS

The Spa at Ventana (48123 CA-1, 831/667-4222, www.ventanainn.com, daily 10am-7pm, massages $70-295) offers a large menu of spa treatments to both hotel guests and visitors. You'll love the serene atmosphere of the

California Condors

With wings spanning 10 feet from tip to tip, the California condors soaring over the Big Sur coastline are some of the area's most impressive natural treasures. But, in 1987, there was only one bird left in the wild, and it was taken into captivity as part of a captive breeding program. The condors' population had plummeted due to its susceptibility to lead poisoning along with deaths caused by electric power lines, habitat loss, and being shot by indiscriminate humans.

a California condor in Big Sur

Now the reintroduction of the high-soaring California condor, the largest flying bird in North America, to Big Sur and the Central Coast is truly one of conservation's greatest success stories. In 1997, the Monterey County-based nonprofit Ventana Wildlife Society (VWS) began releasing the giant birds back into the wild. Currently, over 60 wild condors soar above Big Sur and the surrounding area, and in 2006, a pair of condors were found nesting in the hollowed-out section of a redwood tree.

The species recovery in the Big Sur area means that you might be able to spot a California condor flying overhead while visiting the rugged coastal region. Look for a tracking tag on the condor's wing to determine that you are actually looking at a California condor and not just a big turkey vulture. Or take a two-hour tour with the **Ventana Wildlife Society** (831/455-9514, 2nd Sun. every month, $50 pp), which uses radio telemetry to track the released birds. You can also visit the **VWS Discovery Center** (Andrew Molera State Park, CA-1, 22 miles south of Carmel, 831/624-1202, www.ventanaws.org, Memorial Day-Labor Day Sat.-Sun. 9am-4pm), where there's an exhibit that details the near extinction of the condor and the attempts to restore its population. For a once-in-a-lifetime condor viewing experience, opt for the **Condor Sanctuary Tour** (831/455-9514, May-Dec. by appointment, $1,000/up to four people), where the VWS executive director drives you up to a remote condor sanctuary in the Santa Lucia Mountains. Here the giant birds are in their element as they ride thermals in the sky overhead and perch on rocks and tree limbs like natural gargoyles. Lunch is included.

treatment and waiting areas. Greenery and weathered wood create a unique space that helps to put you in a tranquil place, ready for your body to follow your mind into a state of relaxation. Indulge in a soothing massage, purifying body treatment, or rejuvenating or beautifying facial. Take your spa experience a step further in true Big Sur fashion with an astrological reading, essence portrait, or a jade stone massage. If you're a hotel guest, you can choose to have your spa treatment in the comfort of your own room or out on your private deck.

Just across the highway from the Ventana, the **Post Ranch Inn's Spa** (47900 CA-1, 831/667-2200, www.postranchinn.com, daily 9am-9pm, massages $160-400) is another ultra-high-end resort spa, only open to those who are spending the evening at the luxurious resort. Shaded by redwoods, the relaxing spa offers massages and facials along with more unique treatments including Big Sur jade stone therapy and craniosacral therapy.

TUBING

Cool off during a hot day by floating in the Big Sur River on an inner tube. During the summer and fall, when the river has lower water levels, you'll be floating in deep pools (rather than traveling along the river) and most likely have to portage around river rocks and shallow areas. There are no places in Big Sur that rent tubes, but a few places, including the **Fernwood Camp Store** (47200 CA-1, 1.9 miles south of Andrew Molera State Park, 831/667-2422, daily 10am-6pm), the **Ripplewood Store** (47047 CA-1, 831/667-2242, www.ripplewoodresort.com, daily 8am-8pm), and **Riverside Campgrounds & Cabin Store** (CA-1, 22 miles south of Carmel, 831/667-2414, www.riversidecampground.com, daily 8am-8pm) sell tubes for less than $25. You can put your tube in the river anywhere below Pfeiffer Big Sur State Park's gorge and head down toward Andrew Molera State Park, where the waterway spills into the ocean.

JADE HUNTING

Spend significant time in Big Sur, and you'll notice locals wearing sea-polished jade jewelry, which is also for sale in many gift shops. Big Sur jade, which is a naturally occurring mineral, can be found on the beaches of Big Sur's south coast. The best places to find jade are at **Willow Creek** (CA-1, 2.4 miles south of Jade Cove, http://campone.com, daily 6am-10pm) and **Jade Cove** (0.7 miles south of Sand Dollar Beach, http://campone.com). Ideal times for jade hunting are after big winter storms. It's not easy to tell jade apart from serpentine, a similar-looking mineral. One way is to get the rock wet and hold it up into the sunlight. If it is somewhat translucent, you may have a piece of jade in your hand. Another way is to scrape a pocketknife across the suspected jade. Serpentine will be scratched easily, while it is difficult to mark jade with a knife. Jade can only be taken from below the high-tide line.

Entertainment and Events

LIVE MUSIC

Over the last few years, Big Sur has become an unexpected hotbed of big music concerts. More than just a place to down a beer and observe the local characters, **Fernwood Tavern** (47200 CA-1, 831/667-2422, www.fernwoodbigsur.com, Sun.-Thurs. 11am-11pm, Fri.-Sat. 11am-1am) also has live music. Most of the big-name acts swing through Big Sur in the summer and fall. Even when it isn't hosting nationally known touring bands, Fernwood has a wide range of regional acts on Saturday nights. You might hear country, folk, or even indie rock from the small stage. Most live music happens on weekends, especially Saturday nights, starting at 10pm.

Down the road, the **Henry Miller Memorial Library** (48603 CA-1, 831/667-2574, www.henrymiller.org) has had some internationally known acts perform on its stage including Arcade Fire, TV on the Radio, and the Fleet Foxes, who typically fill far bigger venues. Check their website for upcoming events.

The manager of the **Big Sur River Inn** (46480 CA-1, 831/667-2700, www.bigsurriverinn.com, concerts late April-early Oct. Sun. 1pm-5pm) jokes that they have been doing Sunday afternoon concerts on their back deck since "Jesus started riding a bicycle." The live music tradition here began in the 1960s with famed local act Jack Stock and the Abalone Stompers. Now it's mostly local jazz bands that play on the restaurant's sunny deck, while a barbecue is set up on the large green lawn. It's a great way to end a weekend.

BARS

The primary watering hole in Big Sur is **Fernwood Tavern** (47200 CA-1, 831/667-2422, www.fernwoodbigsur.com, Sun.-Thurs. noon-midnight, Fri.-Sat. noon-1am), a classic tavern with redwood timbers and a fireplace that warms the place up in the chilly months. It's also a great place to hear a band, especially on Saturday nights. Enjoy a beer or cocktail inside or out back on the back deck under the redwoods. On any given summer

Big Sur Playlist

Big Sur has been a popular subject of many songwriters. The following songs make a great playlist while cruising down Highway 1.

- Alanis Morissette's "Big Sur"—The Jagged Little Pill artist softens up for the Big Sur coast in this song that proclaims: "All roads lead to Big Sur/ All roads home to Big Sur."

- Buckethead's "Big Sur Moon"—This instrumental from the KFC bucket-wearing musician would be an ideal soundtrack for a moonlit drive down Highway 1.

- Johnny Rivers' "Going Back to Big Sur"—The man behind "Secret Agent Man" sings: "I'm going back to Big Sur/ This time I might just stay." He kept his word and is now a Big Sur resident.

- Jay Farrar and Ben Gibbard's "Big Sur"—The Son Volt frontman and the Death Cab for Cutie frontman team up for this acoustic song that soundtracked the 2008 documentary *One Fast Move or I'm Gone: Kerouac's Big Sur.*

- Red Hot Chili Peppers' "Road Trippin'"—This acoustic orchestral track shouts out the region with the line: "In Big Sur, we take some time to linger on."

- Judy Collins' "Big Sur"—The folk singer and songwriter puts her big voice into an ode to Big Sur on this track from 2011's *Bohemian.*

- The Thrills' "Big Sur"—The Irish indie-pop group's debut-album single warns "just don't go back to Big Sur" in a catchy way that suggests they may go against their better judgment.

- Beach Boys' "California Saga (Big Sur)"—The surf-rock band goes country-tinged in this knowing look at Big Sur's natural treasures.

- Ramblin' Jack Elliott's "South Coast"—With lyrics from Big Sur novelist Lillian Bos Ross, this superb acoustic story song capped Elliott's Grammy-winning 1995 album of the same name.

- Mason Jennings' "Big Sur"—The folky singer-songwriter uses Big Sur in this tune with the refrain: "This is a song to bring you hope" from his 1997 self-titled debut.

- Death Cab for Cutie's "Bixby Canyon Road"—Inspired by frontman Ben Gibbard's trip to the canyon where Beat writer Jack Kerouac wrote his dark novel *Big Sur,* this is a highlight of the indie rock group's 2008 album *Narrow Stairs.*

- Jason Aldean's "Texas Was You"—Country artist Jason Aldean recounts experiences across the country including a drive down Big Sur's coastline in this song.

- Siskiyou's "Big Sur"—Canadian indie folk act Siskiyou whispers "Let's party all night long," like they are playing in a tent within a campground of sleeping campers in this seven-minute, 40-second track.

evening Fernwood can be an intriguing mix of longtime locals, international tourists, and everyone in between.

The newest place to grab a beer in Big Sur is the **Big Sur Taphouse** (47250 CA-1, 831/667-2225, www.bigsurtaphouse.com, Mon.-Thurs. noon-10pm, Fri. noon-midnight, Sat. 10am-midnight, Sun. 10am-10pm). The Taphouse has 10 rotating beers on tap, with a heavy emphasis on West Coast microbrews. The cozy interior has wood tables, a gas fireplace, and board games. With two big-screen TVs, the Taphouse is also a good place to catch your favorite sports team in action. Out back is a large patio with picnic tables and plenty of sun. They also serve better-than-average bar food, including tacos and pork sliders.

The **Maiden Publick House** (CA-1, Village Center Shops, 831/667-2355, daily noon-midnight), known simply as "the pub," is in the Village Shops complex just a few feet north of the River Inn Restaurant. With 100 different brands of bottled beer and 16 rotating beers on tap, this is a good stop for craft beer lovers. The only beer that stays on draft is Guinness. Grab a spot at the large wooden bar or sit on the small outdoor patio by the parking lot.

The **Big Sur River Inn Restaurant** (46840 CA-1, 831/667-2700, www.bigsurriverinn.com, daily 8am-11am, 11:30am-4:30pm, 5pm-9pm) is a fine place for a cocktail or beer any time of day. During daylight hours, you can take your drink to the nearby Big Sur River and plop down on a chair in the stream to enjoy it. In the late afternoon and early evening, the intimate bar area gets a fun local crowd.

To have a cocktail with a stunning view, head to the **Restaurant at Ventana Inn** (48123 CA-1, 831/667-4242, www.ventanainn.com, daily 11:30am-4pm and 6pm-9pm). Order a drink at the bar (the Moscow mules and mojitos are quite good) and take it out on the sprawling outdoor deck with a view down the coast.

FESTIVALS AND EVENTS

Tasty things grow in Big Sur's woods—including chanterelle mushrooms. The **Big Sur Foragers Festival** (various locations, www.bigsurforagersfestival.org, Jan.) celebrates found foods with a dinner, foraging hikes, and a cooking competition. Proceeds benefit the Big Sur Health Center.

The **Big Sur International Marathon** (831/625-6226, www.bsim.org, entry $150-300, Apr.) is one of the most popular marathons in the world, due in no small part to the scenery runners encounter on the 26-mile course. The race begins at Big Sur Station and then winds, climbs, and descends again on the way to Carmel's Rio Road. The April race weekend also includes 21-mile runs, 9-mile runs, 5K walks, relay runs, and a 3K kids' fun run.

Every Memorial Day weekend, the Monterey County Free Libraries' Big Sur branch takes advantage of the crowds for their annual **Big Sur Book and Bake Sale** (lawn adjacent to the Big Sur branch of the Monterey County Free Libraries, CA-1 at Ripplewood, 831/667-2537, Memorial Day weekend). There are always some used-book treasures and some tasty baked goods at this benefit, where all of the proceeds go to the library.

Throughout the summer, the **Henry Miller Memorial Library** (48603 CA-1, 831/667-2574, www.henrymiller.org) hosts the **Big Sur International Short Film Screening Series,** where free films from all over the globe are shown on Thursday nights.

Each year, the Pacific Valley School hosts the fund-raising **Big Sur Jade Festival** (Pacific Valley School, 69325 CA-1, http://bigsurjadefest.com, Oct.). Come out to see the artists, craftspeople, jewelry makers, and rock hunters displaying their wares at this early-fall festival. The school is located across CA-1 from Sand Dollar Beach. You can munch snacks as you tap your feet to the live music. Check the website for the exact dates and information about this year's festival.

Not up for the Big Sur Marathon? No problem. Maybe the **Big Sur River Run** (Pfeiffer Big Sur State Park, 831/624-4112, www.bigsurriverrun.org, Oct.) is more your speed. This 10K run is along the flat, paved park road that skirts the Big Sur River. There's also a 5K walk. Proceeds benefit the Big Sur Health Center and the Big Sur Volunteer Fire Brigade.

Nepenthe's **Halloween Bal Masque** (Nepenthe Restaurant, 48510 CA-1, 831/667-2345, www.nepenthebigsur.com, Oct. 31, adults $35, children 12 and under $7) is Big Sur's best party and a way to see this community's creativity in action with some amazing homemade costumes. The ticket price includes all-you-can-eat Ambrosia and veggie burgers. There's also live music or a DJ.

The **Big Sur Food & Wine Festival** (various Big Sur locations, www.bigsurfoodandwine.org, Nov.) combines fine wines and cuisine with Big Sur's stunning views. Events include hiking with stemware along with tastings and dinners. A big part of the money made from the event goes to local nonprofits.

Shopping

There are a few shops in Big Sur that sell the work of local artists and artisans. One of these is the long-running **Local Color** (46480 CA-1, 831/667-0481, www.bigsurlocalcolor.com, daily 10am-6pm), which is located in the Village Shops next to the Big Sur River Inn. It carries locally made items ranging from redwood bowls to tie-dyed clothes.

By the Big Sur Bakery, the **Big Sur Garden Gallery** (Loma Vista Gardens, 47540 CA-1, 831/667-2000, Wed.-Mon. 10am-6pm) sells locally made items including Big Sur jade necklaces, art by Big Sur artists, and vintage clothing. The eclectic and fun shop is housed in a building that appears to have been a greenhouse at one time. Also in the Loma Vista Gardens, **The Altar** (Loma Vista Gardens, 47540 CA-1, 831/238-2828, Fri.-Mon. noon-5pm) bills itself as "the tiniest shop in the world." It is a small store with unique home and garden supplies.

On the same grounds as the ultra-popular Nepenthe Restaurant, **The Phoenix Shop** (48510 CA-1, 831/667-2347, www.phoenix-shopbigsur.com, daily 10:30am-7pm) has jade jewelry, boutique clothing, musical instruments, garden supplies, and books on Big Sur and beyond.

Forgot to bring a book for your vacation? The **Henry Miller Memorial Library** (48603 CA-1, 831/667-2574, www.henrymiller.org, daily 11am-6pm) is here to help with its wonderfully intuitive selection of books for sale, including everything from local titles to Beat writers and French surrealists.

One of the major attractions at Lucia's New Camaldoli Hermitage is the **New Camaldoli Hermitage Bookstore** (62475 CA-1, Lucia, 831/667-2456, http://contemplation.com, daily 8am-11:15am and 1:15pm-5pm). This quiet-as-a-library shop is known for its brandy-dipped fruitcakes and Father Arthur Poulin's art, striking landscape paintings composed of dots of paint. It also has holy medals, incense, crucifixes, candles, and religious books by everyone from C. S. Lewis to Thich Nhat Hanh.

Across the highway from Nepenthe Restaurant, the building that houses the **Hawthorne Gallery** (48485 CA-1, 831/667-3200, www.hawthornegallery.com, daily

Big Sur Garden Gallery

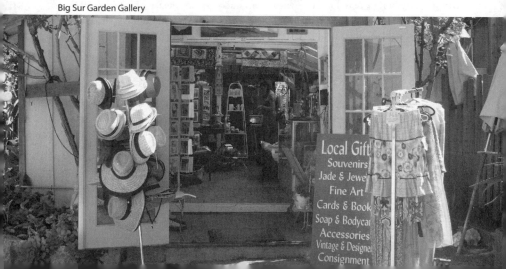

10am-6pm) is a piece of art itself, a work of glass and metal created in collaboration with Post Ranch Inn architect Mickey Muenning. Inside are paintings, sculptures, and glass items created by the Hawthorne family and their artist friends.

Also within a unique structure, the **Big**

Sur Coast Gallery (49901 CA-1, 831/667-2301, www.coastgalleries.com, daily 10am-5pm) is in a pair of buildings that resemble giant wooden wine barrels. They have works by Henry Miller, Marc Chagall, and local artists. They also have a café with outdoor seating on the roof of one of the structures.

Accommodations

$100-150

You'll find a couple of small motels along CA-1 in the valley of Big Sur. One of the more popular of these is the **Fernwood Resort** (47200 CA-1, 831/667-2422, www.fernwood-bigsur.com, motel rooms $135-180, cabins $215). The cluster of buildings includes a 12-room motel, a small convenience store, a restaurant, and a bar that is a gathering place for locals and a frequent host of live music. The motel units are located on either side of the restaurant-bar-convenience store. The nicely priced units start at a simple queen bedroom and go up to a queen bedroom with a fireplace and a two-person hot tub on an outdoor back deck. Down near the Big Sur River, the cabins have fully equipped kitchens and a refrigerator. The cabins are a good deal for groups of two to six people.

Your guest room at **Deetjen's Big Sur Inn** (48865 CA-1, 831/667-2378, www.deetjens. com, $100-270) will be unique, still decorated with the art and collectibles chosen and arranged by Grandpa Deetjen many moons ago. The historic inn prides itself on its rustic construction, so expect thin, weathered walls, funky cabin construction, no outdoor locks on the doors, and an altogether one-of-a-kind experience. Five rooms have shared baths, but you can request a room with private bath when you make reservations. The best budget options are those with the shared bathroom including "Petite Cuisine" ($100) with a single bed, "Little Room" ($115) with a double bed, and "Van Gogh" ($115) with two single beds. Deetjen's prefers to offer a serene

environment, and to that end does not permit children under 12 unless you rent both rooms of a two-room building. Deetjen's has no TVs or stereos, no phones in guest rooms, and no cell phone service. One of the primary sources of entertainment is the rooms' guest journals, which have occupied the evenings of those who have stayed here for years. Decide for yourself whether this sounds terrifying or wonderful.

A night in a cabin is a great way to spend an evening under the Big Sur stars. The **Ripplewood Resort** (47047 CA-1, 831/667-2242 or 800/575-1735, www.ripplewoodresort. com, $130-225) has you covered with 15 cabins and a duplex available for a night's stay. This was one of Big Sur's first resorts, operating before the Bixby Bridge was finished in 1932, allowing visitors to more easily access the area. A lot of the cabins are spread out along the Big Sur River and have riverview decks. Cabin features can include kitchens and/or fireplaces.

To truly soak in Big Sur's solitude, the ★ **New Camaldoli Hermitage** (62475 CA-1, 0.5 miles south of Lucia, 831/667-2456, www.contemplation, $105-250) offers a quiet stay in the mountains above Lucia. The Hermitage is home to a group of Roman Catholic monks, who offer various overnight accommodations for travelers of any or no religious denomination who want to "experience the precious gift of time for a contemplative life." Radios and musical instruments are not permitted here. The many benches on the property offer opportunities to take in the natural beauty at night, from the shining stars freckling the sky to the distant Piedras Blancas Light Station waving its light over the sea. Framed copies of Saint Romauld's Brief Rule hang in the overnight units, summing up the experience: "Sit in your cell as in paradise. Put the whole world behind you and forget it. Watch your thoughts like a good fisherman watching for fish." The five private hermitages available to guests are basically trailers with porches. The trailers are decorated with religious iconography and outfitted with a bed, desk, bathroom, and kitchen with a gas-burning countertop stove. There are also nine private rooms, each with a half bath and a garden, located in the retreat house. Men can opt to stay overnight in a monk's cell within the monastic enclosure, while there are also a few units outside the enclosure that accommodate two guests. The monks are not a talkative bunch, so there are not a lot of instructions. Overnight guests can head to the monastery's kitchen for breakfast, lunch, and dinner. The food is primarily vegetarian and simple. After serving yourself, bring your back to your accommodations to dine alone, so that there is no disruption to the grounds' silence. Staying at the Hermitage is one of the region's best deals.

The accommodations can be rustic, but they are worth it if it's solitude you're after.

$150-250

The best part about staying at the **Big Sur Lodge** (47225 CA-1, 800/424-4787, www.big-surlodge.com, $229-394), inside Pfeiffer Big Sur State Park, is that you can leave your room and hit the trail. In the early 1900s, the park was a resort owned by the pioneering Pfeiffer family. Though the amenities have been updated somewhat, the Big Sur Lodge still evokes the classic woodsy vacation cabin. Set on a sunny knoll, the lodge has 62 units with the majority being family- and group-friendly two-bedroom options. Twelve units also have kitchenettes. The rooms could use a bit of a remodel, but every one has a front or back deck for spending time outdoors. There are no TVs here and connecting to the Internet requires paying an extra fee, but all stays come with a pass that allows you entrance into all of Big Sur's state parks including Pfeiffer Big Sur State Park, Andrew Molera State Park, and Julia Pfeiffer Burns State Park. There are several amenities just a short walk down the hill from the rooms, including the **Big Sur Lodge Restaurant** (daily 8am-9:30pm), the **Deli & Café** (daily 8am-9:30pm), and the **Gift Shop**

overnight retreat at the New Camaldoli Hermitage

& General Store (April-Oct. daily 8am-9pm, Nov.-March daily 9am-7pm). Be sure to take advantage of the lodge's pool (March-Oct. 9am-9pm) during your stay and watch for the semi-wild turkeys that roam the property.

The **Big Sur River Inn** (46480 CA-1, 831/667-2700 or 800/548-3610, www.bigsur-riverinn.com, $200-350) has been lodging guests in Big Sur since 1934. It was formerly the Apple Pie Inn and Rogers Redwood Camp before becoming the River Inn in 1943. The River Inn has 14 rooms on the east side of Highway 1 and six suites on the west side of the road. Units are soundproofed (a big plus given their proximity to the highway) and have all new bedding and flat-screen TVs. (There are almost no lodging options in Big Sur with TVs.) The east side rooms are cozy (read: fairly small) with knotty pine walls and small porch areas out front. The west side suites each have two rooms, one with a king bed and the other with a trundle bed, good for families and small groups. The suites also have decks overlooking the property's grassy lawn and the Big Sur River. Also on site is a seasonally heated outdoor pool. It's proximal to the **River Inn Restaurant** (daily 8am-11am, 11:30am-4:30pm, and 5pm-9pm, $12-32) and the **Maiden Publick House** (Village Center Shops, 831/667-2355, daily noon-midnight).

Filled with creative touches and thoughtful amenities, ★ **Glen Oaks Big Sur** (47080 CA-1, 831/667-2105, www.glenoaksbigsur.com, $225-550) offers the region's best lodging for the price. Its 16 units bring the motor lodge into the new millennium with heated stone bathroom floors, in-room yoga mats, spacious two-person showers, and gas fireplaces that double as art pieces. These combine seamlessly with the classic adobe walls and wood rafters. The king rooms have nice enclosed outdoor courtyards, while all the units have fun items to entertain guests, from board games and a card deck of yoga poses to a copy of Henry Miller's *Big Sur and the Oranges of Hieronymus Bosch*. For those who would rather spend an evening in a stand-alone structure, Glen Oaks has two cottages amid the oak trees and eight cabins in an impressive redwood grove by the Big Sur River. The cabins are clean with a modern rustic feel and have kitchenettes along with outdoor fire pits that are already set up with kindling and firewood. All guests have access to two on-site beaches situated on scenic sections of the Big Sur River. Glen Oaks' redwood grove is home to the Big Sur Valley's second-largest

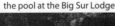
the pool at the Big Sur Lodge

redwood, the Grandmother Pfeiffer Tree. The forward-looking Glen Oaks even has its own electric car charging station. The complex is just feet away from two of Big Sur's restaurants: the **Big Sur Roadhouse** (47080 CA-1, 831/667-2370, www.glenoaksbigsur.com/roadhouse.html, daily 7:30am-9pm, $19-32) and **Ripplewood Café** (47047 CA-1, 831/667-2242, www.ripplewoodresort.com, daily 8am-2pm, $9-16).

Located halfway between Big Sur and Carmel, the privately owned **Severson's Knoll** (seversonland@gmail.com, www.seversonsknoll.com, two-night minimum, $225-250) is a cabin perched on the rim of a canyon with views of the Big Sur backcountry. Three miles inland, including a short drive on a dirt road, this cozy structure has a wood stove, a bath, a romantic outdoor bathtub, a kitchen, and a wooden porch that wraps around three-quarters of the structure. The bedroom is on the second floor and reached by a covered outdoor staircase. Just feet away is a building housing a nice amenity: a wood-fired sauna. The owners also rent a 600-square-foot unit ($175, two-night minimum) attached to their home that has a private bath, a bedroom, a kitchen, and a sunroom.

The **Lucia Lodge** (62400 CA-1, 50 miles south of Carmel, 866/424-4787, www.lucialodge.com, $230-300) has just 10 rooms, 8 of which have a superb view of Big Sur's south coast. The original lodge was built in the 1930s as freestanding cabins, and now feature gas fireplaces and four-poster beds. The other units are more modern but lack telephones and TVs. The lodge was featured in the 1999 film *The Limey* starring Terence Stamp, Peter Fonda, and Leslie Ann Warren.

There are not many lodging choices on Big Sur's south coast. One of the only options is the **Gorda Springs Resort** (CA-1, 65 miles south of Carmel, Gorda, 805/927-3918, www.gordaspringsresort.com, $175-400). Studio suites, cottages, and small house-like structures are available. The Gorda complex includes a restaurant, espresso bar, gift shop, and a gas station (known for a while as selling the most expensive gas in the country). The studio suites all have fireplaces, while some of the cottages and houses have kitchens.

The **Ragged Point Inn and Resort** (19019 CA-1, 85 miles south of Carmel, 805/927-4502, http://raggedpointinn.com, $189-349) is on the southern end of Big Sur, right before the mountains level out and give way to the landscape surrounding San Simeon. The inn has 39 rooms that take

Lucia Lodge

advantage of their position on a seaside cliff. The most expensive units have superb views of the sea and sheltered balconies or decks. They also have gas fireplaces and Jacuzzi tubs. Other rooms are set farther back from the edge. One worthwhile feature of the grounds is a steep 0.6-mile round-trip trail to a black sand beach that is open to guests and non-guests alike. The property also is home to a gift shop, jewelry store, coffee bar, mini-mart, and the **Ragged Point Restaurant** (805/927-5708, daily 8am-11am, noon-4pm, and 5pm-9pm, $22-40).

OVER $250

One of Big Sur's two luxury resorts, **Ventana Inn & Spa** (48123 CA-1, 831/667-2331, www.ventanainn.com, $700-2,500) is a place where the panoramic views begin on the way to the parking lot. Once you reach the inn, there are home-baked pastries, fresh yogurt, in-season fruit, and organic coffee that can be delivered to your room in the morning or eaten in the restaurant. And that's just the beginning of an unbelievable day at the Ventana. Next, don your plush spa robe and rubber slippers and head for the Japanese bathhouses. Choose from two bathhouses, one at each end of the property. Both are clothing-optional and gender segregated, and the upper house has glass and open-air windows that let you look out to the ocean. Two swimming pools offer a cooler respite from your busy life; the lower pool is clothing-optional, and the upper pool perches on a high spot for enthralling views. Even daily complimentary yoga classes can be yours for the asking. The guest rooms range from the "modest" standard rooms with king beds, tasteful exposed cedar walls and ceilings, and attractive green and earth-tone appointments, all the way up through generous and gorgeous suites to full-size multiple-bedroom houses. You can also take an evening stroll down to the **Restaurant at Ventana Inn** (831/667-4242, www.ventanainn.com, daily 11:30am-4pm and 6pm-9pm, 4-course dinner tasting menu $75), which is the only spot on the property where you need to wear

more than your robe and flip-flops. If you're headed to the **Spa at Ventana Inn** (831/667-4222, daily 10am-7pm) for a treatment, you can go comfy and casual. Ventana also has a car service for guests who want to dine at other Big Sur restaurants.

Even though a night at ★ **Post Ranch Inn** (47900 CA-1, 888/524-4787 or 831/667-2200, www.postranchinn.com, $675-2,485) can total more than some people's monthly paycheck, an evening staring at the smear of stars over the vast blue Pacific from one of the stainless steel hot soaking tubs on the deck of Post Ranch's ocean-facing rooms can temporarily cause all life's worries to ebb away. Though it may be difficult to leave the resort's well-appointed units, it is a singular experience to soak in the Infinity Jade Pool, an ocean-facing warm pool made from chunks of the green ornamental stone. Situated on a 1,200-foot-high ridgeline, all the rooms at this luxury resort have striking views, whether it's of the ocean or the jagged peaks of the nearby Ventana Wilderness. The units also blend in well with the natural environment, including the seven tree houses, which are perched 10 feet off the ground. Each one has a king bed, an old-fashioned wood-burning fireplace, a spa tub, and a private deck. In addition, the mini-bars are stocked with complimentary snacks, wine, and cold drinks. During your stay, take advantage of the resort's complimentary activities including yoga classes, nature hikes, garden tours, and stargazing. A night at Post Ranch also includes an impressive breakfast with made-to-order omelets and French toast as well as a spread of pastries, fruit, and yogurt served in the Sierra Mar Restaurant with its stellar ocean views.

CAMPING

Many visitors to Big Sur want to experience the unspoiled beauty of the landscape daily. To accommodate true outdoors lovers, many of the parks and lodges have overnight campgrounds. You'll find all types of camping, from full-service, RV-accessible areas to

A New Age California Experience

The **Esalen Institute** (55000 Hwy. 1, 831/667-3000, www.esalen.org) is known throughout California as the home of Esalen massage technique, a forerunner and cutting-edge player in ecological living, and a space to retreat from the world and build a new and better sense of self. Visitors journey from all over the state and beyond to sink into the haven that's sometimes called "The New Age Harvard."

One of the institute's biggest draws, the bathhouse, sits down a rocky path right on the edge of the cliffs overlooking the ocean. It includes a motley collection of mineral-fed hot tubs looking out over the waves—choose either the Quiet Side or the indoors Silent Side, and then sink into the water and contemplate the Pacific Ocean's limitless expanse, meditate on a perfect sunset or arrangement of stars, or (on the Quiet Side) get to know your fellow bathers—who will be nude.

Esalen's bathhouse area is "clothing optional"; its philosophy puts the essence of nature above the sovereignty of humanity, and it encourages openness and sharing among its guests—to the point of chatting nude with total strangers in a smallish hot tub. You'll also find a distinct lack of attendants to help you find your way around. Once you've parked and been given directions, it's up to you to find your way down to the cliffs. You'll have to find your own towel, ferret out a cubby for your clothes in the changing rooms, grab a shower, and then wander out to find your favorite of the hot tubs. Be sure you go all the way outside past the individual claw-foot tubs to the glorious shallow cement tubs that sit right out on the edge of the cliff with the surf crashing just below.

In addition to the nudity and new-age culture of Esalen, you'll learn that this isn't a day spa. You'll need to make an appointment for a massage (at $165 a pop), which grants you access to the hot tubs for an hour before and an hour after your 75-minute treatment session. If you just want to sit in the mineral water, you'll need to stay up late. Very late. Inexpensive ($20) open access to the Esalen tubs begins on a first-come, first-served basis at 1am and ends at 3am. Many locals consider the sleep deprivation well worth it to get the chance to enjoy the healing mineral waters and the stunning astronomical shows.

If you're not comfortable with your own nudity or that of others, you're uninterested in the all-inclusive spiritual philosophy, or you're unable to enjoy silence, Esalen is not for you. But if this description of a California experience sounds just fabulous to you, make your reservations now. The Esalen Institute accepts reservations by phone if necessary. Go to the website for more information.

environmental tent campsites to wilderness backpacking. You can camp in a state park or out behind one of the small resort motels near a restaurant and a store and possibly the cool, refreshing Big Sur River. Pick the option that best suits you and your family's needs.

In summer months, especially on weekends, campers without reservations coming to Big Sur are frequently turned away from the full campgrounds. A backup option for the desperate is to try and secure one of the 12 first-come, first-served tent campsites at **Bottchers Gap** (Palo Colorado Rd., nine miles east of CA-1, 805/434-1996, http://campone.com, $15). There are few amenities and it can get hot up here, but at 2,100 feet, the camp has some good views of the Big Sur

backcountry. Be aware that the longtime camp host here is a stickler for the rules.

★ **Andrew Molera State Park** (CA-1, 3.1 miles south of Point Sur Light Station, 831/667-2315, www.parks.ca.gov, $25) offers 24 walk-in, tent-only campsites located 0.25-0.5 miles from the parking lot via a level, well-maintained trail. You'll pitch your tent at a pretty meadow near the Big Sur River, in a site that includes a picnic table and a fire ring. No reservations are taken, so come early in summertime to get one of the prime spots under a tree. While you're camping, look out for bobcats, foxes, deer, raccoons (stow your food securely!), and any number of birds. From the camping area, it's an easy one-mile hike to the beach.

State parks are not the only places to camp in designated campsites in Big Sur. The privately owned **Big Sur Campgrounds & Cabins** (47000 CA-1, 831/667-2322, www. bigsurcamp.com, tent sites $55-65, RV sites $65-75, camping cabins $165, cabins $225-415) offers space to pitch a tent beside the redwoods and river. The tent sites come with a fire pit and picnic table, while the RV sites can accommodate vehicles up to 40 feet with electrical and water hookups. A slight step up are the camping cabins, which have a queen bed with linens and blankets but no indoor plumbing or heating. There are also more equipped cabins ranging from one-room units to A-frames to two-bedroom options. They each have a gas or wood-burning fireplace for keeping warm. The on-site facilities include a camp store, a playground, and laundry facilities. Right next door, **Riverside Campground & Cabins** (47020 CA-1, 22 miles south of Carmel, 831/667-2414, www. riversidecampground.com, tent sites $50-55, RV sites $55, cabins $105-210) has 22 tent sites and 12 RV sites on 12 redwood-shaded acres by the Big Sur River. The tent sites include the requisite fire pits and picnic tables. The RV sites have water and electrical hookups. Or opt for one of the cabins that range from a small unit with a shared bathhouse to larger ones with a queen bed, bathroom, and kitchenette.

The **Fernwood Resort** (47200 CA-1, 1.9 miles south of Andrew Molera State Park, 831/667-2422, www.fernwoodbigsur.com, tent site $55, campsite with electrical hookup $65, tent cabin $90, adventure tent $120) offers a range of camping options. There are 66 campsites located around the Big Sur River, some with electrical hookups for RVs. Fernwood also has tent cabins, which are small canvas-constructed spaces with room for four in a double and two twins. You can pull your car right up to the back of your cabin. Bring your own linens or sleeping bags, pillows, and towels to make up the inside of your tent cabin. Splitting the difference between camping and a motel room are the rustic "Adventure Tents," canvas tents draped over a solid floor whose biggest comfort are the fully made queen beds and electricity courtesy of an extension cord run into the tent. All camping options have easy access to the river, where you can swim, inner tube, and hike. Hot showers and restrooms are a short walk away. Also, you will be stumbling distance from Big Sur's most popular watering hole, the Fernwood Bar.

The biggest and most developed campground in Big Sur is at ★ **Pfeiffer Big Sur State Park** (CA-1, 2.7 miles south of Andrew Molera State Park, 800/444-7275, www.parks. ca.gov, www.reserveamerica.com, standard campsite $35, riverside campsite $50). With more than 150 individual sites, each of which can handle two vehicles and eight people or an RV (maximum 32 feet, trailers maximum 27 feet, dump station on site), there's enough room for almost everybody, except during a crowded summer weekend. During those times, a grocery store and laundry facility operate within the campground for those who don't want to hike down to the lodge, and plenty of flush toilets and hot showers are scattered throughout the campground. In the evenings, walk down to the Campfire Center for entertaining and educational programs. Pfeiffer Big Sur fills up fast in the summertime, especially on weekends. Reservations are recommended.

In 2013, tech entrepreneur Sean Parker made national news for his elaborate wedding in the **Ventana Campground** (48123 CA-1, 831/667-2712, www.ventanacamping. com, $55), which was closed at the time. Now you can camp at the site of that opulent fete. On the grounds of the Ventana Inn, the campground has 78 campsites in a redwood-shaded canyon by Post Creek. Each site has a picnic table and fire pit. You can walk to the Ventana Restaurant.

★ **Julia Pfeiffer Burns State Park** (CA-1, 7.7 miles south of Henry Miller Memorial Library, 831/667-2315 or 800/444-7275, www.parks.ca.gov, www.reserveamerica.com, $30) has two walk-in environmental campsites perched over the ocean behind stunning McWay Falls. It's a short 0.33-mile walk to these two sites, which have fire pits, picnic tables, and a shared pit toilet, but there is no running water. More importantly, they have some of the best views of the California coast that you can find in a developed state park campground. At night, fall asleep to the sound of waves crashing into the rocks below. Saddle Rock is the better of the two sites, but you can't go wrong with either one. These two sites book up far in advance, particularly in summer. Reservations can be made seven months in advance, but if you haven't planned that far ahead, there is an option on the Reserve America website that will alert you if there has been a cancellation. Note that you will need to check in at Pfeiffer Big Sur State Park, which is 12 miles north on CA-1.

Limekiln State Park (63025 CA-1, 14.4 miles south of Julia Pfeiffer Burns State Park, 800/444-7275, www.parks.ca.gov, $35) can satisfy your desire to sleep in a redwood grove or near Big Sur's crashing sea. The 32 sites include 12 in the beach area—some with coastal views—while the rest are creekside or in the redwoods. The campground has the standard state park setup where all sites have a picnic table and fire pit. There are also shared hot showers and flush toilets. Of the sites, 29 can

be reserved in advance, while three are overflow sites with no parking. One of the best sites is an overflow site with an ocean view tucked under the towering bridge. It's located behind campsite four.

A popular U.S. Forest Service campground on the south coast of Big Sur, **Kirk Creek Campground** (CA-1, 1.7 miles south of Limekiln State Park, 805/434-1996, www. recreation.gov, $25) has a great location on a bluff above the ocean. Right across the highway is the trailhead for the Vicente Flat Trail and the scenic Nacimiento-Fergusson Road. The sites have picnic tables and campfire rings with grills, while the grounds have toilets and drinking water.

Plaskett Creek Campground (CA-1, seven miles south of Limekiln State Park, 805/434-1996, www.recreation.gov, $25) is located right across the highway from Sand Dollar Beach. The sites are in a grassy area under Monterey pine and cypress trees. There are picnic tables and a campfire ring with a grill at every site along with a flush toilet and drinking water in the campground.

Camping on the Big Sur coast is very popular during the summer. Therefore, if you haven't made reservations for a campsite months in advance, it's going to be difficult

the two-site campground at Julia Pfeiffer Burns State Park

to find a place to pitch your tent. **Nacimiento Campground** (Nacimiento-Fergusson Rd., 11 miles east of CA-1, http://campone.com, first come, first served, $15) is just over 10 miles inland, but it does offer a possible place to stay when the coast is inundated with campers. There are just eight first-come, first-served sites here, all located by the Nacimiento River.

Two miles east of Nacimiento Campground and far more spacious, **Ponderosa Campground** (Nacimiento-Fergusson Rd., 13 miles east of CA-1, http://campone.com, reservations 877/444-6777 or www.recreation. gov, $20) has 23 sites along the Nacimiento River. All of the sites have picnic tables, fire pits, and raised grills. Reservations must be made more than eight days in advance. Fewer than that, you can try your luck by trying to secure a site in person. Be aware that it will be hot and bug-filled during the summer.

For the ultimate high-end California green lodging-cum-camping experience, book a yurt (a circular structure made with a wood frame covered by cloth) at the **Treebones Resort** (71895 CA-1, 877/424-4787, www. treebonesresort.com, $225-355). The yurts at Treebones tend to be spacious and charming, with polished wood floors, queen beds, seating areas, and outdoor decks for lounging. They are really cool structures, but they are not soundproofed. There are also five walk-in campsites ($95-150 for two people, breakfast and use of the facilities included). For a truly different experience, camp in the human nest ($150), a bundle of wood off the ground outfitted with a futon mattress. A stay in any of the facilities includes a complimentary breakfast with make-your-own waffles. In the central lodge, you'll find nice hot showers and usually clean restroom facilities. There is also a heated pool with an ocean view and a hot tub on the grounds. Being away from any real town, Treebones has a couple of on-site dining options: the **Wild Coast Restaurant** (daily noon-2pm and 5:30pm-9pm, $25-36) and the **Oceanview Sushi Bar** (March-Dec. Wed.-Mon. 4:30pm-8pm, $8-19).

yurt at Treebones Resort

Food

As you traverse the famed CA-1 through Big Sur, you'll quickly realize that a ready meal isn't something to take for granted. You'll see no In-N-Out Burgers, Starbucks, or Safeways lining the road here. While you can find groceries, they tend to appear in small markets attached to motels. To avoid paying premiums at the mini-marts, pick up staple supplies in Cambria or Carmel before you enter the area if you don't plan to leave again for a few days.

PUB FOOD

The **Fernwood Bar & Grill** (47200 CA-1, 831/667-2129, www.fernwoodbigsur.com, daily 11am-9pm, $10-25) at Fernwood Resort looks and feels like a grill in the woods ought to. Even in the middle of the afternoon, the aging, wood-paneled interior is dimly lit and strewn with casual tables and chairs. Walk up to the counter to order tacos, burgers, or pizzas, then head to the bar to grab a soda or a beer. Another casual place for a beer and food is the **Maiden Publick House** (Village Center Shops, 831/667-2355, daily noon-midnight, $9-15). There are salads, sandwiches, burgers, and pub fare, including unique fish-and-chips made with beer-battered salmon instead of cod.

The **Big Sur Taphouse** (47250 CA-1, 831/667-2225, www.bigsurtaphouse.com, Mon.-Thurs. noon-10pm, Fri. noon-midnight, Sat. 10am-midnight, Sun. 10am-10pm) is a casual place for a beer and an unfussy but tasty meal. Snack on chicken wings, a charcuterie platter, or an artisan cheese plate, or get something more substantial like a sandwich, taco plate, or trio of barbecued pork sliders.

CASUAL DINING

The **Rocky Point Restaurant** (36700 CA-1, 10 miles south of Carmel, 831/624-2933, www.rockypointrestaurant.com, daily 11:30am-sunset, $15-39) has long had one of Big Sur's best views from a restaurant. Unfortunately,

over the years, the food and service didn't live up to the panoramas. With new management and ownership, there's hope that Rocky Point has turned itself around. Regardless, a drink on the patio with its fire pit and views is a worthwhile endeavor. Go simple with a salad or sandwich or opt for a meat or seafood entrée. They do slow-roasted prime rib every day and a fried chicken special on Thursdays.

One of Big Sur's most popular attractions is ★ **Nepenthe** (48510 CA-1, 831/667-2345, www.nepenthebigsur.com, 4th of July weekend-Labor Day daily 11:30am-4:30 pm and 5pm-10:30pm, Labor Day-4th of July weekend daily 11:30am-4:30pm and 5pm-10pm, $15-44), a restaurant built on the site where Rita Hayworth and Orson Welles owned a cabin until 1947. The deck offers views on par with some of those you might attain on one of Big Sur's great hikes. Sit under multicolored umbrellas on bar-like long tables with stunning south-facing views. At sunset, order a basket of fries with Nepenthe's signature Ambrosia dipping sauce and wash them down with a potent South Coast margarita. During dinner, there is glazed duck and an eight-ounce filet mignon, but the best bet is the restaurant's most popular item: the Ambrosia burger, a ground steak burger drenched in that tasty Ambrosia sauce. When Nepenthe has a line for tables, consider dining at **Café Kevah** (weather permitting, President's Day Weekend-New Year's Day daily 9am-4pm, $9-16), an outdoor deck below the main restaurant that serves brunch, salad, and panini.

The ★ **Big Sur Bakery** (47540 CA-1, 831/667-0520, www.bigsurbakery.com, bakery daily from 8am, restaurant Mon. 9:30am-3:30pm, Tues.-Fri. 9:30am-3:30pm and 5:30pm-close, Sat.-Sun. 10:30am-2:30pm and 5:30pm-close, $18-32) might sound like a casual, walk-up eating establishment, and the bakery part of it is. You can stop in beginning at 8am every day to grab a fresh-baked scone, a homemade jelly donut, or a flaky croissant sandwich to save for lunch later on. But on the dining room side, an elegant surprise awaits diners who've spent the day hiking the redwoods and strolling the beaches. Make reservations or you might miss out on the creative wood-fired pizzas, wood-grilled meats, and seafood. At brunch, they serve their unique wood-fired bacon and three-egg breakfast pizza.

Easing into the day is easy at ★ **Deetjen's** (48865 CA-1, 831/667-2378, www.deetjens. com, Mon.-Fri. 8am-noon and 6pm-9pm, Sat.-Sun. 8am-12:30pm and 6pm-9pm, $10-32). The locals know Deetjen's for their breakfast, and it is an almost required experience for visitors to the area. Among fanciful knickknacks, framed photos of inn founder "Grandpa" Deetjen, and cabinets displaying fine china, diners can fill up on Deetjen's popular eggs Benedict dishes or the equally worthy Deetjen's dip, a turkey and avocado sandwich that comes with some hollandaise dipping sauce. In the evening, things get darker and more romantic as entrées, including the spicy seafood paella and an oven-roasted rack of lamb, are served to your candlelit table.

If it's a warm afternoon, get a table on the sunny back deck of the **Big Sur River Inn Restaurant** (46840 CA-1, 831/667-2700, http://bigsurriverinn.com, daily 8am-11am, 11:30am-4:30pm, and 5pm-9pm, $12-32). On summer Sundays, bands perform on the crowded deck, and you can take your libation out back to one of the chairs situated right in the middle of the cool Big Sur River. If it's chillier out, warm up by the large stone fireplace and then eat in the wood-beamed main dining room. This restaurant serves sandwiches, burgers, and fish-and-chips for lunch along with steak, ribs, and seafood at dinner. For dessert, they still do the famous apple pie that put them on the map back in the 1930s. The bar is known for its popular spicy Bloody Mary cocktails. The cozy atmosphere, outdoor deck, and seats placed in the river make this a worthy stop for a meal.

★ **The Big Sur Roadhouse** (47080 CA-1, 831/667-2370, www.glenoaksbigsur. com, daily 7:30am-9pm, $19-32) is one of the best bets for creative California dining without draining your bank account. The decor inside and out has been dubbed "homegrown modernism," with contemporary artwork hanging on the walls and a comfortable feel. The outdoor seating area has heating lamps and two fire pits, perfect for enjoying a glass

Umbrellas shade Nepenthe's deck.

of wine or beer on a nice Big Sur night. Chef Brendan Esons's seasonal menu and daily specials take advantage of the coastline's superb seafood and other local ingredients, as in the Dungeness crab appetizer. Nightly entrée options include a sautéed whitefish and a house-made pasta. A specialty is the breaded pork loin with its standout mushroom spaetzle. The Roadhouse also does breakfast and lunch. It's worth noting that their ice cream, pita bread, bagels, and pasta are made in-house.

Don't overlook the ★ **Ripplewood Café** (47047 CA-1, 831/667-2242, www.ripplewoodresort.com, daily 8am-2pm, $9-16) for breakfast or lunch. This unassuming spot may save the day on summer weekends when Deetjen's is flooded. Dine inside on the classic breakfast counter or on the outside brick patio among flowering plants. The breakfast menu includes pancakes, three-egg omelets, and a worthwhile chorizo and eggs. Be sure to order the grilled potato gratin with any breakfast dish; it may be the highlight of your meal. Ripplewood shifts to lunch at 11:30am, though it keeps a few breakfast items. Lunch offerings include sandwiches, Mexican food items, and salads.

Dine with views of Pfeiffer Big Sur State Park's redwoods at the **Big Sur Lodge Restaurant** (47225 CA-1, 800/424-4787, www.bigsurlodge.com, daily 8am-9:30pm). The open dining room lacks ambience but has plenty of windows peering out into the woods and a fireplace at one end to warm things up on cool mornings and evenings. There's also an outdoor deck with heating lamps, dining setups, a small bar area, and a view of the Big Sur River. The restaurant serves all three meals of the day, with salads, sandwiches, burgers, and entrées available at lunch and dinner. Adjacent to the restaurant area is the **Deli & Café** (daily 7:30am-9:30pm), which has coffee, sandwiches to go, cold drinks, and snacks.

There aren't many dining options on Big Sur's far south coast. The **Lucia Lodge Restaurant** (62400 CA-1, 50 miles south of Carmel, 866/424-4787, www.lucialodge.com, summer daily 11am-9pm, winter hours vary, $24-38) does breakfast and dinner with a heaping side of amazing views. There's a dining room with a fireplace and plenty of windows looking out on the coast. The deck below is ideal for dining outdoors. You're paying for the views, especially at dinner. The most popular item is the lunch menu fish-and-chips, highly touted by *Coastal Living Magazine*.

The best options for south coast dining

Deetjen's offers the best breakfast in Big Sur.

are available at the Treebones Resort. The **Wild Coast Restaurant** (Treebones Resort, 71895 CA-1, 805/927-2390, daily noon-2pm and 5:30pm-9pm, $25-36) is in the main lodge building of the resort by the check-in counter and gift store. Dine under a high, wooden, yurt-like ceiling on entrees that may include blackened salmon and tofu yellow curry. Treebones Resort's ★ **Oceanview Sushi Bar** (Treebones Resort, 71895 CA-1, 805/927-2390, March-Dec. Wed.-Mon. 4:30pm-8pm, $8-19) offers an intimate place to eat artfully prepared raw fish. Just 10 seats are available at a redwood sushi bar located within a tent-like structure. Dining here is an intimate experience, with the sushi chef helping to guide you through a menu that includes simple rolls, garden rolls, specialty rolls, and hearty rolls designed to resemble burritos. There are two beers on tap along with a menu of sakes, Japanese beers, and California wines. The sushi bar is very popular and very small, with priority given to Treebones' guests.

Gorda is a roadside complex at Big Sur's southern end with a gas station, mini-mart, espresso bar, general store, and the **Whale Watcher's Café** (Gorda Springs Resort, 65 miles south of Carmel, 805/927-1590, www.gordaspringsresort.com, daily 7:30am-9pm, $16-30). There are plenty of seats on the outside decks along with an indoor dining room decorated with nautical paraphernalia including harpoons, anchors, and porthole windows. Lunch has mainly sandwiches and pastas, while dinner ranges from a teriyaki chicken sandwich on the low end up to a surf and turf dinner. This is not the place for budget diners.

You'll probably get more bang from your buck in nearby Cambria, which is 20 miles away, but the **Ragged Point Restaurant** (19019 CA-1, 85 miles south of Carmel, 805/927-5708, daily 8am-11am, noon-4pm, and 5pm-9pm, $22-40) has a nice dining room with stone columns and large glass windows. The seafood is sourced from Morro Bay's popular Tognazzini's Fish Market. Other dinner entrées may include a seven-ounce filet or spiced lentil cakes.

FINE DINING

You don't need to be a guest at the gorgeous Ventana to enjoy a fine gourmet dinner at **The Restaurant at Ventana** (48123 CA-1, 831/667-4242, www.ventanainn.com, daily 11:30am-4pm and 6pm-9pm, 4-course dinner tasting menu $75). The spacious dining room boasts a warm wood fire, an open kitchen, lodge-like wood beams, and comfortable banquettes with plenty of throw pillows to lounge against as you peruse the menu. Request a table outside to enjoy stunning views with your meal on the restaurant's expansive patio. New chef Paul Corsentino has upped the quality of the menu, which at times has wild boar and Monterey sardine courses. You can choose an à la carte main course entrée or go for the five-round prix fixe. Sit in the small bar area for a more casual dining and drinking experience. The Big Sur Burger ($19) is a unique burger with pickled toppings.

The **Sierra Mar** (47900 CA-1, 831/667-2800, www.postranchinn.com, daily 12:15pm-3pm and 5:30pm-9pm, lunch $55, dinner $125-175 pp) restaurant at the Post Ranch Inn offers a decadent four-course prix fixe dinner menu every night ($125) or a nine-course tasting menu ($175). There's also a less formal three-course lunch every day. With floor-to-ceiling glass windows overlooking the plunging ridgeline and the Pacific below, it's a good idea to schedule dinner during sunset. The daily menu rotates, but some courses have included farm-raised abalone in brown butter and a succulent short rib and beef tenderloin duo.

MARKETS

With no supermarkets or chain mini-marts in the entire Big Sur region, the local markets do a booming business. The best of these is the ★ **Big Sur Deli** (47520 CA-1, 831/667-2225, www.bigsurdeli.com, daily 7am-8pm, $3.50-7). Very popular with the locals, the deli has large, made-to-order sandwiches, burritos, tamales, tacos, and pasta salads. If the line is long at the counter, opt for a premade sandwich for a quicker exit. They also have cold drinks, wine, beer, and some basic supplies. This is the best place to stock up for treats for a day hike or beach picnic.

The **River Inn Big Sur General Store** (46840 CA-1, 831/667-2700, summer daily 7:30am-9pm, winter daily 7:30am-8pm, $7-10) has basic supplies, along with beer and a

nice selection of California wines. Even better, it has a wonderful burrito bar and smoothie counter in the back. The burritos range from breakfast burritos to roasted veggie wraps and classic carnitas. These large burritos are some of Big Sur's best deals for the price. The freshly made fruit smoothies hit the spot after a long hike. There are also simple premade turkey and ham sandwiches in a nearby fridge for taking out on a hike or picnic.

Information and Services

There is no comprehensive visitors center in Big Sur, but the website for the **Big Sur Chamber of Commerce** (www.bigsurcalifornia.org) includes up-to-date information about hikes as well as links to lodging and restaurants. Pick up the *Big Sur Guide,* a publication of the Big Sur Chamber of Commerce that includes a map and guide to local businesses, or download one from the website.

Big Sur Station (CA-1, 0.33 miles south of Pfeiffer Big Sur State Park, 831/667-2315, daily 9am-4pm) is the closest thing to a visitors center. The staffed building offers maps and brochures for all the major parks and trails of Big Sur, plus a bookshop. This is also where the trailhead for the popular backcountry Pine Ridge Trail is located. You can get a **free backcountry fire permit** as well as pay the $5 fee for the Pine Ridge Trailhead parking here.

Big Sur has its own **post office** (47500 CA-1, 831/667-2305, www.usps.com, Mon.-Fri. 8:30am-11am and noon-4pm). Pick up a postcard at Big Sur Station or the adjacent

Big Sur Deli and send it to a friend to make them jealous of the stunning natural beauty you are seeing.

Your **cell phone** may not work anywhere in Big Sur, but especially out in the undeveloped reaches of forest and on CA-1 away from the valley. The best places to get cell service are around Andrew Molera State Park and Point Sur, along with the large dirt pullout a quarter mile south of Big Sur Station on Highway 1. Likewise, GPS units may struggle in this region. It's best to have a map in your vehicle, or pick up a free *Big Sur Guide,* which has a general map of the region.

The **Big Sur Health Center** (46896 CA-1, Big Sur, 831/667-2580, http://bigsurhealthcenter.org, Mon.-Fri. 10am-1pm and 2pm-5pm) can take care of minor medical needs, and provides an ambulance service and limited emergency care. The nearest full-service hospital is the **Community Hospital of the Monterey Peninsula** (23625 Holman Hwy., Monterey, 831/624-5311 or 888/452-4667, www.chomp.org).

Transportation

Big Sur is not a town but rather the name for the lightly developed coastline stretching from San Simeon to Carmel. It can only be reached via CA-1. The drive north from San Simeon into Big Sur is where the Pacific Coast Highway gets really interesting, twisting and turning along with the coastline. The largest concentration of businesses is located within the Big Sur Valley, 61 miles north of San Simeon.

The drive from San Simeon to the Big Sur Valley usually takes around 1.5 hours, but it can be slow going, especially if you are behind an RV. You may want to stop every few miles to snap a photo of the stunning coastline. If traffic is backing up behind you, pull into a turnoff to let other cars pass; the local drivers can be impatient with tourist traffic. CA-1 can have one or both lanes closed at times, especially in the winter months when rockslides occur. Check the **Caltrans** website (www.dot.ca.gov) or the **Big Sur California Blog** (www.thebigsurblog.com) for current road conditions.

It is difficult to get around Big Sur without a car. However, on weekends from Labor Day through Memorial Day, **Monterey-Salinas Transit** (888/678-2871, www.mst.org, $3.50, Memorial Day-Labor Day daily, Labor Day-Memorial Day Sat.-Sun., check website for specific times) runs a bus route through Big Sur that stops at Nepenthe, Pfeiffer Big Sur State Park, the Big Sur River Inn, Andrew Molera State Park, Point Sur Light Station, and the Bixby Creek Bridge as it heads to Carmel and Monterey.

Cambria, San Simeon, and Morro Bay

The rugged coastline twists and turns through Cambria and San Simeon and onward to Morro Bay. The hills to the east contain this small coastal region, keeping it distinct both naturally and culturally.

These towns have remained relatively unspoiled, not only in their natural beauty but in the old-fashioned simplicity of the homes and businesses that adorn their streets. Morro Bay still looks much like it did decades ago, a small beach community that fronts the Pacific Ocean, its namesake Morro Rock standing guard at the mouth of the bay. Within the bay is an active fishing fleet as well as a rebounding local sea otter population. Cayucos is an unassuming little beach town with a popular beach and a pier that dates back to the 1800s. Just north of Cayucos, Cambria still has many 1880s storefronts and a feel of yesteryear.

But when it comes to this area, there is only one true sight: palatial Hearst Castle, located about seven miles north of Cambria in San Simeon. Once functioning mainly to service the palatial estate's inhabitant, millionaire William Randolph Hearst, San Simeon hasn't grown much since the beginning of the 20th century.

PLANNING YOUR TIME

These beachside communities are all located along Highway 1. The big draw in this region—and one of the most visited attractions in California—is Hearst Castle. Most visitors plan their itineraries around touring the immense mansion, including visits to its gateway towns, Cambria and Morro Bay. There's no advantage to planning to spend the night specifically in Morro Bay or Cambria, since they are only 15 miles apart. Heading south, stop in Cambria and work your way down the coast, finding accommodations in Morro Bay.

You can stop off at Hearst Castle for the day as part of a longer road trip, but seeing all the area has to offer requires a weekend. One day and a night is enough time to get a feel for Cambria and San Simeon. Similarly, one day and a night can be perfect for just Morro Bay. The village of Cambria can be scouted out in a day, and you'll leave with an appreciation for the area, though you'll undoubtedly want to

Previous: Morro Bay; Morro Rock, as seen from Highway 46; **Above:** elephant seal on a beach near San Simeon.

Look for ★ to find recommended sights, activities, dining, and lodging.

Highlights

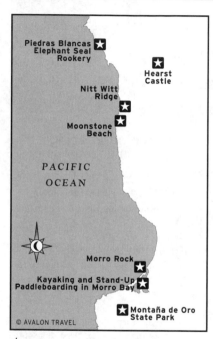

© AVALON TRAVEL

Randolph Hearst spared no expense to construct the ultimate playground (page 227).

★ **Nitt Witt Ridge:** This small, rambling ode to one man's eccentricity is made of abalone shells, car rims, toilet seats, and what others might call garbage (page 229).

★ **Moonstone Beach:** This stretch of beach exemplifies the beauty of this rugged area. It's named for the semi-clear stones that you can find on the sand (page 230).

★ **Piedras Blancas Elephant Seal Rookery:** Every winter elephant seals show up north of San Simeon to birth their pups. The males spar, the females wean their newborns, and the people get a free show (page 231).

★ **Morro Rock:** Primal, austere, and endlessly photogenic, this ancient dormant volcano is a refuge for endangered falcons, a home to native Indian lore, and a traveler's delight (page 248).

★ **Montaña de Oro State Park:** With 7 miles of coastline and almost 50 miles of trails, the park is a great place for wildlife lovers and outdoor recreation enthusiasts (page 249).

★ **Kayaking and Stand-Up Paddleboarding in Morro Bay:** Get on the water for the best chance to see wildlife and the impressive dunes of the Morro Bay Sandspit up close (page 253).

★ **Hearst Castle:** Opulent, erratic, and ultimately all-American, this massive, lavish compound built on a remote hill is the closest thing to a true castle in California. Media mogul William return. Morro Bay and nearby Cayucos can also be explored relatively well in a day and a night. But these places beg for leisure time: the ability to wander the beaches, the hillsides, and the streets with no agenda, which makes for a restful weekend getaway.

Cambria and San Simeon

Cambria, originally known as Slabtown, retains nothing of its original if uninspired moniker. Divided into east and west villages, it is a charming, easily walkable area of low storefronts, with moss covered pine trees as a backdrop. Typically you'll see visitors meandering in and out of the local stores, browsing art galleries or combing Moonstone Beach for souvenir moonstone rocks. The really great thing about Cambria is that, aside from the gas stations, you won't find any chain stores—not one—in town, and Cambrians, and most visitors, like it that way. It truly is an idyllic spot, even during bustling summer months when the crowds swell dramatically. Many of the buildings are original, dating to the 1880s.

Cambria owes much of its prosperity to the immense mansion on the hill, Hearst Castle. Located about seven miles north in San Simeon, Hearst Castle, quite frankly, *is* San Simeon; the town grew up around it to support the overwhelming needs of its megalomaniacal owner and never-ending construction. The town dock provided a place for ships to unload tons of marble, piles of antiques, and dozens of workers.

Today, San Simeon is less a town and more a stopping point for visitors heading to Hearst Castle. Stores, hotels, and restaurants flank both sides of Highway 1. The general store and post office acted as a central gathering place for the community, and you can still walk up the weathered wooden steps and make a purchase here, whether it's a tasty sandwich from Sebastian's Store or a bottle of wine from Hearst Ranch Winery. Around the corner at the building's other door, you can buy a book of stamps or mail a letter at the tiny operating post office.

If there's any strolling to be done, it's along the bluffs or on the rocky beaches. Set amid incredible open space between the hills and the ocean, San Simeon is truly a paradise of natural beauty, with stunning coastlines and gorgeous sunsets casting warm tones of amber light on the craggy rocks at the surf line.

SIGHTS
★ Hearst Castle

There's nothing else in California quite like **Hearst Castle** (Hwy. 1 and Hearst Castle Rd., 800/444-4445, www.hearstcastle.org, tours daily 8:20am-3:20pm). Newspaper magnate William Randolph Hearst conceived the idea of a grand mansion in the Mediterranean style on land his parents bought along the central California coast. His memories of camping on the hills above the Pacific led him to choose the spot where the castle now stands. He hired Julia Morgan, the first female civil engineering graduate from the University of California, Berkeley, to design and build the house for him. She did a brilliant job with every detail, despite the ever-changing wishes of her employer. By way of decoration, Hearst purchased hundreds of European and Renaissance antiquities, from tiny tchotchkes to whole gilded ceilings. Hearst also adored exotic animals, and he created one of the largest private zoos in the nation on his thousands of Central Coast acres. Most of the zoo is gone now, but you can still see the occasional zebra grazing peacefully along Highway 1 south of the castle, heralding the exotic nature of Hearst Castle ahead.

The visitors center is a lavish affair with a gift shop, a restaurant, a café, a ticket booth, and a movie theater. Here you can see the much-touted film *Hearst Castle—Building the Dream,* which will give you an overview

Cambria and San Simeon

PIEDRAS BLANCAS
LIGHT STATION

PIEDRAS BLANCAS
ELEPHANT SEAL
ROOKERY

HEARST CASTLE RD

SEBASTIAN'S
STORE

HEARST
CASTLE

SAN SIMEON
William Randolph Hearst
Memorial State Beach

BEST WESTERN
CAVALIER OCEANFRONT
RESORT
MANTA REY
RESTAURANT

THE MORGAN

San Simeon
State Beach

SEE
"CAMBRIA"
MAP
SAN SIMEON CREEK RD

MOONSTONE BEACH
NITT WITT RIDGE
CAMBRIA

OLALLIEBERRY
INN
SANTA ROSA CREEK RD

HER CASTLE
HOMESTAY B&B

GREEN VALLEY RD

0   3 mi
0   3 km

Villa Creek

PACIFIC

OCEAN
To
San Luis
Obispo

Cayucos
State Beach

OLD CREEK
RD

Morro Strand
State Beach

MORRO
ROCK
ATASCADERO
RD

KAYAKING AND STAND-UP
PADDLEBOARDING IN MORRO BAY
MORRO
BAY

SPOONER'S
COVE

PECHO
VALLEY
RD

LOS OSOS VALLEY RD

TURRI RD

MONTAÑA DE ORO
STATE PARK

© AVALON TRAVEL

of the construction and history of the marvelous edifice, and of William Randolph Hearst's empire. (Only daytime tours offer free showings of the movie. During evening tours, a movie ticket is $6 for adults and $4 for children. To see the movie without going on a tour, tickets cost $10 for adults and $8 for children.) After buying your ticket, board the shuttle that takes you up the hill to your tour. No private cars are allowed on the roads up to the castle. There are several tours to choose from, each focusing on different spaces and aspects of the castle.

THE TOURS

Expect to walk for at least an hour on whichever tour you choose, and to climb up and down many stairs. Even the most jaded traveler can't help but be amazed by the beauty and opulence that drips from every room in the house. Lovers of European art and antiques will want to stay forever.

The **Grand Rooms Museum Tour** (45 minutes, 106 stairs, 0.6 miles, adults $25, children under the age of 12 $12) is recommended for first-time visitors. It begins in the castle's assembly room, which is draped in Flemish tapestries, before heading into the dining room, the billiard room, and the impressive movie theater, where you'll watch a few old Hearst newsreels. The guide then lets you loose to take in the swimming pools: the indoor pool, decorated in gold and blue, and the stunning outdoor Neptune Pool.

For a further glimpse into Hearst's personal life, take the **Upstairs Suites Tour** (45 minutes, 273 stairs, 0.75 miles, adults $25, children under the age of 12 $12). Among the highlights are a stop within Hearst's private suite and a visit to his library, which holds over 4,000 books and 150 ancient Greek vases. At the end of this tour, you can explore the grounds, including the Neptune Pool, on your own.

Epicureans should opt for the **Cottages & Kitchen Tour** (45 minutes, 176 stairs, 0.75 miles, adults $25, children under the age of 12 $12). Visit the wine cellar first, where there

Julia Morgan:
A Woman of Independent Means

Best known for designing and building Hearst Castle over a 21-year period, architect Julia Morgan designed more than 700 buildings in an illustrious career that spanned nearly 50 years. At 5 feet, 2 inches tall, she was a petite woman, but never one to be underestimated. On a cool spring morning in 1919, William Randolph Hearst swaggered into Morgan's office in San Francisco. "Miss Morgan, we are tired of camping out in the open at the ranch in San Simeon, and I would like to build a little something," Hearst said in his high-pitched voice. And that set in motion events that would catapult her into architectural history.

Julia Morgan never married; she was devoted to her work and carved out a lasting legacy for women everywhere. She was the first woman to graduate from the prestigious Ecole des Beaux-Arts in Paris and was one of the first graduates, male or female, from the University of California, Berkeley, with a degree in civil engineering. Her notable California projects include not only the enduring Hearst Castle, but also the Bavarian-style **Wyntoon,** also for William Randolph Hearst; **Asilomar,** located in Pacific Grove; the **Los Angeles Herald Examiner Building** in Los Angeles; the **Margaret Baylor Inn** in Santa Barbara; and a plethora of commercial buildings, YWCAs, private residences, apartments, churches, and educational facilities.

Julia Morgan ultimately gave hope to women and girls everywhere, living a life that proved to them that their vision could someday be realized. Today the **Julia Morgan School for Girls,** an all-girls middle school in Berkeley, provides girls with education and empowerment. Morgan died in 1958 at the age of 85. In 1957 she granted her one and only press interview, stating simply and succinctly: "My buildings will be my legacy. They will speak for me long after I am gone."

are still bottles of wine, gin, rum, beer, and vermouth lining the walls. (After a visit here, actor David Niven once said that "the wine flowed like glue.") Then take in the ornate guest cottages Casa Del Monte and Casa del Mar, where Hearst spent the final two years of his life. The tour concludes in the massive castle kitchen, with its steam-heated metal counters, before leaving you to explore the grounds on your own.

The **Designing the Dream Tour** (75 minutes, 320 stairs, 1.2 miles, adults $30, children under the age of 12 $15) highlights the estate's three-decade evolution in architectural design. This option includes visits to the estate's biggest guesthouse and the north wing of the main house. The guided tour wraps up at the indoor Roman Pool and its dressing rooms. The price of this tour also includes a viewing of the 40-minute film *Hearst Castle—Building the Dream.*

The seasonal **Evening Museum Tour** (100 minutes, 308 stairs, 0.75 miles, adults $36, children under the age of 12 $18) is only given in spring and fall. Volunteers dress in 1930s fashions and welcome guests as if they are arriving at one of Hearst's legendary parties.

Buy tour tickets at least a few days in advance, and even farther ahead on summer weekends. Wheelchair-accessible Grand Rooms and Evening Tours are available for visitors with limited mobility. Strollers are not permitted. The restrooms and food concessions are all in the visitors center. No food, drink, or chewing gum are allowed on any tour.

★ Nitt Witt Ridge

While William Randolph Hearst built one of the most expensive homes ever seen in California, local eccentric Arthur Harold Beal (aka Captain Nit Wit or Der Tinkerpaw) got busy building the cheapest "castle" he could. **Nitt Witt Ridge** (881 Hillcrest Dr., 805/927-2690, tours by appointment, $5) is the result of five decades of scavenging trash and using it as building supplies to create a multistory

Cambria

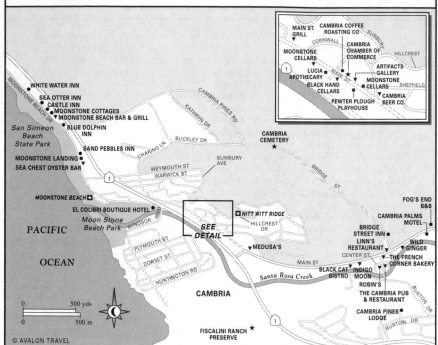

home like no other on the coast. The rambling structure is made of abalone shells, used car rims, and toilet seats, among other found materials. Features like the cobblestone archways reveal a true artist's touch. Today, you can make an appointment with owner Mike O'Malley to take a tour of the property, but don't just drop in. O'Malley is a quirky spirit himself who relishes the chance to spread the gospel about this one-of-a-kind sight. It's weird, it's funky, and it's fun—an oddly iconic experience of the Central Coast.

To find Nitt Witt Ridge, drive on Cambria's Main Street toward Moonstone Beach and make a right onto Cornwall Street. Take the second right onto Hillcrest Avenue and look for the unique structure.

Cambria Cemetery

Artsy isn't a word that's usually associated with graveyards, but in Cambria it fits. The **Cambria Cemetery** (6005 Bridge St., 805/927-5158, www.cambriacemetery.com, daily 9am-4pm) reflects the artistic bent of the town's residents in its tombstone decor. Unlike many cemeteries, at Cambria the family and friends of the deceased are allowed to place all manner of personal objects at their loved ones' graves. You'll see painted tombstones, beautiful panes of stained glass, unusual wind chimes, and many other unique expressions of love, devotion, and art as you wander the 12 wooded acres.

★ Moonstone Beach

Known for its namesake shimmering stone, **Moonstone Beach** (Moonstone Beach Dr.) is a scenic, pebbly slice of coastline with craggy rocks offshore. Cambria's moonstones are bright, translucent pebbles that can be easiest to find at low tides and when the sun shines, highlighting their features. They are fairly easy to collect, especially after winter storms. The moonstones on Moonstone Beach are not gem quality, but they make a fun souvenir. If you can't find any, many Cambria boutiques and galleries carry moonstone jewelry.

Huts constructed from driftwood can be found on some sections of the beach, and there is plenty more than just moonstones on the shoreline. A wooden boardwalk runs along the top of the bluffs above the beach. From here, you can take in the scenery and watch moonstone collectors with buckets wander below in the tide line. Access is at Leffingwell Landing, Moonstone Beach Drive, and Santa Rosa Creek.

Piedras Blancas Light Station

First illuminated in 1875, the **Piedras Blancas Light Station** (tours meet at the Piedras Blancas Motel, 1.5 miles north of the light station on Hwy. 1, 805/927-7361, www.piedrasblancas.gov, tours mid-June-Sept. Mon.-Sat. 9:45am, Sept.-mid-June Tues., Thurs., and Sat. 9:45am, adults $10, ages 6-17 $5, under age 5 free) and its adjacent grounds can be accessed on a two-hour tour. Piedras Blancas means "white rocks" in Spanish. In

1948 a nearby earthquake caused a crack in the lighthouse tower and the removal of a first-order Fresnel lens, which was replaced with an automatic aerobeacon. Since 2001 the lighthouse has been run by the federal Bureau of Land Management.

★ Piedras Blancas Elephant Seal Rookery

Stopping at the **Piedras Blancas Elephant Seal Rookery** (Hwy. 1, seven miles north of San Simeon, 805/924-1628, www.elephantseal. org, free) is like watching a nature documentary in real time. On this sliver of beach, up to 17,000 elephant seals rest, breed, give birth, or fight one another. The rookery is right along Highway 1; turn into the large gravel parking lot and follow the boardwalks north or south to viewing areas where informative plaques give background on the elephant seals. Volunteer docents are available to answer questions (daily 10am-4pm). The beaches themselves are off-limits to humans, since they're covered in the large marine mammals. But thanks to the wheelchair-accessible boardwalks built above the beach, visitors can get just a matter of feet away from the giant creatures. In the fall, most adult seals head out to sea, returning in early to mid-December.

Nitt Witt Ridge

Most of the seal births occur between the end of December and the middle of February.

Fiscalini Ranch Preserve

A terrific place to take in Cambria's natural assets, the **Fiscalini Ranch Preserve** (805/927-2856, www.ffrpcambria.org, daily dawn-dusk, free) is home to abundant plants and animals, including one of the last three remaining native Monterey pine forests and 25 special-status species like American peregrine falcons, western snowy plovers, and California red-legged frogs. Bird-watchers have spotted at least 182 bird species here. The preserve is actually two parcels of land on both the east and west side of Highway 1; head for the 364-acre western portion. There are a few entry points, so to avoid confusion, download the map from the ranch's website or stop in at the **Friends of Fiscalini Ranch Preserve Office** (604 Main St., Thurs.-Fri. 11am-2pm, Sat. 11am-3pm).

The preserve is named for the Fiscalini family, who started a cattle ranch and dairy farm on the land back in the mid-1850s. A housing development was planned here in the 1980s until an organization was formed to maintain the ranch as public open space. The land was finally purchased and preserved in 2000. The **Friends of Fiscalini Ranch Preserve** (www.cambriaranchwalks.com) also offers free monthly docent-guided walks.

William Randolph Hearst Memorial State Beach

Down the hill from Hearst Castle is **William Randolph Hearst Memorial State Beach** (750 Hearst Castle Rd., 805/927-2020, www.parks.ca.gov, daily dawn-dusk, free), a stretch of kelp-strewn sand along a protected cove. The beach's 795-foot-long pier is great for fishing and strolling, and the **Coastal Discovery Center** (805/927-2145, http://montereybay.noaa.gov, Fri.-Sun. 11am-5pm, free), run by California State Parks and Monterey Bay National Marine Sanctuary, warrants a stop. It focuses on local natural history and culture, with exhibits on shipwrecks, a display on elephant seals, and an interactive tidepool. This beach is also an ideal place to try kayaking.

WINE TASTING

Cambria has a handful of tasting rooms showcasing wines made here and in nearby Paso Robles.

Moonstone Cellars

Moonstone Cellars (801 Main St., Ste. C,

elephant seals fighting at the Piedras Blancas Elephant Seal Rookery

The Hearst Legacy

William Randolph Hearst: The name conjures images of wealth beyond belief. And with great wealth comes great responsibility. The William Randolph Hearst Foundation was established by its namesake, publisher William Randolph Hearst, in 1948 under California nonprofit laws, exclusively for educational and charitable purposes. Since then, the Hearst Foundations have contributed more than $735 million in the areas of education, health care, social services, and the arts in every state.

Since Hearst owned 26 newspapers at the height of his power, the foundation has always had a strong affinity for the written word. The **Hearst Journalism Awards Program** (http://hearstfdn.org) was founded in 1960 to provide support, encouragement, and assistance to journalism education at the college and university level. The program awards scholarships to students for outstanding performance in college-level journalism. The 50th annual program, which offered more than $550,000 in awards in 2010, consisted of six monthly writing competitions, three photojournalism competitions, four broadcast news competitions (two in radio and two in television), and a multimedia competition.

Hearst also had political ambitions. His father was a state senator, and thus the foundation also funds programs for service in the public interest. The **United States Senate Youth Program** (www.hearstfdn.org/ussyp) was established in 1962 by a U.S. Senate resolution. It's a unique educational experience for outstanding high school students interested in pursuing a career in public service. Two student leaders from each state, the District of Columbia, and the Department of Defense Education Activity spend a week in Washington DC experiencing their national government in action. Student delegates get the chance to hear major policy addresses by senators, cabinet members, officials from the Departments of State and Defense, and directors of other federal agencies. The students also participate in a meeting with a justice of the U.S. Supreme Court.

805/927-9466, www.moonstonecellars.com, daily 11am-5pm, tasting $7-14) is an appropriate name for this little Cambria winery: Father and son Muril and Todd Clift began their winemaking careers producing wine in a basement near Moonstone Beach. They showcase their passion in the tasting room by pouring two chardonnays, a viognier, a cabernet sauvignon, a merlot, and a zinfandel.

Black Hand Cellars

Although the tasting room of **Black Hand Cellars** (766 Main St., Ste. B, 805/927-9463, www.blackhandcellars.com, daily 11am-5pm, tasting $10) is in Cambria's west village, the vineyard is located northwest of Paso Robles. The focus is on Syrahs, but they also do Rhône-style blends, Bordeaux-style blends, a Grenache, and a dessert wine.

Twin Coyotes Winery

Twin brothers run **Twin Coyotes Winery** (2020 Main St., 805/927-9800, www.twincoyotes.com, Fri.-Sat. noon-6pm, Sun.-Mon. noon-5pm, tasting $6), which offers a wide range of reds and some whites, including a cabernet sauvignon, a petite Syrah, a merlot, a tempranillo, a primitivo, a chardonnay, and a dessert wine. They use sustainable means to farm grapes in their vineyard in Paso Robles.

Hearst Ranch Winery

The **Hearst Ranch Winery** (442 San Simeon Rd., 805/927-4100, www.hearstranchwinery. com, daily 11am-5pm, tasting $10) shares the historic 1852 general store in old San Simeon with the post office and the popular Sebastian's Store Restaurant. This cool little tasting room pours a range of wines, including the award-winning Pico Creek Merlot and the Glacier Ridge Chardonnay.

SHOPPING

This is a town chock-full of unique shops. Antiques, local art, and funky gift and specialty food shops are where Cambria shines.

For antiques lovers, there are multiple options. The three floors of **Antiques on Main** (2338 Main St., 805/927-4292, daily 10am-5pm) have everything from fossils to furniture. The **Country Collectibles Antiques Mall** (2380 Main St., 805/927-0245, daily 10am-5pm) has all kinds of small collectibles, including comic books, French pottery, and Disney memorabilia. In the Redwood Center shopping strip, **Rich Man Poor Man Antiques Mall** (2110 Main St., 805/203-5350, www.richmanpoormanantiques.com, daily 10am-5pm) has two floors of high-quality antiques and collectibles from over 30 dealers, selling everything from furniture to estate jewelry.

Examine the local art scene at **The Vault Gallery** (2289 Main St., 805/927-0300, www.vaultgallery.com, daily 10:30am-6pm), which displays the work of Central Coast photographers, painters, and sculptors, with a large collection of plein air paintings. A large bronze sculpture out front welcomes visitors to the **Artifacts Gallery** (775 Main St., 805/927-4465, www.artifactsgallery.com, Sun.-Thurs.10am-5pm, Fri.-Sat. 10am-6pm), where oil paintings, more bronzes, and fine-art reproductions fill the space. The two-story building includes an in-house framing studio. **Moonstone Gallery** (4070 Burton Dr., 800/424-3827, www.moonstones.com, daily 9am-9pm) specializes in moonstone jewelry, but they also showcase sculptures, kaleidoscopes, metal art, and hardwood jewelry boxes.

The **Lucia Apothecary** (746 Main St., 805/927-1831, www.luciacompany.com, April-Dec. Mon.-Fri. 11am-5pm, Sat. 10am-5pm, Sun. 10am-4pm, Jan.-March call for hours) has body oils, scrubs, creams, washes, and mists in 19 scents inspired by California locales. Located in a beautiful old building that was a blacksmith shop in the 1800s, **Cinnabar** (4121 Burton Dr., 805/395-4111, http://cinnabaronline.com, Sun.-Thurs. 11am-6pm, Fri. 11am-9pm, Sat. 11am-10pm) has unique folk art pieces, home decor, and furnishings, including pieces made from reclaimed wood and even lamps made out of tree leaves.

Fermentations (2306 Main St., 805/927-7141, www.fermentations.com, daily 10am-8pm) has a large selection of gourmet food and wines, with a focus on the products of nearby Paso Robles vineyards.

SPORTS AND RECREATION

Surfing

Cambria is not a popular surfing destination, but there can be waves to ride if you have a board with you. The north end of the strip of businesses in San Simeon is where you'll find **Pico Creek,** a reef break off the spot where Pico Creek enters the ocean. Just south of the creek is a beach where there can be peaky beach break waves. Park in the cul-de-sac at the western end of Pico Avenue. Another option is **Santa Rosa Creek,** at the southern end of Cambria's Moonstone Beach. This is a beach break littered with a few rocks. To get here, turn left into the public parking lot off Moonstone Beach Drive.

Kayaking

William Randolph Hearst Memorial State Beach (750 Hearst Castle Rd., 805/927-2020, www.parks.ca.gov, daily dawn-dusk, free) offers a protected cove that's ideal for kayaking. You may see sea otters, seals, and sea lions while paddling. Located right on the beach, **Sea For Yourself Kayak Outfitters** (805/927-1787, http://kayakcambria.com, mid-June-early Sept. daily 10am-4pm, single kayak $10/hour, double kayak $20/hour, stand-up paddleboard $15/hour) rents out equipment. They also offer two- to three-hour kayak tours of San Simeon Cove ($50 pp). Other tours include fishing excursions and paddles along Cambria's coastal terrace or Moonstone Drive ($95-110).

Lawn Bowling

The **Joslyn Recreation Center** (950 Main St., 805/927-3364, www.joslynrec.org, club hours Mon., Wed., and Fri.-Sat. 8:30am-noon, donation) has a large artificial turf field for lawn bowling. Lawn bowling is similar to bocce, where you try to roll balls closest to a target ball. If you don't know how to play, someone at the recreation center will be able to show you the basics during club hours. Groups can reserve the green during non-club hours.

Hiking

Fiscalini Ranch Preserve (www.ffrpcambria.org, daily dawn-dusk, free) is a wonderful place to take a walk. Hike the **Bluff Trail** (trailheads at the end of S. Windsor Blvd. and N. Windsor Blvd, two miles round-trip, easy) to view wildflower-colored bluffs and rocky shoreline, which includes tidepools and attracts relaxing sea lions. Monterey pines crown the ridgeline above. Multiple spur trails branch out to the bluffs' edges. A wooden boardwalk protects some sensitive areas, while arty driftwood benches provide places to sit and enjoy the scenery. The Bluff Trail can become a two-mile loop by taking the **Marine Terrace Trail** back. This wider trail is higher up on the hill. When you return to the south side of the preserve, you'll have to walk a block down on Wedgewood Street to return to the South Windsor Boulevard parking area. Trail maps are available for download on the preserve's website, or stop into the **Friends of the Fiscalini Ranch Preserve Office** (604 Main St., Thurs.-Fri. 11am-2pm, Sat. 11am-3pm).

In **San Simeon State Park** (500 San Simeon Rd., www.parks.ca.gov, daily dawn-dusk, free), the **San Simeon Creek Trail** (3.5 miles round-trip, moderate) goes through the park's wetlands, up to a grassy ridge studded with Monterey pines. To reach the trailhead, park in the Washburn Day Use Area. Walk east on the service road, and take the trail on the right.

Horseback Riding

Explore Cambria's hills and forests via horseback with **Outback Trail Rides** (805/286-8772, www.outbacktrailrides.com, May-Sept., $55-85). Three possible rides include two different winery trips and one along Cayucos Beach. They also have Moonstone Beach **wagon rides** (May-Sept. Fri.-Sat. 3pm-7pm, $10-15) that depart hourly from the Castle Inn (6620 Moonstone Beach Dr.).

Spas

Therapy By the Sea (816 Main St., 805/927-2956, http://therapybythesea.com, Sun.-Thurs. 8am-8pm, Fri.-Sat. 8am-9pm, massages $30-125) offers a range of massages including Swedish, Reiki, warm stone, and prenatal. They also provide facials and other relaxation packages. In the Cambria Pines Lodge, the **Sojourn Healing Arts & Spa** (2905 Burton Dr., 805/927-8007, www.sojournspa.com, by appointment, $90-170) offers similar massage treatments that also include warm stones and aromatherapy. In addition, they have a unique package called **Yogassage** ($450) that combines an hour-long massage with a 90-minute yoga session.

ENTERTAINMENT AND EVENTS
Nightlife

If touring Hearst Castle leaves you thirsty for a beer, Cambria has a few different options. **Mozzi's** (2262 Main St., 805/927-4767, http://mozzissaloon.com, Mon.-Fri. 1pm-midnight, Sat.-Sun. 11am-2am) is a classic old California saloon—there's been a bar on this site since 1866. Old artifacts like lanterns and farm equipment hang from the ceiling above the long redwood bar, jukebox, and pool tables in this historic watering hole. Save some money on "Two Dollar Tuesdays" when all well drinks and draft beers are just two bucks a pop.

Cambria Pines Lodge Fireside Lounge (Cambria Pines Lodge, 2905 Burton Dr., 805/927-4200, www.cambriapineslodge. com, Mon.-Fri. 3pm-midnight, Sat.-Sun.

noon-midnight) has live music nightly, performed on a stage to the right of a big stone fireplace. Enjoy a cocktail, beer, or wine seated at one of the couches or small tables.

Local craft brewery the **Cambria Beer Company** (821 Cornwall St., 805/203-5265, http://cambriabeerco.com, Mon.-Sat. noon-7pm, Sun. noon-6pm) has anywhere from 6 to 11 beers on tap, with unique offerings like an olallieberry sour, orange wheat, vanilla bourbon porter, and chocolate mole stout. The most popular is the Old Number 23 Porter. Get a taster flight with four samples for $7. The tasting room feels like a small cottage, with local art and vintage Pearl Jam posters on the walls.

The downstairs pub at **The Cambria Pub & Restaurant** (4090 Burton Dr., 805/927-0782, www.thecambriapub.com, winter Thurs.-Tues. 11am-9pm, summer Sun.-Thurs. 11am-9pm, Fri.-Sat. 11am-10pm) is a fine spot for a cold beer. Enjoy one of 12 beers on tap, including local favorites like Firestone and Figueroa, while taking in the latest sporting event on the pub's four TVs.

Performing Arts

Cambria has its own little theater, the **Pewter Plough Playhouse** (824 Main St., 805/927-3877, www.pewterploughplayhouse.org, tickets $15-25). Its 59 seats are named for legendary stars of the stage like Laurence Olivier, Noël Coward, and Vivien Leigh. The theater does a wide range of shows. Catch a stage adaptation of a film like 1972's *Butterflies Are Free*, a one-man tribute to Mark Twain, or a contemporary drama like *The Weir*. Enjoy a drink before or after the show at the piano bar off the lobby.

Festivals and Events

Sample wines from over 35 local wineries, as well as wine and food pairings, at the **Cambria Art and Wine Festival** (various venues, 805/927-3624, www.cambriaartwine. org, Jan., $25-35) in January. The popular three-day event has been known to sell out. It also includes an art show and silent auction.

The Pinedorado Grounds, next to the Veterans Memorial building, are home to **Pinedorado Days** (Pinedorado Grounds, Main St., 805/927-9903, www.pinedorado. com, Labor Day weekend), a community celebration that's occurred here every Labor Day weekend since 1949. Expect a parade and a car show along with barbecues, live music, kids' games, art shows, and food booths.

Throughout October, the Cambria Historical Society sponsors the **Cambria Scarecrow Festival** (805/927-2891, various venues, 805/927-2597, www.cambriascarecrows.com, Oct.), with creative scarecrows lining the streets of town.

ACCOMMODATIONS

Many of the accommodations in Cambria are along the small town's Hotel Row, aka Moonstone Beach Drive. San Simeon has a small strip of hotels on either side of the highway south of Hearst Castle.

Under $150

Located next to a church, the ★ **Bridge Street Inn-HI Cambria** (4314 Bridge St., 805/927-7653, http://bridgestreetinncambria. com, $32-95) used to be the pastor's house. Now it's a clean, cozy hostel with a dorm room and five private rooms. The kitchen has a collection of cast-iron kitchenware, and there's a volleyball court out front. Part of Bridge Street's appeal is its enthusiastic young owner, Brandon Follett, who sometimes books live bands to play at the hostel. Even if there's no band scheduled to play, it doesn't take much to entice Brandon to grab his acoustic guitar and play a song for his guests.

Her Castle Homestay Bed and Breakfast Inn (1978 Londonderry Ln., 805/924-1719, www.hercastle.cc, $130-170) is a bit different from your average B&B, with only two guest rooms available and lots of personal attention from the owners. When you make your reservations, ask about a half-day wine tour or dinner reservations. Her Castle can be the perfect hideaway for two couples traveling together who desire the privacy of "their own house." Although it was established in 1957, **Cambria Palms Motel** (2662 Main St., 805/927-4485, www.cambriapalmsmotel.com, $129-180) has been remodeled and modernized; the 18 guest rooms have free Wi-Fi and cable TV. Some guest rooms also have private patios, and pet-friendly rooms are available. The family-friendly **Castle Inn** (6620 Moonstone Beach Dr., 805/927-8605, www.cambriainns.com, $144-169) has a great location, right across the road from Moonstone Beach, offering excellent ocean views. Guest rooms are unassuming, with wooden bed frames, coffee pots, fridges, and flat-screen TVs. The heated pool and hot tub are sheltered from the coastal winds. A basic continental breakfast is served in the morning.

$150-250

For a great selection of anything from economical standard rooms up to rustic cabins with king beds and a fireplace, pick the **Cambria Pines Lodge** (2905 Burton Dr., 805/927-4200 or 800/927-4200, www.cambriapineslodge.com, $165-365). All guest rooms have plenty of creature comforts, including TVs, private baths, and, in some cases, fireplaces. There's also a nice garden area with flowering plants, benches, and sculptures.

One of San Simeon's best lodging options, **The Morgan** (9135 Hearst Dr., 800/451-9900, www.hotel-morgan.com, $179-349) is named for Hearst Castle architect Julia Morgan, paying tribute to her with reproductions of her architectural drawings in all of the guest rooms. The rooms are clean and well appointed, and some have partial ocean views; eight rooms come with soaking tubs and gas fireplaces. The Morgan also has a wind-sheltered pool and deck. A complimentary continental breakfast is served every morning. **The Massage Center at The Morgan** (805/927-3878, massages $90-145) offers massages, aromatherapy, warm stone therapy, and hand and foot scrubs.

A favorite among the many inns of Cambria, the **Olallieberry Inn** (2476 Main St., 805/927-3233, www.olallieberry.com, $150-225) is in a charming 19th-century Greek Revival home and adjacent cottage. Each of the nine guest rooms features its own quaint Victorian-inspired decor with comfortable beds and attractive appointments. A full daily breakfast, complete with olallieberry jam, rounds out the comfortable personal experience.

A pebble's throw from Moonstone Beach, the ★ **Sand Pebbles Inn** (6252 Moonstone Beach Dr., 805/927-5600, www.cambriainns.com, $159-279) is a two-story gray building where most guest rooms have glimpses of the ocean through bay windows. The clean, tastefully decorated rooms have comfortable beds, mini-fridges, and microwaves. The six west-facing rooms have full ocean views, while the bottom three have patios. Expect nice little amenities such as welcome cookies, a better-than-average continental breakfast, coffee and tea served in the lobby, and a lending library of DVDs.

Located on the north end of Moonstone Beach, the **White Water Inn** (6790 Moonstone Beach Dr., 805/927-1066, www.whitewaterinn.com, $189-339) is a small family-run hotel. The distinct yellow building looks like a collection of connected cottages, with 15 guest rooms and two mini-suites. All of the guest rooms have gas fireplaces; the mini-suites have spas on private patios. The service is notable—continental breakfast is delivered to your room on china, and they'll even clean your car's windshield before your drive home.

Just across the street from Moonstone Beach, the quaint **Sea Otter Inn** (6656 Moonstone Beach Dr., 800/927-5888, www.seaotterinn.com, $139-319) focuses on seaside charm. Standard guest rooms have fireplace heaters, microwaves, fridges, and DVD players. Upgrade to enjoy a whirlpool tub and a view of the ocean.

The sleek, modern **El Colibri Boutique Hotel & Spa** (5620 Moonstone Beach Dr., 805/924-3003, www.elcolibrihotel.com,

$160-300) offers a wine bar in the lobby and a wellness center with two steam rooms and an outdoor Jacuzzi on site. All 34 guest rooms have fireplaces, soaking tubs, and Keurig coffeemakers. On weekends, enjoy live music and wine.

The **Fog's End Bed and Breakfast** (2735 Main St., 805/927-7465, www.fogsend.com, $175-195) offers just five guest rooms on an eight-acre spread just outside Cambria's East Village. The gracious hosts spoil guests with a full breakfast in the morning along with appetizers and wine at night. Play bocce ball or horseshoes on the lawn or enjoy a game of pool in the barn.

The **Best Western Cavalier Oceanfront Resort** (9415 Hearst Dr., San Simeon, 805/927-4688, www.cavalierresort.com, $189-339) occupies a prime piece of real estate in San Simeon on a bluff above the ocean just south of Pico Creek. The highest-priced rooms are oceanfront offerings with wood-burning fireplaces, soaking tubs, and private patios. The grounds include a pool, an exercise room, a day spa, and a restaurant.

Moonstone Landing (6240 Moonstone Beach Dr., 805/927-0012, www.moonstone-landing.com, $225-330) provides inexpensive partial-view guest rooms with the decor and amenities of a mid-tier chain motel, as well as oceanfront luxury guest rooms featuring porches with ocean views, soaking tubs, and gas fireplaces.

Over $250

One of the cuter and more interesting options on Moonstone Beach Drive, **Moonstone Cottages** (6580 Moonstone Beach Dr., 805/927-1366, http://moonstonecottages.com, $319-389) offers peace and luxury along the sea. Each of the three cottages includes a fireplace, a marble bath with a whirlpool tub, a flat-screen TV with a DVD player, Internet access, and a view of the ocean. Breakfast is delivered to your cottage each morning.

Owned by the same family, the adults-only ★ **Blue Dolphin Inn** (6470 Moonstone Beach Dr., 805/927-3300, www.cambriainns.

com, $249-399) offers slightly more upscale guest rooms than its neighbor. The six ocean-view rooms come with fireplaces, Keurig coffeemakers, robes, and slippers. Breakfast is delivered to your room every morning.

CAMPING

At **San Simeon State Park** (500 San Simeon Creek Rd., Cambria, 800/444-7275, www.reserveamerica.com, $20-25), you can experience the opulence of Hearst Castle on a budget. The **San Simeon Creek Campground** ($25) is the more developed option here, with 115 campsites for tents and RVs. All have fire pits and picnic tables. At the time of publication all of the toilets and showers were closed due to the state's water shortage. The **Washburn Campground** ($20) is a primitive campground one mile inland. There are views of the Santa Lucia Mountains and the Pacific Ocean from Washburn's sites.

FOOD
Asian

Dragon Bistro (2150 Center St., 805/927-1622, daily 11am-9pm, $12-19) does Chinese food without the high sodium, fat, or sugar content. The restaurant uses fresh seafood, meat, and vegetables in traditional dishes like orange chicken and black pepper beef. "The Treasures of the Sea" is a hot platter with a fishing net of shrimp, scallop, fish, and clam. The generous lunch menu (11am-3pm) will leave you stuffed.

One of the best bargains in town is **Wild Ginger** (2380 Main St., 805/927-1001, www.wildgingercambria.com, Mon.-Wed. and Fri.-Sat. 11am-2:30pm and 5pm-9pm, Sun. 5pm-9pm, $14-19). This tiny pan-Asian café serves delicious fresh food like Vietnamese caramelized prawns and eggplant curry. There's also an array of take-out fare. Come early for the best selection.

Bakeries

The French Corner Bakery (2214 Main St., 805/927-8227, www.frenchcornerbakery.com, daily 6:30am-6pm, $7) offers a selection of

Olallieberries

You'll see the name olallieberry around Cambria, perhaps spelled differently each time. Part loganberry, part raspberry, this berry grows in and around Cambria, but it was actually created in a laboratory. The original cross was made as early as 1935 as a joint project between Oregon State University and the U.S. Department of Agriculture. Selected in 1937 and tested in Oregon, Washington, and California and referred to as Oregon 609, it was eventually named Olallie and released in 1950. (The name means "berry" in Native American languages.) While developed in Oregon and planted there, it has never been very productive in that environment and is primarily grown in California. It has usually been marketed as olallieberry, just as Marion is sold as marionberry. The taste and structure is similar to a blackberry but a little milder. Make sure you try it while you're in town, or pick up a jar to take with you as a souvenir for people back home, who have probably never heard of it before.

fresh-made bread and pastries behind a glass counter, overseen by a large mural of Paris. There's also a small menu of lunch options, including cold deli sandwiches, Mexican *tortas,* and hot offerings like an Italian meatball sandwich.

Breakfast and Brunch

Take in a hearty breakfast or lunch on the outdoor patio at the family-owned **Creekside Garden Café** (2114 Main St., 805/927-8646, www.creeksidegardencafe.com, Mon.-Sat. 7am-2pm, Sun. 7am-1pm, $5-10). Fuel up with omelets, scrambles, or pancakes. Lunch showcases burgers, sandwiches, salads, and south-of-the-border items.

Cheap Eats

Although Cambria and San Simeon have more than their fair share of fine dining, the places to get a burger or sandwich are actually some of the best and most popular eateries in the area. The best spot to fuel up for a Hearst Castle tour is easily ★ **Sebastian's Store** (442 Slo San Simeon Rd., San Simeon, 805/927-3307, Wed.-Sun. 11am-4pm, $7-12). Housed alongside the Hearst Ranch Winery tasting room and the tiny San Simeon post office, this small eatery showcases tender, juicy beef from nearby Hearst Ranch in burgers, French dips, and unique creations like the Hot Beef Ortega Melt. This is a popular place, and the sandwiches take a few minutes to prepare,

so don't stop in right before your scheduled Hearst Castle tour.

The ★ **Main Street Grill** (603 Main St., 805/927-3194, www.firestonegrill.com, June-Aug. daily 11am-9pm, Sept.-May daily 11am-8pm, $4-18) is a popular eatery housed in a cavernous building located on the way into Cambria. The tri-tip steak sandwich—tri-tip drenched in barbecue sauce and placed on a French roll dipped in butter—is the favorite, even though the ABC burger, with avocado, bacon, and cheese topping the meat, puts most burger joints to shame. The giant Cobb salad comes with lots of diced-up bacon and your choice of chicken or steak.

Coffee and Tea

The **Cambria Coffee Roasting Company** (761 Main St., 805/927-0670, www.cambriacoffee.com, daily 7am-5:30pm) roasts their own beans. Head upstairs to stretch out and enjoy the free Wi-Fi.

Mexican

Every town in California has a taqueria, and Cambria is no different. **Medusa's** (1053 Main St., 805/927-0135, http://medusascambria.com, Mon.-Sat. 7am-8pm, $5-12) offers the usual tacos, burritos, and enchiladas as well as an extensive breakfast menu that includes *chilaquiles,* huevos rancheros, and chorizo and eggs. Get it to go or dine inside under a mural of a jungle pyramid.

New American and Fusion

One of the most popular restaurants in Cambria is the **Black Cat Bistro** (1602 Main St., 805/927-1600, www.blackcatbistro.com, daily 5pm-9pm, $18-30), serving creative seafood, vegetarian, meat, and poultry entrées. The interior is homey, with a fireplace and wood floors. Reservations are recommended at this small spot.

Part of an expansive local family business, **Linn's Restaurant** (2277 Main St., 805/927-0371, www.linnsfruitbin.com, daily 8am-9pm, $14-32) serves tasty, unpretentious American favorites in a casual family-friendly atmosphere. Think potpies, stroganoff, and pot roast. Save room for the olallieberry pie—or purchase a ready-to-bake pie, jam, or even vinegar to take home.

Madeline's Restaurant and Wine Shop (788 Main St., 805/927-4175, www.madelinescambria.com, daily 5pm-9pm, $22-32) pours local wines by day (tasting room 805/927-0990, daily 11am-5pm) and serves French-influenced dinner fare by night, with entrées like seafood gumbo, pan-seared duck, and vegetarian polenta. Or opt for a five course-tasting menu at $55 a person.

The Sow's Ear Café (2248 Main St., 805/927-4865, http://thesowsear.com, daily 5pm-close, $18-31) breathes new life into comfort-food classics. The potpies are stuffed with lobster, while the macaroni and cheese is spiked with sausage and smoked chicken. The chicken-fried steak and chicken and dumplings hew to classic rib-sticking recipes.

Indigo Moon (1980 Main St., 805/927-2911, www.indigomooncafe.com, daily 10am-9pm, $17-35) is another worthy dining destination. The menu is a fusion of American, European, and Asian influences, with entrées like the perfectly breaded calamari *piccata* with a tasty red curry sauce. Dine inside the historic cottage or out on the covered garden patio. Indigo Moon also sells artisanal cheeses and bottles of wine, so it's a good place to stop for picnic supplies.

The eclectic menu at ★ **Robin's** (4095 Burton Dr., 805/927-5007, www.robinsrestaurant.com, Sun.-Thurs. 11am-9:30pm, Fri.-Sat. 11am-10pm, $16-26) has cuisine from around the world, including Thailand (Thai green chicken), India (a selection of curries), the Mediterranean (meze plate), Mexico (wild prawn enchiladas), and the old US of A (flat-iron steak, burgers). What makes it so impressive is that they do it all so well. Start with the signature salmon bisque or the grilled naan pizzette of the day. The menu also has a

the ABC burger at Cambria's Main Street Grill

number of vegetarian and gluten-free dishes. The setting is a historic building erected by Heart Castle's construction foreman as his own residence, with a large dining room and an outdoor deck decorated with hanging vines. Expect fine service from a staff that's proud of their product. Happy hour (Mon.-Fri. 3pm-5pm) has $5 small plates and $5 glasses of wine and sangria.

Seafood

If the smell of the salt air on Moonstone Beach leaves you longing for a seafood dinner, head for the ★ **Sea Chest Oyster Bar** (6216 Moonstone Beach Dr., 805/927-4514, www.seachestrestaurant.com, daily 5:30pm-9pm, $20-30, cash only). No reservations are accepted, so expect a long line out the door at opening time, and prepare to get here early (or wait a long while) for one of the window-side tables. The wait is worth it. The restaurant is located in a wooden cottage with great ocean views. Framed photographs on the walls and books on bookshelves add to the homey feel of the place. Sit at the bar to watch the cooks prepare the impressive dishes like halibut, salmon, and cioppino, which is served in the pot it was cooked in. The menu of oyster and clam appetizers includes the indulgent Devils on Horseback, a decadent dish of sautéed oysters drenched in wine, garlic, and butter and topped with crispy bacon on two slabs of toast. The lightly breaded calamari strips are superb as well.

An unassuming steak and seafood restaurant attached to San Simeon's Quality Inn, the family-owned **Manta Rey Restaurant** (9240 Castillo Dr., 805/924-1032, www.mantareyrestaurant.com, daily 5pm-9pm, $16-40) pleasantly surprises with its artfully done and tasty seafood dishes. Items like sand dabs, salmon, oysters, and sea bass come from nearby Morro Bay when in season. A good place to start is with Manta Rey's oysters Rockefeller appetizer ($14), a rich mix of baked oyster, bacon, cheese, and spinach in an oyster shell. The perfectly breaded sand dabs in a creamy basil and sherry sauce are a recommended entrée, especially if it's caught fresh in nearby Morro Bay. The decor here is basic—white tablecloths, flowers on the table—and there is a view of the highway and the ocean in the distance from the porthole-like windows. Being near Hearst Castle, there is frequently an international clientele. Every day, Manta Rey has an early bird special (5pm-6pm) so that you can save a few dollars on select entrées.

Robin's restaurant

At the very least, the **Moonstone Beach Bar & Grill** (6550 Moonstone Beach Dr., 805/927-3859, www.moonstonebeach.com, Mon.-Sat. 11am-9pm, Sun. 9am-9pm, $20-31) is a great place for a drink. The deck out front—always crowded on summer days—has a nice view of the beach. It's ideal for a late-afternoon beer, local wine, or specialty cocktail. The dinner menu is heavy on grilled seafood, while lunch has a wide variety of sandwiches.

Farmers Market

Stock up on produce, fruit, and honey at the food-only **Cambria Farmer's Market** (Veterans Hall parking lot, 1000 Main St., www.cambriafarmersmarket.com, summer Fri. 2:30pm-5:30pm, winter Fri. 2:30pm-5pm).

INFORMATION AND SERVICES
Maps and Visitor Information

The **Cambria Chamber of Commerce** (767 Main St., 805/927-3624, www.cambria-chamber.org, Mon.-Fri. 9am-5pm, Sat.-Sun. noon-4pm) is probably the best resource for information on the area. It also provides a free annual publication that lists many of the local stores, restaurants, and lodgings. Be sure to pick up a trail guide for additional hikes and walks—Cambria has great places to roam. The **Cambria Public Library** (1043 Main St., 805/927-4336, www.slolibrary.org, Tues.-Thurs. 9am-5pm, Fri. 9am-6pm, Sat. 11am-4pm) offers additional information and local history, including a map for a self-guided historical walking tour.

Emergency Services

Cambria is served by three facilities: **Twin Cities Hospital** (1100 Las Tablas Rd., Templeton, 805/434-3500, www.twincities-hospital.com) in Templeton, 25 miles inland, and **Sierra Vista Regional Medical Center** (1010 Murray Ave., San Luis Obispo, 805/546-7600, www.sierravistaregional.com) and **French Hospital** (1911 Johnson Ave., San Luis Obispo, 805/543-5353, www.frenchmedicalcenter.org), both in San Luis Obispo, 37 miles south. Cambria and San Simeon are policed by the **San Luis Obispo Sheriff's Department** (805/781-4550, www.slosheriff.org). If you have an emergency, dial 911.

Newspapers and Media

The Cambrian (www.sanluisobispo.com/

the Sea Chest Oyster Bar

the-cambrian) is the local paper, published each week on Thursday; copies cost $0.50. **KTEA** (103.5 FM, www.ktea-fm.com) is the local radio station.

Postal Services

There is a **post office** (4100 Bridge St., 805/927-8610, www.usps.com, Mon.-Fri. 9am-4:30pm) currently open weekdays in Cambria, and postal services are available in San Simeon at **Sebastian's General Store** (444 S. San Simeon Rd., 805/927-4156, www. usps.com, Mon.-Fri. 11:30am-3:30pm).

TRANSPORTATION
Car
Cambria and San Simeon are located directly along Highway 1 and are only accessible by this road, whether you're coming from the north or the south. You can access Highway 1 from U.S. 101 via scenic Highway 46, which connects to Highway 1 just south of Cambria. If you use Cambria as a base to explore the Paso Robles wine area, or even

for excursions to Morro Bay (15 miles), a car will be necessary. The only available taxi service is **Cambria Cab** (4363 Bridge St., 805/927-4357).

Bus
The regional bus system, the **RTA** (805/541-2228, www.slorta.org), connects San Luis Obispo, Morro Bay, Cayucos, Cambria, and San Simeon. Fares range $1.50-3.

Train
There is no rail service to Cambria or San Simeon; the nearest Amtrak train station is located in San Luis Obispo, 35 miles south of Cambria.

Air
There are scheduled flights from Los Angeles, San Francisco, and Phoenix to the **San Luis Obispo County Regional Airport** (SBP, 901 Airport Dr., San Luis Obispo, 805/781-5205, www.sloairport.com), which is 35 miles south of Cambria.

Cayucos

Just 13 miles south of Cambria along Highway 1, Cayucos is one of California's best little beach towns. There are no real attractions here except for the small strip of a beach between open hillsides and the Pacific, but there are a good number of nice restaurants and places to stay, so it makes a nice, less touristy place to spend the night while visiting the area's attractions, including Hearst Castle, 30 miles north.

Cayucos is named after the indigenous Chumash people's word for kayak or canoe. One of the early proponents of the town was Captain James Cass, who, with a business partner, built the pier, a store, and a warehouse in the late 1800s. Today, the long, narrow pier still stands, while the warehouse is the town's community center and home of the Cayucos Art Society Gallery.

RECREATION
Beaches
The major attraction in Cayucos is **Cayucos State Beach** (Cayucos Dr., 805/781-5930, www.parks.ca.gov, daily sunrise-sunset) and the pier, which was built in 1875 by Captain James Cass. The beach has volleyball courts, swing sets, and lifeguard stands, which are staffed during the summer months. The pier is lit at night for fishing. Cayucos is not known for consistent surf, but rideable waves can occur on the south side of the pier. This is a usually mellow beach-break spot good for beginners. The relatively calm waters off Cayucos Beach are a good place to try kayaking or stand-up paddleboarding.

Just a few feet from the beach, **Good Clean Fun** (136 Ocean Front Ln., 805/995-1993, http://goodcleanfunusa.com, daily 9am-6pm) rents out surfboards ($10/hour), wetsuits ($8/hour), body boards ($5/hour), stand-up paddleboards ($15/hour), and kayaks ($30-40/hour). They also have surf lessons, a surf camp, kayak tours, and kayak fishing outings. Another place to pick up beach equipment is the **Cayucos Surf Company** (95 Cayucos Dr., 805/995-1000, www.cayucossurfcompany.com, winter daily 10am-6pm, summer daily 9am-6pm). They have wetsuits ($15/day), surfboards ($29/day), body boards ($20/day), and stand-up paddleboards ($40/day) for rent. They also offer private and group surfing lessons.

Hiking

The oceanfront land between Cayucos and Cambria is mostly undeveloped because it's preserved as part of the state park system. The 355-acre **Estero Bluffs State Park** (west of Hwy. 1 from N. Ocean St. to Villa Creek, 805/772-7434, www.parks.ca.gov, free) is a coastal terrace that offers trails into intertidal areas. It includes a pocket cove and a beach at Villa Creek, which is also an important habitat for the endangered snowy plover.

The 784-acre **Harmony Headlands State Park** (Hwy. 1, five miles north of Cayucos, 805/772-7434, www.parks.ca.gov, daily 6am-sunset, $3/vehicle) was ranch and dairy land until the mid-1960s, and it opened as a state park in 2008. The only real way to experience this park is the 1.5-mile hike from the small 10-car parking lot out to the coast. The trail is a mostly flat dirt road. As it begins, it passes over a bridge where you may be able to look down and spot southwestern pond turtles. The trail continues through grasslands and hugs the side of a scenic ravine, then runs north along a marine terrace. It ends at a small finger that juts out between rocks and tidepools. In the spring, wildflowers such as morning glories, California buttercups, and lupine color the grasslands. Keep your eyes peeled for endangered California red-legged frogs and rare southwestern pond turtles. There are no facilities except for a portable toilet located next to a ranch house just a few minutes into the trail, on a short side-spur trail to the right.

Spas

After a tough day of relaxing on Cayucos Beach, you deserve a massage. The **Cayucos Aloha Spa** (196 S. Ocean Ave., 805/995-2222, www.cayucosalohaspa.com, by appointment) has you covered with massages ($65 per hour), pedicures, manicures, and "bacials" (a facial treatment for your back).

Wine Tasting

Cayucos Cellars (131 N. Ocean Ave., 805/995-3036, www.cayucoscellars.com, Wed.-Mon. 11:30am-5:30pm, tasting $10) is a true family affair. All the employees are members of the Selkirk family. Cayucos Cellars produces just 500 to 800 cases of wine per year, including zinfandels and cabernet sauvignons. The winery is in an old barn in the Cayucos hills, but the tasting room is in the bright blue building on the town's main drag.

ENTERTAINMENT AND EVENTS

Bars

The **Old Cayucos Tavern** (130 N. Ocean Ave., 805/995-3209, www.oldcayucostavern.com, daily 10am-2am) is a classic Western saloon, with a poker room in the back and a bar up front. In the barroom, over 10 beers are available on tap, and topless cowgirl paintings adorn the walls. There are also two pool tables and a shuffleboard table for those who want to play games without the fear of losing their money in the card room. Western scenes decorate the walls and wooden barrels serve as tables. Live bands perform on weekends.

If you want to sample some local wines, the **Full Moon Wine Bar and Bistro** (10 N. Ocean Ave., Ste. 212, 805/995-0095, www.fullmoontastingroom.com, Thurs.-Sat. 4pm-10pm, Sun.-Mon. 2pm-7pm) has a large selection of wines from nearby Paso Robles, Monterey, and Santa Barbara as well as Europe. Full Moon serves soups, salads, dips,

In the mid-1800s the hilly land around the present-day community of Harmony was settled by Swiss immigrants interested in dairy farming. The first cheese factory was established in the area in 1869. After that, this portion of San Luis Obispo County became known for its cheese and butter, becoming home to companies like the Excelsior Cheese Factory and the Diamond Creamery. William Randolph Hearst traveled to Harmony to get his milk. Eventually, tensions grew between competing dairy farmers, which led to a feud and a murder. After peace was restored and a truce was made, the farmers decided to name the town Harmony in 1907 to reflect their newly adopted situation.

In 1958, Harmony ceased its cheese and butter making. The population of the town dropped until the 1970s, when some of the old dairy buildings were occupied by artist studios, galleries, and shops. The new influx of residents didn't quite restore Harmony to its former glory of the dairy days.

Currently, Harmony is primarily known for **Harmony Cellars** (3255 Harmony Valley Rd., 805/927-1625, www.harmonycellars.com, fall-spring daily 10am-5pm, summer daily 10am-5:30pm, tasting $7), a winery that makes reds and whites, and **Harmony Glassworks** (2180 Old Creamery Rd., 805/927-4248, http://harmonyglassworks.com, winter daily 9am-5pm, summer daily 9am-6pm), a glass-art gallery, studio, and school. Harmony is also home to the **Harmony Chapel** (805/927-1028, www.harmonychapel.net), a recording studio and café.

tapas, sandwiches, and desserts, all with an ocean view.

Festivals and Events

On New Year's Day, join the locals for the **Carlin Soule Memorial Polar Bear Dip** (Cayucos Pier, www.cayucoschamber.com, New Year's Day, noon). It began with just seven brave souls (including founder Carlin Soule) hopping into the frigid Pacific without wetsuits. Bravery must be contagious: Today there are over 1,000 participants.

Discover the region's bountiful food and wine at the **Cayucos Wine and Food Festival** (Cayucos Visitors Center and Museum, 41 S. Ocean Ave., 805/995-0095, www.cayucoschamber.com, Jan.).

The **Independence Day Celebration** (various venues, 805/995-1200, www.cayucoschamber.com, July 4) is a big deal, with a serious sand sculpture contest on the beach, a parade, a barbecue, and a fireworks show from the pier.

SHOPPING

Remember When (152 N. Ocean Ave., 805/995-1232, daily 10am-5pm) is home to antiques and collectibles. The **Lady Spencer Galleria and Distinctive Gifts** (148 N. Ocean Ave., 805/995-3771, www.ladyspencer.com, Mon.-Tues. and Thurs.-Sat. 10am-5pm, Sun. 10:30am-4pm) carries all sorts of unique items from barbed-wire earrings to soy candles and glass tableware.

Located in a red two-story building on Cayucos's main drag, **Brown Butter Cookie Company** (98 N. Ocean Ave., 805/995-2076, www.brownbuttercookies.com, daily 9am-6pm) bakes and sells original cookie creations, including their original brown butter sea salt cookie and more recent recipes such as coconut lime and cocoa mint. Witness the delectable creative process as it takes place right behind the counter.

ACCOMMODATIONS
Under $150

The **Seaside Motel** (42 S. Ocean Ave., 805/995-3809 or 800/549-0900, www. seasidemotel.com, $110-180) has brightly colored and uniquely decorated guest rooms with names like "Birdhouse Bungalow" and "Sunflower Surprise." Some guest rooms have kitchenettes; all have flat-screen TVs and Internet access. Suites are available for larger groups. All guests have access to the on-site garden.

$150-250

Located right behind the Brown Butter Cookie Company, ★ **The Saltbox** (150 D St., 800/995-2322, www.thesaltbox.com, $150-220) makes a superb home base while you're exploring the coast. The historic blue building, constructed by a ship's captain in the 1880s, is split into three units, each with a fully equipped kitchen, private entrance, and a deck or patio. The ground-floor Captain's Quarters can accommodate six to eight people with three bedrooms, two bathrooms, and an enclosed brick patio area. It's a perfect fit for three couples or a big family. The Crow's Nest is an upstairs apartment with two bedrooms that can accommodate four people and has a nice view of the sea and the pier. The Carriage House is a small studio in the shade of the main house. The place is a bit dated (there's a VCR and a tape

The Saltbox

player in the Crow's Nest), but that is outweighed by lots of character, a great location, and fair rates.

True to its name, the **Shoreline Inn** (1 N. Ocean Ave., 805/995-3681 or 800/549-2244, www.cayucosshorelineinn.com, $149-249) is right on the beach. All of the guest rooms have impressive beach and pier views as well as access to the beach and beachside showers. Everyone also gets a mini-fridge, a microwave, free Wi-Fi, and a flat-screen TV with a DVD player. Start the morning with a deluxe continental breakfast, and snack on complimentary cookies in the afternoon.

The **Cayucos Motel** (20 S. Ocean Ave., 805/995-3670 or 800/965-2699, www.cayucosmotel.com, $145-250) is also all about the beach, with beach access, an outdoor shower, and bodyboards and beach towels that guests can check out to further enjoy the surf and sand. Each of the eight guest rooms is different; some have private patios. The outdoor deck includes a barbecue grill and a Ping-Pong table. The continental breakfast is a good value for the price.

The **Cayucos Sunset Inn Bed and Breakfast** (95 S. Ocean Ave., 805/995 2500 or 877/805-1076, www.cayucossunsetinn.com, $189-349) has five two-room suites with private balconies, soaking tubs, and fireplaces. The innkeepers provide a full hot breakfast in the morning that is served in the dining room as well as milk and cookies delivered to your unit every evening.

The modern rooms at **On the Beach Bed & Breakfast** (181 N. Ocean Ave., 805/995-3200, www.californiaonthebeach.com, $179-389) have gas fireplaces, private balconies, and jetted tubs. The rooftop hot tub offers views of the ocean and pier. Enjoy wine and appetizers in the evening and wake up to complimentary breakfast in the morning.

FOOD
Coffee and Tea
Grab your morning caffeine jolt at **Top Dog Coffee Bar** (14 N. Ocean St., 805/900-5194, http://topdogcoffeebar.com, daily 6am-11pm).

Mexican and Italian
If you can't decide between Mexican and Italian food, head to **Martin's Restaurant** (49 S. Ocean St., 805/995-2626, www.martinsrestaurantcayucos.com, daily 8am-9pm, $9-17); they do both. Fish tacos, shrimp enchiladas, tostadas, and burritos appear on the menu alongside pizza, calzones, and full entrées like chicken parmesan and salmon fettuccine.

Pizza
A blue building just a few feet from Cayucos Beach, **Ocean Front Pizza** (156 1/2 Ocean Front Ave., 805/995-2979, www.oceanfrontpizza.com, daily 11:30am-8:30pm, $10-22) offers classic pizza combos, build-your-own pies, specialty pizzas like pesto and Thai, and barbecued chicken. All feature hand-tossed dough and homemade sauce.

Seafood
Cayucos is a place for seafood, and there is probably nothing in town as revered as ★ **Rudell's Smokehouse** (101 D St., 805/995-5028, www.smokerjim.com, daily 11am 6pm, $4 11). Rudell's is nothing more than a little shack near the beach, but this place serves some of the tastiest fish tacos you'll ever eat, including salmon and albacore variations. The seafood is smoked, and the unexpected but welcome presence of chopped apples gives the fixings a sweet crunch. The seating options are limited to a few outdoor tables, so plan on taking your taco to the nearby beach.

Living up to its name, **Schooners Wharf** (171 N. Ocean Ave., 805/995-3883, Sun.-Thurs. 11am-9pm, Fri.-Sat. 11am-10pm, $9-28) has a serious nautical theme going: It's a two-story compound of corrugated metal and wood decorated heavily with marine flotsam and jetsam. The menu here is seafood-heavy, with a range of items from hearty cioppino to seared ahi. But the burgers, made with local Hearst Ranch beef, are also worthy of your attention. If you are looking for somewhere to eat in Cayucos later at night, Schooners will probably be the only option.

At **Duckies Chowder House** (55 Cayucos Dr., 805/995-2245, www.duckieschowder.com, daily 11am-8pm, $6-12.50), you can get your chowder New England or Manhattan style and served in a cup, bowl, or bread bowl. Other seafood options are mostly fried; there are also salads and sandwiches on the menu. Pitchers of beer and the company of friends make it all go down easy.

The **Sea Shanty** (296 S. Ocean Ave., 805/995-3272, www.seashantycayucos.com, winter daily 8am-9pm, summer daily 8am-10pm, $10-25) serves gut-busting portions for breakfast, lunch, and dinner. The carb-loaded Cayucos Breakfast is biscuits drenched in eggs and gravy alongside a small mound of diced Swiss sausage. Lunches focus on charbroiled and fried seafood. Noteworthy desserts include a range of pies and cobblers. Dine inside under hundreds of hanging baseball caps—or better yet, sit outside on the covered wooden deck.

Markets

Cayucos has its own **farmers market** (Cayucos Veterans Hall parking lot, 10 Cayucos Dr., 805/296-2056, summer Fri. 10am-12:30pm).

INFORMATION AND SERVICES

The website **Cayucos by the Sea** (www.cayucosbythesea.com) has information on everything from the town's history to its current lodging and restaurant options. Visit the brick-and-mortar location or the website of the **Cayucos Chamber of Commerce** (41 S. Ocean Ave., 805/995-8552, www.cayucoschamber.com, winter Fri.-Sun. 11am-4pm, summer Fri.-Mon. 11am-4pm).

Cayucos has a few basic services, including a **post office** (97 Ash Ave., 805/995-3479, www.usps.com, Mon.-Fri. 9am-4pm). The **Cayucos Super Market** (301 S. Ocean Ave., 805/995-3929, daily 8am-8pm) has all the basic supplies you'll need. It's also home to the **Cayucos Sausage Company** (www.cayucossausagecompany.com), which has an array of homemade sausages.

Morro Bay

The picturesque fishing village of Morro Bay is dominated by Morro Rock, a 576-foot-high volcanic plug that looms over the harbor. In 1542, Juan Rodríguez Cabrillo, the first European explorer to navigate the California coast, named the landmark Morro Rock because he thought it resembled a moor's turban.

With a view of the rock, the small city's Embarcadero is a string of tourist shops, restaurants, and hotels strung along Morro Bay, a large estuary that includes the harbor, the Morro Bay State Marine Recreational Management Area, and the Morro Bay State Marine Reserve. Uphill from the water, more restaurants, bars, and stores are located in Morro Bay's Olde Towne section.

With natural attractions that include the stunning Montaña de Oro State Park just miles from town and with a nice waterfront focus, Morro Bay is a worthy destination or detour for a weekend, even though a lot of the area's lodgings fill up during high-season weekends.

SIGHTS
★ Morro Rock

It would be difficult to come to the town of Morro Bay and not see **Morro Rock.** The 576-foot-high volcanic plug, which has been called the "Gibraltar of the Pacific," dominates the town's scenery, whether you are walking along the bayside Embarcadero or beachcombing on the sandy coastline just north of the prominent geologic feature. The rock was an island until the 1930s, when a road was built connecting it to the mainland. The area around the rock is accessible, but the rock itself is off-limits because it is home to a group of endangered peregrine falcons. Indeed, a multitude of birds always seems to be swirling around the rock they call home.

★ Montaña de Oro State Park

Montaña de Oro State Park (Pecho Rd., seven miles south of Los Osos, 805/528-0513, www.parks.ca.gov, daily 6am-10pm, free) is for those seeking a serious nature fix on the Central Coast. This sprawling 8,000-acre park with seven miles of coastline has coves, tidepools, sand dunes, and almost 50 miles of hiking trails. A great way to get a feel for the park's immense size is to hike up the two-mile **Valencia Peak Trail** (four miles round-trip). In springtime the sides of the trail are decorated with blooming wildflowers, and the 1,347-foot-high summit offers commanding views of Montaña de Oro's pocked coastline and Morro Rock jutting out in the distance. From this vantage point in spring, the park's sticky monkey flower, wild mustard, and California poppies dust the hillsides in gold. The hike is steep and exposed so make sure to bring plenty of water on warm days.

For a feel of the coast, park right in front of **Spooner's Cove** and walk out on its wide coarse-grained beach. On the cove's north end, Islay Creek drains into the ocean. There's also a picturesque arch across the creek in the rock face on the north side. The **Spooner Ranch House Museum** informs visitors about early inhabitants of the park's land, the Spooner family. There are also displays about the area's plants, mountain lions, and raptors in the small facility.

Morro Bay State Park

Morro Bay State Park (Morro Bay State Park Rd., 805/772-7434, www.slostateparks.com, $8/vehicle) is not a typical state park. It has hiking trails, a campground, and recreational opportunities, but this park also has its own natural history museum, a golf course, and a marina. Located just south of town, the park is situated on the shores of Morro Bay. One way to get a feel for the park is to hike the **Black Hill Trail** (three miles round-trip).

A unique aspect of Morro Bay State Park is the **Morro Bay Museum of Natural History** (Morro Bay State Park Rd., 805/772-2694, www.ccnha.org, daily 10am-5pm, adults $3, under age 16 free). Small but informative, the museum has displays that explain the habitats of the Central Coast and some interactive exhibits for kids. An observation deck hanging off the museum allows for a great view of Morro Bay. Beside the museum is a

Morro Rock towers over Morro Bay.

garden that shows how the area's original inhabitants, the Chumash people, utilized the region's plants.

Play a round of golf at the **Morro Bay State Park Golf Course** (201 State Park Rd., 805/772-1923, www.slocountyparks.com, Mon.-Fri. $40, Sat.-Sun. $49), or head out on the water in a kayak, a canoe, or a stand-up paddleboard rented from the **Kayak Shack** (10 State Park Rd., 805/772-8796, www.morrobaykayakshack.com, Sept.-June daily 9am-4pm, July-Aug. 9am-5pm, kayaks $12-16/hour, canoes $14/hour, stand-up paddleboards $12/hour).

Morro Bay Harbor Walk

The **Morro Bay Harbor Walk** (0.5 miles, easy) is a great way to take in Morro Bay's harbor. Beginning at the north end of the Embarcadero, the boardwalk and bike trail runs along the harbor to towering Morro Rock. The harbor views are nice, and you can get some scenic photos of the picturesque town and the hills behind it. You may also spot some sea otters in the water. Along the way, the walk passes through **Coleman Park** (101 Coleman Dr., 805/772-6278, www.morro-bay.ca.us, daily dawn-dusk), a small city park with a picnic area, a basketball court, and a swing set for kids.

One way to do the Morro Bay Harbor Walk is by pedal power. Located near the start of the trail is **Farmer's Kites** (1108 Front. St., 805/772-0113, daily 9am-6pm). This store rents beach cruisers ($10/hour) along with two-person and four-person surrey bikes ($20-30/hour).

Giant Chessboard

Morro Bay's most unusual sight is the 16-by-16-foot **Giant Chessboard** (Centennial Pkwy., 805/772-6278). The waist-high chess pieces used in the game weigh as much as 30 pounds. Four picnic tables adjoin the Giant Chessboard; each has a chessboard where the local chess fiends play. You can reserve the board for a small fee (Mon.-Fri. 8am-5pm).

Or join the Morro Bay Chess Club when they play on Saturdays starting at noon.

Morro Bay Estuary Nature Center

Run by the Morro Bay National Estuary Program, the **Morro Bay Estuary Nature Center** (601 Embarcadero, Ste. 11, 805/772-3834, www.mbnep.org, Mar.-Dec. daily 10am-6pm, Jan.-Feb. daily 10am-5pm) explains the significance of the 2,300-acre estuary that is a focal point of the town. A watershed exhibit shows where rainfall goes, while an aquarium has live steelhead trout. Another aquarium houses eelgrass along with hermit crabs and anemones. There are also windows looking out on the estuary, where you may be able to spot sea otters, harbor seals, and sea lions in the water.

Morro Bay Skateboard Museum

California is the birthplace of skateboarding, and the **Morro Bay Skateboard Museum** (601 Embarcadero, Ste. 4, 805/610-3565, www.mbskate.com, daily 10am-5pm, donations appreciated) celebrates skating with a collection of over 200 boards dating from the 1950s to the present. There are homemade boards, boards autographed by skate pros, a Budweiser promotional board, and several boards that have been ridden all the way across the country. Scooters and framed skateboarding trading cards are also on display. The small one-room museum also sells skateboards, skate shoes, and T-shirts.

SPAS

The **Bay Beauty Spa** (1140 Front St., Unit C, 805/772-5038, www.baybeautyspa.com, daily 9am-5pm) offers several massage options ($75-100), including popular couples massages and HydroMassage, which employs jets of hot water beneath a cushioned mattress. It's like a soak in a whirlpool tub, but you can do it fully clothed and stay completely dry. Other procedures include pedicures, facials, microdermabrasion, and waxing. The location has a nice view of the harbor.

Spa By the Bay (895 Napa Ave., Ste. A1, 805/234-6922, http://spamorrobay.com, Mon.-Sat. by appointment) provides massages ($65-130) in a relaxing, Asian-influenced setting. Their signature Coastal Massage utilizes stretching, acupressure, and hot rocks.

ENTERTAINMENT AND EVENTS
Bars

With old gas and oilcans hanging from the ceiling, **The Fuel Dock** (900 Main St., 805/772-8478, Mon.-Wed. 2pm-2am, Thurs. 1pm-2am, Fri. 11am-2am, Sat.-Sun. 10am-2am) lives up to its name. Behind the bar is a good selection of liquor and beer to act as social lubricants. The front room has a stage that hosts live bands on weekends, while the back room has a couple of pool tables.

Across the street, **Legends Bar** (899 Main St., 805/772-2525, daily noon-2am) has a red pool table and a giant moose head poking out from behind the bar. Grab a drink and look at the framed historic photos covering the walls.

Down on the Embarcadero, **The Libertine Pub** (801 Embarcadero, 805/772-0700, www.thelibertinepub.com, Mon.-Wed. noon-11pm, Thurs.-Sun. noon-midnight) is the place for the discerning beer drinker, with 48 rotating craft beers on tap including some made in-house. One of the beers on tap will always be a sour. You can also order craft cocktails (a basil bourbon drink that counts marmalade as one of its ingredients) and pub food (including fish tacos, burgers, and *moules frites*). The bartenders also act as DJs, playing selections from the Libertine's stash of vinyl.

Stax Wine Bar & Bistro (1099 Embarcadero, 805/772-5055, www.stax-wine.com, Sun.-Thurs. noon-8pm, Fri.-Sat. noon-10pm) has a nice sidelong view of the harbor. Sit at the long, black granite bar or at the handful of tables to sample the selection of over 100 wines, many from local wineries. Five to eight rotating wines are served by the glass. The small food menu includes crostinis, paninis, salads, cheese plates, and local oysters.

A new Morro Bay place to sip wine is the **Waves Wine Bar** (845 Embarcadero, Ste. H, 805/225-1628, http://waveswinebar.wix.com/waves, Mon. and Wed.-Thurs. 2pm-8pm, Fri. 2pm-10pm, Sat. noon-10pm, Sun. noon-8pm), where the focus is on Paso Robles reds. There's also a limited food menu that includes a couple of pizzas and cheese plates.

Borderline kitschy, with marine decorations that match its harborside location, the **Otter Rock Café** (885 Embarcadero, 805/772-1420, www.otterrockcafe.com, Mon. and Thurs. 11am-10pm, Wed. and Fri. 11am-midnight, Sat. 8am-midnight, Sun. 8am-10pm) draws a crowd that knows how to have fun. Wednesday is karaoke night, and there's usually a band on either Friday or Saturday. The outdoor seating offers views of the harbor and the rock.

Cinema

There's only one movie house in town, the **Bay Theatre** (464 Morro Bay Blvd., 805/772-2444, www.morrobaymovie.com), and it has only one screen, so you're pretty limited unless you drive 20 minutes south to San Luis Obispo. This small-town theater has been screening films since the 1940s.

Festivals and Events

Bird-watchers flock to the **Morro Bay Winter Bird Festival** (various venues, 805/234-1170, www.morrobaybirdfestival.org, free-$90, Jan.). Some 200 species are typically spotted during the three-day event, which includes birding classes and tours of local birding spots.

Strong winds kick up on the Central Coast in the spring. The **Morro Bay Kite Festival** (Morro Bay Beach, 200 Coleman Dr., 800/231-0592, www.morrobaykitefestival.org, last weekend in Apr.) takes advantage of these gales with pro kite fliers twirling and flipping their kites in the sky. The festival also offers kite-flying lessons.

Held in July, the **Rock to Pier Run**

Water Farms

Aquaculture is the practice of farming aquatic organisms. The Cambria and Morro Bay area has two fine examples of aquaculture operations. The **Morro Bay Oyster Company** (1287 Embarcadero, 805/234-7102, www.morrobayoysters.com) uses environmentally sustainable techniques to raise Pacific Gold oysters in the cold, nutrient-rich waters of Morro Bay. The oysters start off as small as a pencil eraser, encased in mesh nets, and are "farmed" for 12 to 24 months until they have developed into tasty bivalve mollusks with a shell. Farther up the road in Cayucos, **The Abalone Farm** (8077/367-2271, www.abalonefarm.com) is the largest aquaculture facility in the nation. They produce an impressive 100 tons of California red abalone per year. The natural California red abalone population was decimated by years of overharvesting, so the Abalone Farm is a way for seafood lovers to once again dine on the large edible sea snail. Though there are currently no tours available for visitors to view these facilities, seafood enthusiasts can seek out these tasty, sustainably farmed products while dining at local restaurants.

(starting line at Morro Rock, 805/772-6281, July) is an annual beach run from Morro Rock to Cayucos Pier and back.

The **Avocado and Margarita Festival** (714 Embarcadero, http://avomargfest.com, Sept.) celebrates great food and drink, all complementing and inspired by the ever-popular locally grown avocado. The festival includes live music performances, a sombrero contest, and a raffle for a year's supply of avocados.

For over 30 years, the **Morro Bay Harbor Festival** (Embarcadero between Marina St. and Harbor St., 800/366-6043, www.mbhf. com, Oct.) has showcased the best of the region, including wines, seafood, live music, and a clam chowder contest.

SHOPPING

The Embarcadero is a fine place to stroll and pop into shops. One of the best is **The Shell Shop** (590 Embarcadero, 805/772-8014, www. theshellshop.net, winter daily 9:30am-5pm, summer daily 9:30am-7pm), which has imported shells from over 22 countries. Beautiful marine items on sale include nautilus shells, abalone shells, and decorative pieces of coral as well as seashell jewelry.

Run by a community of artists, the **Gallery at Marina Square** (601 Embarcadero, Ste. 10, 805/772-1068, http://galleryatmarinasquare. blogspot.com, daily 10am-6pm) showcases local art including the work of sculptors,

photographers, jewelry makers, glassworkers, and woodworkers. A public reception on the second Friday of every month (5pm-8pm) celebrates a member artist and a guest artist.

The Garden Gallery (680 Embarcadero, 805/772-4044, www.thegardengalleryinc. com, daily 10am-5pm) occupies a two-story building designed and built by one of its owners. The indoor and outdoor areas are filled with cacti and other succulents, along with garden decorations like fountains and pottery and indoor items like clocks and candles.

Wavelengths Surf Shop (998 Embarcadero, 805/772-3904, daily 9:30am-6pm) has a good selection of new surfboards, skateboards, wetsuits, and surf wear, including hoodies and T-shirts. Browse the outlet store located right across the street to find deals on used boards and wetsuits. It's also where you can rent a surfboard or wetsuit.

Stock up on Central Coast wines at the **Morro Bay Wine Seller** (601 Embarcadero, Ste. 5, 805/772-8388, www.morrobaywineseller.com, Sun.-Thurs. 10am-6pm, Fri.-Sat. 10am-8pm, tasting $5). They also have beer, cheese, and wine accessories.

SPORTS AND RECREATION
Beaches

There are several beaches in and around Morro Bay. Popular with surfers and beachcombers,

Morro Rock Beach (west end of Embarcadero, 805/772-6200, www.morro-bay.ca.us) lies within the city limits, just north of Morro Rock. Two lifeguard towers are staffed from Memorial Day to Labor Day (10am-6pm). The **Morro Bay Sandspit** (805/772-6200, www.morro-bay.ca.us) is a four-mile-long line of dunes and beach that separates Morro Bay from the ocean. The northernmost mile is within city limits, while the southern portion is located in Montaña de Oro State Park. You can access this area by walking in from the state park or by paddling across Morro Harbor to the land south of the harbor mouth.

Just north of town is **Morro Strand State Beach** (two miles south of Cayucos, CA-1, 805/772-2560, www.parks.ca.gov). The three-mile strand of sand is popular with anglers, windsurfers, and kite fliers. **North Point** (Hwy. 1 at Toro Ln., 805/772-6200, www.morro-bay.ca.us) is a bluff-top city park with a stairway to the beach and great tidepools. From here, you can also walk north all the way to Cayucos or head south toward looming Morro Rock. The wetlands at **Cloisters Park** (San Jacinto St. and Coral St., 805/772-6200, www.morro-bay.ca.us) are home to fish and birds. This city park also offers access to the beach.

Surfing

Morro Rock Beach (west end of Embarcadero, 805/772-6200, www.morro-bay.ca.us) has a consistent beach break. It's a unique experience to be able to stare up at a giant rock while waiting for waves. **Wavelengths Surf Shop** (998 Embarcadero, 805/772-3904, daily 9:30am-6pm, board rental $20/day, wetsuit rental $10/day), on the Embarcadero on the way to the beach, rents boards and wetsuits, as does **TKD Surf Shop** (911 Main St., 805/772-2431, daily 10am-6pm, soft-top surfboard rental $10/day, wetsuit rental $10/day).

★ Kayaking and Stand-Up Paddleboarding

Paddling the protected scenic waters of Morro Bay, whether you're in a kayak or on a stand-up paddleboard, is a great way to see wildlife up close. You might see otters lazily backstroking in the estuary or clouds of birds gliding just above the surface of the water.

Paddle over to the **Morro Bay Sandspit**, a finger of dunes located in the northern section of Montaña de Oro State Park that separates the bay from the ocean. Then beach your vessel and climb over the dunes to the mostly isolated beach on the ocean side. Parts of the

The Shell Shop is a store like no other.

dunes can be closed to protect the snowy plover. Away from the harbor area, the estuary can be very shallow; plan your paddling at high tide to avoid too much portaging.

Central Coast Stand-Up Paddling (1215 Embarcadero, 805/395-0410, www.centralcoastsup.com, daily 9am-6pm) rents stand-up paddleboards and kayaks ($18/hour). They also offer a 2.5-hour Morro Bay Tour ($75 pp). **Kayak Horizons** (551 Embarcadero, 805/772-6444, www.kayakhorizons.com, daily 9am-5pm) rents kayaks ($12-18/hour) and paddleboards ($12/hour) and hosts a three-hour paddle around the estuary ($59). **Central Coast Outdoors** (805/528-1080, www.centralcoastoutdoors.com, kayak tours $55-110 pp) has a range of kayaking tours that depart from the **Morro Bay State Park Marina** (100 State Park Rd.). Options include short paddles, sunset paddles, full-moon paddles, half-day paddles, and a kayak trip to the sandspit for a dinner in the dunes. Visit their website for more information. In Morro Bay State Park, you can secure a canoe or kayak from **A Kayak Shack** (10 State Park Rd., 805/772-8796, www.morrobaykayakshack.com, Sept.-June daily 9am-4pm, July-Aug. 9am-5pm, kayaks $12-16/hour, canoes $14/hour, stand-up paddleboards $12/hour).

Boat Tours

Sub Sea Tours (699 Embarcadero, 805/772-9463, www.subseatours.com, adults $17, seniors and students $14, children $9) is like snorkeling without getting wet. The yellow 27-foot semisubmersible vessel has a cabin outfitted with windows below the water. The 45-minute tour takes you around the harbor is search of wildlife. Expect to see sea lions sunning on a floating dock and sea otters playing in the water. At a much-touted secret spot, fish congregate for feeding. You'll typically see smelt, appearing like silver splinters, but you may also catch a glimpse of salmon, lingcod, perch, and sunfish. The captain may even cue up the Beatles' "Yellow Submarine" on the sound system. Kids will love it. Sub Sea Tours also schedules 2-3.5-hour whale-watching excursions (adults $45, seniors and students $40, under age 12 $35) to see California gray whales and humpback whales.

If you'd rather cruise the bay with the benefit of adult beverages, try **Lost Isle Adventure Tours** (845 Embarcadero, 805/771-9337, http://baycruisers.com, adults $10, under age 13 $5), which take place on a ramshackle floating tiki bar. They also rent electric boats ($75/hour) that can accommodate up to eight people. **Chablis Cruises** (800/979-3370, http://chabliscruises.com) are held on a two-story riverboat with a rooftop deck. Options include a two-hour weekly champagne brunch excursion (11am, adults $42, under age 12 $21) and two-hour harbor cruises ($20). **Virg's Landing** (1169 Market Ave., 805/772-1222, http://virgslanding.com, $49-89) sends four boats out for daily fishing trips, searching for rock cod, albacore, king salmon, and halibut. They also offer whale-watching excursions from December to April.

Bird-Watching

Morro Bay is one of California's great birding spots. **Morro Bay State Park** is home to a **heron rookery,** located just north of the Museum of Natural History. At **Morro Rock,** you'll see endangered peregrine falcons, ever-present gulls, and the occasional canyon wren. On the northwest end of **Morro Bay State Park Marina Area** (off State Park Dr.) birders can spot loons, grebes, brants, and ducks; you may also see American pipits and Nelson's sparrows. The cypress trees host roosting black-crowned night herons.

In **Montaña de Oro State Park,** along the **Sandspit,** you might find wrentits, blue-gray gnatcatchers, and California thrashers. **Islay Creek** hosts gulls at the beach in the winter. Farther upstream, clay-colored sparrows, chipping sparrows, and rare migrating warblers have been spotted. The region can be accessed via the park's **Islay Creek Trail.** The **Morro Coast Audubon Society** (805/772-1991, www.morrocoastaudubon.org) conducts birding field trips to local hotspots;

check their website for information on the up-coming trips.

Hiking

Morro Bay State Park (Morro Bay State Park Rd., 805/772-2560, www.parks.ca.gov) has 13 miles of hiking trails. One of the most popular is the **Black Hill Trail** (three miles round-trip, moderate), which begins from the campground road. This climb gains 600 vertical feet and passes through chaparral and eucalyptus on the way to the 640-foot-high Black Hill, part of the same system of volcanic plugs that produced nearby Morro Rock.

Montaña de Oro State Park (Pecho Rd., seven miles south of Los Osos, 805/528-0513, www.parks.ca.gov) has almost 50 miles of hiking trails. Take in the park's coastline along the **Montaña de Oro Bluffs Trail** (four miles round-trip, easy). The trailhead begins about 100 yards south of the visitors center and campground entrance and runs along a marine terrace to the park's southern boundary. On the way it passes **Corallina Cove,** where you may see harbor seals and sea otters. Starting at the parking area just south of the visitors center, **Valencia Peak Trail** (four miles round-trip, moderate) leads to its

namesake 1,347-foot-high peak, which offers a nice view of the coastline spread out below. The **Hazard Peak Trail** (six miles round-trip, moderate-strenuous) starts at Pecho Valley Road and climbs to the summit of 1,076-foot Hazard Peak, with unobstructed 360-degree views. The **Islay Canyon Trail** (six miles round-trip, moderate) takes you through the park's inland creekbeds and canyons. Starting at the bottom of Islay Creek Canyon, this wide dirt path is popular with birders because of the 25 to 40 different bird species that frequent the area. An abandoned barn makes a good marker to turn back toward the trailhead.

Just south of Montaña de Oro State Park, the **Point Buchon Trail** (3.5 miles round-trip, easy, Apr.-Oct. Thurs.-Mon. 8am-5pm, Nov.-Mar. Thurs.-Mon. 8am-4pm) leads along pristine shoreline, passing a natural sinkhole and jagged sea-sculpted cliffs. The trail begins at Montaña de Oro State Park's Coon Creek Parking Lot. It's located on a parcel of land owned by utility company PG&E. In order to preserve the area's natural resources, the number of hikers each day is limited; make a reservation via the PG&E website (http://pge.modwest.com/pgereservations).

Located in nearby Los Osos, the **Elfin**

trail within Montaña de Oro State Park

Forest Boardwalk Trail (0.75 miles, easy, www.elfin-forest.org, daily dawn-dusk) offers an easy boardwalk trail through 90 acres of marsh, dune scrub, and pygmy oak woodland. While some California live oaks reach heights of 50 feet, the persistent winds and poor soil keep these tiny specimens just 4-20 feet tall. Parking is off any of Los Osos' 11th to 17th Streets, which end at the edge of the forest. The 16th Street entrance offers the best access for people using wheelchairs or strollers.

Horseback Riding

No Worries Trail Rides (805/286-1338, http://jennerroseranch.webs.com) offers one-hour ($74), two-hour ($100), and all-day ($190) rides on Montaña de Oro State Park's trails and beaches. You meet your horse for the day at the park. Your transportation will be one of the rare horse breeds fostered at Jenner Rose Ranch, including haflingers, gypsy horses, and friesians.

City Parks

A couple of small city parks appeal to families or those who want a break from browsing in the Embarcadero's shops. Tiny **Anchor Memorial Park** (931 Embarcadero, 805/772-6278, www.morro-bay.ca.us) is dedicated to local people who have been lost at sea on fishing boats. This bayfront space has a statue of an anchor and nifty benches that resemble boat cleats. Two-acre **Tidelands Park** (300-394 Embarcadero, 805/772-6278, www.morro-bay.ca.us) has a kid's play area with a pirate ship and some seal statues. A staircase leads to the mudflats below. There's also a fish-cleaning station.

Golf

How many state parks have their own golf course? People call the **Morro Bay Golf Course** (201 State Park Rd., 805/772-1923, www.golfmorrobay.com, greens fees Mon.-Fri. $44, Sat.-Sun. $52) the "poor man's Pebble Beach," probably because of the hilly terrain and great ocean views. It also has a driving range, rental clubs, a pro shop, and a bar and grill.

ACCOMMODATIONS
Under $150

The **Sundown Inn** (640 Main St., 805/772-3229 or 800/696-6928, http://sundowninn.com, $89-189) is a well-priced motel within walking distance of Morro Bay's downtown and waterfront areas. Guest rooms have fridges, microwaves, and—here's something different—coin-operated vibrating beds.

The owners of the **Marina Street Inn Bed & Breakfast** (305 Marina St., 805/772-4016, www.marinastreetinn.com, $125-145) honeymooned here, so they know what visitors want. The four suites are individually decorated; one has a nautical theme, while another features a willow-limb bedpost and a birdhouse table. Each suite shares a balcony or porch with the adjoining room. The hot breakfast may include a crustless quiche or buttermilk waffles.

Just up from the Embarcadero, the **Blue Sail Inn** (851 Market Ave., 805/772-2766 or 800/971-6910, www.bluesailinn.com, $129-229) is another relatively inexpensive place to lay your head. Most guest rooms include balconies; there's also a hot tub and complimentary continental breakfast.

The 16-room **Back Bay Inn** (1391 2nd St., Los Osos, 805/528-1233, www.backbayinn.com, $110-210) is located in a scenic setting on the south end of the estuary in Los Osos, about three miles from the Morro Bay Embarcadero. Most guest rooms have a view of the bay; the second-floor units come with a balcony or fireplace. There is also a cottage, a loft, and a studio for rent. All guests receive an evening wine reception and a hot breakfast.

Located just inside Morro Bay State Park, the recently renovated **Inn at Morro Bay** (60 State Park Rd., 805/772-5651 and 800/321-9566, http://innatmorrobay.com, rooms $135-229, cottage $350-375) offers easy access to the golf course and the Museum of Natural History. The Cape Cod-style guest rooms offer views of the bay. There's also a spa (805/772-5651, massages $55-120) with a range of treatments.

$150-250

The ★ **Masterpiece Hotel** (1206 Main St., 805/772-5633 or 800/527-6782, www.masterpiecehotel.com, $189-249) is a great place to stay for art enthusiasts and lovers of quirky motels. Each guest room is decorated with framed prints from master painters, and the hallways also have prints of paintings by Henri Matisse, Vincent Van Gogh, and Norman Rockwell. There's also a large indoor spa pool decorated like a Roman bathhouse that further differentiates this motel from other cookie-cutter lodging options. Expect a deluxe breakfast in the morning and a wine-and-cheese serving in early evening.

Built in 1939, the bright ★ **Beach Bungalow Inn and Suites** (1050 Morro Ave., 805/772-9700, www.morrobaybeachbungalow.com, $139-299) have been extensively renovated. The 12 clean, spacious, and modern guest rooms have hardwood floors, local art on the walls, and flat-screen TVs. Eleven of the guest rooms have gas fireplaces. Family suites accommodate four people, while king deluxe suites have full kitchens. Two bicycles are available for cruising around town. There's also a fire pit outside to enjoy the Central Coast evenings. In the morning, a hot breakfast is served to your room.

The unique **Front Street Inn and Spa** (1140 Embarcadero, 805/772-5038, www.frontstreetinn.net, $199-250) offers just two large guest rooms that share a floor with a spa. The spacious high-ceilinged rooms are oriented around large windows, with superb views of the harbor and the rock. Both have deep soaking tubs, fridges, and gas fireplaces. Expect to wake to the aroma of the bakery on the first floor. The adjacent **Bay Beauty Spa** (805/772-8548, www.baybeautyspa.com, massages $75-150) is known for its couples massages.

From the outside, the **Ascot Suites** (260 Morro Bay Blvd., 805/772-4437 or 800/887-6454, www.ascotsuites.com, $159-319)

resembles an English country inn. The theme continues in the guest rooms with English country fabrics and fireplaces. A rooftop garden showcases views of Morro Rock and the bay. Deluxe guest rooms include jetted tubs. Expect a full hot breakfast as well as a complimentary afternoon wine tasting.

All of the 33 guest rooms at the recently renovated **Embarcadero Inn** (456 Embarcadero, 805/772-2700 or 888/223-5777, www.embarcaderoinn.com, $148-220) have at least a partial view of the bay. Many also include a private balcony and a fireplace. The family suite comes with two bedrooms and a fully equipped kitchen. Other amenities include a spa room with a hot tub and complimentary continental breakfast.

The **Estero Inn** (501 Embarcadero, 805/772-1500, www.esteroinn.com, $159-299) is located right on the waterfront. All eight guest rooms are suites with microwaves and fridges. They each have a balcony or ocean view. Continental breakfast is served in the morning.

Over $250

The family-run **Anderson Inn** (897 Embarcadero, 805/772-3434, www.andersoninnmorrobay.com, $249-389) is an eight-room boutique hotel located right on Morro Bay's busy Embarcadero. Three of the guest rooms are perched right over the estuary with stunning views of the nearby rock. Those premium guest rooms also include fireplaces and jetted tubs.

CAMPING

Located a couple of miles outside downtown Morro Bay, the **Morro Bay State Park Campground** (Morro Bay State Park Rd., 800/444-7275, www.parks.ca.gov, tents $35, RVs $50) has 140 campsites, many shaded by eucalyptus and pine trees; right across the street is the Morro Bay estuary. Six miles southwest of Morro Bay, **Montaña de Oro State Park** (Pecho Rd., seven miles south of Los Osos, 800/444-7275, www.parks.ca.gov, $25) has more primitive camping facilities.

There are walk-in environmental campsites and a primitive campground behind the Spooner Ranch House that has pit toilets.

One mile north of Morro Rock, **Morro Strand State Beach** (Yerba Buena St. and CA-1, 800/444-7275, www.reserveamerica.com, $35) has over 80 sites within spitting distance of the beach.

FOOD
Breakfast and Brunch

★ **Frankie and Lola's** (1154 Front St., 805/771-9306, www.frankieandlolas.com, daily 6:30am-2:30pm, $4-13) does breakfast right. Creative savory dishes include the fried green tomato Benedict topped with creole hollandaise sauce and tasty, colorful *chilaquiles* with red chorizo, avocado, and tomatillo salsa. Lunch focuses on salads and sandwiches with creations including an edamame flatbread and a more traditional tri-tip avocado sandwich.

The Coffee Pot Restaurant (1001 Front St., 805/772-3176, http://morrobaycoffeepot.com, daily 7am-1:30pm, $7-13) has been serving up breakfast since 1960, an impressive career for any restaurant. They also make more than just traditional fare: try an omelet drenched in enchilada sauce and or french toast stuffed with cream cheese, walnuts, and marmalade.

On the road toward Montaña de Oro State Park, **Celia's Garden Café** (1188 Los Osos Valley Rd., Los Osos, 805/528-5711, http://celiasgardencafe.com, daily 7:30am-2:30pm, $9-12) is an ideal place to fuel up for a day of hiking. Fill up on a pork chop and eggs or the chicken-fried steak. Other options include omelets, benedicts, and hotcakes. Located in a plant nursery, the café has an indoor dining room and a dog-friendly outdoor patio.

Cheap Eats

In the mood for a darn fine hamburger? In nearby Los Osos, **Sylvester's Burgers** (1099 Santa Ynez Ave., Los Osos, 805/528-0779, www.sylvestersburgers.com, daily 11am-9pm, $5-8) attracts carnivores with juicy beef slathered in signature sauce. The yellow shack has a range of juicy, tasty, never-frozen beef burgers, including The Sylvester Burger, a pound of beef topped with cheddar cheese, onion rings, bacon—and of course, Sylvester's sauce. Four beers are available on tap to wash it down. Eat on the outdoor deck or inside,

Frankie and Lola's

where the walls are decorated with photos of the regulars.

La Parisienne (1140 Front St., 805/772-8530, Mon. and Wed.-Sat. 7:30am-5pm, Sun. 7:30am-4pm, $4-7) is a bakery that also serves a lot of inexpensive sandwiches. The breakfast sandwiches can be served on a baguette or a croissant, while the lunch menu includes sandwiches, salads, and burgers.

Classic American

The giant parking lot outside **Carla's Country Kitchen** (213 Beach St., 805/772-9051, daily 6:30am-2pm, $6-12) attests to the popularity of this breakfast and lunch spot. With blue-and-white checkered tablecloths, Carla's serves heaping portions of breakfast classics, including scrambles and omelets, along with sandwiches and burgers. The Pooney scramble is a tasty mess of spinach, cheeses, eggs, bacon, and mushrooms. The biscuits can be on the dry side.

Within Morro Bay State Park, the **Bayside Café** (10 State Park Rd., 805/772-1465, www.baysidecafe.com, Mon.-Wed. 11am-3pm, Thurs. and Sun. 11am-8:30pm, Fri.-Sat. 11am-9pm, $8-25), true to its name, is right by the bay. The lunch menu skews toward burgers and fish-and-chips, while dinner features fancier fare such as lobster scampi.

Locals head to **The Hungry Fisherman** (399 Beach St., 805/772-3444, daily 6am-9pm, $10-30) for budget breakfasts and hearty egg dishes. At night there's classic diner fare like fried chicken and chicken-fried steak as well as seafood.

Coffee and Tea

Popular **Top Dog Coffee** (875 Main St., 805/772-9225, www.topdogcoffeebar.com, daily 6am-11pm) is the place to get caffeinated, with all of the usual options as well as a few creative beverages like mango chai and Mexican mocha. The coffee beans are roasted right here. For lunch (6:30am-4pm), they also serve café fare: bagels, burritos, paninis, and sandwiches. There are tables inside and out front on the sidewalk. Right around

the corner, **The Rock Espresso Bar** (275 Morro Bay Blvd., 805/772-3411, Sun.-Thurs. 6am-5pm, Fri.-Sat. 6am-6pm) makes espressos, cappuccinos, lattes and mochas. Enjoy the cottage-like interior or the garden out back. They also sell 20 kinds of coffee beans.

German

The roast beef brings people back to the **Hofbrau** (901 Embarcadero, 805/772-2411, www.hofbraumorrobay.com, daily 11am-9pm, $7-15). It has been serving up popular half-pound hand-carved roast beef sandwiches au jus since 1971. The informal waterfront eatery also cooks up clam chowder, burgers, and fish-and-chips alongside German fare like bratwurst and sauerkraut. There's also a salad bar to balance your meat intake.

Mexican

People worship the crab cake and fish tacos at ★ **Taco Temple** (2680 N. Main St., 805/772-4965, Wed.-Mon. 11am-9pm, $5-22, cash only). Housed in a big multicolored building east of Highway 1, where colorful surfboards hang on the walls, this is not the standard taqueria. Their California take on classic Mexican dishes includes sweet potato enchiladas and tacos filled with soft-shell crab or calamari. The tacos are served like salads, with the meat and greens piled on tortillas. The chips and salsa are terrific.

You'll find more traditional taqueria fare at **Tacos de Mexico** (980 Main St., 805/772-5796, Mon.-Thurs. 8am-9pm, Fri.-Sun. 8am-10pm, $4.50-7.50). The menu includes tacos, of course, as well as wet and dry burritos, with options like *chile verde* and *chile colorado*. The large tostadas are popular with the local crowd.

Seafood

Seafood is the way to go when dining in the fishing village of Morro Bay. An unassuming fish house with views of the fishing boats and the bay, ★ **Tognazzini's Dockside Restaurant** (1245 Embarcadero,

805/772-8100, www.bonniemarietta.com, summer Sun.-Thurs. 11am-9pm, Fri.-Sat. 11am-10pm, winter Sun.-Thurs. 11am-8pm, Fri.-Sat. 11am-9pm, $18-27) has an extensive seafood menu as well as art depicting sultry mermaids hanging on the wall. Entrées include albacore kebabs and wild salmon in a unique tequila marinade. If you're an oyster lover, you simply can't go wrong with Dockside's barbecued oysters appetizer, which features the shellfish swimming in garlic butter studded with scallions. Behind the main restaurant is the **Dockside Too Fish Market** (summer daily 10am-8pm, winter Sun.-Thurs. 10am-6pm, Fri.-Sat. 10am-8pm), a local favorite with beer, seafood, and live music.

Giovanni's Fish Market & Galley (1001 Front St., 877/552-4467, www.giovannisfishmarket.com, market daily 9am-6pm, restaurant daily 11am-6pm, $5-10) is a real working market, with live abalone and sushi-grade fish pulled right out of the bay. The fish-and-chips wins raves, and the clam chowder wins awards. Try the barbecued oysters in garlic or Sriracha butter, or Rockefeller-style with bacon and jalapeños. During summer months, expect long lines to dine on the outdoor patio.

Located on a hill above the Embarcadero, ★ **Dorn's Original Breakers Café** (801 Market St., 805/772-4415, www.dornscafe. com, daily 7am-9pm, $13-30) offers a great view of Morro Rock from its dining room. It has been family owned and operated since 1942. Dinner begins with bread and a dish of garlic, olive oil, vinegar, and cheese. The large menu of seafood and steak includes fresh daily specials like snapper, petrale sole, salmon, and halibut from local waters.

Elegant **Windows on the Water** (699 Embarcadero, Ste. 7, 805/772-0677, www. windowsmb.com, Sun.-Thurs. 5pm-8:30pm, Fri.-Sat. 5pm-9pm, $23-39) showcases local seafood like abalone, oysters, halibut, and sand dabs. The wine list is heavy with local vintages.

The upscale **Galley Seafood Bar & Grill** (899 Embarcadero, 805/772-7777, http://galleymorrobay.com, daily 11am-2:30pm and 5pm-close, $18-46) is popular for items like pan-seared scallops. The menu changes daily depending on the fresh catch.

Thai

Thai Bounty (560 Embarcadero, 805/772-2500, http://thethaibounty.com, Thurs.-Tues.

Taco Temple

11am-9pm, $11-14) has won second place for its oyster entry in the Central Coast Oyster Festival, so the chefs know seafood. They take advantage of the local bounty—both fresh seafood and vegetables and herbs from their own garden—to create daily specials with preparations like panang curry, garlic pepper, and spicy stir-fry. Dine indoors or out on the patio.

In nearby Los Osos, **Noi's Little Thai Takeout** (1288 2nd St., 805/528-6647, Mon.-Fri. 11am-7:30pm, $8-13) is a local favorite. They have a different curry dish for every day of the week along with noodle and rice plates. Expect to get your food to go because there is very limited seating.

Vegetarian

Run by the folks who own the adjacent Sunshine Health Foods store, the **Shine Café** (427 Morro Bay Blvd., 805/771-8344, www.sunshinehealthfoods-shinecafe. com, Mon.-Fri. 11am-5pm, Sat. 9am-5pm, Sun. 10am-4pm, $4.50-11) is a vegetarian's dream, focusing on local and organic ingredients in their smoothies, sandwiches and salads. The BLT uses bacon-flavored tempeh, and the namesake hummus wrap is big enough to sate even a carnivore's appetite. Gluten-free tempeh tacos are a house specialty. Order at the inside kitchen counter, then dine indoors under local art or out at sidewalk tables.

Farmers Market

Morro Bay has two weekly farmers markets: the **Thursday farmers market** (Spencer's Fresh Markets parking lot, 2650 Main St., 805/544-9570, www.slocountyfarmers.org, Thurs. 2:30pm-5pm) and the **Saturday farmers market** (Main St. and Harbor St., 805/602-1009, Sat. 3pm-6pm).

INFORMATION AND SERVICES

The **Morro Bay Chamber of Commerce** (845 Embarcadero, Ste. D, 800/225-1633, www.morrobay.org) has a wonderful visitors center overlooking the bay at the end of a small boardwalk. It has a vast array of printed material you can take with you.

French Hospital Medical Center (1911 Johnson Ave., San Luis Obispo, 805/543-5353, www.frenchmedicalcenter.org) and **Sierra Vista Regional Medical Center** (1010 Murray Ave., San Luis Obispo, 805/546-7600, www.sierravistaregional.com) are the closest hospitals. Both are in San Luis Obispo, 13 miles from Morro Bay. If you have an emergency, dial 911. The local police are the **Morro Bay Police Department** (850 Morro Bay Blvd., 805/772-6225).

To access the **post office** (898 Napa Ave., 805/772-0839, Mon.-Fri. 9am-5pm, Sat. 9am-1pm), you'll need to leave the Embarcadero area and head uptown.

TRANSPORTATION
Car

As with most towns on the Central Coast, CA-1 cuts through Morro Bay. If you're traveling south from San Francisco, take U.S. 101 south to Atascadero, take Highway 41 west, and then head south on Highway 1. Exit at Main Street in Morro Bay. If you're traveling from Los Angeles, the best route is U.S. 101 north to San Luis Obispo, and then north on Highway 1 to Morro Bay; take the Morro Bay Boulevard exit into town.

Morro Bay is 30 miles south of Hearst Castle on CA-1. Simply look for the Main Street exit to get to downtown Morro Bay.

Bus

There is no direct bus service to Morro Bay, although **Greyhound** (805/238-1242, www.greyhound.com) travels along U.S. 101 and stops at 1460 Calle Joaquin Street in San Luis Obispo. From there you'll need to connect with **Regional Transit Authority** (805/781-4472, www.slorta.org, $1.50-3) buses to get to Morro Bay. There are various weekday and weekend routes.

Trolley

The **Morro Bay Trolley** (595 Harbor Way, 805/772-2744, Memorial Day weekend-first weekend in Oct. Mon. 11am-5pm, Fri.-Sat. 11am-7pm, Sun. 11am-6pm, $1 per ride, children under 5 free) operates three routes. The **Waterfront Route** runs the length of the Embarcadero, including out to Morro Rock. The **Downtown Route** runs through the downtown (as in uptown) area all the way out to Morro Bay State Park. The **North Morro Bay Route** runs from uptown through the northern part of Morro Bay, north of the rock, along Highway 1. An all-day pass (not a bad idea if you plan on seeing a lot of sights) is $3.

Background

The Landscape

The Monterey Bay region and Central Coast were formed by tectonic events occurring over the past 30 million years. The inland section of Monterey County is on the very active San Andreas Fault, the boundary between the Pacific Plate and North American Plate. The fault line frequently causes earthquakes in the historic town of San Juan Bautista. Santa Cruz was the epicenter of the Loma Prieta Earthquake, a magnitude 6.9 event that rocked the region in 1989.

The area's coastal mountain ranges were also formed by tectonic activity. Both the Santa Lucia Mountains and Santa Cruz Mountains parallel the coastline and help contribute to the area's stunning scenery and many recreation opportunities. The Santa Cruz Mountains begin on the San Francisco Peninsula and run south into the Salinas Valley. Their highest point is 3,786-foot Loma Prieta Peak.

The dramatic Santa Lucia Mountains form the backdrop for Big Sur. They traverse Monterey County and the northern portion of San Luis Obispo County. The highest point in the range is 5,857-foot Junipero Serra Peak on the eastern flank of the mountains, while 5,155-foot Cone Peak has the most dramatic rise from sea to summit.

Rivers and streams bisect the area on their way to the sea. The San Lorenzo River begins in the Santa Cruz Mountains and spills into the sea just south of the Santa Cruz Beach Boardwalk. The largest river in the region is the Salinas River, which runs through the Salinas Valley before turning its course to the ocean south of Moss Landing. The Carmel River originates in the Santa Lucia Mountains and hits the Pacific just a shade south of Carmel-by-the-Sea.

The entire section of the Pacific Ocean offshore of this region is part of Monterey Bay National Marine Sanctuary, which stretches from Marin County above San Francisco down to Cambria. Monterey Bay is a Pacific Ocean bay between Santa Cruz and Monterey. It is known for its abundant kelp forests and the Monterey Submarine Canyon, an underwater valley off Moss Landing in the middle of the bay. The canyon plunges to a depth of two miles, twice as deep as Arizona's Grand Canyon.

CLIMATE

Like most of coastal California, the Monterey Bay area is known for its mostly mild Mediterranean climate. This means that summer and fall are warm and dry, while winter and spring are chillier and see more rainfall. Precipitation is rare in the region from May to October, while pretty much all of the rain falls between November and April. Unfortunately, the last few years have seen minimal rainfall throughout the year, a phenomenon that is contributing to California's drought.

Summers on the coast can be chillier that expected due to fog. This effect is caused by hot inland air meeting up with cool air coming off the Pacific Ocean. The best places to get out of the fog are the inland sections of Monterey County including Carmel Valley and Salinas Valley. Big Sur Valley also offers sunny relief when the coast is socked in with fog. On many summer days, the Monterey Peninsula is obscured by fog, while Santa Cruz across the bay is sunny and a few degrees warmer.

Previous: the Big Sur coastline; Morro Bay and Morro Rock.

ENVIRONMENTAL ISSUES

Californians face several major environmental issues. The state battles drought, and water for crops, farms, and human consumption is always in short supply. Monterey Bay is not immune to this problem and is even considering desalination plants that transform seawater into drinking water. Water conservation measures can include limiting development and urban sprawl, restricting water usage, and designating set periods for personal and recreational use, such as watering lawns.

Water pollution is also an issue. Most tap water is safe to drink, but swimming in bays, lakes, and rivers, as well as the Pacific Ocean, requires more caution. Pollution may cause *E. coli* outbreaks at beaches, affecting wildlife and beachgoers alike. Santa Cruz's Cowell's Beach and Capitola Beach have been known to have bacteria in their waters after winter rains.

Many of the state's grand oak trees have succumbed to sudden oak death, a disease that spreads through spores to eventually kill live oaks, black oaks, and tan oaks. To control its spread, travelers are advised to clean all camping equipment thoroughly and to buy and burn local firewood rather than importing it from elsewhere.

Plants and Animals

PLANTS
Redwoods

The **coast redwood** *(Sequoia sempervirens)* grows as far south as Big Sur. Coast redwoods are characterized by their towering height, flaky red bark, and moist understory. Among the tallest trees on earth, they are also some of the oldest, with some individuals almost 2,000 years old. Because they collect moisture from the ocean and fog, coast redwoods occupy only a narrow strip of coastal California; they grow no more than 50 miles inland. Their tannin-rich bark is crucial to their ability to survive wildfires and regenerate afterward. Big Basin State Park is the region's best place to marvel at the giants.

Oaks

California is home to many native oaks. The most common are the **valley oak, black oak, live oak,** and **coastal live oak.** The deciduous black oak grows throughout the foothills of the Coast Range; the coastal live oak occupies the Coast Range itself. The acorns of all these oaks were an important food supply for California's Native American populations and continue to be an important food source for wildlife.

Wildflowers

The state flower is the **California poppy** *(Eschscholzia californica).* The pretty little perennial grows just about everywhere, even on the sides of the busiest highways. The flowers of most California poppies are bright orange, but they also appear occasionally in white, cream, and an even deeper red-orange.

ANIMALS
Mountain Lions

Mountain lions *(Felis concolor)* are an example of powerful and potentially deadly beauty. Their solitary territorial hunting habits make them elusive, but human contact has increased as more homes are built in mountain lion habitat throughout California. Many parks in or near mountain lion territory post signs with warnings and advice: Do not run if you come across a mountain lion, instead make noise and raise and wave your arms so that you look bigger. The California Department of Fish and Wildlife (www.dfg.ca.gov) offers a downloadable brochure on encounters and other tips.

Whales

The massive, majestic **gray whale** *(Eschrichtius robustus)* was once endangered, but its numbers have rebounded with international protection. The gray whale measures about 40 feet long and has mottled shades of gray with black fins; its habitat is inshore ocean waters, so there is a chance to get a glimpse of them from headlands up and down the coast. Gray whales generally migrate south along the coast November-January, and closer to shore February-June when they return northward.

Perhaps a more recognizable behemoth is the **humpback whale** *(Megaptera novaeangliae)*. At 45-55 feet long, the humpback is the only large whale to breach regularly; it then rolls and crashes back into the water, providing one of the best shows in nature. The whale also rolls from side to side on the surface, slapping its long flippers. Humpbacks generally stay a little farther from shore, so it may be necessary to take a whale-watching cruise to catch a glimpse of them, but their 20-foot spouts can help landlubbers spot them from shore. Look for humpbacks April-early December off the coast near Big Sur, particularly at Julia Pfeiffer Burns State Park.

The **blue whale** *(Balaenoptera musculus)* is the largest animal on earth. At 70-90 feet long, the blue whale even exceeds most dinosaurs in size. Sporting a blue-gray top and a yellowish bottom, the blue whale has a heart the size of a small car—and two blowholes—but, alas, does not breach. They can be seen June-November off the California coast, especially at Monterey.

California Sea Lions

Watching a beach full of California sea lions *(Zalophus californianus)* sunning themselves and noisily honking away can be a pleasure. Sea lions are migratory, so they come and go at will, especially in the fall when they head to Southern California for breeding.

Sea Otters

Even higher on the cuteness scale is the sea otter *(Enhydra lutris),* which can be spotted just offshore in shallow kelp beds. Once near

California poppies near Monterey

extinction, the endearing and playful sea otter has survived; now there are more than 2,000 in California waters. It can be a bit mesmerizing to witness a sea otter roll on its back in the water and use a rock to break open mollusks for lunch. Sea otter habitat runs from Monterey Bay to Big Sur.

Birds

California has a wide range of habitat with accessible food and water that makes it perfect for hundreds of bird species to nest, raise their young, or just stop over and rest during long migrations. Nearly 600 species have been spotted in California.

Among the most regal of California's bird species are raptors. The **red-tailed hawk** *(Buteo jamaicensis)* is found throughout California and is frequently sighted perched in trees along highways and even in urban areas. The red-tailed hawk features a light underbelly with a dark band and a distinctive red tail that gives the bird its name.

Although not as common as it once was,

Swainson's hawk *(Buteo swainsoni)* has been an indicator species in California's environment. The Swainson's hawk population has declined due to loss of habitat and excessive pesticide use in agricultural lands; its main diet consists of the locusts and grasshoppers that feed on these crops, passing the contaminants on to the birds. These hawks are smaller than the red-tailed hawk, with dark brown coloring and some white underparts either on the chest or under the tail.

With wings spanning 10 feet from tip to tip, the **California condor** *(Gymnogyps californianus)* is the largest flying bird in North America. In the recent past, the condor's population had plummeted due to its susceptibility to lead poisoning, along with deaths caused by electric power lines, habitat loss, and gunshots from indiscriminate humans. In 1987, there was only one California condor left in the wild; it was taken into captivity as part of a breeding program. In 1997, a Monterey County-based nonprofit, the Ventana Wildlife Society (VWS), began releasing the giant birds back into the wild. Currently, 70 wild condors soar above California's Central Coast. The species' recovery is one of conservation's great success stories.

Reptiles

Several varieties of **rattlesnakes** are indigenous to the state. If you spot California's most infamous native reptile, keep your distance. All rattlesnakes are venomous, although death by snakebite is extremely rare in California. Most parks with known rattlesnake populations post signs alerting hikers to their presence; hikers should stay on marked trails and avoid tromping off into meadows or brush. Pay attention when hiking, especially when negotiating rocks and woodpiles, and never put a foot or a hand down in a spot you can't see first. Wear long pants and heavy hiking boots for protection from snakes as well as insects, other critters, and unfriendly plants you might encounter.

Butterflies

California's vast population of wildflowers attracts an array of gorgeous butterflies. The **monarch butterfly** *(Danaus plexippus)* is emblematic of the state. These large orange-and-black butterflies have a migratory pattern that's reminiscent of birds. Starting in August, they begin migrating south to cluster in groves of eucalyptus trees. As they crowd together and close up their wings to hibernate, their dull outer wing

California condor near Big Sur

color camouflages them as clumps of dried leaves, thus protecting them from predators. In spring, the butterflies begin to wake up, fluttering lazily in the groves for a while before flying north to seek out milkweed on which to lay their eggs. Pacific Grove and Santa Cruz are great places to visit these "butterfly trees."

History

THE FIRST RESIDENTS

The diverse ecology of California allowed Native Americans to adapt to the land in various ways. These groups included the Ohlone. More than 100 Native American languages were spoken in California, and each language had several dialects, all of which were identified with geographic areas.

Ohlone

The Ohlone·people once occupied what is now Santa Cruz, Monterey, and the lower Salinas Valley, as well as land to the north. The Ohlone lived in permanent villages, only moving temporarily to gather seasonal foods such as acorns and berries. The Ohlone formed an association of about 50 different communities with an average of 200 members each. The villages interacted through trade, marriages, and ceremonies. Basket weaving, ceremonial dancing, piercings and tattoos, and general ornamentation indicated status within the community and were all part of Ohlone life. Like other Native Americans in the region, the Ohlone depended on hunting, fishing, gathering, and agrarian skills such as burning off old growth each year to get a better yield from seeds.

The Ohlone culture remained fairly stable until the first Spanish missionaries arrived to spread Christianity and to expand Spanish territorial claims. Spanish explorer Sebastián Vizcaíno reached what is now Monterey in December 1602, and the Rumsen group of Ohlone were the first natives he encountered. Father Junípero Serra's missionaries built seven missions on Ohlone land, and most of the Ohlone people were brought to the missions to live and work. For the next 60 years, the Ohlone suffered, as did most indigenous people at the missions. Along with the culture shock of subjugation came the diseases for which they had no immunity—measles, smallpox, syphilis, and others. It wasn't until 1834 that the California missions were abolished and the Mexican government redistributed the mission land holdings.

The Ohlone lost the vast majority of their population between 1780 and 1850 because of disease, social upheaval from European incursion, and low birth rates. Estimates are that there were 7,000-26,000 Ohlone when Spanish soldiers and missionaries arrived, and about 3,000 in 1800 and 864-1,000 by 1852. There are 1,500-2,000 Ohlone people today.

THE MISSION PERIOD

In the mid-1700s, Spain pushed for colonization of Alta California, rushing to occupy North America before the British beat them to it. The effort was overly ambitious and underfunded, but missionaries started to sweep into present-day California.

The priest Junípero Serra is credited with influencing the early development of California. A Franciscan monk, Serra took an active role in bringing both Christianity and European diseases to Native American people from San Diego north to Sonoma County. The Franciscan order built a string of missions; each was intended to act as a self-sufficient parish that grew its own food, maintained its own buildings, and took care of its own people. However, mission structures were limited by a lack of suitable building materials and skilled labor. Later, the forced labor of Native Americans was used to cut and haul timbers and to make adobe bricks. By the time the missions were operating, they claimed about 15 percent of the land in California, or about one million acres per mission.

Missions in this region include Santa Cruz Mission, San Juan Bautista Mission, San Carlos Borromeo de Carmelo Mission (better known as the Carmel Mission), Soledad's Mission Nuestra Senora de la Soledad, and inland Monterey County's Mission San Antonio de Padua.

Spanish soldiers used subjugation to control indigenous people, pulling them from their villages and lands to the missions. Presidios (royal forts) were built near some of the missions to establish land claims, intimidate indigenous people, and carry out the overall goal of finding wealth in the New World. The presidios housed the Spanish soldiers that accompanied the missionaries.

The city of Monterey was founded in 1770 with the establishment of the Presidio of Monterey and Mission San Carlos. At this time, Monterey became the capital of Spain's Alta California territory. Junípero Serra moved the mission to Carmel in 1771 to be closer to a better water supply.

In 1821, Mexico gained independence from Spain along with control of Alta California and the missions. The Franciscans resisted giving up the land and free labor, and Native Americans continued to be treated as slaves. From 1824 to 1834 the Mexican government handed out 51 land grants to colonists for land that had belonged to Native Americans and was held by nearby missions. From 1834 to 1836 the Mexican government revoked the power of the Franciscans to use Native American labor, and it began to redistribute the vast mission land holdings.

STATEHOOD

The dramatic population boom caused by the Gold Rush that began in 1848 ensured that California would be on the fast track to admission into the United States, bypassing the territorial phase. Monterey was integral to California's burgeoning statehood and hosted California's first constitutional convention at Colton Hall in 1849. The next year, California became a state. It had gone from a Mexican province to the 31st U.S. state in little more than four years. Monterey is known for having many of the state's firsts, from its first government building to its first theater to its first newspaper.

BACKGROUND
HISTORY

Carmel Mission

HOTEL DEL MONTE AND THE RISE OF THE TOURISM INDUSTRY

In 1880, a sprawling seaside resort called the Hotel Del Monte opened in Monterey, establishing the peninsula's reputation as a vacation destination. Its on-site features included a polo field, a horse track, a hedge maze, and a golf course. The buildings and grounds would be leased by the U.S. government in 1942 before becoming the still-operating Naval Postgraduate School.

THE GREAT DEPRESSION

The stock market crash of 1929 led to the Great Depression. Many property owners lost their farms and homes, and unemployment in California hit 28 percent in 1932; by 1935, about 20 percent of all Californians were on public relief.

The Great Depression transformed the nation. Beyond the economic agony was an optimism that moved people to migrate to California. Many migrants from the Midwest settled in California, preserving their ways and retaining identities separate from other Californians. The Midwestern migrants' plight was captured in John Steinbeck's 1939 novel *The Grapes of Wrath*. Steinbeck, a Salinas native, gathered information by viewing firsthand the deplorable living and labor conditions under which Okie families existed. The novel was widely read and was turned into a movie in 1940. Government agencies banned the book from public schools, and libraries and large landowners campaigned to have it banned elsewhere. That effort lost steam, however, when Steinbeck won the 1940 Pulitzer Prize.

SARDINE CAPITAL OF THE WORLD

The first half of the 1900s found Monterey Bay's fishing industry flourishing. The center of the activity was Cannery Row, a road in Monterey lined with sardine-canning factories. The fishermen and canneries were extremely busy in the 1930s and early 1940s, gaining Monterey the title "Sardine Capital of the World." The catch began decreasing in 1945 and never recovered. The time and place were immortalized that same year with the publication of John Steinbeck's *Cannery Row*. The street is now a popular tourist attraction due in large part to the Monterey Bay Aquarium, which opened there in 1984.

Government and Economy

GOVERNMENT

California is home to what many consider liberal views: support of political protests and free speech, legalized medical marijuana use, environmental activism, and gay and lesbian rights. These beliefs are not incorporated as a whole throughout the state, however. Major metropolitan and coastal areas have become havens for artists, musicians, and those seeking alternatives to mainstream America. Inland populations, however, often show more conservative leanings at the polls.

California is overwhelmingly Democratic, but when it comes to politics, not everything is predictable. In 2008 California voters approved Proposition 8, which outlawed same-sex marriage, by 52.2 percent to 47.8 percent; voters in some counties approved the ban by more than 75 percent. A ballot measure to legalize marijuana use was defeated that same year. Yet Californians also voted for Democrat Barack Obama as president the same year by a definitive majority, 61 percent to 37 percent. Obama took the state again in the 2012 election with 53 percent of the votes.

ECONOMY

California boasts the eighth-largest economy in the world, although the ongoing global economic downturn may put a dent in that ranking in the years to come. Still, California's contribution to the United States outpaces even its immense size and population, and it continues to be the country's number-one economy.

California's number-one economic sector is farming. Sweet strawberries and spiky artichokes grow in abundance in the cooler Central Coast region. The Salinas Valley is a world-renowned agricultural region. Agriculture, including fruit, vegetables, nuts, dairy, and wine production, help make California the world's fifth-largest supplier of food and agriculture commodities.

Today, organic farms and ranches are proliferating across the state. An increasing number of small farms and ranches growing crops use organic, sustainable, and even biodynamic practices. Most of these farmers sell directly to consumers by way of farmers markets and farm stands—almost every town or county in California has a weekly farmers market in the summer, and many are held year-round.

And then there's the wine. It seems like every square inch of free agricultural land has a grapevine growing on it. The vineyards that were once seen primarily in Napa and Sonoma can now be found in Monterey, Carmel Valley, and the Santa Cruz Mountains. It's actually the wine industry that's leading the charge beyond mere organic and into biodynamic growing practices.

Essentials

Transportation

FLYING INTO MONTEREY

The **Monterey Regional Airport** (MRY, 200 Fred Kane Dr., 831/648-7000, www.montereyairport.com) is the easiest way to travel to the Monterey Bay area. Five airlines (Alaska Airlines, American Airlines, Allegiant, United, U.S. Airways) fly commuter flights to and from San Francisco, San Diego, Los Angeles, Phoenix, and Las Vegas. The airport is just 3.5 miles from downtown. Most of the time you can get better deals flying into San Jose or San Francisco, but it is worth looking at Monterey Regional Airport, as there are occasionally good deals.

FLYING INTO SAN JOSE

The largest and closest airport to the Monterey region is **Mineta San Jose International Airport** (SJC, 1701 Airport Blvd., San Jose, 408/392-3600, www.flysanjose.com). This is a large, easily navigable airport that's a 75-minute drive from downtown Monterey. **Monterey Airbus** (831/373-7777, www.montereyairbus.com, $35-10) is a shuttle service that takes travelers from San Jose Airport to downtown Monterey. You can save five dollars by booking online.

FLYING INTO SAN FRANCISCO

San Francisco International Airport (SFO, 650/821-8211, www.flysfo.com) is a major airport that's an under-two-hour drive from downtown Monterey if traffic goes in your favor. The **Monterey Airbus** (831/373-7777, www.montereyairbus.com, $45-50) is a shuttle service that takes travelers from San Francisco Airport to downtown Monterey. You can save five dollars by booking online.

TRAIN

There is one **Amtrak** (www.amtrak.com) train route that serves the region: The *Coast Starlight* travels down the West Coast, but stops only as close as Salinas before cutting inland. Amtrak has Thruway stations and stops in Santa Cruz, Monterey, and Carmel that bus passengers to the nearest Amtrak station.

CAR

CA-1, which is also known as **Highway 1,** is the major highway that runs along the coast from Santa Cruz through Monterey, Carmel, and Big Sur down to Cambria and Morro Bay. **U.S. 101** runs through the inland areas of Monterey including Salinas before heading out to the coast south of Morro Bay at San Luis Obispo.

The easiest route to get to the Monterey Peninsula is to take U.S. 101 south from the San Francisco or San Jose airports and then take CA-156 east to CA-1. Head south on CA-1 for Monterey, Carmel, and all communities to the south. **CA-17** is a mountainous highway that can be used as a shortcut to get from San Jose to Santa Cruz.

Road closures are not uncommon in winter. CA-1 along the coast and CA-17 can shut down due to flooding or landslides. Traffic jams, accidents, mudslides, fires, and snow can affect highways and interstates at any time. Before heading out on your adventure, check road conditions online at the **California Department of Transportation** (Caltrans, www.dot.ca.gov). The **Thomas Guide Road Atlas** (www.thomasguidebooks.com, $20-130) is a reliable and detailed map and road guide and a great insurance policy against getting lost.

Previous: the Big Sur Coast Highway; Bixby Bridge.

Car and RV Rental

Most car-rental companies are located at the airports. To reserve a car in advance, contact **Budget Rent A Car** (inside U.S. 800/218-7992, outside U.S. 800/472-3325, www.budget.com), **Dollar Rent A Car** (800/800-4000, www.dollar.com), **Enterprise** (800/261-7331, www.enterprise.com), or **Hertz** (inside U.S. and Canada 800/654-3131, outside U.S. 800/654-3131, www.hertz.com).

To rent a car, drivers in California must be at least 21 years of age and have a valid driver's license. California law also requires that all vehicles carry liability insurance. You can purchase insurance with your rental car, but it generally costs an additional $10 per day, which can add up quickly. Most private auto insurance will also cover rental cars. Before buying rental insurance, check your car insurance policy to see if rental car coverage is included.

The average cost of a rental car is $40 per day or $210 per week; however, rates vary greatly based on the time of year and distance traveled. Weekend and summer rentals cost significantly more. Generally, it is more expensive to rent from car rental agencies at an airport. To avoid excessive rates, first plan travel to areas where a car is not required, then rent a car from an agency branch in town to further explore more rural areas. Rental agencies occasionally allow vehicle drop-off at a different location from where it was picked up for an additional fee.

Another option is to rent an RV. You won't have to worry about camping or lodging options, and many facilities, particularly farther north, accommodate RVs. However, RVs are difficult to maneuver and park, limiting your access to metropolitan areas. They are also expensive, both in terms of gas and the rental rates. Rates during the summer average $1,300 per week and $570 for three days, the standard minimum rental. **Cruise America** (800/671-8042, www.cruiseamerica.com) has branches in San Francisco, San Mateo, and San Jose. **El Monte RV** (800/337-2214, www.elmonterv.com) operates out of San Francisco, San Jose, and Santa Cruz.

Jucy Rentals (800/650-4180, www.jucyrentals.com) rents minivans with pop-up tops. The colorful vehicles are smaller and easier to manage than large RVs, but still come equipped with a fridge, gas cooker, sink, DVD player, and two double beds. Rent one just south of San Francisco (1620 Doolittle Dr., San Leandro, Mon.-Fri. 9am-4:30pm, Sat. 9am-noon) and cruise down the coast.

BUS

Greyhound (800/231-2222, www.greyhound.com) has stations in Santa Cruz (920 Pacific Ave., 831/423-4082) and Salinas (3 Station Pl., 831/424-4418). Greyhound routes generally follow the major highways, traveling U.S. 101.

Visas and Officialdom

PASSPORTS AND VISAS

Visiting from another country, you must have a valid passport and a visa to enter the United States. If you hold a current passport from one of the following countries, you may qualify for the Visa Waiver Program: Andorra, Australia, Austria, Belgium, Brunei, Chile, Czech Republic, Denmark, Estonia, Finland, France, Germany, Greece, Hungary, Iceland, Ireland, Italy, Japan, Latvia, Liechtenstein, Lithuania, Luxembourg, Malta, Monaco, the Netherlands, New Zealand, Norway, Portugal, San Marino, Singapore, Slovakia, Slovenia, South Korea, Spain, Sweden, Switzerland, Taiwan, and the United Kingdom. To qualify, you must apply online with the Electronic System for Travel Authorization and hold a return plane or cruise ticket to your country of origin dated less than 90 days from your date of entry.

Holders of Canadian passports don't need visas or visa waivers.

In most other countries, the local U.S. embassy should be able to provide a tourist visa. The average fee for a visa is US$160. While a visa may be processed as quickly as 24 hours on request, plan at least a couple of weeks, as there can be unexpected delays, particularly during the busy summer season (June-Aug.).

CUSTOMS

Before you enter the United States from another country by sea or by air, you'll be required to fill out a customs form. Check with the U.S. embassy in your country or **Customs and Border Protection** (inside the U.S. 877/227-5511, outside the U.S. 202/325-8000, www.cbp.gov) for an updated list of items you must declare.

If you require medication administered by injection, you must pack your syringes in a checked bag; syringes are not permitted in carry-ons coming into the United States.

Also, pack documentation describing your need for any narcotic medications you've brought with you. Failure to produce documentation for narcotics on request can result in severe penalties in the United States.

If you're driving into California along I-5 or another major highway, prepare to stop at Agricultural Inspection Stations a few miles inside the state line. You don't need to present a passport, a visa, or even a driver's license; instead, you must be prepared to present all your fruits and vegetables. California's largest economic sector is agriculture, and a number of the major crops grown here are sensitive to pests and diseases. In an effort to prevent known pests from entering the state and endangering crops, travelers are asked to identify all produce they're carrying in from other states or from Mexico. If you've got produce, especially homegrown or from a farm stand, it could be infected by a known problem pest or disease. Expect it to be confiscated on the spot.

You'll also be asked about fruits and veggies on your U.S. Customs form, which you'll be asked to fill out on the airplane or ship before you reach the United States.

Travel Tips

CONDUCT AND CUSTOMS

The legal **drinking age** in California is 21. Expect to have your ID checked if you look under age 30, especially in bars and clubs, but also in restaurants and wineries.

Smoking has been banned in many places throughout California. Don't expect to find a smoking section in any restaurant or an ashtray in any bar. Smoking is illegal in all bars and clubs, but your new favorite watering hole might have an outdoor patio where smokers can huddle. Taking the ban one step further, many hotels, motels, and inns throughout California are strictly nonsmoking, and you'll be subject to fees of hundreds of dollars if your room smells of smoke when you leave.

There's no smoking in any public building, and even some of the state parks don't allow cigarettes. There's often good reason for this; the fire danger in California is extreme in the summer, and one carelessly thrown butt can cause a genuine catastrophe.

ACCESS FOR TRAVELERS WITH DISABILITIES

Most attractions, hotels, and restaurants are accessible for travelers with disabilities. State law requires that public transportation must accommodate the special needs of travelers with disabilities and that public spaces and businesses have adequate restroom facilities and equal access. This includes national parks and historic structures, many of which have been refitted with ramps and wider

Coasting California with the Kids

- The **Santa Cruz Beach Boardwalk** (page 146) offers nonstop amusement.

- Families flock to **Monterey Bay Aquarium** (page 33) to see cute sea otters and scary sharks up close.

- If your kids just want to play, you can't beat Monterey's **Dennis the Menace Park** (page 39) which has all sorts of slides, bridges, and swing sets.

- To see underwater sea life without donning snorkeling gear, hitch a ride with Morro Bay's **Sub Sea Tours** (page 254) where families ride in a mini-submarine.

doors. Many hiking trails are also accessible to wheelchairs, and most campgrounds designate specific campsites that meet the Americans with Disabilities Act standards. The state of California also provides a free telephone TDD-to-voice relay service; just dial 711.

If you are traveling with a disability, there are many resources to help you plan your trip. **Access Northern California** (http://accessnca.org) is a nonprofit organization that offers general travel tips, including recommendations on accommodations, parks and trails, transportation, and travel equipment. **Access-Able** (www.access-able.com) is another travel resource, as is **Gimp-on-the-Go** (www.gimponthego.com). The message board on the **American Foundation for the Blind** (www.afb.org) website is a good forum to discuss travel strategies for the visually impaired. For a comprehensive guide to wheelchair-accessible beaches, rivers, and shorelines on the Central Coast, contact the **California Coastal Conservancy** (510/286-1015, www.scc.ca.gov), which publishes a free and downloadable guide (www.wheelingcalscoast.org). **Wheelchair Getaways** in San Francisco (800/638-1912, www.wheelchairgetaways.com, $95-110 per day) rents wheelchair-accessible vans and offer pickup and drop-off service from airports ($100-300). Likewise, **Avis Access** (800/669-9585, www.avis.com) rents cars, scooters, and other products to make traveling with a disability easier; click on the "Services" link on their website.

TRAVELING WITH CHILDREN

Many spots in this region are ideal destinations for families with children of all ages. Amusement parks, interactive museums, zoos, parks, beaches, and playgrounds all make for family-friendly fun. On the other hand, there are a few spots that beckon more to adults than to children. Before you book a room at a B&B that you expect to share with your kids, check to be sure that the inn can accommodate extra people in the guestrooms and whether they allow guests under age 16.

SENIOR TRAVELERS

You'll find senior discounts nearly every place you go, including restaurants, golf courses, major attractions, and even some hotels, although the minimum age can range 50-65. Just ask, and be prepared to produce ID if you look young or are requesting a senior discount. You can often get additional discounts on rental cars, hotels, and tour packages as a member of **AARP** (888/687-2277, www.aarp.org). If you're not a member, its website can also offer helpful travel tips and advice. **Elderhostel** (800/454-5768, www.roadscholar.org) is another great resource for senior travelers. Dedicated to providing educational opportunities for older travelers, Elderhostel provides package trips to beautiful and interesting destinations. Called "Educational Adventures," these trips are generally 3-9 days long and emphasize history, natural history, art, music, or a combination thereof.

GAY AND LESBIAN TRAVELERS

As with much of the country, the farther you venture into rural and agricultural regions, the less likely you are to experience the liberal acceptance California is known for. The **International Gay and Lesbian Travel Association** (954/630-1637, www.

iglta.org) has a directory of gay- and lesbian-friendly tour operators, accommodations, and destinations.

Santa Cruz is a quirky town specially known for its lesbian-friendly culture. A relaxed vibe informs everything from underground clubs to unofficial nude beaches to live-action role-playing games in the middle of downtown. Even the lingerie and adult toyshops tend to be woman-owned and operated.

Health and Safety

MEDICAL SERVICES

For an emergency, **dial 911.** Inside hotels and resorts, check your emergency number as soon as you get to your guest room. In urban and suburban areas, full-service hospitals and medical centers abound, but in more remote regions, help can be more than an hour away.

If you're planning a **backcountry expedition,** follow all rules and guidelines for obtaining **wilderness permits** and for self-registration at trailheads. These are for your safety, letting the rangers know roughly where you plan to be and when to expect you back. National and state park visitors centers can advise in more detail on any health or wilderness alerts in the area. It is also advisable to let someone outside your party know your route and expected date of return.

Being out in the elements can present its own set of challenges. Despite California's relatively mild climate, **heat exhaustion** and **heat stroke** can affect anyone during the hot summer months, particularly during a long, strenuous hike in the sun. Common symptoms include nausea, lightheadedness, headache, or muscle cramps. **Dehydration** and loss of electrolytes are the common causes of heat exhaustion. If you or anyone in your group develops any of these symptoms, get out of the sun immediately, stop all physical activity, and drink plenty of water. Heat exhaustion can be severe, and if untreated can

lead to heat stroke, in which the body's core temperature reaches 105°F. Fainting, seizures, confusion, and rapid heartbeat and breathing can indicate the situation has moved beyond heat exhaustion. If you suspect this, call 911 immediately.

Similar precautions hold true for **hypothermia,** which is caused by prolonged exposure to cold water or weather. For many in California, this can happen on a hike or backpacking trip without sufficient rain gear, or by staying too long in the ocean or another cold body of water without a wetsuit. Symptoms include shivering, weak pulse, drowsiness, confusion, slurred speech, or stumbling. To treat hypothermia, immediately remove the wet clothing, cover the person with blankets, and feed him or her hot liquids. If symptoms don't improve, call 911.

WILDERNESS SAFETY

Many places are still wild, making it important to use precautions with regard to wildlife. **Mountain lions** can be found in the Coast Range, as well as grasslands and forests. Because of their solitary nature, it is unlikely you will see one, even on long trips in the backcountry. Still, there are a couple things to remember. If you come across a kill, probably a large partly eaten deer, leave immediately. And if you see a mountain lion and it sees you, identify yourself as human, making your body appear as big as possible, just as with a bear. And remember: Never run. As with any cat, large or small, running triggers its hunting instincts. If a mountain lion should attack, fight back; cats don't like to get hurt.

The other treacherous critter in the back-country is the **rattlesnake**. It can be found in summer in generally hot and dry areas. When hiking in this type of terrain—many parks will indicate if rattlesnakes are a problem in the area—keep your eyes on the ground and an ear out for the telltale rattle. Snakes like to warn you to keep away. The only time this is not the case is with baby rattlesnakes that have not yet developed their rattles. Unfortunately, they have developed their fangs and venom, which is particularly potent. If you're bitten by a rattlesnake, seek immediate medical attention.

Mosquitoes can be found throughout the state. At higher elevations they can be worse, prompting many hikers and backpackers to don head nets and apply potent repellents, usually DEET. The high season for mosquitoes is late spring-early summer.

Ticks live in many of the forests and grasslands throughout the state, except at higher elevations. Tick season generally runs late fall-early summer. If you are hiking through brushy areas, wear pants and long-sleeved shirts. Ticks like to crawl to warm, moist places (armpits are a favorite) on their host. If a tick is engorged, it can be difficult to remove. There are two main types of ticks found in California: dog ticks and deer ticks. Dog ticks are larger, brown, and have a gold spot on their backs, while deer ticks are small, tear-shaped, and black. Deer ticks are known to carry Lyme disease. While Lyme disease is relatively rare in California—there are more cases in the northernmost part of the state—it is very serious. If you get bitten by a deer tick and the bite leaves a red ring, seek medical attention. Lyme disease can be successfully treated with early rounds of antibiotics.

There is only one major variety of plant in California that can cause an adverse reaction in humans if you touch the leaves or stems: **poison oak,** a common shrub that inhabits forests throughout the state. Poison oak has a characteristic three-leaf configuration, with scalloped leaves that are shiny green in the spring and then turn yellow, orange, and red in late summer-fall. In fall, the leaves drop, leaving a cluster of innocuous-looking branches. The oil in poison oak is present year-round in both the leaves and branches. Your best protection is to wear long sleeves and long pants when hiking, no matter how hot it is. A product called Tecnu is available at most California drugstores—slather it on before you go hiking to protect yourself from poison oak. If your skin comes into contact with poison oak, expect a nasty rash known for its itchiness and irritation. Poison oak is also extremely transferable, so avoid touching your eyes, face, or other parts of your body to prevent spreading the rash. Calamine lotion can help, and in extreme cases a doctor can administer cortisone to help decrease the inflammation.

CRIME AND SAFETY PRECAUTIONS

The outdoors are not the only place that harbors danger. In both rural and urban areas, theft can be a problem. When parking at a trailhead or in a park or at a beach, don't leave any valuables in the car. If you must, place them out of sight, either in a locked glove box or in the trunk. The same holds true for urban areas. Furthermore, avoid keeping your wallet, camera, and other expensive items, including lots of cash, easily accessible in backpacks; keep them within your sight at all times. Certain urban neighborhoods are best avoided at night. If you find yourself in these areas after dark, consider taking a cab to avoid walking blocks and blocks to get to your car or to wait for public transportation. In case of a theft or any other emergency, call 911.

Information and Services

MONEY

Most businesses accept the major credit cards Visa, MasterCard, Discover, and American Express. ATM and debit cards work at many stores and restaurants, and ATMs are available throughout the region. In more remote areas, some businesses may only accept cash, so don't depend entirely on your plastic.

You can change currency at any international airport. Currency-exchange points also crop up in some of the major business hotels in urban areas.

Banks

As with anywhere, traveling with a huge amount of cash is not recommended, which may make frequent trips to the bank necessary. Fortunately, most destinations have at least one major bank. Usually Bank of America or Wells Fargo can be found on the main drags through towns. Banking hours tend to be Monday-Friday 8am-5pm, Saturday 9am-noon. Never count on a bank being open on Sundays or on federal holidays. If you need cash when the banks are closed, there is generally a 24-hour ATM available. Furthermore, many cash-only businesses have an on-site ATM for those who don't have enough cash ready in their wallets. The unfortunate downside to this convenience is a fee of $2-4 per transaction. This also applies to ATMs at banks at which you don't have an account.

Tax

Sales tax in California varies by city and county, but the average rate is around 7.5 percent. All goods are taxable with the exception of food not eaten on the premises. For example, your bill at a restaurant will include tax, but your bill at a grocery store will not. The hotel tax is another unexpected added expense to traveling. Most cities have enacted a tax on hotel rooms largely to make up for budget shortfalls. As you would expect, these taxes are higher in areas more popular with visitors.

Tipping

Tipping is expected and appreciated, and a 15 percent tip for restaurants is about the norm. When ordering in bars, tip the bartender or wait staff $1 per drink. For taxis, plan to tip 15-20 percent of the fare, or simply round up the cost to the nearest dollar. Cafés and coffee shops often have tip jars out. There is no consensus on what is appropriate when purchasing a $3 beverage. Often $0.50 is enough, depending on the quality and service.

COMMUNICATIONS AND MEDIA

With the exception of rural and wilderness areas, California is fairly well connected. Cell phone reception is good except in places far from any large town, including Big Sur. Likewise, you can find Internet access just about anywhere. The bigger cities are well wired, but even in small towns you can log on either at a library or in a café with a computer in the back. Be prepared to pay a per-minute usage fee or purchase a drink.

Because of California's size both geographically and in terms of population, you will have to contend with multiple area codes— the numbers that prefix the seven-digit phone number—throughout the state. The 800 or 866 area codes are toll-free numbers. Any time you are dialing out of the area, you must dial a 1 plus the area code followed by the seven-digit number.

To mail a letter, find a blue post office box, which are found on the main streets of any town. Postage rates vary by destination. You can purchase stamps at the local post office, where you can also mail packages. Stamps can also be bought at some ATMs and online at www.usps.com, which can also give you the location and hours of the nearest post office.

Post offices are generally open Monday-Friday, with limited hours on Saturday. They are always closed on Sunday and federal holidays.

MAPS AND VISITOR INFORMATION

If you are looking for maps, almost all gas stations and drugstores sell maps both of the place you're in and of the whole state. **California State Automobile Association** (CSAA, http://calstate.aaa.com) offers free maps to auto club members.

Many local and regional visitors centers also offer maps, but you'll need to pay a few dollars for the bigger and better ones. But if all you need is a wine-tasting map in a known wine region, you can probably get one for free along with a few tasting coupons at the nearest regional visitors center. Basic national park maps come with your admission payment. State park maps can be free or cost a few dollars at the visitors centers.

The state's **California Travel and Tourism Commission** (916/444-4429, www.visitcalifornia.com) also provides helpful and free tips, information, and downloadable maps and guides. The **Monterey County Convention & Visitors Bureau** (www.seemonterey.com) has a superb website for travel information about attractions, lodging, and restaurants along with insider tips, a great blog, and a comprehensive events calendar.

California is in the Pacific time zone (PST and PDT) and observes daylight saving time March-November.

Resources

Suggested Reading

Monterey County has been home to some of the world's most revered writers, including John Steinbeck, Henry Miller, and Robinson Jeffers. Other writers like Robert Louis Stevenson, Jack Kerouac, and Richard Brautigan were inspired after spending a little time in the area. The Monterey Bay region has also been the focus of works on the natural world and human history.

LITERATURE

Jeffers, Robinson. *Selected Poems.* New York: Vintage Books, 1965. The superb nature poems in this collection include "The Place For No Story," set in present-day Garrapata State Park; "The Purse-Seine," about a boat off the Santa Cruz coast; and "Tor House," named for the author's self-constructed residence on Carmel Point.

Kerouac, Jack. *Big Sur.* New York: Penguin Books, reprint 2013. The Beat writer made famous by *On the Road* goes dark in this 1962 novel about a man's mental deterioration and struggle with alcoholism that takes place mostly at a cabin in Big Sur.

Miller, Henry. *Big Sur and the Oranges of Hieronymus Bosch.* New York: Pocket Books, reprint 1975. The controversial author spent 18 years residing in Big Sur and wrote this 1957 portrait about the rural region and his life there.

Steinbeck, John. *Cannery Row.* New York: Penguin Books, reprint 2014. Pulitzer Prize-winning writer John Steinbeck set many of his novels in Monterey County, but *Cannery Row,* originally published in 1945, is a favorite among many for its depiction of a marine biologist and the other colorful inhabitants of Monterey's old fish-canning neighborhood.

CULTURAL AND NATURAL HISTORY

Bignell, Steven, and Susan Brujines. *228 Interesting, Odd, Beautiful and Historic Things to See in Santa Cruz County.* Santa Cruz, CA: Journeyworks Publishing, 2013. A fun book that covers major Santa Cruz sights including the Santa Cruz Mission and the Giant Dipper Roller Coaster, along with lesser-known gems like the Bigfoot Discovery Museum and Kitchen's Temple, a West Side lot filled with detailed minarets and walls.

Henson, Paul, Donald J. Unser, and Valerie A. Kells. *The Natural History of Big Sur.* Oakland: University of California Press, 1996. The in-depth book covers Big Sur's plants, animal species, geology, significant places, and human history.

Lundy, A. L. "Scrap." *Real Life on Cannery Row: Real People, Places and Events that Inspired John Steinbeck.* Santa Monica, CA: Angel City Press, 2008. A thin volume packed with historic photos and anecdotes about the people and places that shaped John Steinbeck's novel *Cannery Row.*

Norman, Jeff. *Big Sur: Images of America.* Mount Pleasant, SC: Arcadia Publishing, 2004. Big Sur historian and biologist Jeff Norman wrote this photo-heavy book about the rugged region.

Palumbi, Stephen R. and Carolyn Sotka. *The Death and Life of Monterey Bay: A Story of Revival.* Washington DC: Island Press, 2012. The director of Pacific Grove's Hopkins Marine Station tells the story of Monterey Bay from its pristine past to its overfished days to its eventual renewal.

Internet Resources

It should come as no surprise that the California travel industry leads the way in the use of the Internet as a marketing, communications, and sales tool. The overwhelming majority of destinations have their own websites—even tiny towns in the middle of nowhere proudly tout their attractions on the Web.

Big Sur Chamber of Commerce
www.bigsurcalifornia.org
This website has visitors information and a blog about highway and emergency conditions.

California Department of Transportation
www.dot.ca.gov
Check here for a state map and highway information before planning a coastal road trip.

California Outdoor and Recreational Information
www.caoutdoors.com
This recreation-focused website includes links to maps, local newspapers, festivals, and events as well as a wide variety of recreational activities throughout the state.

California State Parks
www.parks.ca.gov
The official website lists hours, accessibility, activities, camping areas, fees, and more information for all parks in the state system.

Cambria Chamber of Commerce
www.cambriachamber.org
It's a good idea to visit this site before a trip for information about Cambria's lodging, shops, attractions, and restaurants.

CarmelCalifornia.com
www.carmelcalifornia.com
This website has information on restaurants, shopping, art galleries, spas, and more along with exclusive offers including reduced-rate accommodations and two-for-one wine tastings.

Hilltromper Santa Cruz
http://hilltromper.com
A website that covers Santa Cruz outdoor recreation and environmental issues in depth.

Monterey County Weekly
www.montereycountyweekly.com
The local alternative weekly's website has lots of information on local events and dining.

Monterey County Convention & Visitors Bureau
www.seemonterey.com
This fantastic website has the usual visitor information (lodging, attractions, and restaurants) and other creative components including videos, a blog, insider tips, and a comprehensive calendar of events.

Santa Cruz County Conference and Visitors Council
www.santacruz.org

The Santa Cruz County Conference and Visitors Council puts their comprehensive Santa Cruz Traveler's Guide online at this site.

State of California
www.ca.gov

This website offers outdoor resources for California state and government organizations. Check for information about fishing and hunting licenses, backcountry permits, boating regulations, and more.

Ventana Wilderness Alliance
www.ventanawild.org

This website provides the best and most up-to-date details on conditions in Big Sur's Ventana Wilderness.

Visit California
www.visitcalifornia.com

Before your visit, check out the official tourism site of the state of California.

Index

List of Maps

Photo Credits

Title page photo: © Dreamstime.com

All photos © Stuart Thornton except page 6 (top left) © Dreamstime.com, (top right) © Dreamstime.com, (bottom) © Dreamstime.com; page 7 (top) © Dreamstime.com, (bottom right) © Dreamstime.com; page 8 © Dreamstime.com; page 10 © Dreamstime.com; page 22 © timla/123rf.com; page 25 © Dreamstime.com; page 27 © Dreamstime.com; page 84 (top) © Dreamstime.com, (bottom) © Dreamstime.com; page 91 © Alan Stacy/Tor House Foundation; page 121 (top) © Dreamstime.com, (bottom) © Dreamstime.com; page 123 © Mel Surdin | Dreamstime.com; page 142 © Dreamstime.com; page 181 © Dreamstime.com; page 183 © Dreamstime.com; page 224 © Dreamstime.com; page 225 © Dreamstime.com; page 249 © Stuart Thornton; page 263 (top) © Dreamstime.com, (bottom) © Dreamstime.com; page 266 © Dreamstime.com; page 267 © Dreamstime.com; page 269 © Dreamstime.com; page 272 (top) © Dreamstime.com, (bottom) © Dreamstime.com

Acknowledgments

It has been a true honor writing about the Monterey Bay area and Big Sur. I have lived in this area for almost 20 years and researching this book further enriched my appreciation for the region.

I'd like to thank all of my wonderful pals from Monterey Bay that are truly the area's best attraction. This includes Wendy Burnett, Joe Burnett, Dan Linehan, Trey Kropp, Bob Cole, Adam Joseph, Mark Anderson, Chris Smith, "Kansas City" Shane Dolbier, Dave Schmalz, Walter Ryce, Ryan McGlynn, "Windy Apple" Gabe Skvor, "Wolverine" Mike Allen, Michelle Micalizio Johnson, Pam McDonald, and, especially, my girlfriend Sarah Kenoyer.

A big thanks to Grace Fujimoto, Elizabeth Hansen, Darren Alessi, Leah Gordon, and Albert Angulo at Avalon Travel for this opportunity and all their tremendous help with making this dream a reality.

I have to give the biggest thanks to my wonderful parents John and Ronnie Thornton for all of their love and support through the years. And a big shout out to my nephew Hayes Thornton!

Also Available

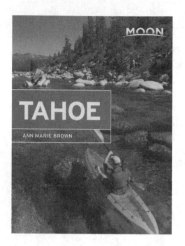

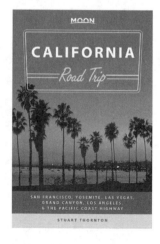

MAP SYMBOLS

Expressway	★	Highlight	✕	Airfield	⚲	Golf Course
Primary Road	○	City/Town	✈	Airport	🅿	Parking Area
Secondary Road	⊛	State Capital	▲	Mountain	▲	Archaeological Site
Unpaved Road	⊛	National Capital	✛	Unique Natural Feature	🛉	Church
Trail	★	Point of Interest				Gas Station
Ferry	•	Accommodation	🌫	Waterfall	🥔	Glacier
Railroad	▾	Restaurant/Bar	▲	Park		Mangrove
Pedestrian Walkway	▪	Other Location	▣	Trailhead		Reef
Stairs	⋀	Campground	⛷	Skiing Area		Swamp

CONVERSION TABLES

°C = (°F - 32) / 1.8
°F = (°C x 1.8) + 32
1 inch = 2.54 centimeters (cm)
1 foot = 0.304 meters (m)
1 yard = 0.914 meters
1 mile = 1.6093 kilometers (km)
1 km = 0.6214 miles
1 fathom = 1.8288 m
1 chain = 20.1168 m
1 furlong = 201.168 m
1 acre = 0.4047 hectares
1 sq km = 100 hectares
1 sq mile = 2.59 square km
1 ounce = 28.35 grams
1 pound = 0.4536 kilograms
1 short ton = 0.90718 metric ton
1 short ton = 2,000 pounds
1 long ton = 1.016 metric tons
1 long ton = 2,240 pounds
1 metric ton = 1,000 kilograms
1 quart = 0.94635 liters
1 US gallon = 3.7854 liters
1 Imperial gallon = 4.5459 liters
1 nautical mile = 1.852 km

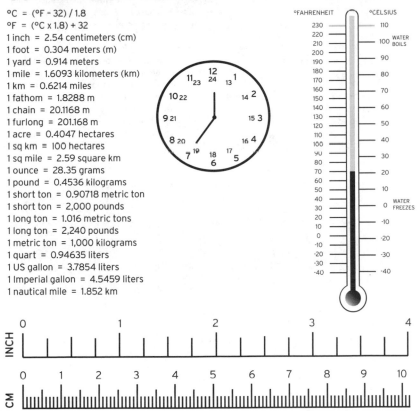

MOON MONTEREY & CARMEL
Avalon Travel
a member of the Perseus Books Group
1700 Fourth Street
Berkeley, CA 94710, USA
www.moon.com

Editor: Leah Gordon
Series Manager: Kathryn Ettinger
Copy Editor: Brett Keener
Graphics Coordinators: Darren Alessi,
  Kathryn Osgood
Production Coordinator: Darren Alessi
Cover Design: Faceout Studios, Charles Brock
Moon Logo: Tim McGrath
Map Editor: Albert Angulo
Cartographer: Brian Shotwell
Indexer: Rachel Kuhn

ISBN-13: 978-1-63121-243-7
ISSN: 1539-9656

Printing History
1st Edition — 2002
5th Edition — January 2016
5 4 3 2 1

Text © 2016 by Stuart Thornton & Avalon Travel.
Maps © 2016 by Avalon Travel.
All rights reserved.

Some photos and illustrations are used by
permission and are the property of the original
copyright owners.

Front cover photo: Carmel Beach © Pgiam/Getty

Printed in Canada by Friesens

Moon Handbooks and the Moon logo are the
property of Avalon Travel. All other marks and logos
depicted are the property of the original owners.
All rights reserved. No part of this book may be
translated or reproduced in any form, except brief
extracts by a reviewer for the purpose of a review,
without written permission of the copyright owner.

All recommendations, including those for sights,
activities, hotels, restaurants, and shops, are based
on each author's individual judgment. We do not
accept payment for inclusion in our travel guides,
and our authors don't accept free goods or services
in exchange for positive coverage.

Although every effort was made to ensure that
the information was correct at the time of going
to press, the author and publisher do not assume
and hereby disclaim any liability to any party for any
loss or damage caused by errors, omissions, or any
potential travel disruption due to labor or financial
difficulty, whether such errors or omissions result
from negligence, accident, or any other cause.

32953012474666